For Reference

Not to be taken from this room

D-Day

D-Day

THE ESSENTIAL REFERENCE GUIDE

Spencer C. Tucker, Editor

ABC-CLIO™

An Imprint of ABC-CLIO, LLC
Santa Barbara, California • Denver, Colorado

Copyright © 2018 by ABC-CLIO, LLC

All rights reserved. No part of this publication may be reproduced, stored in a retrieval system, or transmitted, in any form or by any means, electronic, mechanical, photocopying, recording, or otherwise, except for the inclusion of brief quotations in a review, without prior permission in writing from the publisher.

Library of Congress Cataloging-in-Publication Data

Names: Tucker, Spencer, 1937– editor.
Title: D-Day : the essential reference guide / Spencer C. Tucker, editor.
Other titles: D-Day, the essential reference guide
Description: Santa Barbara, CA : ABC-CLIO, [2018] | Includes bibliographical
  references and index.
Identifiers: LCCN 2017016648 (print) | LCCN 2017019312 (ebook) |
  ISBN 9781440849756 (ebook) | ISBN 9781440849749 (alk. paper)
Subjects: LCSH: World War, 1939–1945—Campaigns—France—Normandy—
  Encyclopedias. | Operation Overlord—Encyclopedias. | Normandy (France)—History,
  Military—Encyclopedias.
Classification: LCC D756.5.N6 (ebook) | LCC D756.5.N6 D255 2018 (print) |
  DDC 940.54/21421—dc23
LC record available at https://lccn.loc.gov/2017016648

ISBN: 978-1-4408-4974-9 (print)
      978-1-4408-4975-6 (ebook)

22 21 20 19 18   1 2 3 4 5

This book is also available as an eBook.

ABC-CLIO
An Imprint of ABC-CLIO, LLC

ABC-CLIO, LLC
130 Cremona Drive, P.O. Box 1911
Santa Barbara, California 93116-1911
www.abc-clio.com

This book is printed on acid-free paper ∞

Manufactured in the United States of America

For Dr. Richard and Claire Griffith,
whose friendship over the years is deeply treasured

Contents

List of Entries, ix

List of Primary Documents, xi

Maps, xiii

Preface, xvii

Introduction: The Normandy Invasion (D-Day, June 6, 1944) and Campaign, xix

A–Z Entries, 1

Primary Documents, 221

Appendix A: Ground Forces Order of Battle on D-Day, June 6, 1944, 237

Appendix B: Number of Troops Killed on June 6, 1944, 239

Appendix C: Army, Corps, and Division Units Involved in the Battle of Normandy (June 6–August 29, 1944), 241

Appendix D: Estimated Casualties in the Battle of Normandy (June 6–August 29, 1944), 243

Chronology, 245

Bibliography, 255

Editor and Contributors, 261

About the Editor, 265

Index, 267

List of Entries

Airborne Forces, British and American
Aircraft, Bombers
Aircraft, Fighters and Fighter-Bombers
Aircraft, Gliders
Aircraft, Transports
Air Warfare, Ground-Attack Aviation
Amphibious Warfare in the European Theater
Antitank Guns and Antitank Warfare
Artillery and Fire Support
Atlantic, Battle of the
Atlantic Wall
Barton, Raymond Oscar "Tubby" (1889–1963)
BLUECOAT, Operation (July 30–August 7, 1944)
Bradley, Omar Nelson (1893–1981)
Brooke, Sir Alan Francis (First Viscount Alanbrooke) (1883–1963)
Caen, Battle to Secure (June 6–July 18, 1944)
Cemeteries, Normandy Invasion
Cherbourg, Capture of (June 22–29, 1944)
Churchill, Sir Winston Leonard Spencer (1874–1965)
COBRA, Operation (July 25–31, 1944)
Cole, Robert George (1915–1944)
Collins, Joseph Lawton "Lightning Joe" (1896–1987)
Command Structure, Allied
Command Structure, German
Coningham, Sir Arthur "Mary" (1895–1948)
Cota, Norman Daniel "Dutch" (1893–1971)
Cotentin (Cherbourg) Peninsula
Crerar, Henry Duncan Graham (1888–1965)
Crocker, Sir John Treddinick (1896–1963)
Culin, Curtis Grubb, III (1915–1963)
de Gaulle, Charles (1890–1970)
Dempsey, Miles Christopher (1896–1969)
Dietrich, Josef "Sepp" (1892–1966)
Dollman, Friedrich (1882–1944)
Doohan, James Montgomery (1920–2005)
Double-Cross System
Ehlers, Walter David (1921–2014)
Eisenhower, Dwight David (1890–1969)
English Channel
Falaise–Argentan Pocket (August 12–24, 1944)
Festung Europa
Films Treating the Normandy Invasion
FORTITUDE, Operation (1944)
France, Campaign (June 6–September 15, 1944)
French Resistance
Gale, Sir Richard Nelson (1896–1982)
Gerhardt, Charles Hunter (1895–1976)
Gerow, Leonard Townsend (1888–1972)
Geyr von Schweppenburg, Leo Dietrich Franz Freiherr (1886–1974)
Hand Grenades
Higgins, Andrew Jackson (1886–1952)
Hitler, Adolf (1889–1945)
Hobart, Sir Percy Cleghorn Stanley (1885–1957)

Howard, John (1912–1999)
Huebner, Clarence Ralph (1888–1972)
Jodl, Alfred (1890–1946)
JUBILEE, Operation (Dieppe Raid, August 19, 1942)
Kirk, Alan Goodrich (1888–1963)
Kluge, Günther Adolf Ferdinand von (1882–1944)
Krancke, Theodor (1893–1973)
La Fière Causeway, Battle of the (June 6–9, 1944)
Landing Craft
Lee, John Clifford Hodges (1887–1958)
Leigh-Mallory, Sir Trafford (1892–1944)
LÜTTICH, Operation (Mortain Counteroffensive, August 7–13, 1944)
Lyme Bay, Battle of (April 28, 1944)
Machine Guns
Marshall, George Catlett (1880–1959)
Millin, William "Piper Bill" (1922–2010)
Montgomery, Sir Bernard Law (First Viscount Montgomery of Alamein) (1887–1976)
Moon, Don Pardee (1894–1944)
Morgan, Frederick Edgeworth (1894–1967)
Mulberries
NEPTUNE, Operation (June 6–July 3, 1944)
Normandy
OVERLORD, Operation, Planning for
Patton, George Smith, Jr. (1885–1945)
Pegasus and Horsa Bridges, Battle for (June 6, 1944)
PLUTO
Pointe du Hoc, Seizure of (June 6, 1944)

Quesada, Elwood Richard "Pete" (1904–1993)
Ramsay, Sir Bertram Home (1883–1945)
Ridgway, Matthew Bunker (1895–1993)
Rifles
Rommel, Erwin Johannes Eugen (1891–1944)
Roosevelt, Franklin D. (1882–1945)
Roosevelt, Theodore, Jr. (1887–1944)
ROUNDUP, Operation (1943)
Rudder, James Earl (1910–1970)
Rundstedt, Karl Rudolf Gerd von (1875–1953)
Sainte-Mère-Église
Saint-Lô, Battle of (July 11–19, 1944)
Simonds, Guy Granville (1903–1974)
SLEDGEHAMMER, Operation
Smith, Walter Bedell (1895–1961)
Stagg, James Martin (1900–1975)
Steele, John Marvin (1912–1969)
Tanks
Taylor, Maxwell Davenport (1901–1987)
Tedder, Sir Arthur William (1st Baron Tedder) (1890–1967)
Tehran Conference (November 28–December 1, 1943)
Terrain and Tactical Problems on D-Day
Todt Organization
TOTALIZE, Operation (August 7–13, 1944)
TRACTABLE, Operation (August 14–21, 1944)
Vian, Sir Philip Louis (1894–1968)
Warships, Allied
Winters, Richard D. (1918–2011)
World War II, European Theater: Overview

List of Primary Documents

Allied Planning for the Normandy Invasion (July 1943)

Anglo-American Combined Chiefs of Staff, Directive to Supreme Commander Allied Expeditionary Force, February 12, 1944

Eisenhower's Statement in the Event the D-Day Landings Failed, June 5, 1944

Order of the Day and Letter to the Troops, Supreme Commander of the Western Allied Expeditionary Force General Dwight D. Eisenhower, June 6, 1944

U.S. President Franklin D. Roosevelt's Remarks by Radio, June 6, 1944

Forrest C. Pogue on D-Day, June 6–7, 1944

General Dwight D. Eisenhower to General George C. Marshall, July 5, 1944

General Erwin Rommel, Teletype Message to Hitler, July 15, 1944

U.S. Army General Dwight D. Eisenhower on Sergeant Curtis G. Culin's Invention of the "Rhino" Tank Modification Preceding Operation COBRA (July 25–31, 1944)

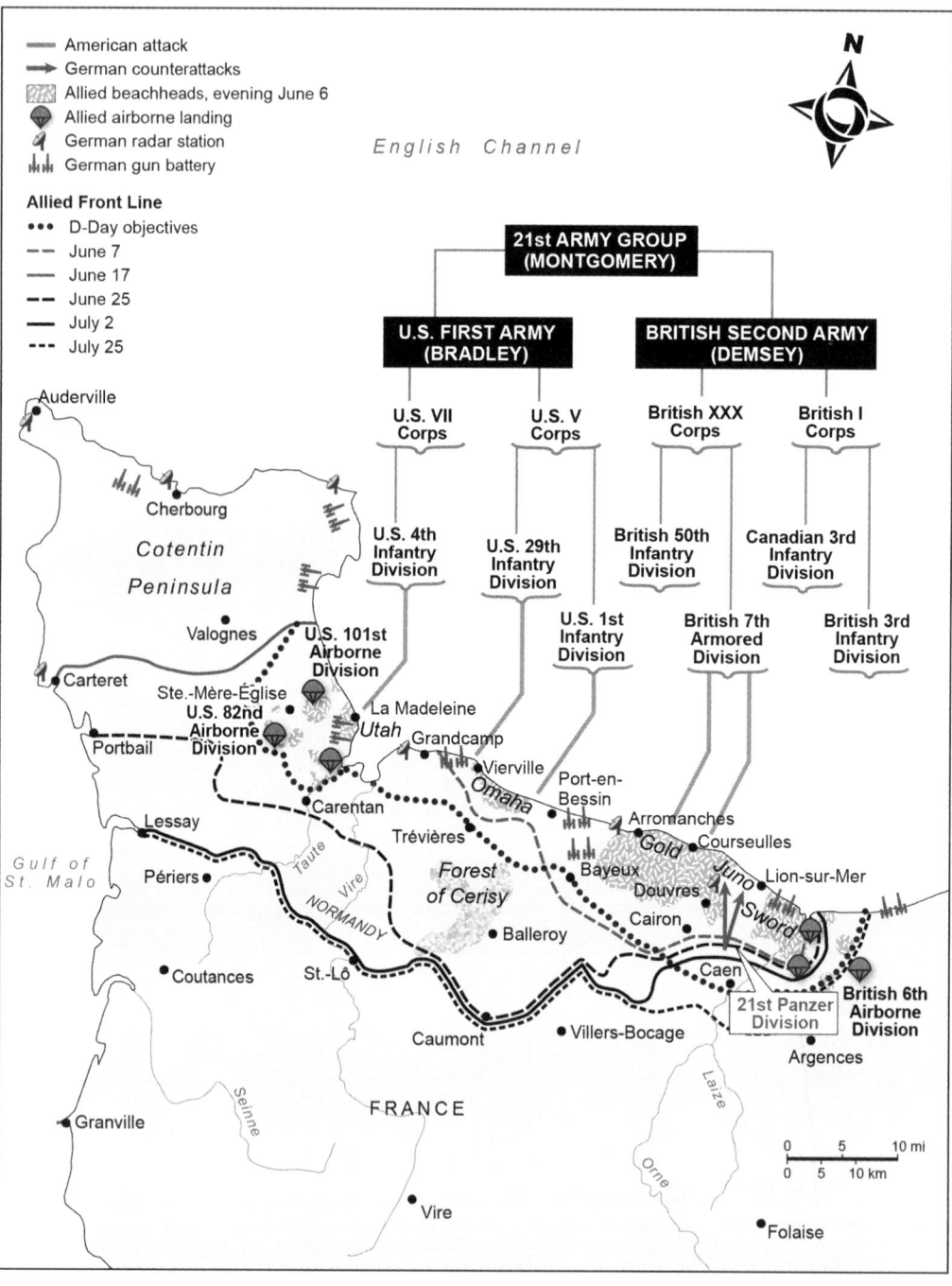

COLLAPSE OF GERMANY, 1945

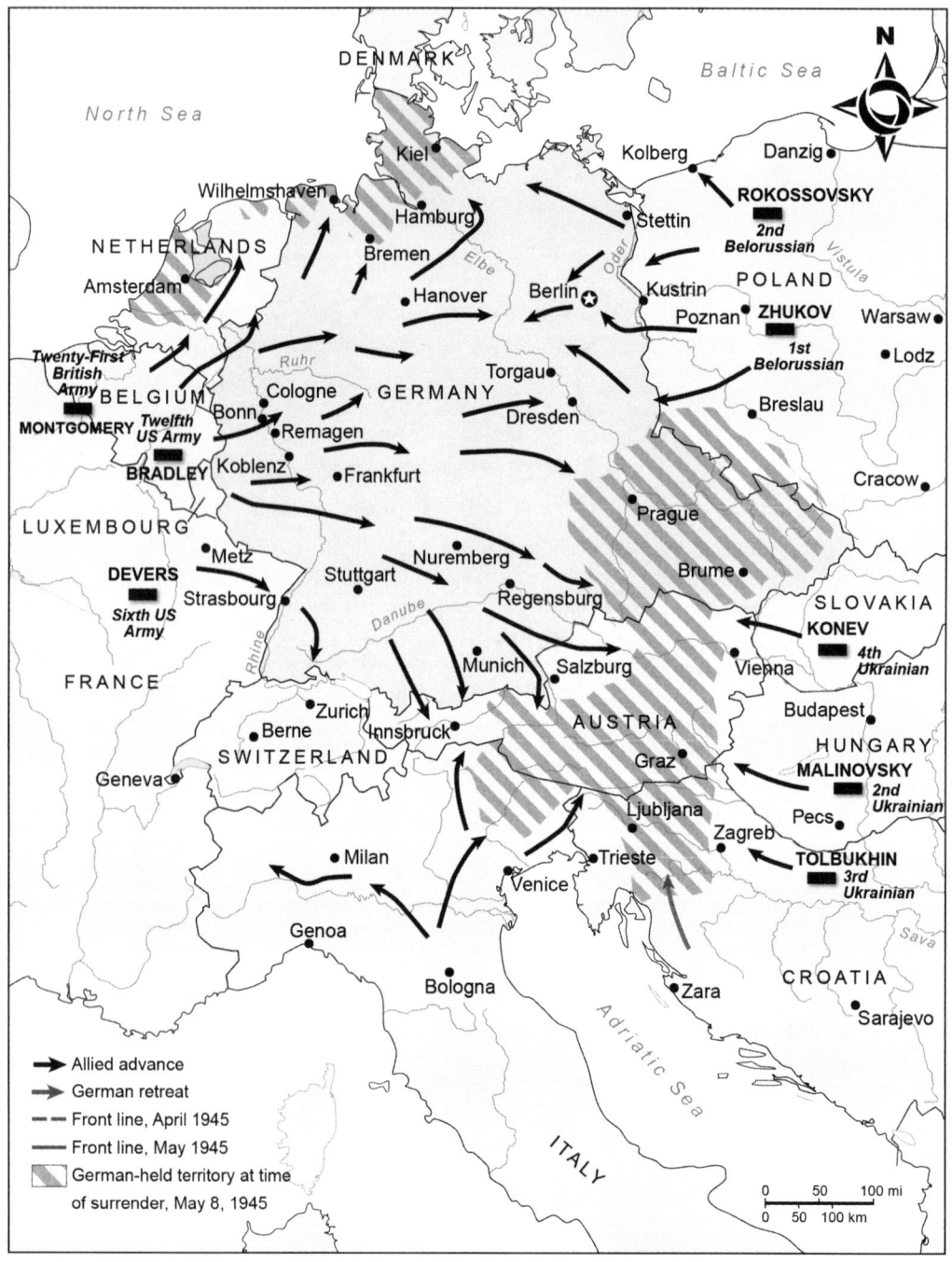

Preface

The Allied invasion of Normandy on June 6, 1944, was history's largest amphibious operation. Nothing of its scale had ever been attempted before, nor is it likely to be attempted in the future. Following years of debate and planning, the Americans had gotten their way, overriding both British prime minister Winston Churchill's fears that an invasion of France would be a bloodbath comparable to World War I in Flanders and his oft-stated preference for a Mediterranean option. On the first day some 130,000 men came ashore, and 1 million men had landed within a month. The logistics of all of this were staggering, as were the risks. There was no way to conceal the preparations, and the likelihood of the Germans learning the location of the landings was considerable, but an elaborate deception worked to perfection.

Deciding on June 6 was a considerable risk. Bad weather had delayed the invasion and supreme commander of the Allied Expeditionary Force General Dwight D. Eisenhower made the decision on the advice of his meteorologists that a break in the weather appeared likely. Indeed, the foul weather worked to the Allied advantage, for although poor conditions did have negative impacts on the landing operations, the Germans were convinced that the invasion would not then occur, and it thus caught them off guard.

The invasion of Normandy was, above all, an Allied effort. One of the enduring myths about D-Day ("D" stands simply for "Day"), for Americans at least, is that it was largely a U.S. operation. Indeed, the British bore the brunt of it. Of the 1,213 warships involved, 200 were American and 892 were British; of the 4,126 landing craft involved, 805 were American and 3,261 were British. Some 31 percent of all supplies used by U.S. forces during D-Day came directly from Britain. Two-thirds of the 12,000 aircraft involved were also British. Of those who landed in occupied France on June 6, 75,215 were British and Canadian troops, and 57,500 were from the United States.

The invaders sustained some 10,300 casualties—4,300 British and Canadian and 6,000 U.S. The higher U.S. losses were largely a result of the fighting for Omaha Beach, one of the three designated American landing beaches, where there was strong opposition and indeed fears that the men there might have to be evacuated, but the Americans ultimately persevered.

Although the landing was successful at all five beaches, the initial goals were not met. The British had hoped to take Caen by midnight the first day. Caen to the Orne River was not secured until July 9. The Americans had hoped to take the important English Channel port of Cherbourg in 15 days.

Resistance there ended only on June 30, and the damage to the port facilities was such that it would be months before substantial cargoes could be unloaded there and moved inland.

Yet in the end, the Battle of Normandy was a success. The Allies managed to figure out ways to break the tenacious German resistance in the ideal defensive terrain of the Norman *bocage* country, and they also controlled the skies. The British were able to draw off the bulk of German armor in their own effort to secure Caen, greatly aiding the Americans in breaking free in Operation COBRA (July 25–31). Although the Allies were slow to realize the opportunity and close the trap of the Falaise pocket, which allowed substantial German forces to escape eastward, the Battle of Normandy was a success.

Casualties, although high, were less than feared. Allied losses—including some 12,000, most of them aircrew—in the several months preceding the invasion to August 29, 1944, totaled some 237,606 killed, wounded, or missing. German casualties are largely guesswork, but the number killed, wounded, or taken prisoner range from some 288,875 to 400,000.

On August 15 in Operation DRAGOON, the Allies also invaded southern France. Paris was liberated during August 19–25, and France was largely cleared of the Germans by mid-September. Although opportunities that might have ended the war in 1944 were missed, the Western Allies and the Soviets now clearly had the upper hand, and the defeat of Germany—barring some kind of miracle weapon—was merely a matter of time, as most of the German leaders, though not Adolf Hitler, clearly understood. The fighting in Europe ended on May 8, 1945.

I learned a great deal working on this project, especially about the British, Canadian, Polish, and French Resistance contributions to the success of the invasion and the subsequent battle to secure Normandy. Other individuals have made major contributions to this project. Distinguished military historians Colonel Jerry Morelock, USA Rtd., and Major General David Zabecki, USA Rtd., PhD, both reviewed my initial entry list and made many useful suggestions. I am also grateful to General Zabecki for taking the time from his own busy scholarly schedule to write a number of the important entries. Dr. Paul Pierpaoli Jr., my close collaborator on so many encyclopedia projects, has been a tremendous help, writing a number of entries and compiling oral histories and unpublished memoirs related to D-Day. Although we are not able to include any of these oral histories and memoirs in this book for copyright reasons, I do encourage readers to look them up at the Veteran's History Project website (https://www.loc.gov/vets/stories/onthebeach.html#stories). As always, I take full responsibility for any errors of content or omissions.

Spencer C. Tucker

Introduction: The Normandy Invasion (D-Day, June 6, 1944) and Campaign

U.S. officials, principally army chief of staff General George C. Marshall, had long sought the earliest possible invasion of France as the way to win World War II in the shortest possible time. They supported both Operation GYMNAST, a British cross–English Channel invasion contingency plan for late 1942, and Operation ROUNDUP, a 48-division invasion of France projected to occur by April 1943. The failure of the Allied raid on Dieppe, France (Operation JUBILEE), on August 19, 1942, however, led the Americans to concede the British position that a cross-channel invasion was many months, if not years, in the future. Prime Minister Winston L. S. Churchill and British planners meanwhile sought to interest the United States in a more opportunistic approach that would include operations in the Mediterranean theater, and the Americans reluctantly acceded.

This led to Operation TORCH, the Allied invasion of North Africa (November 8, 1942), and to subsequent British and U.S. landings in Sicily and Italy. The United States insisted, however, that the 1943–1945 Italy campaign would be a secondary effort. At the Tehran Conference in November 1943, Soviet leader Joseph Stalin had pressed U.S. president Franklin D. Roosevelt and Churchill for the cross-channel invasion. Stalin agreed to mount a major offensive by the Soviets on the Eastern Front to coincide with the landing. He also pressed Roosevelt to name the commander of the invasion force, and shortly after the conference Roosevelt appointed General Dwight D. Eisenhower to the post of supreme commander, Allied Expeditionary Force.

Festung Europa (Fortress Europe) and its coasts of Holland, Belgium, and France bristled with all manner of German fortifications and booby traps. The Todt Organization had begun erecting defenses there in mid-1942, and during the next two years the Germans used some 17.3 million cubic yards of concrete and 1.2 million tons of steel in thousands of fortifications. Field Marshal Erwin Rommel, appointed in November 1943 to command Army Group B and the coastal defenses in France, disagreed with German commander in chief, West, Field Marshal Gerd von Rundstedt.

Rommel, well aware from the campaign in North Africa what complete Allied domination of the air would mean, believed that if an Allied invasion of France was to be stopped at all, it had to be defeated on the beaches. Rommel told Adolf Hitler, "If we don't manage to throw them back at once, the invasion will succeed in spite of the Atlantic Wall."

Rundstedt and Hitler, however, placed their hopes in a large mobile armor reserve that would defeat the Allied forces once they were ashore. Hitler seems to have welcomed the invasion as a chance to engage and destroy the British and U.S. forces. In Britain, they could not be touched; in France, the Western Allied armies could be destroyed. Hitler was convinced that the Allied effort would result in another Dieppe. "Let them come," he said. "They will get the thrashing of their lives."

Rommel did what he could, supervising the construction of elaborate defenses, the placement of half a million foreshore obstacles, and the laying of some 4 million mines. Rommel had the Fifteenth Army in northern France and the Seventh Army in Normandy—a total of 25 static coastal divisions, 16 infantry and parachute divisions, 20 armored and mechanized divisions, and 7 reserve divisions. The Germans were weak in air and naval assets, however. The Third Air Fleet in France deployed only 329 aircraft on D-Day, and German naval forces in the area consisted of 4 destroyers and 39 E-boats. Germany also deployed several dozen U-boats, most from French ports, during the subsequent Normandy campaign.

Meanwhile, U.S. and British aircraft worked to soften the German defenses and isolate the beachheads. Between April 1 and June 5, 1944, Allied aircraft flew 200,000 sorties in support of the coming invasion and dropped 195,000 tons of bombs. The Allies lost 2,000 aircraft in the process, but by D-Day they had largely isolated the landing areas and achieved virtually total air supremacy.

The Germans also greatly strengthened the French channel port defenses, which Hitler ordered turned into fortresses. All of this was for naught, because as German minister of armaments Albert Speer noted, the Allies came over the beaches and "brought their own port with them. . . . Our whole plan of defense had proved irrelevant." In one of the greatest military engineering achievements in history, thousands of men labored in Britain for months to build two large artificial harbors known as Mulberries A and B. Plans called for these, after the initial Allied landings, to be hauled across the English Channel from Britain and sunk in place. Their importance to the Allied cause can be seen in that by the end of October, 25 percent of stores, 20 percent of personnel, and 15 percent of vehicles had passed through Mulberry B.

The Allies worked out precise and elaborate plans for the mammoth cross-channel invasion, code-named OVERLORD, to occur on the Cotentin Peninsula in Normandy. British admiral Bertram H. Ramsay had overall command of the naval operation, code-named NEPTUNE, while British general Bernard Montgomery exercised overall command of the land forces. The object of the operation was "to secure a lodgement on the continent, from which further offensive operations can be developed."

The landing would be preceded by a night drop of paratroops. General Marshall, an enthusiastic supporter of airborne forces, urged the use of five airborne divisions, but Eisenhower had his doubts, and as it transpired, only three were employed: the British 6th and the U.S. 82nd and 101st. The lightly armed paratroopers, operating in conjunction with the French Resistance, had the vital task of securing the flanks of the lodgment and destroying key transportation choke points to prevent the Germans from reinforcing their beach defenses. The German 21st Panzer and 12th Schutzstaffel (SS) Panzer Divisions were stationed just outside Caen. If they were permitted to reach the beaches, they could strike the amphibious forces from the flank and roll them up.

The amphibious assault would occur early in the morning after the airborne assault, with five infantry divisions wading ashore along the 50-mile stretch of coast, divided into five sectors. The designated beaches were, from west to east, the U.S. 4th Infantry Division (Utah), the U.S. 1st Infantry and 29th Infantry Divisions (Omaha), the British 50th Infantry Division (Gold), the Canadian 3rd Infantry Division (Juno), and the British 3rd Infantry Division (Sword).

Operation OVERLORD proved to be a vast undertaking. The airborne forces alone would require 1,340 C-47 transports and 2,500 gliders. Ten thousand aircraft would secure the skies. Naval support for the invasion would come from 138 bombardment warships, 221 destroyers and other convoy escorts, 287 minesweepers, 495 light craft, and 441 auxiliaries. In addition, there were some 4,000 landing ships and other craft of various sizes.

Eisenhower faced a difficult decision, given terrible weather in the days preceding the planned landing. Informed by his chief meteorologist that a break in the weather might occur, Eisenhower decided to proceed. This decision worked to the Allies' advantage, for the Germans did not expect a landing in such poor weather. The French Resistance was informed by radio code, and the airborne forces took off.

The airborne operation involving 23,400 U.S. and British parachutist and glider troops occurred on schedule on the night of June 5–6, but thick cloud banks over Normandy caused pilots to veer off course to avoid midair collisions. German antiaircraft fire, jumpy flight crews, and Pathfinders who were immediately engaged in firefights on the ground and unable to set up their beacons led to premature drops and to paratroopers being scattered all over the peninsula. Some were even dropped into the English Channel, where they drowned, dragged down by their heavy equipment. Gliders crashed into obstacles, and they and the paratroopers came down in fields that had been deliberately flooded by the Germans as a defensive measure. Much equipment was thus lost.

Nonetheless, the wide scattering of forces caused confusion among the defenders as to the precise Allied plans. Officers collected as many men as they could, and improvised units were soon moving on the objectives, most of which were secured.

Success was likely if the Allies could establish a bridgehead large enough to allow them to build up their strength and overcome the German defenders. Once the Allies broke out they would have the whole of France for maneuver, because their armies were fully mechanized and the bulk of the defending German forces were not. The only possibility of German success was for the defenders to rapidly commit panzer reserves, but this step was fatally delayed by two factors.

The first was Allied naval gunfire support and air superiority of 30 to 1 over Normandy itself (there were large numbers of ground-support aircraft, especially the U.S. Republic P-47 Thunderbolt and North American P-51 Mustang and the British Hawker Typhoon). The second was Hitler's failure to immediately authorize commitment of the armored reserves. Hitler was convinced that the invasion at Normandy was merely a feint and that the main thrust would come in the Pas de Calais sector. Allied deception measures played a key role in deluding him.

The British "double-cross" system worked to perfection. Every German agent in Britain was either dead, jailed, or working for British intelligence. The British actually controlled the entire German spy network in the United Kingdom and used it to feed disinformation to the Germans. Operations FORTITUDE NORTH and FORTITUDE SOUTH also deceived Hitler. Operation FORTITUDE NORTH caused him to believe that the Allies intended to invade Norway from Scotland, leading him to maintain and even reinforce substantial German units there; FORTITUDE SOUTH led Hitler to believe that the main Allied effort in France would be a subsequent landing in the Pas de Calais area, the narrowest point of the English Channel, and that the lodgment in Normandy was only a feint.

To this end the Allies created the "First U.S. Army Group" under Lieutenant General George S. Patton, still without command following an incident in which he had slapped two soldiers suffering from combat fatigue in Sicily. The Germans expected that the aggressive Patton would command any Allied invasion of the continent. The First U.S. Army Group, an imaginary formation of 18 divisions and 4 corps headquarters, contributed nothing to OVERLORD but did confuse the Germans.

Not until late July did Hitler authorize the movement of the Fifteenth Panzer Army from the Pas de Calais to Normandy. In effect, the deception totally immobilized 19 German divisions east of the Seine. Although units of the Fifteenth Army were moved west to Normandy before that date, this was done piecemeal, and hence they were much easier for the Allies to defeat.

Meanwhile, the actual Normandy invasion began. In the days before the invasion, some 2,700 vessels manned by 195,000 men were on the move. Operation NEPTUNE transported by ship 130,000 troops, 2,000 tanks, 12,000 other vehicles, and 10,000 tons of supplies. At about 5:30 a.m. on June 6, 1944, the bombardment ships opened up against the 50-mile invasion front, engaging the German shore batteries. The first U.S. assault troops landed 30 to 40 minutes later, and the British landing craft were ashore two hours later.

The landing was in jeopardy only on Omaha Beach, where because of rough seas only 5 of 32 amphibious duplex-drive tanks reached the shore. Support artillery was also lost when DUKW amphibious trucks were swamped by the waves. Some landing craft were hit and destroyed, and those troops of the 1st Infantry Division who gained the beach were soon pinned down by withering German fire. U.S. First Army commander Lieutenant General Omar N. Bradley even considered withdrawal.

At 9:50 a.m., the gunfire support ships opened up against the German shore batteries. Destroyers repeatedly risked running aground to provide close-in gunnery to assist the troops ashore; indeed, several destroyers actually scraped bottom. It was nearly noon before the German defenders began to give way. The 1st Infantry and 29th Divisions overcame German opposition with sheer determination, reinforced by the knowledge that there was no place to retreat.

The landings on the other beaches were not as difficult. Overall, for the first day the Allies sustained some 10,300 casualties—4,300 British and Canadian and 6,000 U.S. A recent study suggests that a night landing would have produced fewer casualties. The Allies had used night landings with great success in the Mediterranean, but Montgomery believed that overwhelming Allied air and naval power would make a daytime landing preferable. Still, the losses were comparatively light.

The Allies put ashore 75,215 British and Canadian troops and 57,500 U.S. forces on D-Day and 1 million men within a month. Unfortunately for the Allies, during June 19–20 a force 6–7 storm blew out of the northwest and severely damaged Mulberry A in the American sector. The storm also sank well over 100 small craft and drove many more ashore, bringing to a halt the discharge of supplies. Vital ammunition stocks had to be flown in. Mulberry A was abandoned, but a strengthened Mulberry B provided supplies to both armies until the end of the war.

Eventually the United States committed 60 divisions to the battle for the continent. The British and Canadians never had more than 20, and as the disparity grew, so too did U.S. influence over military and political strategy. Churchill was understandably insistent that Montgomery exercise prudence and not sacrifice his men needlessly, which would further reduce British influence.

The Allied ground offensive proceeded more slowly than expected. Hitler ordered his armies to fight for every inch of ground rather than withdraw along phase lines, as his generals wanted. At first this delayed the Allied timetable; however, it also greatly accelerated the ultimate defeat and ensured that it would be costly. Complete Allied air superiority devastated the Germans by day and forced them to move largely at night. The French Resistance also played an important role, providing the invading Allied forces with intelligence information and impeding German resupply efforts through sabotage and the destruction of rolling stock and bridges.

The Normandy countryside proved to be ideal defensive terrain. Over the centuries, the dividing lines between individual fields had been allowed to grow up into tangled hedgerows. This *bocage* resisted passage and slowed the Allied advance to a crawl. The Germans blocked Montgomery's early efforts to take the city of Caen. Major General J. Lawton Collins's U.S. VII Corps had more success on the Allied right, gradually pushing across the base of the Cotentin Peninsula. On June 18 it turned north to liberate the important port of Cherbourg, while the remainder of Bradley's army maintained an aggressive defense. Cherbourg fell on June 30, but its German defenders destroyed the harbor facilities, and it would take U.S. engineers under Major General Lucius Clay six weeks to get the harbor facilities back in operation.

Not until Operation COBRA on July 25–31 were the Allies able to break out. With the British effort to secure Caen drawing off the bulk of the German armor, Bradley's U.S. First Army forced the German line west of Saint-Lô, and Collins's VII Corps made the main effort. All of northern France was open for the highly mechanized Allied units to maneuver. On August 15, Allied forces also came ashore on the French Mediterranean coast in Operation DRAGOON. The German defenders were now in full retreat, but it remained to be seen if the Allies could maintain their fast-lengthening supply lines and end the war in the west before the Germans had a chance to recover.

Spencer C. Tucker

Further Reading

Ambrose, Stephen E. *D-Day, June 6, 1944: The Climactic Battle of World War II.* New York: Simon and Schuster, 1994.

Blair, Clay. *Ridgway's Paratroopers: The American Airborne in World War II.* Garden City, NY: Dial, 1985.

D'Este, Carlo. *Decision in Normandy.* New York: E. P. Dutton, 1983.

Hartcup, Guy. *Code Name Mulberry: The Planning, Building and Operation of the Normandy Harbours.* London: David and Charles, 1977.

Hastings, Max. *Overlord: D-Day, June 6, 1944.* New York: Simon and Schuster, 1984.

Hesketh, Roger. *Fortitude: The D-Day Deception Campaign.* New York: Overlook, 2000.

Keegan, John. *Six Armies in Normandy: From D-Day to the Liberation of Paris, June 6th–August 25th, 1944.* New York: Viking, 1982.

Lewis, Adrian R. *Omaha Beach: A Flawed Victory.* Chapel Hill: University of North Carolina Press, 2001.

Masterman, J. C. *The Double-Cross System in the War of 1939–1945.* New Haven, CT: Yale University Press, 1972.

Mitcham, Samuel W., Jr. *Rommel's Last Battle: The Desert Fox in the Normandy Campaign.* New York: Stein and Day, 1983.

Schofield, B. B. *Operation Neptune.* London: Ian Allan, 1974.

Airborne Forces, British and American

The concept of airborne forces originated in 1918 during World War I, when Colonel William Mitchell, director of U.S. air operations in France, proposed landing part of the U.S. 1st Division behind German lines on the Western Front. Thus was born the idea of parachuting, or air-landing troops behind enemy lines to create a new flank, what would be known as vertical envelopment. The concept was put into action in the 1930s.

The U.S. Army carried out some small-scale experiments at Kelly and Brooks fields in 1928 and 1929, and in 1936 the Soviets demonstrated a full-blown parachute landing, with some 5,000 men taking part. British reaction to the reports of experiments with airborne forces in the Soviet Union was of mild interest only, although the Eastern Command staged some antiparachutist exercises. There the matter rested until the Germans showed how effective parachute and air-landing troops were when they carried out their spectacular air assaults in Norway, Denmark, and the Netherlands in 1940.

Although manpower demands in Britain in 1940 were such that it should have been impossible to raise a parachute force of any significance, at the urging of Prime Minister Winston L. S. Churchill, 500 men were undergoing training as parachutists by August 1940. Fulfillment of Churchill's order that the number be increased to 5,000 had to await additional equipment and aircraft, however. Inevitably, such a new branch of infantry was beset with problems, mainly of supply, but there was also resistance to the concept within the regular units of the British Army. This often led battalions to post their least effective men to such new units merely to get rid of them.

The War Office, representing the British Army, and the Air Ministry, representing the Royal Air Force (RAF), had to agree on aircraft. Because the Bomber Command was becoming aggressively conservative of aircraft, the only plane initially available for training and operations was the Whitley bomber. Aircraft for the airborne forces were thus severely limited until a supply of Douglas C-47 Dakota (Skytrain, in U.S. service) aircraft was established, whereupon the parachute troops found their perfect drop aircraft. The British were also the first Allied nation to develop gliders as troop-carrying aircraft.

Progress in developing British airborne forces was slow; RAF objections were constant, in view of the pressure to carry the continental war to Germany via the strategic bombing campaign. Once the United States entered the war, however, the situation eased enormously, and equipment that Britain was unable to manufacture became readily available.

To provide more men for the airborne forces, the War Office decided in 1941 that whole battalions were to be transferred, even though extra training would be needed to bring many men up to the standards of fitness required of airborne troops. At the same time, the Central Landing Establishment became the main training center for airborne forces. The 1st Parachute Brigade, consisting of four parachute battalions, was established under Brigadier Richard N. "Windy" Gale. Initially three battalions were formed, which exist to this day in the British Army as the 1st, 2nd, and 3rd Battalions, Parachute Regiment.

The Glider Pilot Regiment was also formed in 1941. Pilots were selected from army and RAF volunteers, but they were part of the army once trained. Airborne forces are infantry, but they had to be fitter than the average soldier, and training was rigorous. Troops were trained to endure in the cold, in wet weather, and in heat. They also had to be fit to withstand the impact of the landing, to fight alone with light weapons, and to fight without support for some days.

The airborne concept at that time was twofold: to raid, in which case troops would be extracted by land or sea after the operation (such as the attack on the German radar station at Bruneval in northern France on February 27–28, 1944), or to land at the rear of the enemy to capture a strategic target. Two examples of the latter are the Orne bridge landing on D-Day, June 6, 1944, and Operation MARKET GARDEN (MARKET was the airborne portion) on September 17–26, 1944, when the 1st Airborne Division tried to secure the bridges across the Rhine at Arnhem in Holland.

U.S. Army chief of staff General George C. Marshall was an enthusiastic advocate of airborne forces. The first U.S. airborne division was the 82nd, a conversion of the 82nd Infantry (all-America) Division, formed in March 1942. Major General Omar N. Bradley commanded the division, with Brigadier General Matthew B. Ridgway as his assistant. Ridgway was appointed divisional commander as a major general in June 1942, and the division became the 82nd Airborne Division that August.

The 82nd went to North Africa in April 1943, just as German resistance in that theater was ending. The division took part in operations in Sicily and Normandy and, under the command of Major General James M. Gavin, participated in Operation MARKET GARDEN in the Nijmegen-Arnhem area and also in the Ardennes Offensive (December 16, 1944–January 16, 1945).

The 101st Airborne Division was activated in August 1942 with a nucleus of officers and men from the 82nd Airborne Division. The 101st was commanded by Major General William C. Lee, one of the originators of U.S. airborne forces, and left for England in September 1943. Lee had a heart attack in the spring of 1944, and Major General Maxwell D. Taylor took over, leading the division through D-Day and Operation MARKET GARDEN, when it secured the bridge at Eindhoven. The division distinguished itself in the defense of Bastogne during the German Ardennes Offensive.

Three other U.S. airborne divisions were established: the 11th, which served in the Pacific, jumped onto Corregidor Island, and fought in the February 3–March 4, 1945, Battle of Manila; the 17th, which was rapidly moved to Europe for the German Ardennes Offensive and then jumped into the Rhine crossing with the British 6th Airborne Division; and the 13th, which, although it arrived in France in January 1945, never saw action. British airborne forces also saw limited service in the Pacific theater.

There was close cooperation between British and U.S. airborne forces. When the U.S. 101st Airborne arrived in England, it was installed in a camp close to the training area for the British 6th Airborne Division. Training and operational techniques were almost identical, and there were common exercises and shoots to create close bonds among troops. There were also frequent personnel exchanges to cement friendship. Similar arrangements were made between the U.S. 82nd Airborne and the British 1st Airborne Division.

Parachute training in the United States was centered at Fort Benning, Georgia, and in 1943 some 48,000 volunteers commenced training, with 30,000 qualifying as paratroopers. Of those rejected, some were kept for training as air-landing troops.

One great contribution made by the United States to the common good was the formation and transfer to England of the U.S. Troop Carrier Command. As noted, transport aircraft shortages bedeviled airborne forces' training and operations from the outset. The arrival of large numbers of C-47 aircraft was a major assist. The RAF in 1944 had nine squadrons of aircraft, or a total of 180 planes, dedicated to airborne forces.

Polish troops were also trained in Britain as parachutists to form the Polish 1st Parachute Brigade, which fought at Arnhem in MARKET GARDEN. Contingents from France, Norway, Holland, and Belgium were also trained, many of whom served operationally in the Special Air Service Brigade. The British Commonwealth also raised parachute units. The 1st Australian Parachute Battalion served in the Far East, and the Canadian 1st Parachute Battalion served in Europe.

Several small-scale operations had been carried out before 1943 with mixed success, but the big date for airborne forces was June 6, 1944. Plans for D-Day required the flanks of the invasion beaches to be secured in advance, and only airborne forces could guarantee this. Available in Britain for the invasion were two British airborne divisions (the 1st and 6th) and two American airborne divisions (the 82nd and 101st). The plan was to use all the available airborne and gliderborne troops in the initial stages of the operation. Unfortunately, even in June 1944 transport aircraft available were insufficient for all troops to be dropped at once. All aircraft were organized in a common pool so that either British or American troops could be moved by mainly American aircraft. This was another fine example of the cooperation that existed at all levels within the Allied airborne forces.

Operation OVERLORD (D-Day) began for the paratroopers and gliders in the dark early on June 6. To the west, American paratroopers dropped at the base of the Cotentin Peninsula to secure the forward areas of what were to be Omaha and Utah Beaches. Despite many dispersal problems, most of the troops managed to link up and were soon in action, denying the Germans the ability to move against the beachheads. The troops fought with great gallantry despite their weakened strength (caused by air transport problems), and by the end of the day contact had been established with the invasion forces from the beachheads. In the east, Britain's 6th Airborne Division was charged with controlling the left flank of the British invasion beaches.

Perhaps the most startling operation (for the Germans) was the coup de main attack by glider-borne air-landing troops of 11th Battalion, Oxford and Buckinghamshire Light Infantry, who landed so close to their target that they were able to capture bridges over the Caen Canal and the Orne River. On a larger scale, the 3rd Parachute Brigade was ordered to take out the Merville Battery, which posed a threat to the invasion beaches. The 9th Parachute Battalion, which planned to attack with 700 men, was so spread out on landing that only 150 men were available. With virtually no support, the men attacked the battery and captured it. The battalion lost 65 men and captured 22 Germans; the remainder of the German force of 200 were either killed or wounded.

All Allied parachute and glider troops in the war were of a high standard, and their fighting record bears this out. Even when things went wrong, as often happened when troops were dropped from aircraft, the men made every effort to link up and carry out the task they had been given.

David Westwood

Further Reading

Gale, Sir Richard Nelson. *With the 6th Airborne Division in Normandy.* London: Smason Law, Marston, 1948.

Harclerode, Peter. *Para.* London: Arms and Armour, 1992.

Imperial General Staff. *Airborne Operations.* London: War Office, 1943.

Otway, T. B. H. *Official Account of Airborne Forces.* London: War Office, 1951.

Rottman, Gordon. *World War II Airborne Forces Tactics.* Oxford, UK: Osprey, 2006.

Wright, Robert K., and John T. Greenwood. *Airborne Forces at War.* Annapolis, MD: Naval Institute Press, 2007.

Aircraft, Bombers

Bombers are aircraft designed to attack enemy targets including troop concentrations, installations, and shipping. During the 1930s, bomber designs underwent something of a revolution; performance increased to the point that many bombers were faster than the fighters then in service. The prevailing wisdom, according to Italian aviation theorist General Giulio Douhuet, was "the bomber will always get through." It was assumed that bombers would be sufficiently fast to evade most defending fighters and that defensive armament could deal with any that did intercept. The bomber was therefore seen as something of a terror weapon. Events in the 1936–1939 Spanish Civil War, including the German bombing of Guernica, and the early German experience in World War II tended to reinforce this view.

Operational experience early in World War II led the European powers to retrofit their aircraft with armor and self-sealing fuel tanks. The Germans had essentially a tactical air force geared to the support of ground troops and embraced dive-bombing. All of their bombers had to be able to dive-bomb, but the required structural changes greatly added to the planes' weight and decreased bomb loads.

Defensive armament of the majority of bombers at the start of the war proved inadequate in number and caliber of weapons and/or their field of fire, largely because of the assumption that interceptions at 300-plus miles per hour were difficult and would therefore be rare. Early U.S. Boeing B-17s, for example, had blind spots and single manually aimed weapons. Later B-17 models had much better defensive armament deployed as multiple weapons in power turrets, making them much more difficult to shoot down. An alternative tactic was to dispense with all defensive weapons and rely on speed and performance to evade defenses. The British De Havilland Mosquito, which carried out many pinpoint attacks from 1942 onward, epitomized this approach.

The following describes the most significant bombers employed by the British, Americans, and Germans in the months leading up to the Normandy invasion, during D-Day itself, and in the campaign that followed.

Germany

The Heinkel He-177 "Greif" (Griffin) was a long-range heavy bomber with a crew of six. Ordered in 1939, it entered service in 1942. It was 72 feet 2 inches in length with a wingspan of 103 feet 2 inches. The He-177 had a maximum takeoff weight of 70,548 pounds. Powered by two Daimler-Benz DB 610 24-cylinder liquid-cooled piston engines of 2,700 horsepower each, it had a maximum speed of 351 miles per hour, a ceiling of 26,250 feet, and a combat radius of 957 miles. Armed with two 20mm cannon, one 7.92mm, and four 13mm machine guns, the He-177 could carry up to 13,227 pounds of ordnance internally and up to 15,873 pounds externally, including three glide bombs.

The He-177 was limited in capability owing to engine and structural problems that led to crews calling it the "Luftwaffe Lighter" and the "Flaming Coffin." Also, its considerable fuel consumption rate came at a time when Germany was experiencing major petroleum shortages. During the Normandy campaign the He-177 was employed chiefly on night bombing raids as well as in dropping sea mines in the English Channel to disrupt Allied shipping. Some 1,146 He-117s were built during the war.

Great Britain

The Handley Page Halifax I heavy bomber entered service early in 1941 and was found to be a good bomber, but it lacked adequate defensive armament. The B.III version, which joined the Royal Air Force (RAF) in late 1943, was the most numerous model, using the more powerful Bristol Hercules engine in place of the earlier Merlin. Although the Halifax's main role was as a bomber, it was also employed as a transport, glider tug, and maritime reconnaissance aircraft.

The Halifax had a crew of seven. It was 71 feet 7 inches in length and 104 feet 2 inches in wingspan. It had a maximum weight of 54,400 pounds. Powered by four 1,615-horsepower Bristol Hercules radial engines, it had a maximum speed of 282 miles per hour and an operational ceiling of 24,000 feet. The Halifax had a range of 1,985 miles with 7,000 pounds of bombs. It was armed with nine .30-caliber machine guns and could carry up to 13,000 pounds of bombs. During the Normandy campaign, Halifax heavy bombers flew 75,532 missions, most of them at night, dropping nearly 227,000 tons of bombs. A total of 6,176 Halifaxes were built.

The Avro Lancaster heavy bomber entered operational service with the RAF in early 1942 and soon became the primary RAF strategic bomber. It suffered fewer losses per ton of bombs dropped than the Halifax. The Lancaster had a large bomb bay and was designed to carry 4,000-pound bombs; successive modifications enabled it to carry 8,000- and 12,000-pound weapons, and the B.I (special) carried a single 22,000-pound "Grand Slam" armor-piercing bomb.

The Lancaster had a crew of seven. It was 69 feet 4 inches in length with a wingspan of 102 feet. Powered by four 1,180-horsepower Rolls-Royce Merlin V-type engines, it had a maximum speed of 287 miles per hour and a ceiling of 24,500 feet. It had a maximum weight of 68,000 pounds and a range of 1,730 miles with 12,000 pounds of bombs. Armed with eight .30-caliber machine guns, it could carry up to 18,000 pounds of bombs. A total of 7,366 Lancasters were built.

The De Havilland Mosquito was constructed largely from a plywood/balsa sandwich and was designed to be sufficiently fast to outrun enemy fighters. The Mosquito had excellent handling characteristics. It joined the RAF in the bomber role early in 1942 and quickly demonstrated that it could carry out extremely accurate attacks, including a daring low-level attack on the Gestapo headquarters in Oslo, Norway, in late 1942. Mosquitoes originally equipped the RAF's pathfinder force, and they were able to roam across Germany largely unmolested. Operationally, the Mosquito had by far the lowest loss rate of any aircraft in Bomber Command (about 0.6 percent), as its speed enabled it to avoid most interception, and its structure tended to absorb cannon hits.

The Mosquito had a crew of two. It was 40 feet 6 inches in length and had a wingspan of 54 feet 2 inches. Its maximum weight was 19,093 pounds. Powered by two 1,680-horsepower Rolls-Royce Merlin V-type engines, it had a maximum speed of 408 miles per hour and a ceiling of 37,000 feet. It had a range of 1,370 miles with 4,000 pounds of bombs, its maximum armament. Mosquitoes were employed on D-Day itself and throughout the Normandy campaign, chiefly in a ground-attack role. A total of 6,439 Mosquitoes were built.

United States

The Boeing B-17 Flying Fortress heavy bomber was designed in 1934 and sold to Congress by the U.S. Army Air Corps as an offshore antishipping bomber. The B-17B entered service late in 1939; it was fast and had a high operational ceiling, but the initial versions were not particularly capable. The B-17E, which entered service early in 1942, had much-improved defensive armament, including a tail-gun turret, and the B-17G (late 1943) introduced an additional chin turret, which was later fitted to some F models. The F and G models formed the mainstay of the U.S. heavy day-bomber force in Europe and remained in service until the end of the war.

A Boeing B-17 Flying Fortress, shown here bombing Germany. The B-17 was the principal U.S. strategic bomber in the European Theater of World War II and played an important role in the Normandy invasion. (Library of Congress)

The B-17 had a crew of 9–10 men. It was 74 feet 9 inches in length with a wingspan of 103 feet 10 inches. It had a maximum takeoff weight of 55,000 pounds. Powered by four 1,200-horsepower Wright Cyclone radial engines with a maximum speed of 299 miles per hour and a ceiling of 37,500 feet, it had a range of 2,000 miles with 6,000 pounds of bombs. The G model was armed with 13 .50-caliber machine guns and could carry up to 12,800 pounds of bombs. A total of 8,685 B-17s were built.

The Consolidated B-24 Liberator heavy bomber was designed with a high aspect-ratio wing that, together with its Davis high-lift airfoil, provided very good range/payload performance. The first Liberators entered service with RAF Coastal Command in mid-1941, and the type went on to serve with the U.S. Army Air Forces and the U.S. Navy. The Liberator developed a reputation for fragility in the European theater and was prone to catching fire when hit, but its long range made it the preeminent strategic bomber in the Pacific theater.

The Liberator had a crew of 8–12 men. It was 67 feet 2 inches in length with a wingspan of 110 feet. It had a maximum weight of 56,000 pounds. Powered by four 1,200-horsepower Wright Cyclone radial engines, it was capable of a speed of 290 miles per hour. It had a ceiling of 28,000 feet and a range of 1,700 miles with 5,000 pounds of bombs. It was armed with 10 .50-caliber machine guns and could carry up to 8,000 pounds of bombs.

The B-24 was employed as a reconnaissance, antisubmarine, and transport aircraft as well as in its primary strategic bombing role, and it was produced in greater quantities than any other American aircraft, with 18,188 being built to May 1945.

The North American B-25 Mitchell entered service in late 1940. It had self-sealing fuel tanks and armor protection. The Mitchell had good handling characteristics and was probably the best all-around medium bomber of the war. The B-25 achieved lasting fame when 16 of them, flying from the carrier *Hornet,* attacked Tokyo on April 18, 1942. The Mitchell performed multiple missions including ground strafing, torpedo-bombing, antisubmarine work, and reconnaissance.

The B-25 had a crew of five. It was 52 feet 11 inches in length with a wingspan of 67 feet 7 inches. It had a maximum weight of 33,450 pounds. Powered by two 1,700-horsepower Wright Cyclone radial engines, it was capable of a speed of 275 miles per hour and had a ceiling of 25,000 feet. It had a range of 1,175 miles with 3,200 pounds of bombs. The B-25 mounted a variety of armament, including up to 18 .50-caliber machine guns in the B-25J and a 75mm cannon in the B-25H. It could carry 4,000 pounds of bombs. Mitchells were flown by most Allied air forces, and approximately 11,000 were built.

The Martin B-26 Marauder medium bomber entered service early in 1942 and initially gained a reputation as a difficult aircraft to fly, partly because of its weight and high landing and takeoff speeds. Certainly it required skill and practice to master. In later models (B-26F onward), the wing incidence was increased to reduce the landing and takeoff speeds.

The B-26 had a crew of seven. It was 58 feet 3 inches in length with a wingspan of 71 feet. It had a maximum weight of 37,000 pounds. Powered by two 1,920-horsepower Pratt & Whitney radial engines, it had a maximum speed of 282 miles per hour and a ceiling of 21,700 feet. It had a range of 1,150 miles with 3,000 pounds of bombs. The B-26 was armed with 11 .50-caliber machine guns and could carry up to 5,200 pounds of bombs.

The B-26 could absorb significant damage and was an effective bomber; its final combat loss rate was less than 1 percent. A total of 5,157 were built.

 Andy Blackburn and Spencer C. Tucker

Further Reading

Green, William. *Famous Bombers of the Second World War.* 2nd ed. London: Book Club Associates, 1979.

Jarrett, Philip, ed. *Aircraft of the Second World War.* London: Putnam, 1997.

Munson, Kenneth. *Bombers, Patrol, and Transport Aircraft, 1939–45.* Poole, UK: Blandford, 1975.

Aircraft, Fighters and Fighter-Bombers

Fighters are aircraft designed to shoot down other aircraft. Fighter-bombers are those aircraft capable of engaging enemy aircraft but also well suited to tactical bombing and ground-attack missions. World War II was a period of transition for such aircraft, and by 1945 aircraft weight, armament, and performance had all increased dramatically. The following were the most significant fighters of the Normandy campaign.

Germany

The Messerschmitt Bf-109 (commonly called the Me-109) entered service in its earliest form (Bf-109B) in 1937 and remained in service throughout the war, being constantly modified. It received progressively more powerful engines, and in common with many other aircraft, its handling qualities and maneuverability degraded with successive versions. The Bf-109 could not turn tightly, but it was an effective fighter when handled correctly, possessing excellent dive and zoom climb capabilities. The later versions were better at high altitude, but the controls became stiff at high speeds, and cockpit visibility was poor.

The Bf-109G had a crew of one. It was 29 feet 7 inches in length with a wingspan of 32 feet 6 inches. It had a loaded weight of 6,940 pounds. Powered by a Daimler-Benz DB 605-A liquid-cooled inverted V12 1,455-horsepower engine, it had a maximum speed of 398 miles per hour. Normal range was 528 miles with a service ceiling of 29,370 feet. It was armed with two 13mm machine guns and one 20mm cannon. It could carry a single 551-pound bomb or four 110-pound bombs. Approximately 35,000 Bf-109s were built.

The Focke-Wulf Fw-190A entered service in mid-1941 and became one of the best low- and medium-altitude fighters of the war. It had light and effective controls and possibly the best rate of roll of any World War II fighter. It was superior to the contemporary Spitfire Mk V in all areas except turning circle and was generally regarded as a strong and rugged aircraft. The Germans sent hundreds of Fw-190s into the fight for Normandy.

The Fw-190A8 entered service in February 1944. It had a crew of one. The plane was 29 feet 5 inches in length with a wingspan of 34 feet 5 inches. It had a loaded weight of 9,735 pounds and was powered by a BMW 801 D-2 radial engine of 2,100 horsepower that gave it a maximum speed of 408 miles per hour. It had a range of 500 miles and a ceiling of 37,430 feet. Armament consisted of four 20mm cannon and two 13mm machine guns. A total of 20,001 Focke-Wulf Fw 190s were built.

The twin-engine Messerschmitt Bf-110, designed as a long-range escort fighter, entered service with the Luftwaffe in 1939. It was fast and well armed, but it could not meet contemporary single-engine fighters on equal terms. It was not a success as an escort fighter, but from 1943 the Bf-110G4 enjoyed much success as a radar-equipped night fighter.

The Bf-110 had a crew of two. The Bf-110G2 had a length of 40 feet 6 inches and a wingspan of 53 feet 4 inches. It weighed 17,158 pounds loaded. Powered by two Daimler-Benz DB 605B liquid-cooled inverted V-12 1,455-horsepower engines, it was capable of 370 miles per hour. It had a normal range of 558 miles and a ceiling of 36,000 feet. It was armed with two 20mm cannon and five 7.92mm machine guns. Approximately 6,150 were built.

Great Britain
The Hawker Hurricane entered service in 1937 and was the first monoplane fighter of the Royal Air Force (RAF), serving on all fronts. The Hurricane Mk I was the major RAF fighter during the Battle of Britain. On paper it was average, but it had hidden strengths; it was an excellent gun platform and was more maneuverable than the Spitfire. The Mk I's controls did not stiffen appreciably at high speed, and it was strong, able to withstand maneuvers that would literally pull the wings off its contemporaries. Later versions (Mk IID, Mk IV) were mainly built as fighter-bombers.

The Hurricane Mk 2C had a crew of one. It was 32 feet 3 inches in length with a wingspan of 40 feet. It had a loaded weight of 7,670 pounds. Powered by a Rolls-Royce Merlin XX liquid-cooled V-12, 1,185-horsepower engine, it was capable of 340 miles per hour. It had a range of 600 miles and a ceiling of 36,000 feet. Armament consisted of four 20mm cannon and two 250-pound bombs. A total of 14,233 Hurricanes were manufactured.

The Supermarine Spitfire was an advanced design when the Mk I entered service in 1938 and was able to accept progressively more powerful engines and heavier armament as the war continued, with only a slight reduction in handling qualities. The "Spit" was fast and maneuverable and was widely regarded as a pilot's aircraft. In performance terms, it was usually considered superior to its direct opponents. The Spitfire was continuously updated and revised with many specialist high- and low-altitude versions, and the late-war marks had a particularly impressive performance.

The Spitfire Mk VB had a a crew of one. The plane was 29 feet 11 inches in length with a wingspan of 36 feet 10 inches. It had a loaded weight of 6,622 pounds and was powered by a Rolls-Royce Merlin 45 supercharged V12 engine producing 1,470 horsepower with an aircraft speed of 370 miles per hour. It had a combat radius of 410 miles and a ceiling of 36,500 feet. Armament varied from eight .303 machine guns to two 20mm cannon and four .303 machine guns. A total of 20,351 Spitfires were built.

The Hawker Typhoon was rushed into service late in 1941 to combat the German Fw-190 threat but suffered from teething troubles. Its performance at low altitude was good, particularly its acceleration and dive, but its performance above about 20,000 feet was poor because of its thick wing. Eighteen squadrons of Typhoons were available during the Normandy campaign and savaged the German armor formations. During Operation GOODWOOD (July 18–20, 1944) alone, Typhoon pilots claimed 222 German tanks destroyed by rockets. Allied commander General Dwight D. Eisenhower claimed that "[t]he chief credit in smashing the enemy's spearhead, however, must go to the rocket-firing Typhoon aircraft of the Second Tactical Air Force. . . . The result of the strafing was that the enemy attack was effectively brought to a halt, and a threat was turned into a great victory."

The Typhoon Mk1B had a crew of one. The plane was 31 feet 11 inches in length with a wingspan of 41 feet 7 inches. It had a loaded weight of 11,400 pounds and was powered by a Napier Sabre IIA, IIB, or IIC liquid-cooled H-24 piston engine of 2,180, 2,200, or 2,260 horsepower, producing a maximum speed of 412 miles per hour. It had a maximum range of 510 miles and a ceiling of 35,200 feet. It was armed with four 20mm cannon and eight air-to-ground rockets or two 500- or 1,000-pound bombs. A total of 3,317 Typhoons were built.

The Hawker Tempest appeared early in 1944 and was an aerodynamically cleaner Typhoon with a thinner laminar-flow wing. The Tempest was fast and one of the best late-war fighters. It could be maneuvered easily at high speed and had outstanding dive acceleration and zoom climb capabilities. It was, however, not easy to fly to its limits.

The Tempest V had a crew of one. The Tempest was 33 feet 8 inches in length and had a wingspan of 41 feet. Loaded weight was 11,400 pounds. Powered by a Napier Sabre IIA, IIB, or IIC liquid-cooled H-24 sleeve-valve engine with 2,180 horsepower, it had a maximum speed of 432 miles per hour, a range of 740 miles, and a ceiling of 36,500 feet. Armament consisted of four 20mm cannon, along with eight 3-inch (76.1mm) rockets or two 500-pound bombs. A total of 800 Tempests were built.

The De Havilland Mosquito was conceived as a bomber but was also produced in radar-equipped night-fighter and fighter-bomber versions. The NF.II entered service with the RAF in May 1942 and was successful on night-intruder missions; Mosquito night fighters were used over Germany from late 1944 onward and seriously hampered German night-fighter operations. A total of 1,053 Mosquito night fighters of all versions were built. Mosquitoes also served as reconnaissance aircraft. (Specifications for the Mosquito can be found in the entry Aircraft, Bombers.)

The most numerous Mosquito fighter version was the FB.VI, of which 2,718 were built.

United States
The twin-engine, twin-boom Lockheed P-38 Lightning entered service in numbers early in 1942 and was possibly the ultimate long-range tactical fighter of the war. Its long range made it the primary U.S. Army Air Forces fighter in the Pacific theater. Not as maneuverable as a single-engine fighter, it was fast with effective armament and an outstanding zoom climb. Compressibility problems handicapped diving maneuvers, however. The P-38L was the most numerous Lightning variant and entered service in time to participate in the Normandy campaign, during which it was employed largely as a fighter-bomber in a ground-attack role but also in reconnaissance.

The P-38L had a crew of one. It was 37 feet 10 inches in length and had a wingspan of 52 feet. It had a loaded weight of 17,500 pounds. Powered by two Allison V-1710–111/113 V-12 piston engines with 1,600 horsepower, it was capable of a speed of 414 miles per hour and had a range of 1,300 miles. It was armed with one 20mm cannon and four .50-caliber machine guns. It could also carry 12 4.5-inch (122mm) rockets or two 2,000-pound bombs. A total of 9,923 Lightnings were built.

The North American P-51 Mustang was one of the most successful fighters of World War II. Offered to the British Air Purchasing Commission in April 1940 as an alternative to the Curtiss P-40, the P-51A entered service early in 1942 and was appreciably faster than the P-40 because of its laminar-flow wing and efficient cooling system. It had an excellent dive and zoom climb and was quite maneuverable, but it lacked performance at high altitude. The Mustang's performance was transformed by the substitution of a 1,620-horsepower Rolls-Royce Merlin engine in the P-51B, increasing the ceiling by nearly 10,000 feet and providing a marked performance advantage over Luftwaffe piston-engine fighters, particularly above 20,000 feet.

The P-51D Mustang had a crew of one. The aircraft was 32 feet 3 inches in length with a wingspan of 37 feet. It had a loaded weight of 9,200 pounds, and its Packard V-1650–7 liquid-cooled V-12, with a two-stage intercooled supercharger engine, produced 1,490 horsepower, enabling a top speed of 437 miles per hour. It had a range of 1,650 miles and a ceiling of 39,370 feet. It was armed with 6 .50-caliber machine guns and 6–10 5-inch (127mm) rockets or 1,000 pounds of bombs. A total of 15,686 P-51s were built.

The Republic P-47 Thunderbolt was designed for high-altitude combat and was the heaviest single-engine fighter of the war. Entering service early in 1943, the P-47B was at its best at high speed and altitude. Maneuverability was quite good at high speed, but it became ponderous at lower speeds. Although its climb rate was poor, it had exceptional dive acceleration and was very rugged. The major production model was the P-47D, which had provision for bombs and rockets and was an effective ground-attack aircraft.

The P-47D-30 had a crew of one. It was 36 feet 1 inch in length and 40 feet 9 inches in wingspan. The aircraft had a loaded weight of 12,731 pounds. Powered by a single Pratt & Whitney R-2800–59B twin-row radial engine with 2,600 horsepower, it was capable of a speed of 443 miles per hour. It had a range of 800 miles and a ceiling of 43,000 feet. It was armed with 8 .50-caliber machine guns, along with 10 5-inch (127mm) rockets or up to 2,500 pounds of bombs. A total of 15,683 Thunderbolts were built.

Andy Blackburn and Spencer C. Tucker

Further Reading

Green, William. *Famous Fighters of the Second World War.* 2nd ed. London: Book Club Associates, 1979.

Jarrett, Philip, ed. *Aircraft of the Second World War.* London: Putnam, 1997.

Munson, Kenneth. *Fighters, Attack and Training Aircraft, 1939–45.* Poole, UK: Blandford, 1975.

Price, Alfred. *World War II Fighter Conflict.* London: Macdonald and Janes, 1975.

Aircraft, Gliders

A glider is an aircraft without an engine that is most often released into flight from an aerial tow aircraft. During World War II, both the Axis and Allied militaries developed gliders to transport troops, supplies, and equipment into battle. Although this technique had been discussed prior to the war, it had not been implemented. Gliders were to land behind enemy lines, often at night, and the men carried by them would then become infantrymen once on the ground.

The Germans were first to recognize the potential of gliders in the war, in large part because of extensive pre–World War II scientific research and sporting use. The Germans embraced gliding because it did not violate military prohibitions in the 1919 Treaty of Versailles. Gliding clubs, which developed in other countries as well, increased interest in the sport worldwide. Sport gliders used air currents to climb and soar for extended periods, while military gliders simply descended on release from aerial tows.

The Germans employed gliders in their invasion of Belgium and the Netherlands in May 1940, especially in securing Fort Eben Emael (May 10), the key to overrunning Belgium. The Germans also used gliders in the invasion of Crete (May 21–June 1, 1941) and during fighting in the Soviet Union in the Battle of Stalingrad (August 23, 1942–February 2, 1943).

Great Britain was the first Allied nation to deploy gliders. The Air Ministry's Glider Committee encouraged the use of the Hotspur to transport soldiers in late 1940. The Hotspur had a wingspan of 61 feet 11 inches, a length of 39 feet 4 inches, and a height of 10 feet 10 inches. It weighed 1,661 pounds empty and 3,598 pounds fully loaded. The Hotspur was designed to transport two crewmen and six soldiers. A total of 1,015 were built.

In 1941, the British developed the Airspeed A.S. 51 Horsa. It had a wingspan of 88 feet, a length of 68 feet, and a height of 20 feet 3 inches. It weighed 8,370 pounds empty and 15,750 pounds fully loaded. It had a crew of two men and was capable of carrying 25 passengers or two trucks. In all, some 5,000 Horsas were built. They were employed in Operation OVERLORD east of the British invasion beaches, most noteworthy in the successful effort to seize control of Bénouville Bridge (Pegasus Bridge) spanning the Caen Canbal.

The largest Allied glider was the British General Aircraft Limited GAL 49 Hamilcar. With a wingspan of 110 feet, a length of 68 feet 6 inches, and a height of 20 feet 3 inches, it weighed 18,000 pounds empty and 36,000 pounds fully loaded. It had a crew of 2 and could transport 40 troops, a light tank, or artillery pieces. A total of 412 were built.

By the time of the Normandy invasion, only 50 Hamilcars had been produced. Thirty-four were employed as part of Operation MALLARD in support of the British 6th Airborne Division. They transported Tetrarch light tanks and antitank 17-pounder guns. Several gliders were damaged on landing and their cargo lost.

The U.S. Navy explored the possibility of military applications for gliders as early as the 1930s. In February 1941, chief of the Army Air Corps Major General Henry H. "Hap" Arnold ordered specifications drawn up for military gliders. The Waco Aircraft Company in Troy, Ohio, received the first U.S. government contract to build training gliders, and the army began organizing a glider training program.

Constructed of plywood and canvas with a skeleton of steel tubing, the Waco CG-4A had a wingspan of 83 feet 6 inches, a length of 48 feet 4 inches, and a height of 12 feet 7 inches. Its empty weight was 3,300 pounds, and its loaded weight was 7,500 pounds. It had a crew of 2 men and could carry 13 troops or 3,800 pounds of cargo, including artillery pieces, a bulldozer, or a jeep. The Ford Motor Company plant at Kingsford, Michigan, manufactured most of the U.S. gliders, although 15 other companies also produced the Waco. In all 13,908 Wacos were built, making it the most heavily produced glider of the entire war by any power.

Towed by the Douglas C-47 transport, the Waco was first employed in the July 1943 Allied invasion of Sicily. A number of Waco gliders were used in Operation OVERLORD to land men and equipment east of the invasion beaches. A number were damaged or lost, and there were heavy casualties.

Because the gliders were so fragile, soldiers dubbed them "canvas coffins." Men and cargo were loaded through the wide, hinged nose section, which could be quickly opened. Moving at an airspeed of 110–150 miles per hour at an altitude of several thousand feet, C-47s towed the gliders with a 300-foot rope toward a designated landing zone and then descended to release the glider several hundred feet above the ground.

En route to the release point, the glidermen and plane crew communicated with each other either by a telephone wire secured around the towline or via two-way radios. Glider duty was quite hazardous; sometimes the gliders were released prematurely and

Aircraft, Gliders | 13

Oblique aerial view of parachutes and Airspeed Horsa gliders on Landing Zone N of the British 6th Airborne Division near Ranville, France, on the morning of June 6, 1944. (Royal Air Force Official Photographer/IWM via Getty Images)

did not reach the landing zones, and on occasion gliders collided as they approached their destination.

The U.S. 11th, 13th, 17th, 82nd, and 101st Airborne Divisions were organized with two glider infantry regiments, a glider artillery battalion, and glider support units. U.S. gliders were sent to North Africa in 1942 and participated in the July 9–August 22, 1943, Sicily invasion, accompanied by British gliders. High casualties sustained in that operation led General Dwight D. Eisenhower to question the organization of airborne divisions and to threaten to disband glider units. A review board of officers convinced the military authorities to retain them, however. Improvements were also made in structural reinforcement of the glider and in personnel training.

By mid-1944, gliders had become essential elements of Allied invasion forces. Occasionally they were used to transport wounded to hospitals. During the Normandy invasion, U.S. glidermen with the 82nd and 101st Airborne Divisions flew across the English Channel in 2,100 gliders to participate in the D-Day attack. Many gliders and crews were lost. New gliders were manufactured for Operation MARKET GARDEN, the assault on the Germans in the Netherlands, three months later.

Initially the military did not authorize hazardous-duty pay for glidermen, who also did not qualify for wing insignia worn by parachutists. Some of the men created posters; one read "Join the Glider Troops! No Jump Pay. No Flight Pay. But Never a Dull Moment." By July 1944 glider wings were authorized for glider soldiers, and they received hazardous-duty pay. Also in 1944, the modified Waco CG-15A appeared, offering improved crash absorption. The Waco CG-18A could carry 30 soldiers and was deployed during the 1945 Rhine campaign. Gliders were gradually phased out of military inventories after the war, although the Soviet Union retained them through the 1950s.

Elizabeth D. Schafer

Further Reading

Devlin, Gerard M. *Silent Wings: The Saga of the U.S. Army and Marine Combat Glider Pilots during World War II.* New York: St. Martin's, 1985.

Lowden, John L. *Silent Wings at War: Combat Gliders in World War II.* Washington, DC: Smithsonian Institution Press, 1992.

Masters, Charles J. *Glidermen of Neptune: The American D-Day Glider Attack.* Carbondale: Southern Illinois University Press, 1995.

Mrazek, James E. *Fighting Gliders of World War II.* New York: St. Martin's, 1977.

Mrazek, James E. *The Glider War.* New York: St. Martin's, 1975.

Seth, Ronald. *Lion with Blue Wings: The Story of the Glider Regiment, 1942–1945.* London: Gollancz, 1955.

Smith, Claude. *The History of the Glider Pilot Regiment.* London: Leo Cooper, 1992.

Aircraft, Transports

Transport aircraft have the primary purpose of the movement of personnel and supplies. By the early 1930s, improvements in aircraft design and, more important, aircraft engines resulted in the emergence of civil aviation aircraft, such as the Douglas DC-3, for commercial passenger service. Military planners were quick to note these developments, which raised the prospect of rapidly deploying large numbers of men and supplies to the battle zone, including behind enemy lines. By the beginning of World War II, most of the powers that would become involved in the war had either already developed military variants of these civil aircraft or had introduced specially designed military transport aircraft.

Two main types of transport aircraft were employed during the war: large multiengine land-based aircraft or flying boats designed to move many troops or supplies (some of which also served in bombing and reconnaissance roles) and assault or transport gliders designed to be towed and then released so they could glide silently to a landing behind enemy lines (see the entry Aircraft, Gliders).

The following are the most significant aircraft employed primarily for transport by both sides during the Normandy campaign.

Germany

Designed originally in 1930 as a three-engine passenger carrier for Deutsche Lufthansa, the Junkers Ju-52/3m served as the primary transport aircraft of the German Army in World War II. The aircraft made its military debut as a bomber and troop transport during the 1936–1939 Spanish Civil War. Successive versions of the Ju-52/3m incorporated more powerful engines that provided greater load capacity and interchangeable wheel, ski, or float landing gear that allowed it to operate in a variety of conditions.

The Ju-88G-1 had a crew of three. It was 58 feet 9 inches in length with a wingspan of 65 feet 10 inches. Empty weight was 20,020 pounds, with a loaded weight of 28,880 pounds. Powered by two BMW 801G-2 double-row radial engines of 1,677 horsepower each, it had a maximum speed of 342 miles per hour, a ceiling of 32,480 feet, a range of 1,553 miles, and a flight endurance of four hours. It was armed with 4–6 20mm and 1–2 13mm machine guns.

In addition to its transport duties, the Ju-52 served as a bomber, an air ambulance, a glider tug, and a paratrooper transport. Including the approximately 200 civil models constructed prior to the war, a total of 4,800 Ju-52/3ms were built by the end of 1944.

United States

Of all the powers in World War II, the United States had by far the largest number and variety of transport aircraft, in part because it was conducting simultaneous campaigns in the European and Pacific theaters.

Without question, the twin-engine Douglas C-47 Skytrain was the most famous transport aircraft of World War II. As the DC-3, it had revolutionized civil air travel before the war. Once the United States entered the war, the Skytrain went into full-scale military production; 10,665 were produced by war's end, including 4,878 in 1944 alone.

The C-47 could tow two CG-4 Waco assault gliders or one large British Horsa glider. As an aerial ambulance, it was capable of transporting 18 stretcher cases and a medical crew of three. Seven basic C-47 versions were built, and the aircraft had at least 22 separate designations.

Of its variants, the C-47 Skytrain (known as the Dakota in British service) accounted for more than 9,000 of the total produced, approximately 1,800 of which went to Great Britain through Lend-Lease. An additional 2,500 were constructed on license by the Soviet Union as the Lisunov Li-2. Even the Japanese built 485 as the Nakajima L2D through a 1938 license.

The C-47 Skytrain had a crew of 4 and could carry 28 troops. It was 63 feet 9 inches in length with a wingspan of 95 feet 6 inches. It had an empty weight of 18,135 pounds and a loaded weight of 36,600 pounds. Powered by two Pratt & Whitney R-1830 radial engines of 1,200 horsepower each, it had a maximum speed of 224 miles per hour, a service ceiling of 26,400 feet, and a range of 1,600 miles.

The C-47 saw service in every theater of the war and gained renown as the primary glider tow and transport aircraft for airborne forces in the Normandy invasion. During the invasion, more than 12,000 C-47 Skytrains transported 13,100 paratroopers and 3,900 glider troops. The C-47 saw notable service in the 1948 Berlin Airlift as well as the Korean War, and even the Vietnam War.

Justin D. Murphy and Spencer C. Tucker

Further Reading

Jarrett, Philip, ed. *Aircraft of the Second World War.* London: Putnam, 1997.

Munson, Kenneth. *Bombers, Patrol, and Transport Aircraft, 1939–45.* Poole, UK: Blandford, 2002.

Murphy, Justin D., and Matthew A. McNiece. *Military Aircraft, 1919–1945: An Illustrated History of Their Impact.* Santa Barbara, CA: ABC-CLIO, 2008.

Wilson, Stewart. *Aircraft of WWII.* Fyshwick, Australia: Aerospace Publications, 1998.

Air Warfare, Ground-Attack Aviation

Ground-attack aviation refers to the dedicated use of combat aircraft to attack ground combat units and their supporting echelons on or near the front lines in support of friendly ground forces. The practice of supporting infantry ground attack with aircraft gained acceptance late in World War I. Air attacks increasingly were employed both in immediate support of ground operations at the front and also on rear-echelon enemy units.

During the interwar period military theory and doctrine bifurcated, with two distinct schools of thought developing regarding the proper use of airpower. One school followed the precepts of Italian theorist Giulio Douhet and advocated concentration on strategic bombing by heavy self-defending "battle planes" on targets far behind the battle lines, with the intent of collapsing an enemy nation's will. Most British and U.S. airpower advocates supported this concept.

The second school of thought, generally adhered to by the Soviet Union, France, and Germany, advocated airpower as direct support for ground operations. Aircraft would primarily attack targets on the front lines or behind the front, as much as 150 miles. These theorists saw such strikes as enabling ground forces later to move farther in the attack or to yield less terrain in the defense. The German Luftwaffe was essentially a tactical air force, intended for close air support and geared to ground operations.

Each school drove aircraft design in particular directions. Thus, the United States and Great Britain came up with four-engine "strategic" bombers such as the American Boeing B-17 Flying Fortress (Douhet's self-defending "battle plane") and the British Avro Lancaster. The Germans, however, concentrated on fast fighters such as the Bf-109 (also known as the Me-109) to secure air superiority over the battlefield for fast, medium-size, dual-engine bombers such as the Heinkel He-111 and the Dornier Do-17.

The Germans, having learned from U.S. Marine Corps operations in Latin America, also embraced dive-bombing and developed their important single-engine Junkers Ju-87 Stuka, which could deliver its ordnance with great accuracy and proved vital during the war's early campaigns. The prototype Ju-87 flew in 1935 and entered service with the Luftwaffe in the spring of 1937. Examples sent to Spain with the Kondor Legion in 1938 demonstrated highly accurate bombing under conditions of air superiority. Stukas were highly effective in the invasions of Poland in 1939 and France in 1940, but during the Battle of Britain (July 10–September 30, 1940), they suffered such heavy losses from opposing British fighters that they were withdrawn from operations partway through the campaign. They continued to serve in the Mediterranean theater, however, and on the Eastern Front in dive-bombing and close ground-support roles. The Ju-87 was easily recognizable, with its inverted gull wings and fixed spatted landing gear that mounted the Jericho-Trompete (Jericho Trumpet) wailing sirens. Some 6,000 of all versions were built.

The multiple German blitzkriegs against Poland (1939), Norway (1940), and France (1940) demonstrated the great importance of the ground-attack school of thought. Luftwaffe units, especially of the Ju-87, working in close coordination with advancing columns of German infantry and armor, were a key element in allowing those columns to cut through opposing forces with seeming ease, although German air-to-ground coordination was far from perfect, and a number of German soldiers became casualties of friendly fire.

Beginning with British forces in eastern North Africa and then with the Americans in French North Africa, the Western Allies developed their own system of close air support. Almost immediately, the Americans discovered that their own system of command and control for ground-attack operations, developed before the war, was inefficient and unable to keep up with rapidly shifting operations on the ground. Capitalizing on their great strength of adapting to circumstance, the Americans jettisoned their own doctrine nearly wholesale and adopted a modified version of the British system. Thereafter their efficiency in ground-attack operations increased markedly.

At the same time, the Soviet Air Force, which had suffered heavily in the German invasion in June 1941, perfected its own system of ground-support aviation. The Soviets developed highly successful ground-attack fighters and fighter-bombers in the Yakovlev Yak-4 and especially the heavily armored Ilyushin Il-2 Sturmovik. Flying low and employing rockets, Sturmoviks were efficient tank killers and were perhaps the best ground-attack aircraft of the war. In testimony to its success, the Sturmovik remained in production until 1955; the Soviets produced some 36,000 of them.

Simultaneously, the Western Allies began to specialize—in use if not in design—their own aircraft. Great Britain and the United States entered the war with credible, if not outstanding, medium bombers such as the North American B-25 Mitchell and the British Bristol Blenheim. The British added other aircraft, including the versatile De Havilland Mosquito, while the Americans produced excellent fighters in the ground-attack role, such as the Vought F4U Corsair, the twin-engine Lockheed P-38 Lightning, the Republic P-47 Thunderbolt, and the North American P-51 Mustang.

The P-38, P-47, and P-51 were originally designed as bomber escorts or classic conventional pursuit planes (hence the "P" in the nomenclature). The P-51 Mustang, a superb aircraft, may have been the best all-around fighter of the war, but the P-38 and P-47 each had characteristics that made them more suited to lower-level work and the rigors of close air support. For the Thunderbolt, it was the fact that the aircraft could absorb significant damage and continue flying. Its air-cooled engine was less susceptible to failure from damage than that of the Mustang, and ground-attack work generally meant taking ground fire while flying at low altitude. The Lightning had twin engines on twin booms with a pod for the pilot slung between them, and it combined decent range with the heavy punch of five .50-caliber machine guns that fired straight ahead from the central pod. (The guns of most conventional aircraft were aimed inward to a single point.) This gave the Lightning lethal accuracy; the dual air-cooled engines gave the pilot a decent chance to make it home even if one engine shut down. On the British side was the Hawker Typhoon, an underappreciated contender for the title of best ground-attack aircraft of the war.

Ground-attack aviation was immensely important in the success of the Normandy invasion and the subsequent breakout. (The expectation of losses to friendly ground fire prompted the painting of black and white stripes on all Allied aircraft from 1944.) On D-Day alone the Allies flew 14,674 sorties (a sortie being one flight by one aircraft). These attacks destroyed few German aircraft on the ground, however. Most of those claimed destroyed, however, were actually obsolete types or dummy aircraft set up by the Germans to attract attack. Repair facilities and fuel supply areas did take heavy punishment, however, and this significantly impacted German air operations against the invaders.

Within a few days of the invasion, the Luftwaffe had deployed some 800 aircraft to France. The X Air Corps took delivery of 45 Ju-88 torpedo bombers, while the IX Air Corps received 90 bombers. Half of the fighter aircraft in France with the II Air Corps were immediately assigned to ground-attack missions. Although the Focke Wolfe 190 was an excellent ground-attack aircraft, the pilots who accompanied it had little training as interceptor pilots and no training in ground-attack operations. The latter proved so ineffective that on June 12 the II Air Corps ordered a halt to all ground-attack missions and went back to a purely interceptor role.

By June 9 in an extraordinary effort, the Luftwaffe was able to fly 500 sorties a day against the invasion, but this effort met scant success in part because the Allies had been able to destroy most of the German radar sites in France. Owing to their few reconnaissance flights and poor intelligence, the German aircraft were largely reduced to fighter sweeps in the direction of the Allied lodgments. Mining operations against Allied resupply efforts in the English Channel were somewhat more successful, and within 10 days they had sunk two minesweepers and damaged two dozen other vessels. By the end of June the Germans had sown some 4,000 mines. During June the Germans sent more than 1,100 aircraft to France as reinforcements, but most of these were soon lost. Indeed, June was the worst month in 1944 for the Germans in terms of aircraft losses.

The air-ground team for the Western Allies in the European theater of operations truly came into its own in the summer of 1944 with Major General Elwood "Pete" Quesada's IX Tactical Fighter Command. Quesada developed the "armored column cover," in which on-call fighter-bombers could be utilized for ground advances, thus allowing armor units to continue their

Bearing special striped markings on wings and fuselage, a B-26 Marauder of the U.S. Ninth Air Force flies at low altitude over the English Channel on June 6, 1944, to attack gun installations and coastal defenses as landing craft below head toward the Normandy coast. (Photo12/UIG/Getty Images)

advances even when they had outrun their own artillery. Quesada also placed pilots in frontline tanks as forward air controllers, and he employed VHF radios and microwave early warning radar to vector fighter-bombers in real time to their targets. In July 1944 Quesada provided VHF aircraft radios to tank crews, enabling the tank commanders to communicate directly with the fighter-bombers.

Such air-to-ground coordination was manifest following the Allied breakout from Normandy in the complete linkage between Lieutenant General George S. Patton's Third Army, the widest-ranging and fastest-moving element of the Allied sweep across France, and the XIX Tactical Air Command, commanded by Quesada's friend Major General Otto P. Weyland, who employed similar tactics. Patton's rapid advance left his southern flank exposed, and he relied on flank protection by the XIX TAC. Ground-attack aviation was undoubtedly a key factor in the rapid advance and success of the Third Army in its advance across France and into Germany.

Robert L. Bateman and Spencer C. Tucker

Further Reading

Boyne, Walter J. *Clash of Wings: World War II in the Air.* New York: Simon and Schuster, 1994.

Buckley, John. *Air Power in the Age of Total War.* London: UCL Press, 1999.

Hallion, Richard P. *Strike from the Sky: The History of Battlefield Air Attack, 1911–1945.* Washington, DC: Smithsonian Institution Press, 1989.

Hughes, Thomas Alexander. *Overlord: General Pete Quesada and the Triumph of Tactical Air Power in World War II.* New York: Free Press, 1995.

Murray, Williamson. *Luftwaffe.* Baltimore: Nautical and Aviation Publishing, 1985.

Amphibious Warfare in the European Theater

Amphibious warfare is the projection of sea-based ground forces onto land. Amphibious warfare was more widely conducted in World War II than in any previous conflict and on a greater scale than ever before or since. Involving all aspects of naval and military operations—from mine warfare to air and ground combat—amphibious operations are the riskiest and most complex of all military endeavors. The basic principles had been established during World War I and in the postwar period, but the lessons were largely ignored by most military leaders except those in the Soviet Union, the U.S. Marine Corps, and Germany's Landungspionieren (Landing Pioneers). The Royal Navy concluded that the British Gallipoli operation of 1915 had demonstrated the great difficulty of a successful amphibious assault in modern war.

Japan's navy and army developed separate procedures, forces, and equipment to conduct amphibious operations, and they had the good fortune to carry out their early assaults from 1937 against undefended beaches in China and at the beginning of the Pacific war. The German Navy had no interest in amphibious operations before the war, but ironically, Germany initiated the war's first large-scale amphibious operation when it invaded Norway in April 1940. It was the Allies, however, who demonstrated true mastery of the amphibious art. In the end, they landed more than 4 million troops in five major amphibious assaults, dozens of tactical landings, and countless raids along German-occupied coasts of Europe. Amphibious operations provided the Western Allies with their only means of taking the ground war to the European Axis countries. In the Pacific theater, there could have been no Allied victory without amphibious warfare.

Amphibious operations come in three levels—strategic, operational, and tactical—depending on the intended objectives. The Allied landings in France, the Philippines, and Italy and the planned invasion of Japan are examples of strategic landings intended to have decisive impact on the war. The November 8, 1942, North African landings (Operation TORCH), the German assaults in the Dodecanese Islands beginning in October 1943, and most of the Allied assaults in the Pacific were operational-level landings that supported a specific campaign, each part of an overall strategic effort. Soviet landings and most Allied commando raids were tactical-level operations for limited objectives, although some had a strategic impact (capturing German codes, radars, and so on). The Dunkerque (May 26–June 4, 1940) and Crete (May 1941) evacuations are difficult to categorize, but most observers would describe them as operational-level efforts.

Amphibious operations fall into four types: raids, assaults, evacuations, and administrative (noncombat) landings. The first of these is the most dangerous, as it generally is executed against superior enemy forces and involves elements of both an assault and an evacuation. An administrative landing is the safest, being conducted in a benign environment with no enemy ground, air, or naval forces present. Assaults and evacuations face varying levels of risk, depending on the defender's strength and support. The 1940 German invasion of Norway is an example of an assault, although many of its forces came ashore in circumstances approaching that of an administrative landing. Britain's Dunkerque evacuation was the war's first major combat evacuation, while Germany's naval evacuation of its forces from the Baltic in the war's final months was the conflict's largest such operation.

In 1939 the German Army was the only service to recognize the need to rehearse landings and procedures for a specific landing. By 1943, every major military leader realized the necessity for such. Then as today, amphibious operations were broken down into five phases: planning, embarkation, rehearsal, movement to the objective area, and the assault. Soviet doctrine added a sixth phase, the landing of the follow-on army forces.

Germany did not generate a capacity to land troops against determined opposition until well into 1942. By then, Germany's strategic situation precluded such operations except in limited and special circumstances, such as the landings during the Dodecanese campaign. Despite its prewar aversion to amphibious operations, the German Navy conducted World War II's largest amphibious evacuation during the war's final six months. Carried out under desperate circumstances of Soviet air superiority and naval parity, Germany's withdrawal of more than 2 million troops, civilians, and critical equipment from the Baltic is one of the war's more remarkable military achievements. Nonetheless, amphibious warfare was never more than a useful adjunct to German military operations and usually was conducted as an ad hoc affair before 1942.

Necessarily, the Japanese military was much interested in amphibious warfare in the 1930s. The Japanese pioneered development of ramp–front-end landing craft, later copied by other countries, including the United States. The Imperial Japanese Army used amphibious landings to outflank British forces in Malaya and to invade the Philippines, the Netherlands East Indies, and other Pacific islands.

The Soviet Union had a specialized amphibious force of naval infantry at war's start, but it lacked equipment and training. Soviet amphibious forces were expected to land on the beach using ships' boats or other improvised transport. Soviet doctrine called for naval infantry to conduct amphibious raids and support the army's landing by seizing and holding the beachhead while conventional forces disembarked behind them. This approach proved costly in combat, because any delays in the follow-on landing left the naval infantry dangerously exposed to counterattack. As a result, Soviet naval infantry suffered heavy casualties in their amphibious assaults.

On September 23, 1941, the Soviet Black Sea Fleet conducted the Allies' first amphibious assault when a naval infantry regiment was landed against the flank of the Romanian forces besieging Odessa. In fact, amphibious raids and assaults figured prominently in Soviet naval operations along Germany's Black Sea and Arctic Sea flanks, with the Soviets conducting more than 150 amphibious raids and assaults during the war.

Prime Minister Winston L. S. Churchill forced Britain to develop an amphibious warfare capability with the formation of Combined Operations Command. Beginning in June 1940, this organization conducted amphibious commando raids along the coasts of German-occupied Europe. Such raids became more effective as lessons were learned, expertise was expanded, and training was improved.

Britain's assault tactics and equipment were driven primarily by lessons learned from the unsuccessful Dieppe Raid (Operation JUBILEE) on August 19, 1942. The German beach obstacles, extensive minefield belts, and overlapping antitank and artillery fire proved devastating, suggesting to the British a need for specialized vehicles and equipment. Those "funnies," as they came to be known, were ready by the June 6, 1944, Normandy landings but not in time for the earlier Allied landings in North Africa, Sicily, and Italy.

The U.S. Army, present in only a limited capacity at Dieppe, saw little requirement for specialized amphibious equipment other than landing craft, but it did see a need to remove beach obstacles and isolate the beachhead from enemy reinforcement. The smaller land areas and the lack of a heavily mechanized counterattack threat obviated the need to isolate Pacific assault beaches from reinforcements. Hence, airborne operations were not endemic to Pacific theater amphibious assaults, although they were planned for the invasion of Japan.

Operation TORCH in North Africa on November 8, 1942, was the Western Allies' first amphibious assault against a defended beach in the European theater, albeit not a heavily contested one, but it provided the foundations for U.S. amphibious warfare doctrine in Europe. The TORCH landings saw the first employment of underwater demolition teams (UDTs) and the specialized amphibious landing ships that were so critical to getting forces ashore quickly. The tank landing ships (LSTs) were particularly important, as they enabled tanks to land directly on the assault beach.

Although many mistakes were made in the planning and execution of TORCH, it established the basic foundations for all future Allied assaults in the West. All subsequent landings were preceded by special forces, such as UDTs and commandos, to remove obstacles and seize key terrain and defensive features before the main assault force approached the beach. Operation TORCH also exposed the need to rehearse the actual landings well in advance of the assault to ensure a smooth and rapid disembarkation.

Costly Allied naval antiaircraft fire against Allied aircraft carrying the airborne assault force during the Sicily landing (Operation HUSKY) of July 9–August 22, 1943, demonstrated the need for reliable coordination and identification procedures. The operation involved two armies—one British and one U.S.—of two corps each. The six-week battle for Sicily opened the 1943–1945 Italian campaign and drove Benito Mussolini from power; however, it was a close-run affair.

The Germans launched an armored counterattack on the landing's second day, July 10, that nearly cut the beachhead in half and was stopped only by intensive naval gunfire support. The Germans' near success here convinced Allied planners that the early assault waves needed tanks, placing a premium on tank-landing ships in naval construction.

Additional lessons about air and naval support were gained there and at the September 9, 1943, Salerno landings (Operation AVALANCHE), where naval gunfire support proved critical to stopping German armored counterattacks. More significant, procedures and equipment were developed to accelerate the pace of force buildup ashore. That it was a successful effort can best be measured by the success of the Normandy landings (Operations NEPTUNE and OVERLORD) on June 6, 1944, that placed six divisions ashore in less than 24 hours and nearly 1 million men and their equipment in France in less than a week—a phenomenal accomplishment. The subsequent August 15, 1944, landings in southern France (Operation DRAGOON) were not as large, landing a total of fewer than 250,000 troops, but were equally impressive and, coming only two months after the Normandy landings, highlighted the Allies' growing amphibious capacity.

The pinnacle of amphibious operations in the war was achieved in the Pacific theater by the U.S. Marine Corps, which made amphibious assault its raison d'être. Indeed, the first U.S. offensive actions of the war were its landings at Guadalcanal and Tulagi in August 1942. Although mistakes were made in the early going, specialized equipment and vehicles were introduced, and doctrine was modified. This culminated in Operation ICEBERG, the U.S. invasion of Okinawa (March–June 1945), which was the Western Allies' final amphibious operation.

Amphibious operations were critical to the Allied victory in the war. Lacking a land border with Axis territory after 1940, the Western Allies could never have contributed to Germany's defeat or beaten Japan had they not mastered amphibious operations, the most complex of all military activities. The war firmly established the amphibious operations procedures that are employed by all Western nations to this day.

Carl Otis Schuster

Further Reading

Achkasov, V. I., and N. B. Pavlovich. *Soviet Naval Operations in the Great Patriotic War.* Annapolis, MD: Naval Institute Press, 1981.

Clifford, Kenneth J. *Amphibious Warfare Development in Britain and America from 1920–1940.* New York: Edgewood, 1983.

Miller, Nathan. *War at Sea.* New York: Oxford University Press, 1995.

Morison, Samuel E. *History of United States Naval Operations in World War II,* Vols. 2, 4, 5, 9, 10, and 11. Boston: Little, Brown, 1947–1952.

Roskill, Stephen W. *The War at Sea, 1939–1945.* 3 vols. London: HMSO, 1957–1961.

Antitank Guns and Antitank Warfare

The evolution of antitank (AT) warfare in World War II was a continual trade-off between technology and tactical doctrine. At the start of the war, most armies believed that the tank itself was the most effective AT weapon. In the earliest days of the fighting, however, it became clear that the smaller-caliber guns on most tanks were ineffective against opposing armor. The light, towed AT guns that were supposed to be the backup system were even less effective.

Thus, field artillery firing in the direct-fire mode became the primary AT system in 1941 and 1942 on the Eastern Front and in North Africa. Field artillery was only able to return to its primary direct-support mission in late 1942 after large numbers of heavier AT guns had been fielded. Infantry armed with AT rifles, supposed to be the third line of AT defense, proved mostly worthless and were quickly replaced with projector-type weapons such as the U.S. bazooka, the British PIAT, and the German *Panzerfaust*.

Well before the war, German doctrine recognized that high-velocity, flat-trajectory antiaircraft guns could be used in an AT role in emergency situations. In North Africa, the Germans quickly discovered that their 88mm flak guns were devastatingly effective against British tanks.

Most armies used field artillery crews to man AT units. As the war progressed, AT guns became larger and more powerful, and many were mounted on self-propelled carriages to give them mobility equal to the tank. The Germans on the Eastern Front pioneered the use of self-propelled AT guns in an offensive role. The Soviets also developed a wide range of self-propelled weapons. Almost all American self-propelled AT guns were turret-mounted, but the Germans and especially the Soviets favored turretless vehicles. They were simpler and cheaper to build, and the lack of a turret produced a lower profile that made the vehicles smaller targets. The Soviets spent the first two years of the war on the defensive, and as a result they mastered defensive AT tactics.

The U.S. Army organized AT guns into tank-destroyer battalions. In 1942, a tank-destroyer battalion had three companies of three platoons with four guns each, either towed or self-propelled. American self-propelled tank destroyers did not do well in North Africa. The operational area was too vast for the guns to mass effectively, and the terrain was too open for the self-propelled vehicles to find good defensive hull-down positions.

Many American commanders shifted to the British system of towed AT guns, but these proved far less effective when combat operations later moved to Western Europe. In that more restricted terrain the towed guns moved too slowly, and they were too close to the ground to shoot over hedgerows, as in Normandy. By July 1944, the U.S. Army started reequipping all tank-destroyer battalions with self-propelled guns, but some units still had towed guns by the time of the Battle of the Bulge/Ardennes Offensive (December 16, 1944–January 15, 1945).

As World War II progressed, the balance shifted back and forth between heavier and more powerful AT guns and thicker and heavier tank armor. Tank designers were faced with the challenge of developing tanks with guns powerful enough to defeat enemy armor yet with armor strong enough to resist the fire from enemy tanks and AT guns. Larger guns produced more recoil, which required a larger and heavier turret. This combined with stronger armor added to the overall weight of the tank, decreasing the tank's mobility and creating a larger target.

Most World War II tanks had heavier armor on the front and sides, where the tank was more likely to be attacked.

No single system stood out in World War II as the premier tank killer, although certain systems predominated at certain times and in certain theaters. Throughout the war, German tanks were generally better armed and more powerful than their British and American counterparts. This meant that Allied tanks destroyed far fewer panzers than the other way around.

David T. Zabecki

Further Reading

Bailey, Jonathan B. A. *Field Artillery and Firepower.* 2nd ed. Annapolis, MD: Naval Institute Press, 2003.

Gabel, Christopher R. *Seek, Strike, and Destroy: U.S. Army Tank Destroyer Doctrine in World War II.* Ft. Leavenworth, KS: Combat Studies Institute, U.S. Army Command and General Staff College, 1986.

Hogg, Ian V. *German Artillery of World War Two.* Mechanicsburg, PA: Stackpole Books, 1975.

Weeks, John S. *Men against Tanks: A History of Antitank Warfare.* New York: Mason/Charter, 1975.

Artillery and Fire Support

When the Allies landed in Normandy on June 6, 1944, their fire-support systems included field artillery, infantry mortars, close air support, and naval gunfire. The German defenders had field artillery, infantry mortars, close air support, and coastal guns mounted in reinforced concrete bunkers.

Field Artillery

During the early stages of the landings, one of the tactical imperatives for the Allies was to get their field artillery ashore as fast as possible so they could support land operations. By the end of June 6, the British and Canadians had managed to land 240 field guns on Gold, Juno, and Sword Beaches. The Americans, facing much tougher resistance on Omaha and Utah, landed far fewer. The German artillery had the advantage of being in place already, with its target areas registered. By the time the Allies linked up all five beachheads on June 12 they had large numbers of heavier guns and extensive ammunition stores ashore, with more landing every day.

The general organizational structure of the field artillery was similar for all three armies. The division was the primary echelon with its own organic artillery. Normally there was one light artillery battalion to provide direct support to each of the division's three regiments and a medium artillery battalion to provide general support throughout the division's sector. Heavier guns were held at the corps level, and these fired in general support within the corps' sector. American and German infantry regiments also had an organic Cannon Company, or an Infantry Gun Company, that accompanied the regiment in close support, engaging targets directly to the regiment's front. An American Cannon Company was armed with six 105mm howitzers. A German Infantry Gun Company had three 7.5cm infantry guns and one 15cm infantry gun.

World War II field artillery fired a number of different types of rounds. The standard high-explosive projectile could be armed with a point-detonating fuze or a mechanical time fuze to achieve an airburst, which was deadly against troops in the open. Illumination rounds were set to burst high in the air, releasing a parachute flare to illuminate a target area during periods of limited visibility. Smoke rounds provided smoke screens to obscure enemy visibility or to mark targets. White phosphorus (WP) burned very quickly, producing a thick white cloud. It also produced an incendiary effect in the immediate target area. The slower-burning hexachloroethane smoke produced white and colored smoke. Colored smoke was generally used to mark targets. The standard procedure for establishing a smoke screen was to fire WP initially to build up the screen and then follow with white hexachloroethane to maintain it. Although field artillery guns were not designed for an antitank role, they were capable of engaging tanks at close range if armed with high-explosive antitank rounds.

America's two airborne divisions were armed with the 75mm M-1A1 pack howitzer. It was designed for easy disassembly, which allowed it to be landed in gliders and transported on the ground by six mules. It fired a 14-pound projectile to a range of 5.4 miles. Infantry division direct-support artillery was the 105mm M-2A1 howitzer, the most widely used artillery piece in history. It was accurate and reliable and could withstand a great deal of punishment and mishandling. It fired a 33-pound projectile to a maximum range of 6.8 miles. The M-2A1 was towed by a 2.5-ton truck, which also carried the gun's crew and its basic load of ammunition. The armored divisions used the M-2A1's tube and gun carriage mounted on one of several self-propelled platforms. The standard was the M-7B1 Priest, which utilized a Sherman tank chassis.

The 155mm M-1A1 towed howitzer was the standard American medium artillery piece employed in the general support of battalions. It was a successful and popular design but was heavy and somewhat difficult to handle. The cannoneers on the gun crews called these weapons "pigs," short for "pig iron." It fired a 95-pound projectile to a range of 7.4 miles. At corps level the 155mm M-1 towed gun was two and a half times as heavy as the 155mm M-1A1 howitzer and fired a projectile of the same weight (95 pounds) to a range of 19 miles. The 155mm gun had a 19-foot barrel and was known as the "Long Tom."

The primary British and Canadian close-support gun was the 25-pounder Mk-II, which fired a 3.45-inch projectile to 7.6 miles. It had a box trail and an innovative central firing platform that allowed the crew to traverse the gun a full 360 degrees. British medium artillery included the 4.5-inch Mk-II and 5.5-inch Mk-III guns, which used the same carriage. The 4.5-inch gun fired a 55-pound projectile to 11.6 miles, and the 5.5-inch gun fired a 100-pound projectile to 9.2 miles. Both guns were grouped together in medium field artillery regiments. The British also adopted the American 155mm Long Tom.

The lightest German field artillery piece was the 7.5cm leichtes Infanteriegeschütz (le IG 18). It fired a 13.2-pound projectile to a maximum range of 2.1 miles. The towed 10.5cm leichte Feldhaubitze 18 (le FH 18) was the principal German divisional direct-support gun. It fired a 32.7-pound projectile to a range of 6.6 miles. A late World War I–vintage design, it remained a capable weapon throughout World War II. The main problems were that the Germans never had enough of them, and in almost all units right up until the end of the war they were drawn by horses. The divisional general support artillery included the 15cm Kanonne 18 (K 18) and the 15cm schwere Feldhaubitze 18 (s FH 18). The gun fired a 94.8-pound projectile to a range of 15.4 miles, and the heavy howitzer fired a 95.2-pound projectile to 8.2 miles. In the panzer divisions the self-propelled version of the 10.5cm le FH 18, called the *Wespe* (Wasp), was mounted on a PzKpfw-II tank chassis, and the 15cm s FH 18, called the Hummel (Bumblebee), was mounted on a PzKpfw-IV chassis. Although not a field artillery piece, the antiaircraft 8.8cm Flak 18 (and Flak 36 and Flak 39) was also a devastatingly effective antitank weapon when firing armor-piercing ammunition, and in emergency situations it was pressed into service as field artillery. The famous "German 88" had a horizontal range of 8.7 miles. The upgraded 8.8cm Flak 41 had a range of 12.2 miles. The Germans also used multiple rocket launchers in a field artillery role. The towed Nebelwerfer 41 (NbW 41) fired five 15cm rockets to a maximum range of 4.3 miles.

Infantry Mortars

In most World War II armies, mortars provided the organic fire support for infantry battalions and companies. In general, infantry companies had a platoon of small-caliber light mortars, battalions had a platoon of medium mortars, and higher echelons had companies of heavy mortars. Mortars are relatively short-range indirect-fire weapons that fire only at high angles (i.e., at angles of elevation greater than 45 degrees, or 800 mils). The light mortars were man-portable, as were the mediums to a limited extent. This enabled the Allies to establish shore-based fire support with the initial landing waves. As long as the ammunition supply held, mortars had very high rates of fire, up to 15 rounds per minute. Routinely, a unit in close contact received supporting fires from both artillery and mortars. The artillery forward observer assigned to the infantry or armor unit coordinated and synchronized the fires from both systems.

During World War I the British introduced the Stokes Mortar, the first of the modern gravity-fed "stovepipe type" mortars. When the British and Canadians landed on D-Day their light mortar was the 2-inch Mk-II, with a range of about half a mile; the medium mortar was the 3-inch Mk-II, with a range of 1.6 miles; and the heavy mortar was the 4.2-inch, with a range of 2.3 miles. The American 60mm M-2 mortar had a range of 1.1 miles, the 81mm M-1 mortar had a range of 1.8 miles, and the 4.2-inch M-2 mortar had a range of 2.5 miles. Called the "four-deuce" by the troops, it was officially designated a chemical mortar because it could fire chemical and smoke rounds as well as high-explosive rounds. During World War II, however, it was never used to fire chemical projectiles.

The German light mortar was the 5cm Granatwerfer 36 (GrW-36), with a range of .3 mile. The 8cm (actually 81.4mm) GrW-34 had a range of 1.4 miles, and the heavy 12cm GrW-42 had a range of 3.7 miles.

Close Air Support

On June 6 and in the days following, the Allies had a decisive advantage in airpower. While the strategic air forces, the Royal Air Force (RAF) Bomber Command and the U.S. Eighth Air Force, continued to hit key targets far beyond the beachhead, the RAF's Second Tactical Air Force and the U.S. Ninth Air Force's IX Tactical Air Command provided close support to the troops on the beach and also struck at interdiction targets immediately beyond the beachhead. The British and American combined tactical air forces had 2,434 fighters and fighter-bombers as well as 700 light and medium bombers for the interdiction mission.

Unchallenged Allied air supremacy is ironic considering that the German Army that entered World War II had placed far more emphasis on close air support than it did on artillery direct support. The Ju-87 Stuka dive-bomber, working in coordination with the panzers, proved to be an effective combination in Poland in 1939 and in France in 1940. But by June 1944 the Luftwaffe had been ground down by the large-scale fighting in Russia. The British and U.S. Combined Bomber Offensive also took a huge toll on Luftwaffe fighters (and pilots) in the skies over Germany. Thus, on D-Day the Third Air Fleet in the west had only 570 fully operational aircraft, 247 of which were bombers. On June 6 the Luftwaffe managed to fly only 327 daylight sorties and on June 6–7 only 217 night sorties.

Naval Gunfire Support

The Germans had no effective naval presence off Normandy, while the Allies possessed a massive invasion fleet. Almost all of the German senior commanders, including Field Marshal Erwin Rommel, who had command of the coastal defenses, had no experience facing naval gunfire, and they were unprepared for what hit them. Naval warships were capable of carrying guns far heavier than the heaviest field artillery. The Allied warships committed to Operation NEPTUNE included 6 battleships, 2 monitors, 23 cruisers (5 heavy and 18 light), and 105 destroyers and destroyer escorts. Of these, 138 were assigned to shore bombardment. The battleships' main batteries consisted of 12-inch, 14-inch, 15-inch, or 16-inch guns. The BL 16-inch Mk-I naval gun carried on HMS *Rodney* fired a 2,048-pound projectile to a maximum effective range of 19.9 miles. Heavy cruisers typically mounted 8-inch guns, light cruisers mounted 6-inch guns, and destroyers mounted 5-inch guns.

Another valuable naval fire-support asset was the British-designed landing craft tank–rocket (LCT-R). Each LCT-R carried a basic load of 5,000 60-pound RP-3 rockets with a maximum range of one mile. The LCT-R had 1,060 launch tubes on deck, which were fired in ripple salvos. Reloading time, however, was labor-intensive.

Coastal Artillery

Although the Germans had virtually no naval presence, they did have a line of coastal defense batteries mounted in ferro-cement casemates. These ran from the mouth of the Seine to the tip of the Cotentin Peninsula. The guns generally were from 10cm to 15cm in caliber, and all were capable of hitting Allied ships in the Seine Bay. The coastal batteries were therefore priority targets for the battleships and heavy cruisers. Two batteries were at the western end of Omaha Beach, while eight were positioned across Gold, Juno, and Sword Beaches. Five more batteries were positioned from east of Merville to the mouth of the Seine. There were no coastal batteries directly behind Utah Beach, but from its immediate right flank nine batteries ran north along the Cotentin Peninsula.

The two most dangerous batteries to the landing force were at Merville and at Pointe du Hoc, between Omaha and Utah. The guns at Pointe du Hoc were captured French Canon de 155L mle 1932 field guns. They were positioned on a high cliff directly overlooking Utah and had a range of 16.8 miles. Rather than using fixed fortress mounts, the guns remained mounted on their mobile field carriages and were set into special casemates designed for easy emplacement and removal of the guns. In fact, when the U.S. 2nd Ranger Battalion assaulted Pointe du Hoc early on June 6, the Germans already had withdrawn the guns and hid them in a wood line to the rear. The rangers, however, soon located and destroyed the guns.

Merville Battery, just east of the Orne River, had four Czech-made 10cm le FH 14/19 (t) howitzers. With a range of 5.2 miles, they were capable of bringing flanking fire on Sword Beach. Allied intelligence, however, had estimated the battery to be 15cm heavy guns with a range of about 8 miles. The British 9th Parachute Battalion captured Merville Battery early on June 6 but then was forced to withdraw after suffering heavy losses. The Germans reoccupied the position and opened fire on Sword. The Germans managed to hold out at Merville Battery until August 17.

David T. Zabecki

Further Reading

Bailey, Jonathan B. A. *Field Artillery and Fire Power.* 2nd ed. Annapolis, MD: Naval Institute Press, 2003.

Boog, Horst, Werner Rahn, Reinhard Stumpf, and Bernd Wegner. *Germany and the Second World War,* Vol. 6, *The Global War.* Oxford, UK: Clarendon, 2001.

Ellis, L. F. *Victory in the West,* Vol. 1. United Kingdom Military Series. London: HMSO, 1962.

Harrison, Gordon A. *United States Army in World War II: The European Theater of Operations; Cross Channel Attack.* Washington, DC: U.S. Army, Office of the Chief of Military History, 1951.

Hogg, Ian V. *British and American Artillery of World War II.* New York: Hippocrene Books, 1978.

Hogg, Ian V. *German Artillery of World War Two.* Mechanicsburg, PA: Stackpole Books, 1975.

Hogg, Ian V. *The Guns, 1939/45.* New York: Ballantine Books, 1970.

Atlantic, Battle of the

The Battle of the Atlantic was the longest campaign of World War II. In it, the German Navy tried to sever the Allied sea lines of communication along which supplies necessary to fight the war were sent to Great Britain. Without an Allied victory in the long Battle of the Atlantic, the Normandy invasion would have been impossible. To carry out the battle the Germans employed a few surface raiders and long-range aircraft, but principally they fought the battle with submarines (U-boats).

At the beginning of the war, the German Navy possessed not the 300 U-boats deemed necessary by their commander, Commodore Karl Dönitz (he was promoted to rear admiral in October 1939), but 57 boats, of which only 27 could reach the Atlantic from their home bases. Although an extensive building program was immediately begun, only in the second half of 1941 did U-boat numbers begin to rise.

On the Allied side, Royal Navy leaders were at first confident that their asdic (sonar) location device would enable their escort vessels to defend the supply convoys against the submerged attackers so that shipping losses might be limited until new merchant ships built by Britain, Canada, and the United States could settle the balance. Dönitz planned to concentrate groups of U-boats (called wolf packs by the Allies) against the convoys to permit attacks by multiple submarines on the surface at night. It took time, however, before the battles of the convoys really began. The Battle of the Atlantic became a running match between numbers of German U-boats and the development of their weapons against the Allied merchant ships, their sea and air escorts (with improving detection equipment), and new weapons.

The Battle of the Atlantic can be subdivided into eight phases. During the first of these, from September 1939 to June 1940, a small number of U-boats, seldom more than 10 at a time, made individual cruises west of the British Isles and into the Bay of Biscay to intercept Allied merchant ships. Generally, these operated independently because the convoy system, which the British Admiralty had planned before the war, was slow to take shape. Thus, the U-boats found targets, attacking at first according to prize rules by identifying the ship and providing for the safety of its crew. When Britain armed its merchant ships, however, the German submarines increasingly struck without warning.

Dönitz's plan to counter the convoy system with group or pack operations of U-boats—also developed and tested before the war—was put on trial in October and November 1939 and February 1940. The results confirmed the possibility of vectoring a group of U-boats to a convoy by radio signals from whichever U-boat first sighted the convoy. At this time, though, the insufficient numbers of U-boats available and frequent torpedo failures prevented real successes.

The German conquest of Norway and western France provided the U-boats with new bases much closer to the main operational area off the Western Approaches and brought about a second phase from July 1940 to May 1941. During this time the U-boats, operating in groups, were directed by radio signals from the shore against the convoys, in which were now concentrated most of the maritime traffic to and from Great Britain. Even if the number of U-boats in the operational area still did not rise to more than 10 at a time, peak efficiency was attained in terms of the relationship between tonnage sunk and U-boat days at sea.

This was made possible partly by the weakness of the convoy escort groups—because the Royal Navy held back destroyers to guard against an expected German invasion of Britain and maintained large forces in the Mediterranean to offset the loss of the French Navy. In addition, British merchant shipping losses were increased during this phase by the operations of German surface warships in the North and Central Atlantic; by armed merchant raiders in the Atlantic, Pacific, and Indian Oceans; by the attacks of German long-range bombers against the Western Approaches; and by heavy German air attacks against British harbors. The Germans were also aided by Italian submarines based at Bordeaux and sent into the Atlantic, the numbers of which in early 1941 actually surpassed the number of German U-boats.

In late 1940 and the spring of 1941, when the danger of an invasion of the British Isles had receded, London released destroyers for antisubmarine operations and redeployed Coastal Command aircraft to support the convoys off the Western Approaches. Thus, in the third phase of the Battle of the Atlantic, from May to December 1941, the U-boats were forced to operate at greater distances from shore. Long lines of U-boats patrolled across the convoy routes to intercept supply ships. This forced the British in June to begin escorting their convoys along the whole route from Newfoundland to the Western Approaches and—when the U-boats began to cruise off West Africa—the route from Freetown to Gibraltar and the United Kingdom as well.

In March 1941, the Allies captured cipher materials from a German patrol vessel. Then on May 7, 1941, the Royal Navy succeeded in capturing the German Arctic meteorological vessel *München* and seizing its Enigma machine intact. Settings secured from this encoding machine enabled the Royal Navy to read June U-boat radio traffic practically currently. On May 9 during a convoy battle, the British destroyer *Bulldog* captured the German submarine *U-110* and secured the settings for the high-grade officer-only German naval signals. The capture on June 28 of a second German weather ship, the *Lauenburg,* enabled British decryption operations at Bletchley Park to read July German home-waters radio traffic currently.

This led to the interception of German supply ships in the Atlantic and the cessation of German surface ship operations in the Atlantic. Beginning in August 1941, Bletchley Park operatives could decrypt signals between the commander of U-boats and his U-boats at sea. The Allies were thus able to reroute convoys and save perhaps 1.5 million gross tons of shipping. During this third phase, the U.S. Atlantic Fleet was first involved in the battle.

The entry of the United States into the war ushered in the fourth phase of the battle, presenting the U-boats with a second golden opportunity from January to July 1942. Attacking unescorted individual ships off the U.S. East Coast, in the Gulf of Mexico, and in the Caribbean, German U-boats sank greater tonnages than during any other period of the war.

Sightings and sinkings off the U.S. East Coast dropped off sharply after the introduction of the interlocking convoy system there, though, and Dönitz found operations by individual U-boats in such distant waters uneconomical. Thus, in July 1942 he switched the U-boats back to the North Atlantic convoy route. This began the fifth phase, which lasted until May 1943 and proved to be the decisive period of the conflict between the U-boat groups and the convoys with their sea and air escorts. Increasingly, the battle was influenced by technical innovations. Most important in this regard were efforts on both sides in the field of signals intelligence.

On February 1, 1942, the Germans had introduced their new M4 cipher machine, leading to a blackout in decryption that lasted until the end of December 1942. This accomplishment was of limited influence during the fourth phase because the German U-boats operated individually, and there was no great signal traffic in the operational areas. When the convoy battles began again, the Germans could at first decrypt Allied convoy signals.

When Bletchley Park was able to decrypt German signals anew, rerouting convoys again became possible, although this was at first limited by rising numbers of German U-boats in patrol lines. In March 1943 the U-boats achieved their greatest successes against the convoys, and the entire convoy system—the backbone of the Allied strategy against Festung Europa (Fortress Europe)—seemed in jeopardy. But now Allied decryption allowed the dispatch of additional surface and air escorts to support threatened convoys. This development, in connection with the introduction of new weapons and high-frequency direction finding, led to the collapse of the U-boat offensive against the convoys only eight weeks later, in May 1943.

This collapse came as a surprise to Dönitz. Allied success could be attributed mainly to the provision of centimetric radar equipment for the sea and air escorts and the closing of the air gap in the North Atlantic. In the sixth (intermediate) phase from June to August 1943, the U-boats were sent to distant areas where the antisubmarine forces were weak, while the Allied air forces tried to block the U-boat transit routes across the Bay of Biscay.

The change to a new Allied convoy cipher in June, which the German decryption service could not break, made it more difficult for the U-boats to locate the convoys in the seventh phase, from September 1943 to June 1944. During this time, the German U-boat command tried to deploy new weapons (acoustic torpedoes and increased antiaircraft armament) and new equipment (radar warning sets) to force again a decision with the convoys, first in the North Atlantic and then on the Gibraltar routes. After short-lived success, these operations failed and tapered off as the Germans tried to pin down Allied forces until new revolutionary U-boat types became available for operational deployment.

The eighth and final phase, from June 1944 to May 1945, began with the Allied invasion of Normandy. The U-boats, now equipped with snorkel breathing masts, endeavored to attack individual supply ships in the shallow waters of the English Channel and in British and Canadian coastal waters. The U-boats' mission was to pin down Allied supply traffic and antisubmarine forces to prevent the deployment of warships in offensive roles against German-occupied areas. Construction of the new U-boats (of which the Allies received information by decrypting reports sent to Tokyo by the Japanese embassy in Berlin) was delayed by the Allied bombing offensive, however, and the German land defenses collapsed before significant numbers of these boats were ready.

The Battle of the Atlantic lasted without interruption for 69 months, during which time German U-boats sank 2,850 Allied and neutral merchant ships, 2,520 of them in the Atlantic and Indian Oceans. The U-boats also sank many warships, from aircraft carriers to destroyers, frigates, corvettes, and other antisubmarine vessels. The Germans lost in turn the battleship *Bismarck,* the pocket battleship *Graf Spee,* some armed merchant raiders, and 650 U-boats, 522 of them in the Atlantic and Indian Oceans.

The Allied victory in the Battle of the Atlantic resulted from the vastly superior resources on the Allied side in shipbuilding and aircraft production (the ability to replace lost ships and aircraft) and from superior antisubmarine detection equipment and weapons. Allied signals intelligence was critical to the victory.

Jürgen Rohwer

Further Reading

Beesly, Patrick. *Very Special Intelligence: The Story of the Admiralty's Operational Intelligence Centre, 1939–1945.* London: Greenhill Books, 2000.

Blair, Clay. *Hitler's U-Boat War.* Vol. 1, *The Hunters, 1939–1942;* Vol. 2, *The Hunted, 1942–1945.* New York: Random House, 1996, 1998.

Gardner, W. J. R. *Decoding History: The Battle of the Atlantic and Ultra.* Annapolis, MD: Naval Institute Press, 1999.

Niestlé, Axel. *German U-Boat Losses during World War II: Details of Destruction.* Annapolis, MD: Naval Institute Press, 1998.

Rohwer, Jürgen. *Axis Submarine Successes of World War Two: German, Italian and Japanese Submarine Successes, 1939–1945.* London: Greenhill Books, 1999.

Rohwer, Jürgen. *The Critical Convoy Battles of March 1943.* Annapolis, MD: Naval Institute Press, 1977.

Runyan, Timothy J., and Jan M. Copes, eds. *To Die Gallantly: The Battle of the Atlantic.* Boulder, CO: Westview, 1994.

Sebag-Montefiore, Hugh. *Enigma: The Battle for the Code.* London: Weidenfeld and Nicolson, 2000.

Syrett, David. *The Defeat of the German U-Boats: The Battle of the Atlantic.* Columbia: University of South Carolina Press, 1994.

Wynn, Kenneth. *U-Boat Operations of the Second World War,* Vol. 1, *Career Histories, U1–U510;* Vol. 2, *Career Histories, U511–UIT25.* London: Chatham, 1998, 1999.

Atlantic Wall

The Atlantic Wall was the name for German defenses along the European coast, the last of the great defensive lines to be built (1941–1944). As German plans to invade Britain faded late in 1940, it became clear to the German High Command that thousands of miles of European coast had to be defended from possible Allied invasion. The German submarine bases in France, the occupied Channel Islands, and the Dover-Calais narrow point in the English Channel were heavily protected from the beginning. Following its June 1941 invasion of the Soviet Union and U.S. entry into the war in December 1941, Germany went on the defensive in the west. Formal work on the Atlantic Wall began in May 1942.

There never was a continuous wall per se. Such a defensive system would have been impossible to build or man. What the Germans built was a series of defended zones consisting of artillery and infantry positions overlooking likely invasion beaches and ports. Rivalries and different designs among army and navy units and civilian construction battalions often held up progress, as did strategic arguments about the comparative value of fixed defenses versus mobile reserves. So did Allied bombing of transport of construction materials. The three-year effort by Germany was massive nevertheless, involving huge quantities of men, money, and material.

Thousands of emplacements were built along the coast of France, with lesser facilities in the Low Countries and Denmark and along the Norwegian coast. Where possible, existing fortifications and weapons were used. Highlights of the wall were the often extensive artillery batteries built into extensive steel-reinforced cement casemates designed to deflect air attacks. A typical position might include four separate 8-inch gun casemates (which, while protecting the gun and its crew, also limited the weapon's field of fire) plus one or more observation and combat-direction posts, all built close to the coastline. The largest positions might feature mobile 14-inch railway-mounted artillery or

A German machine gun nest along the Atlantic Wall, captured by Canadian troops on June 8, 1944, following the Allied invasion of Normandy. A scaling ladder leans on the barbed wire in front of the concrete emplacement. (AP Photo)

huge turret-mounted guns. Some of the latter, installed in massive emplacements built near the French coast, could actually shell England directly across the channel.

Among German defenses were scores of smaller emplacements for machine guns, observation, personnel, command posts, and minefields. Some were camouflaged to look like houses or other structures, and most were at least partly built into the ground for further protection. A large number of so-called standard bunker designs were employed, although each service had its own set of standards. Extensive propaganda made the wall seem impregnable.

When he was placed in command of German defenses in France in November 1943, Field Marshal Erwin Rommel made the high-tide mark into the main line of defense, adding obstacles and intervening emplacements covering possible landing points. There were half a million beach obstacles along the English Channel alone, many armed with mines.

In the end, the stupendous construction project was largely for naught. Although two-thirds of a planned 15,000 emplacements were completed, few of them fired in anger. D-Day (June 6, 1944) was hardly hindered by the several emplacements in Normandy (some were shelled from the sea, while others were taken by paratroopers or special ranger attacks, as at Pointe du Hoc), and the rest of the coastal forts were generally captured from behind by advancing Allied forces. Extensive remains of the Atlantic Wall exist to this day.

Christopher H. Sterling

Further Reading

Kaufmann, J. E., and J. M. Jurga. "Atlantic Wall." In *Fortress Europe: European Fortifications of World War II,* 381–406. Conshohocken, PA: Combined Publishing, 1999.

Rolf, Rudi. *Atlantic Wall Typology.* Revised ed. Nieuw Weerdinge, Netherlands: Fortress Books, 1998.

Saunders, Anthony. *Hitler's Atlantic Wall.* Stroud, UK: Sutton, 2001.

Schmeelke, Karl-Heinz, and Michael Schmeelke. *German Defensive Batteries and Gun Emplacements on the Normandy Beaches.* Atglen, PA: Schiffer, 1995.

Virilio, Paul. *Bunker Archeology.* New York: Princeton Architectural, 1994.

Wilt, Alan F. *The Atlantic Wall: Hitler's Defenses in the West, 1941–1944.* Ames: Iowa State University Press, 1975.

B

Barton, Raymond Oscar "Tubby" (1889–1963)

U.S. Army officer. Born in Granada, Colorado, on August 22, 1889, Raymond Oscar "Tubby" Barton graduated from the U.S. Military Academy, West Point, in 1912. Following U.S. entry into World War I, Barton commanded a battalion of the 8th Infantry Regiment in France, then in occupation duties in Germany, until 1923, when his unit was the last U.S. military formation to depart.

Barton then commanded the 8th Infantry Regiment. He assumed command of the 4th Infantry Division as a major general in July 1942, and he led the division in the Normandy invasion and subsequent campaign, although assistant division commander Brigadier General Theodore Roosevelt actually led the division ashore on Utah Beach on June 6, 1944. Barton's division took part in the liberation of Paris in August, the drive to the German Siegfried Line, the Battle of the Bulge (December 16, 1944–January 15, 1945), and the Battle of Hürtgen Forest (September 19, 1944–February 10, 1945). Health problems forced Barton to relinquish his command on December 27, 1944. He retired from the army in 1946.

Barton died on February 27, 1963, in Augusta, Georgia.

Spencer C. Tucker

Further Reading

Carhart, Tom. *West Point Warriors: Profiles of Duty, Honor, and Country in Battle.* New York: Warner Books, 2002.

Harrison, Gordon A. *United States Army in World War II: The European Theater of Operations; Cross Channel Attack.* Washington, DC: U.S. Army, Office of the Chief of Military History, 1951.

BLUECOAT, Operation (July 30–August 7, 1944)

BLUECOAT was a British military operation during the Battle of Normandy. It was waged by VIII Corps and XXX Corps of the British Second Army, commanded by Lieutenant General Sir Miles Dempsey, in support of the Normandy breakout by the U.S. First Army in Operation COBRA (July 25–31, 1944). Fought between July 30 and August 7, BLUECOAT had as its objectives securing the road hub of Vire and the high ground of Mount Pinçon while also exploiting the withdrawal, confirmed by signals intelligence, of the German 2nd Panzer Division on July 21 in preparation for the German counteroffensive against the Americans, Operation LÜTTICH.

The British ultimately committed to BLUECOAT VIII Corps, commanded by Lieutenant General Richard O'Connor, with two armored divisions and an armor brigade, and two infantry divisions as well as XXX Corps, commanded by Lieutenant General Gerard Bucknall, of one armor division, one armor brigade, and two infantry divisions. German strength reached four panzer divisions and two infantry divisions under the command of General of the Waffen-SS Paul Hausser.

During July 18–20, the British Second Army had carried out Operation GOODWOOD southeast of the city of Caen on the eastern flank of the Allied lodgment in Normandy. This southward thrust was designed to cause the Germans to maintain the bulk of their armor strength in the British sector, preventing the Germans from concentrating it against COBRA. In preparation for BLUECOAT the boundary between British and U.S. forces was moved westward, with British forces taking over part of the area previously held by the U.S. V Corps. The British VIII Corps headquarters with the 7th, 11th, and Guards Armour Divisions was moved westward toward Caumont. Meanwhile, the German 326th Division had taken over the previously well-organized defenses of a 10-mile-wide stretch of the front south of Caumont that had been previously occupied by the 2nd Panzer Division.

As with COBRA, the British attack on July 30 was immediately preceded by carpet bombing. Although visibility was poor, the bombing raid carried out by 1,000 bombers was much more accurate than that of COBRA. Some 2,000 tons of bombs were expended. Damage to the German defenses was not what the planners had hoped, however, because much of the German equipment was south of the target area. When the British advance began, some of the units were held up by the extensive German minefields and the natural defensive advantages presented by the hedgerows (*bocage*) and sunken rows of the Norman countryside in this area. Nonetheless, by the end of the first day British forces in the center of the front had pushed the lines forward as much as five miles.

Soon, however, the British ran up against German reinforcements and units forced into the British sector by the American advance to the west. Delay was also imposed by confusion between the British and American forces regarding the boundaries and rights to utilize certain roads. Thus, Vire was on the American side of the boundary. XXX Corps had been unable to keep up with VIII Corps, which was then forced to slow in order to protect its flank. Concerns over what was perceived to be the relatively poor performance of XXX Corps brought the dismissal on August 2 of its commander, General Bucknall, replaced by Lieutenant General Brian Horrocks on August 2, while Major General George Erskine, commanding the 7th Armoured Division of the same corps, suffered the same fate on August 3.

The British advance came to a temporary halt on August 4. The Americans captured Vire on August 6, while that same day the British took Mont Pinçon. During BLUECOAT, the British VIII Corps suffered 5,114 casualties. German casualties are unknown.

Operation BLUECOAT succeeded in its overall goal of fixing the German armor units on the eastern (British) part of the front and contributed to the general wearing down of German armored strength in Normandy, thereby lengthening the odds of success for the German counteroffensive in Operation LÜTTICH.

Spencer C. Tucker

Further Reading

Daglish, Ian. *Operation BLUECOAT.* Barnsley, UK: Pen and Sword, 2009.

Ellis, Lionel F., G. W. G. Allen, A. E. Warhurst, and James Robb. *Victory in the West,* Vol. 1, *The Battle of Normandy.* London: HMSO, 1962.

Jackson, G. S. *Operations of VIII Corps: Account of Operations from Normandy to the River Rhine.* London: St. Clementa, 1948.

Bocage. *See* Terrain and Tactical Problems on D-Day

Bradley, Omar Nelson (1893–1981)

U.S. Army general. Born in Clark, Missouri, on February 12, 1893, Omar Nelson Bradley secured an appointment to the U.S. Military Academy at West Point in 1911. He graduated in 1915, a member of what would become known as the "class the stars fell on," and was commissioned a second lieutenant of infantry.

Assigned to the 14th Infantry Regiment in Spokane, Washington, Bradley saw service along the Mexican border during the 1916 crisis that followed Pancho Villa's raid on Columbus, New Mexico. Like his classmate Dwight D. Eisenhower, Bradley missed combat in World War I. During the interwar period his career followed a familiar pattern, with a number of troop commands interspersed with assignments at various military schools, including West Point. His most significant assignment was as chief of the Weapons Section during Colonel George C. Marshall's tenure as deputy commandant at the Infantry School at Fort Benning, Georgia.

Bradley graduated from the Army War College in 1934. Following service in General Marshall's secretariat of the General Staff between 1939 and 1941, Bradley was promoted directly from lieutenant colonel to brigadier general on February 24, 1941, and assigned command of the Infantry School. Promotion to major general followed on February 18, 1942, and Bradley successively commanded the 82nd Infantry Division and the National Guard 28th Infantry Division. In February 1943, Marshall dispatched him to North Africa, where General Dwight D. Eisenhower assigned Bradley as deputy commander of Lieutenant General George S. Patton's II Corps in the wake of the Kasserine Pass debacle (February 14–22, 1943). When Patton assumed command of the Seventh Army, Bradley took command of II Corps and led it with great distinction both in Tunisia and in Sicily. Bradley was promoted to lieutenant general on June 9, 1943.

In October 1943, Bradley assumed command of the First Army and transferred to Britain to prepare for the cross–English Channel invasion. Eisenhower named him to command U.S. ground forces on D-Day (June 6, 1944) in Operation OVERLORD and during the ensuing Normandy campaign. On July 26, the First Army broke the German

Omar N. Bradley, then a lieutenant general, commanded U.S. Army ground forces during the invasion of Normandy. (U.S. Department of Defense)

lines outside Saint-Lô in Operation COBRA (July 25–31), Bradley's operational masterpiece. On August 1, 1944, he assumed command of the 12th Army Group, which then encompassed General Courtney Hodges's First Army and General George Patton's Third Army.

During the subsequent drive across France, Bradley performed well but not spectacularly. His failure to close the Falaise–Argentan gap reflected poorly on his ability as a strategist and undoubtedly extended the war in the west. When the Germans launched the December 16, 1944–January 16, 1945, Ardennes Offensive (Battle of the Bulge), Bradley was slow to react, but in the subsequent campaign he renewed Marshall's and Eisenhower's confidence by carefully orchestrating the advance of the American armies on Field Marshal Bernard L. Montgomery's right flank. By war's end, Bradley had clearly emerged as Eisenhower's most trusted military adviser. As the 12th Army Group grew to include four separate armies, the largest purely American military force in history, Bradley was promoted to general on March 29, 1945, on the eve of Germany's capitulation.

Following the war Bradley headed the Veterans Administration, and in February 1948 he succeeded Eisenhower as army chief of staff. In this post, Bradley championed the continued unification of the nation's armed forces. One year later he became the first chairman of the Joint Chiefs of Staff and was subsequently promoted to the five-star rank of general of the army on September 22, 1950. During the 1950–1953 Korean War, Bradley supported President Harry S. Truman's relief of General Douglas MacArthur in April 1951 and opposed expansion of the war. Bradley retired from active military service in August 1953 to become chairman of the board of the Bulova Watch Corporation. During the Vietnam War, he served as an adviser to President Lyndon Johnson. Bradley died on April 8, 1981, in Washington, D.C.

Cole C. Kingseed

Further Reading

Bradley, Omar N. *A Soldier's Story.* New York: Henry Holt, 1951.

Bradley, Omar N., and Clay Blair. *A General's Life.* New York: Simon and Schuster, 1983.

DeFelice, Jim. *Omar Bradley: General at War.* Washington, DC: Regnery, 2011.

Weigley, Russell F. *Eisenhower's Lieutenants.* Bloomington: Indiana University Press, 1981.

Brooke, Sir Alan Francis (First Viscount Alanbrooke) (1883–1963)

British Army general and chief of the Imperial General Staff from December 1941 to January 1946. Born on July 23, 1883, in Bagnères de Bigorre, France, Alan Francis Brooke graduated from the Royal Military Academy at Woolwich and was commissioned in the Royal Artillery in December 1902. He served in Ireland and India in the years before World War I. On World War I's Western Front, he rose from captain to lieutenant colonel. Between the wars, Brooke was an instructor at the Staff College (1923–1926), commandant of the School of Artillery (1929–1932), and inspector of artillery as a major general by 1935. In 1938, he was promoted to lieutenant general on assuming command of the Anti-Aircraft Corps. Early on, it was clear that his was one of the strongest intellects in the British Army.

On the eve of war (August 31, 1939), Brooke was assigned command of II Corps of the British Expeditionary Force (BEF) in France, a position that lasted until his evacuation with many of his troops at the end of May 1940. Brooke briefly returned to France from June 12 to 18, 1940, this time as nominal commander of the BEF. He became commander of the Home Forces on July 19, 1940, working to improve readiness for the expected German invasion.

Brooke was named chief of the Imperial General Staff on December 25, 1941, and held the post until January 25, 1946, serving concurrently (from March 1942) as chairman of the Chiefs of Staff Committee. In January 1944, he was promoted to field marshal. He attended all summit conferences from 1942 through 1945 concerned with the strategic direction of the war. Brooke held off the premature American desire for a cross–English Channel invasion while supporting action in North Africa and Italy to spread and destroy German forces prior to an invasion of France.

Brooke's feelings toward Prime Minister Winston L. S. Churchill varied from admiration to exasperation. Churchill's penchant for late-night meetings, his impetuosity and interference in military affairs, and his focus on detail at the expense of broader strategic thinking constantly tried Brooke's patience. Brooke's diaries, first published in highly edited fashion in the mid-1950s (and only made available in their full form in 2001), include some of the first postwar criticism of Churchill. Brooke grew to hate the meetings of the Combined Chiefs of Staff for the constant wrangling that arose—especially given his dim view of the strategic thinking of U.S. military leaders, particularly Generals George C. Marshall and Dwight D. Eisenhower. A firm supporter of General Bernard Montgomery, Brooke had little patience for those he believed to be of limited abilities.

Brooke was created a baron (becoming Lord Alanbrooke of Brookborough in September 1945) and a viscount (in January 1946). In 1946 he was made a Knight of the Order of the Garter. He died on June 17, 1963, at Ferney Close, England.

Christopher H. Sterling

Further Reading

Bryant, Arthur. *The Turn of the Tide, 1939–43: Based on the Diaries of Field Marshal Viscount Alanbrooke.* London: Collins, 1955.

Bryant, Arthur. *Victory in the West, 1943–45: Based on the Diaries of Field Marshal Viscount Alanbrooke.* London: Collins, 1957.

Danchev, Alex, and Daniel Todman, eds. *War Diaries, 1939–1945: Field Marshal Lord Alanbrooke.* Berkeley: University of California Press, 2001.

Fraser, David. *Alanbrooke.* London: Collins, 1982.

C

Caen, Battle to Secure (June 6–July 18, 1944)

Securing the city of Caen was a major Allied objective, assigned to the British and Canadians to occur on D-Day, June 6, 1944. The city of William the Conqueror, Caen is the prefecture of the Calvados department and the capital and largest city of the Basse-Normandie region. In Normandy, Caen trails only Rouen and Le Havre in population. Before the Allied invasion the population numbered some 60,000 people.

Located a little more than nine miles inland from the English Channel and bisected by the Orne River, Caen lies in open country suitable for airfields. Possession of Caen and the surrounding countryside would allow the Allies to engage in maneuver warfare, which is what they sought. Caen would be a staging area from which the Allies could drive south against Falaise, then pivot right for an advance to Argentan and the Touques River. If, however, the Germans could prevent the Allies from pushing across these, it would materially strengthen their defensive position. As it turned out, taking Caen on June 6

Devastation in Caen, Normandy, following its liberation by Allied forces on July 18, 1944. Little remained of the old city and its medieval structures. (Keystone/Getty Images)

was overly ambitious. Far from the British 3rd Infantry Division capturing Caen that day as Allied land force commander General Bernard Montgomery had hoped, the struggle to secure the city became an intense meatgrinder battle that consumed much of the Anglo-Canadian Second Army and German Panzergruppe West and left Caen in ruins.

The struggle to secure Caen was not what Montgomery had planned. With the British running out of manpower in 1944, Montgomery was extremely conscious of the need to keep casualties low. U.S. strength was continuing to grow while that of Britain was static or declining, and this growing imbalance translated into increased U.S. influence, as British prime minister Winston Churchill made clear. The British Second Army was well equipped and well supplied, and Montgomery anticipated that this would make the difference and curtail casualties. Although the men of the Second Army were well trained, the Germans had an edge in combat experience and in motivation, especially the SS divisions known for their fanaticism. Montgomery hoped to be able to fight a battle that would maximize British advantages while keeping casualties at a minimum.

The Allies had expected to break out of the beachhead early on and fight a mobile battle in the interior. It did not work out that way, because the Germans dug in and were able to use the *bocage* country to great advantage. Overwhelming Allied airpower could not locate and take out the German tanks, which were more heavily gunned and armored than those of the Allies and were also in camouflaged, hull-down defensive positions. British medium tanks were outgunned and outarmored by the German Tiger heavy tanks, and British artillery—while able to arrest German counterattacks—was not able to overcome the German defenses.

This meant that the bulk of the fighting was left to the infantry, which in turn meant high casualties.

With securing Caen an important Allied objective in the fight for Normandy and following the failure to take it in the initial invasion, Montgomery wrote on June 8 that "I have decided not to have a lot of casualties by battling against the place." Instead, he would envelop Caen from the west and the east. Delays in getting men and supplies ashore, however, enabled the Germans to bring up reinforcements and greatly strengthen their defenses.

Operation TONGA (June 6)
In the airborne operation that preceded the Allied beach landings of June 6, the British 6th Airborne Division and the attached 1st Canadian Parachute Battalion were inserted behind Sword Beach with the assignments in Operation TONGA of securing the important bridges over the Caen Canal and the Orne River to prevent German access to the beach area to contest the landing of the 3rd Infantry Division. They were also charged with taking out the German artillery battery at Merville. The paratroopers and glidermen were able to accomplish these tasks and managed to secure a beachhead on the east bank of the Orne, northeast of Caen. By the afternoon of June 6 the 3rd Infantry Division had pushed to about 3.7 miles of Caen, but its progress was halted by the 21st Panzer Division, with the British failing to secure their principal objective of the Caen-Bayeux road.

Operation PERCH (June 7–14)
With the effort to secure Caen on June 6 having failed and being unwilling to incur the heavy casualties that would likely be associated with a frontal assault on the city, Montgomery decided on the indirect approach of threatening a British breakout southeast of

Caen. The task went to XXX Corps with the 50th (Northumbrian) Infantry Division, charged with capturing Bayeux and the road to Tilly-sur-Seulles, while the 7th Armoured Division advanced toward Mont Pinçon.

On June 9, Montgomery made the effort a pincer movement. While XXX Corps continued its advance, the 7th Armoured Division would proceed east, crossing the Odon River and taking Évrecy. The attack bogged down, however. In endeavoring to take Tilly-sur-Seulles, XXX Corps encountered stubborn German resistance by the Panzer Lehr Division and elements of the 12th SS Panzer Division, greatly aided by the formidable natural defensive barrier of centuries-old hedgerows (the *bocage*) that divided the fields of the region. Fighting for the village of Tuilly-sur-Seulles seesawed back and forth.

In support of the 50th Infantry Division and the 7th Armoured Division, on June 11 the Canadian 6th Armoured Regiment and the Queen's Own Regiment of Canada attempted to secure high ground southwest of Caen. In what was known as the Battle of Le Mesuil-Patry, the 12th SS Panzer Division caught the Canadians in an ambush in a grain field near Le Mesuil-Patry. Employing the handheld antitank *Panzerfaust* weapon introduced in 1943 as well as *Panzerschrecks* and antitank guns with great effect, the Germans knocked out 51 of the 53 Canadian M-4 Sherman tanks. The two Canadian units also sustained 116 killed or missing in action, 35 wounded, and 22 taken prisoner. One English newspaper likened it to the October 1854 Crimean War Charge of the Light Brigade.

I Corps meanwhile was delayed in getting into its attack positions, so that attack was put off until June 12. On commencement of the attack, the 51st (Highland) Division immediately encountered stiff resistance and counterattacks by the 21st Panzer Division. With the 51st Division unable to advance, the drive east of Caen was terminated on June 13.

American forces on the right flank of XXX Corps had, however, forced the Germans to withdraw southward, and this opened a gap in the German front lines of more than seven miles. On learning of this, British Second Army commander Lieutenant Genera Miles Dempsey ordered the 7th Armoured Division diverted from the fighting at Tilly-sur-Seulles to exploit the gap, secure the town of Villers-Bocage, and, hitting the Panzer Lehr Division in a flanking attack, force it to fall back. Following two days of hard fighting that included the Battle of Villers-Bocage, on June 14 the 7th Armoured Division was ordered to withdraw toward Caumont. In one engagement near the village of Cristot, the 6th Green Howards Regiment attached to the 7th Armored lost 250 men when the tanks ranged too far ahead and became separated from the infantry, and heretofore concealed German defenders were able to concentrate on the infantry alone, then turn and attack the tanks from the rear with *Panzerfausts*. A handful of German Tiger heavy tanks also exacted a heavy toll of the leading elements of the 7th Armoured Division.

Dempsey had hoped to renew the offensive once the 7th Armoured had been reinforced, but this plan was shelved following the arrival of a great storm in the English Channel that wrecked a number of Allied freighters and small craft and destroyed one of the Mulberry artificial harbors supplying the troops ashore, sharply curtailing resupply.

Meanwhile, on the evening of June 15 Panzer Lehr Division commander Lieutenant General Fritz Bayerlein utilized all his available tanks and managed to contain an attack by the 49th (West Riding) Infantry

Division and the 50th Division. The next day the British renewed the attack and on June 17 finally took for good what remained of Tilly-sur-Seulles, which reportedly had changed hands 23 times.

Operation MARTLET (June 25–July 1)
On June 25 the 50th Infantry Division, the 49th (West Riding) Infantry Division, and the 8th Armored Brigade (all from XXX Corps) launched Operation MARTLET (also known as Operation DAUNTLESS), a preliminary attack designed to support Operation EPSOM, which began a day later. The goal of MARTLET was to capture a series of villages, chiefly Rauray, and the area around Noyers in order to secure high ground on the right flank of XXX Corps. Success here would prevent German forces from flanking MARTLET from the west. In hard fighting the British had secured their objectives, beating back several counterattacks before the Germans finally withdrew on June 1.

Operation EPSOM (June 26–30)
Also known as the First Battle of the Odon, Operation EPSOM was the code name for the British Second Army operation to secure high ground south of Caen. The attack was mounted by Lieutenant General Sir Richard O'Connor's newly arrived VIII Corps of more than 60,000 men. Although British warships provided long-range gunfire support, poor weather precluded preliminary bombing planned for 250 Bomber Command aircraft. Although XXX Corps was to assist VIII Corps, delays in resupply and reinforcements occasioned by the great storm sharply reduced its role.

In addition to Operation MARTLET, several days after the start of EPSOM (June 26) I Corps was to carry out two operations supporting it. In the first of these, Operation ABERLOUR, the British 3rd Infantry Division, supported by the 8th Canadian Brigade, was to attack north of Caen, while in Operation OTTAWA the 3rd Canadian Division with tank support was to capture the village of Carpiquet and the nearby airfield. Neither attack occurred, however.

On June 26, the first day of EPSOM, the 15th (Scottish) Infantry Division, supported by the 31st Tank Brigade, pushed through the German defensive perimeter. During the next two days the British established a position across the Odon River. The 43rd (Wessex) Infantry Division was ordered forward in an effort to expand this holding but encountered major German counterattacks by I SS and II SS Panzer Corps that forced the withdrawal of some British units from across the river by the end of EPSOM on June 30. VII Corps had advanced some six miles, but by committing their last reserves the Germans had brought the offensive to a halt.

Operation EPSOM had cost the Second Army 470 men killed, 2,187 wounded, and 706 missing in action. The Germans sustained some 3,000 casualties and 126 tanks knocked out. Although the attack had not achieved its goals, EPSOM preempted a major German armor counterattack against the Normandy beaches and had drawn off German units from the American sector.

Operation WINDSOR (July 4–5)
Operation WINDSOR was designed to secure the D-Day goal of securing the airfield at Carpiquet near Caen. Considerable German artillery and antiaircraft assets defended the airfield. The task of taking the airfield was assigned to the 8th Canadian Infantry Brigade, the Royal Winnipeg Rifles of the 7th Canadian Infantry Brigade, tanks of the 10th Armoured Regiment (the Fort Garry Horse), and three squadrons of specialist tanks, including flamethrower tanks, of the 7th Armoured Division. Substantial firepower

support was provided by the nine 16-inch guns of the battleship *Rodney,* substantial numbers of land artillery, and two squadrons of the highly effective RAF Hawker Typhoon ground-attack aircraft with antitank rockets.

Benefitting from French Resistance information on German defensive dispositions, on July 5 the Canadians took the village of Carpiquet. On July 9 following the withdrawal of the 12th SS Panzer Division during Operation CHARNWOOD, the 8th Canadian Infantry Brigade secured both the airfield itself and several nearby villages.

Operation CHARNWOOD (July 8–9)

Operation CHARNWOOD was one of the major Second British Army efforts to secure Caen. In it, three infantry divisions and three tank brigades of I Corps were to drive southward and secure both Caen and bridgeheads across the Orne River in the southern part of the city. British planners hoped that this would allow an advance on Falaise. This time the British attack would be preceded by heavy bombers. In addition to ground-support aircraft, the attackers could rely on 656 artillery pieces.

On the night of July 7, bombers dropped some 1,800 tons of bombs on Caen. The ground attack began at 4:30 a.m. on July 8, followed by another bombing attack several hours later. That evening the Germans authorized the withdrawal across the Orne and into the southern part of Caen of their remaining heavy weapons and the 16th Luftwaffe Field Division. The 12th SS Panzer Division provided cover and then also withdrew across the river.

Early on July 9 British and Canadian forces entered what remained of the city of Caen, and by noon they had reached the north bank of the Orne. Although some bridges remained intact, these were obstructed with rubble and covered by fire from German units south of the river anticipating their use in a counterattack.

Operation JUPITER (July 10–11)

On July 10 the 43rd (Wessex) Infantry Division and the 4th Armoured Brigade of the British VIII Corps mounted an attack to capture several villages and recapture Hill 112, after which the attack would continue to the Orne River. Although the attackers had the benefit of a preliminary artillery and mortar fire, naval gunfire, and ground-attack aircraft, the Germans were aided by the ability of the 88mm gun on the Tiger heavy tank outranging the guns on the British Churchill and Sherman medium tanks and the commitment from reserve status of the 9th SS Panzer Division. Although the British did capture several villages, they did not secure Hill 112 until the Germans withdrew in August.

Operation GOODWOOD (July 18–20)

In Operation GOODWOOD of July 18–20, VIII Corps, with three armored divisions, attacked in the direction of German-held Bourguébus Ridge with the goal of seizing it and securing the area between Bretteville-sur-Laize and Vimont. The British hoped to force the Germans to commit their remaining armor formations, destroying as many of the tanks as possible so as to give the U.S. Operation COBRA the greatest chance of success. GOODWOOD was preceded by Allied secondary attacks resulting in the Second Battle of the Odon, designed to focus German attention on the eastern end of the Allied beachhead. On July 18, I Corps advanced on the eastern flank of VIII Corps to secure a number of villages across the Orne, while on VII Corps' western flank the II Canadian Corps captured the remainder of Caen south of the Orne, including its industrial areas.

The Germans were hit hard by the extensive preliminary bombardment preceding the VIII Corps attack. Some 1,000 aircraft dropped 5,800 tons of bombs, while 400 artillery pieces rained shells on the German positions. Unfortunately, Bourguébus Ridge was beyond the range of the Allied artillery. Casualties were heavy. The attacking forces suffered some 4,800 casualties and lost probably 140 tanks destroyed and another 174 damaged. GOODWOOD remains the largest armor battle ever fought by the British Army. By the end of the operation on July 20, the British had significantly expanded the Orne bridgehead. The most extensive advance was to the east of Caen, with an advance of some seven miles.

Regarding the British thrust as the area of greatest threat, the Germans sent there what remained of the mobile elements of the 2nd Panzer Division. This meant that the Anglo-Canadian forces on the eastern flank of the Normandy beachhead faced some 6.5 panzer divisions, while U.S. and other Allied forces on the western flank had to contend with only 1.5 panzer divisions. This proved to be of great advantage to the Americans in their breakthrough of the German Seventh Army in Operation COBRA (July 25–31).

Operation ATLANTIC (July 18–21)
Mounted in conjunction with Operation GOODWOOD, the 4th and 6th Canadian Infantry Brigades, which were to be supported by the 27th Armoured Regiment and Hawker Typhoon ground-attack aircraft, were to secure the 90-foot-high Verrières Ridge dominating the Caen–Falaise road. The Germans had committed four divisions here in order to prevent the Allies from breaking out into the open countryside south of Caen.

This attack on July 18, Operation ATLANTIC, occurred in heavy rains, removing air support and affecting armor mobility. Counterattacks by two panzer divisions of the I SS Panzer Corps both drove back and inflicted heavy casualties on the attackers. By the end of the operation on July 21 the Canadians had secured several footholds on the ridge, but the Germans still held the bulk of it. Fighting here had cost the Allies some 1,300 casualties. By July 26 that figure had grown to 2,600.

Although British and Canadian forces now held Caen south of the Orne, the fact that the Germans still held Verrières Ridge would lead Montgomery on July 22 to order a new offensive, a "holding attack" to take place within a few days in conjunction with the U.S. planned break out of Operation COBRA. This was Operation SPRING.

Operation SPRING (July 25–27)
Strongly urged by Montgomery, on July 25, the same date as the start of Operation COBRA, Lieutenant General Guy Simonds, commander of the II Canadian Corps, began Operation SPRING. Again, the chief goal was to hold in place German units that might otherwise be sent to the American sector to deal with COBRA, but Simonds also hoped to be able to secure Verrières Ridge. The fighting for the ridge was intense, with July 25 marking the single bloodiest day for a Canadian battalion since the Dieppe Raid in 1942. Two German divisions pushed the Canadians back to beyond their start line, forcing Simonds to call up reserves. Despite this setback, Operation SPRING achieved its overall goal of holding the Germans in place during U.S. Operation COBRA.

Summary
Of seven British infantry divisions in the fight to secure Caen, all had lost three-quarters of their original strength by the end of August, with most of this occurring in the battles for Caen. The rifle companies were the hardest hit, and the fighting was particularly costly

for the officers, who had only a 10 percent chance of surviving unscathed. In all, by August 7 the British, Canadian, and Polish units that fought to take Caen sustained 50,539 killed or wounded. It is worth noting here, however, that the British War Office had forecast 65,751 casualties. German casualties in the Battle for Caen are unknown.

Allied aircraft had dropped leaflets on Caen on June 6 urging the inhabitants to leave, but few had done so. On the afternoon of June 6, British heavy bombers struck the city in order to impede German reinforcements attempting to reach the Allied beaches. Some 800 civilian inhabitants of Caen died during June 6 and 7, and perhaps 15,000 took refuge in quarry tunnels south of the city. Foraging parties managed to get some food to the city inhabitants, and some aid also got there from the Vichy French government. On July 6 the Germans ordered all civilians to leave Caen, although a number remained.

Some 35,000 inhabitants were rendered homeless by the fighting, and after the war the West German government provided reparations to the families of those who were killed or rendered homeless by the fighting. After the liberation of Caen on July 18, little remained of the old city and its many medieval buildings. Reconstruction began in 1948 but was not completed until 1962.

While the Battle for Caen was extremely costly for both sides, Germany's decision to commit to this sector the bulk of its resources here, especially the armor units, weakened its defenses against the Americans and certainly helped facilitate the breakout of the latter in Operation COBRA.

Spencer C. Tucker

Further Reading

Daglish, Ian. *Operation Goodwood: Over the Battlefield.* Barnsley, UK: Pen and Sword, 2005.

Ford, Ken, and Howard Gerrard. *Caen 1944.* Oxford, UK: Osprey, 2004.

Forty, George. *Villers Bocage: Battle Zone Normandy.* Stroud, Gloucestershire, UK: Sutton, 2004.

Hastings, Max. *Overlord: D-Day and the Battle for Normandy.* New York: Simon and Schuster, 1984.

Reynolds, Michael. *Steel Inferno: I SS Panzer Corps in Normandy; The Story of the 1st and 12th SS Panzer Divisions in the 1944 Normandy Campaign.* New York: Sarpedon, 1997.

Trew, Simon, and Stephen Badsey. *Battle for Caen.* Stroud, UK: Sutton, 2004.

Cemeteries, Normandy Invasion

Normandy, France, the site of the D-Day (June 6, 1944) invasion, has a number of cemeteries containing the graves of those who died during the beach landings as well as in the ensuing Normandy campaign. There are cemeteries administered by the United States, Great Britain, Germany, and Poland. Some are relatively small, while others are vast, with many thousands of graves. These sites attract visitors and tourists from around the world.

The largest of the cemeteries is the La Cambe German War Cemetery located near Bayeux. Managed and maintained by the German War Graves Commission, the burial ground contains the bodies of more than 21,200 Germans who died in the region. The site was originally part of a U.S. cemetery, but in the mid-1950s all the bodies of Americans buried there were either transferred to the United States or relocated to the American Cemetery and Memorial at Colleville-sur-Mer. German war dead were also buried in small, isolated battlefield cemeteries throughout Normandy. Many of these were later transferred to La Cambe.

The second-largest war cemetery is the American Cemetery and Memorial at Colleville-sur-Mer, situated on a bluff above Omaha Beach, one of the two principal landing zones for American troops during D-Day. It encompasses 172 acres of land and contains 9,397 graves. Meticulously maintained by the U.S. government, the cemetery features row upon row of identical white crosses and Stars of David. On the walls of a semielliptical memorial set in a garden are the names of 1,557 Americans who died in combat in Normandy but could not be found or precisely identified. A time capsule was placed underneath a pink granite marker opposite the old visitors' center. The marker is simply engraved "To be opened on June 6, 2044."

The Bayeux War Cemetery is Great Britain's largest cemetery in Normandy. It contains 4,648 graves of British Commonwealth soldiers who died in the area in 1944. The cemetery features white headstones engraved with the person's religious affiliation or with any war medals he may have won. The Bayeux Memorial, located within the cemetery, is dedicated to some 1,800 soldiers who were never recovered or identified. A description in Latin adorns the memorial. Translated, it reads "We, once conquered by William, have now set free the Conqueror's native land." At the Ranville War Cemetery outside that place and also maintained by the British, 2,235 graves hold the remains of Commonwealth soldiers, many of them from the 6th Airborne Division. That burial ground also houses the graves of 330 German soldiers.

There are two Canadian cemeteries in Normandy. The first, containing 2,958 graves, is the Bretteville-sur-Laize Canadian War Cemetery in Cintheux. The second, containing 2,048 graves, is the Bény-sur-Mer Canadian War Cemetery, near Reviers. Like the other war cemeteries, they are perfectly maintained and are moving to visit.

A Polish war cemetery, containing the graves of more than 600 Polish soldiers who died during pitched fighting in August 1944, is located near Grainville-Langannerie. It features several beautiful memorials and sculptures.

Paul G. Pierpaoli Jr.

Further Reading

Marriott, Leo, and Simon Forty. *The Normandy Battlefields and the Bridgehead.* Philadelphia: Casemate, 2014.

Power, Stephen T., and Kevin Dennehy. *The D-Day Assault: A 70th Anniversary Guide to the Normandy Landings.* Denver, CO: GTCI Press, 2014.

CHARNWOOD, Operation (July 8–9, 1944). *See* Caen, Battle to Secure

Cherbourg, Capture of (June 22–29, 1944)

Securing the French port city of Cherbourg on the northern shore of the Cotentin Peninsula was a major Allied goal following the D-Day landing. Being able to utilize a major port for resupply was essential if the Allies were to build up their resources faster than the Germans in order to break free for a drive across France.

Lieutenant General Karl-Wilhelm von Schlieben commanded two German battle groups totaling four infantry divisions in defense of the Cotentin Peninsula. German chancellor Adolf Hitler's orders, however, forced Schlieben to defend a line stretching across the entire peninsula, from St. Vaast de la Hogue in the east to Vauville in the west, rather than concentrating his forces in a semicircle south of Cherbourg. This greatly complicated the defense of the port and meant that for the actual defense of the city he had only some 21,000 men, drawn from a variety of sources. German armor was kept to the east because of the British threat to the city of Caen. Hitler's decision to defend the entire peninsula also meant that much of the stores of ammunition in Cherborg were gone before the actual battle for the city had begun. Von Schlieben did, however, have the advantage of concrete fortifications built into three ridges that controlled the approaches to the city. The Cherbourg Arsenal was also a powerful fortress, while the German Navy had constructed fortifications protecting the harbor from seaward attack.

On June 7, 1944, the day after the Allied landings in Normandy, Major General J. Lawton Collins, commanding the U.S. Army VII Corps, launched the 4th, 9th, and 79th Infantry Divisions westward from the Utah Beach lodgment to isolate Cherbourg from the land side. The 9th Division accomplished this task when it reached the Cotentin west coast on June 18. The next day the 4th Division broke through the German defenses on the peninsula's east coast.

That same day, June 19, a tremendous storm hit Normandy. It destroyed the artificial harbor (Mulberry A) at Omaha Beach and rendered the capture of Cherbourg even more urgent. By the end of June 20, meanwhile, all three U.S. divisions had reached the German defensive lines at Cherbourg. The next day was spent reconnoitering the German defenses before Collins issued a demand for surrender, which von Schlieben ignored.

On June 22, the Allies carried out heavy bombing to open the final phase of the battle. The attack opened with a strike by four squadrons of Royal Air Force (RAF) Hawker Typhoons and six squadrons of RAF P-51 Mustangs. This was followed by all 12 fighter-bomber groups in the U.S. Army Air Forces Ninth Air Force and 11 groups from the Ninth Bomber Command. In all, the aircraft dropped some 1,100 tons of bombs on the German positions.

Collins ordered the main attacks in the center and west, conducted by the 79th and 9th Infantry Divisions, while the 4th Infantry Division supported in the east. By the end of June 22, the Americans had managed to establish some positions on all three German-held ridges. That same day, Hitler ordered von Schlieben to fight to the last and leave nothing but ruins.

Fighting was intense for the concrete pillboxes, which the attackers had to destroy one by one. As Allied aircraft kept the defenders inside the pillboxes, the infantrymen would advance to a distance of several hundred yards, then lay down heavy fire as combat engineers worked their way into position to blow the doors off the pillboxes with explosive charges.

By June 23 the U.S. infantry had reached Cherbourg's outer suburbs of Octeville and Tourlaville. These were taken on June 24. Continued air attacks dampened German morale, and on June 25 a naval task force headed by three battleships supported the final attack on Cherbourg proper with naval gunfire.

The 4th and 9th Infantry Divisions seized their objectives inside the city by nightfall on June 25. The 79th Infantry Division had a more difficult fight around Fort du Roule, which finally fell on June 26. Von Schlieben made his final radio message that afternoon and was captured shortly thereafter, but he refused to order a general surrender of forces.

On June 27 Major General Robert Sattler, commanding the city of Cherbourg, agreed to surrender the arsenal following a token attack. After the Americans fired a few shells, Sattler and 400 men marched out. Fighting continued, however, as VII Corps reduced several strongpoints that had been previously bypassed, including Cap de la Hague at the northwest corner of the peninsula, the port facilities, and other resistance pockets on the Cotentin Peninsula. The harbor strongpoints, although under heavy dive-bomber attack, held out until June 29, and when the 9th Division seized Cap de la Hague on June 30, the battle was over.

The heavy fighting to take Cherbourg and the deliberate German demolitions had nonetheless severely damaged the port facilities. VII Corps found landing berths blocked by sunken ships, the harbor mined, the breakwater ripped open, and dock facilities demolished. Three weeks passed before the docks were able to receive cargo, and it was several months before shipments could be received in quantity—a serious blow to Allied logistical planning. Fortunately, the remaining Mulberry and over-the-beaches supply deliveries were greater than originally thought possible.

The fighting for Cherbourg and the deliberate German destruction of its port facilities impacted Allied strategy. The plan to secure the Brittany ports was now scrapped, and the ports were simply isolated and besieged. Several of these ports did not surrender until the end of the war.

Thomas D. Veve and Spencer C. Tucker

Further Reading

Breuer, William B. *Hitler's Fortress Cherbourg: The Conquest of a Bastion*. New York: Stein and Day, 1984.

Harrison, Gordon A. *United States Army in World War II: The European Theater of Operations; Cross Channel Attack*. Washington, DC: Office of the Chief of Military History, 1951.

Ludewig, Joachim. *Rückzug: The German Retreat from France, 1944*. Lexington: University Press of Kentucky, 2012.

Churchill, Sir Winston Leonard Spencer (1874–1965)

British political leader, cabinet minister, and prime minister (1940–1945, 1951–1955). Born at Blenheim Palace, Oxfordshire, on November 30, 1874, Winston Leonard Spencer Churchill was the eldest son of Lord Randolph Churchill, third son of the duke of Marlborough and a rising Conservative politician, and his wife, Jennie Jerome, an American heiress. Educated at Harrow and the Royal Military College, Sandhurst, from 1895 to 1899, Winston Churchill held a commission in the British Army. He visited Cuba on leave and saw active service on the Afghan frontier and in the Sudan, where he took part in the Battle of Omdurman. Captured by South African forces in 1899 while reporting on the Boer War as a journalist, he made a dramatic escape from Pretoria and went to Durban, winning early popular fame.

Churchill emulated his father—who attained the position of chancellor of the exchequer before a premature death ended his political career—by entering politics in 1900 as a Unionist member of Parliament. In 1904 his party's partial conversion to protectionism caused him to join the Liberals, who made him president of the Board of Trade (1908–1910) and home secretary (1910–1911) after they returned to power.

As first lord of the admiralty (1911–1915), Churchill enthusiastically backed the campaign of first sea lord Admiral Sir John "Jackie" Fisher to modernize the Royal Navy with faster battleships and more efficient administration. One of the few initial cabinet supporters of British intervention in

World War I, Churchill was blamed for the disastrous 1915 Dardanelles expedition against the Ottoman Empire, prompting his resignation. He spent the six months up to May 1916 on active service on the Western Front but regained high political office in July 1917, when Prime Minister David Lloyd George made Churchill minister of munitions in his coalition government.

In December 1918 Churchill moved to the War Office, where he unsuccessfully advocated forceful Allied action against Russia in the hope of eliminating that country's new Bolshevik government. In late 1920 he became colonial secretary. Two years after Lloyd George's 1922 defeat, Churchill returned to the Conservatives, who made him chancellor of the exchequer in November 1924, a post he held for five years. He reluctantly acquiesced in Britain's return to the gold standard, and his determination to suppress the 1926 general strike won him the lasting enmity of much of the labor movement.

By 1928 Churchill believed that the postwar peace settlement represented only a truce between wars, a view forcefully set forth in his book *The Aftermath* (1928). When Labour won the 1929 election, Churchill lost office but soon began campaigning eloquently for major British rearmament, especially the massive enhancement of British airpower, to enable the country to face a revived Italian or German military threat. From 1932 onward he sounded this theme eloquently in Parliament, but Conservative leaders remained unsympathetic. Churchill also became perhaps the most visible and vocal critic of the appeasement policies of the successive governments of Prime Ministers Stanley Baldwin and Neville Chamberlain, who effectively tolerated German rearmament, Chancellor Adolf Hitler's deliberate contravention of the provisions of the Treaty of Versailles, and Germany's and Italy's territorial demands on their neighbors.

When Britain declared war on Germany in September 1939, Churchill resumed his old position as first lord of the admiralty. Despite the German attacks on the British aircraft carrier *Courageous* and the battleship *Royal Oak*, as well as the responsibility he bore for the Allied disaster in Norway during April and May 1940, he succeeded Chamberlain as prime minister on May 10, 1940, the day Germany invaded France and the Low Countries. During the next three months Britain sustained repeated disasters as German troops rapidly overran the Low Countries and France, forcing the British Expeditionary Force to withdraw in disarray from northern France at Dunkerque during May 26–June 4, 1940, abandoning most of its equipment. During the Battle of Britain (July 10–September 30, 1940), German airplanes fiercely attacked Britain in an apparent prelude to a full-scale invasion across the English Channel.

Churchill responded vigorously. Although he was 65 years old, he still possessed abundant and unflagging energy; his vitality was fueled by his habit of an afternoon siesta, after which he normally worked until 2:00 or 3:00 the next morning. His fondness for sometimes fanciful and questionable strategic plans often exasperated his closest advisers, as did his attachment to romantic individual ventures—such as those launched by the Special Operations Executive covert action agency, whose establishment he backed enthusiastically. Although he acted forcefully, he did not always make the best decisions.

Even so, Churchill was an outstanding war leader. On taking office he delivered a series of rousing and eloquent speeches, affirming Britain's determination to continue fighting even without allies and voicing his conviction of ultimate triumph. He also followed a demanding schedule of morale-boosting personal visits to British cities, factories, bomb targets, and military installations, a practice he continued throughout the war.

Besides rallying the British people to endure military defeat in France and the bombing campaign that Germany soon launched against Britain's industrial cities, Churchill's speeches, which caught the international imagination, were designed to convince the political leaders and people of the United States—the only quarter from which Britain might anticipate effective assistance—of his country's commitment to the war. U.S. president Franklin D. Roosevelt responded by negotiating the Destroyers for Bases Agreement of August 1940 whereby the United States transferred 50 World War I–vintage destroyers to Britain in exchange for naval basing rights in British Caribbean Islands and North America.

Since the beginning of the war, Britain had purchased war supplies in the United States on a cash-and-carry basis. By December 1940 British resources were running low, and Churchill wrote to Roosevelt to request more extensive U.S. aid. Roosevelt responded by devising the Lease-Lend Act, which was passed by Congress the following spring.

In August 1941 Churchill and Roosevelt met for the first time, in Placentia Bay off the Newfoundland coast, and agreed to endorse a common set of liberal war aims—the Atlantic Charter—and to coordinate their two countries' military strategies. Churchill also agreed to allow British scientists to pool their expertise in nuclear physics with their American counterparts in the Manhattan Project, a largely U.S.-financed effort to build an atomic bomb; the project reached fruition in the summer of 1945.

Churchill was relieved by Japan's December 7, 1941, attack on Pearl Harbor, Hawaii, and the subsequent German and Italian declarations of war on the United States because these events brought the United States fully into the war and, from his perspective, guaranteed an ultimate Allied victory. In the interim, Churchill needed all his talents to sustain British resolution through various disasters, including Japan's conquest of Hong Kong, Malaya, Singapore, and Burma and British defeats in North Africa.

After Germany invaded the Soviet Union in June 1941, Churchill also welcomed the Soviet Union as an ally, although his relations with Soviet leader Joseph Stalin were never close. Churchill made repeated visits to the United States and met Roosevelt at other venues. In addition, all three leaders gathered at major international summit conferences at Tehran in November 1943 and Yalta in February 1945, and Churchill also met Stalin separately on several occasions. Churchill traveled abroad more than any of the other Allied leaders, often at substantial personal risk.

Stalin resented the Anglo-American failure to open a second front in Europe until June 1944, a decision due in considerable part to Churchill's fear that if Britain and the United States launched an invasion of Western Europe too soon, the campaign would degenerate into bloody trench warfare resembling that between 1914 and 1918. With the successful Allied invasion of North Africa, Churchill convinced the Americans to proceed with invasions of Sicily and Italy but was unsuccessful in his efforts to convince Roosevelt to abandon an invasion of France in favor of concentration on the eastern Mediterranean, what Churchill saw as "the soft underbelly of Europe," in order to secure control of the Balkans. Churchill continued to believe that shifting resources for an invasion of France rather than concentrating on the defeat of Italy and the invasion of the Balkans was a major strategic blunder. Meeting Roosevelt in May 1943 in Washington, Churchill finally succumbed to American pressure to open the long-awaited second front in France the following summer but continued to express his opposition to the decision almost up to the invasion itself and also continued to press for his East European strategy months after the invasion had occurred. He also resented intensifying U.S. pressure for phasing out British colonial rule, a prospect made increasingly probable by Britain's growing international weakness.

As the war proceeded and Soviet forces began to push back German troops, Churchill feared that the Soviet Union would dominate postwar Eastern Europe. This was behind his push for the Western Allies to invade the Balkans. Soviet support for communist guerrillas in occupied countries and for the so-called Lublin government in Poland reinforced his apprehensions. In October 1944 Churchill negotiated an informal agreement with Stalin whereby the two leaders delineated their countries' respective spheres of influence in Eastern Europe. At the February 1945 Yalta Conference, Churchill and Roosevelt both acquiesced in regard to effective Soviet domination of most of that region. The three leaders also agreed to divide Germany into three separate occupation zones, to be administered by their occupying military forces but ultimately to be reunited as one state. In April 1945, Churchill unsuccessfully urged the United States to disregard existing understandings with Soviet forces and take Berlin. Despite the creation of the United Nations in 1945, Churchill hoped that close Anglo-American understanding would be the bedrock of the international world order, a perspective intensified by his continuing fears of Germany.

In July 1945 the British electorate voted Churchill out of office while he was attending a meeting at Potsdam, replacing his administration with a reformist Labour government. Churchill was still honored, however, as "the greatest living Englishman" and the war's most towering figure. He used his prestige to rally American elite and public opinion in favor of taking a stronger line against Soviet expansionism in Europe and elsewhere, a position he advanced to enormous publicity in his famous March 1946 "Iron Curtain" speech at Fulton, Missouri. Churchill's six best-selling volumes of memoirs titled *The Second World War* presented a somewhat roseate view of Anglo-American wartime cooperation and were carefully designed to promote the continuing alliance between the two countries, which had become his most cherished objective.

From 1951 to 1955, Churchill served again as Conservative prime minister. Declining health eventually forced him to resign from office. A House of Commons man to the core, he consistently refused the peerage to which his services entitled him. In 1953, however, he did accept a knighthood in the Order of the Garter, the most prestigious and exclusive of all British orders.

Among Churchill's many honors was the Nobel Prize in Literature in 1953 for his many published works. He also was the first person to be made an Honorary Citizen of the United States, by a special act of Congress. And in 1995 the United States named the guided missile destroyer *Winston S. Churchill* (DDG-81) in his honor.

Churchill died in London on January 24, 1965. For many, his death marked the symbolic final passing of Great Britain's imperial age. Churchill received the first state funeral for any British commoner since the death of the Duke of Wellington over a century before. An idiosyncratic political maverick whose pre-1939 record was at best mixed, Churchill rose to the occasion to become the greatest British war leader since the first Earl of Chatham in the 18th century.

Priscilla Roberts

Further Reading

Gilbert, Martin S. *Winston S. Churchill.* 8 vols. New York: Random House, 1966–1988.

Jablonsky, David. *Churchill and Hitler: Essays on the Political-Military Direction of Total War.* Portland, OR: Cass, 1994.

Jenkins, Roy. *Churchill.* London: Macmillan, 2001.

Larres, Klaus. *Churchill's Cold War: The Politics of Personal Diplomacy.* New Haven, CT: Yale University Press, 2002.

Lukacs, John. *Churchill: Visionary, Statesman, Historian.* New Haven, CT: Yale University Press, 2002.

Ramsden, John. *Man of the Century: Winston Churchill and His Legend since 1945.* New York: HarperCollins, 2002.

Stafford, David. *Roosevelt and Churchill: Men of Secrets.* London: Little, Brown, 1999.

COBRA, Operation (July 25–31, 1944)

U.S. Army breakout from the Cotentin Peninsula in July 1944, seven weeks after the D-Day landings. The success of the Allied invasion of June 6, 1944, turned to frustration when tenacious German defenses stifled efforts to expand beyond the initial beachheads. In order to expand the toehold in France and greatly increase supply, the original invasion plan had called for British and Canadian forces of Lieutenant General Miles C. Dempsey's British Second Army to secure early on the important city of Caen to the east of the Allied landing areas, while the American First Army under Lieutenant General Omar N. Bradley broke out and wheeled westward from its landing zones to capture the important deepwater port of Cherbourg. Allied land forces commander General Sir Bernard L. Montgomery had envisioned taking Caen on the first day and Cherbourg within 15 days. It did not work out that way, as both Allied armies soon stalled. The *bocage* Norman countryside just beyond the beaches, with its patchwork of centuries-old thick hedgerows and sunken lanes that defined ancestral agricultural holdings, presented a formidable natural defensive barrier, which the Germans, who were determined to contain the Allies against the coast, utilized with great effectiveness. The German Tiger heavy tank had heavier armor and a more powerful gun than its Allied counterpart medium tanks, and the Germans also made excellent use of the handheld *Panzerfaust* and other antitank weapons. Bradley halted his advance in the western sector before the town of Saint-Lô in order to concentrate on securing Cherbourg.

Supreme commander of the Allied Expeditionary Force General Dwight D. Eisenhower had grown impatient with the disrupted timetable. With no French port in Allied hands, all supplies and reinforcements had to come over the beaches or through two artificial harbors known as Mulberries, and one of these was wrecked in the great storm that blew in on June 19 and had to be abandoned. Securing a port was essential for the Allies to proceed. To break the deadlock, two offensive plans were developed. A series of British operations led by Second Army commander Dempsey would fix German attention on the British and Canadians as they moved to capture Caen. Meanwhile, Bradley planned Operation COBRA, a mobile ground attack in which the

U.S. First Army would break out of the Cotentin Peninsula and drive west into Brittany. This would culminate in a wide sweep to the southeast to stretch German defenses to the breaking point. Although the British and Canadian effort to take Caen turned into a protracted slugfest with heavy casualties on both sides, it did have the positive effect for the Allies of drawing off the bulk of German panzer forces to that threatened front.

Following the end of Operation CHARNWOOD (July 8–9), one of the British efforts against Caen, Montgomery met on July 10 with both Bradley and Dempsey to assess the situation. During that meeting Bradley presented to Montgomery his plans for COBRA, to be launched on July 18, and Montgomery approved. The plan called for the British and Canadians to draw off such German reserves, especially panzer formations, as possible in what became Operation GOODWOOD (July 18–20).

Tactical command for COBRA fell to aggressive VII Corps commander Major General J. Lawton Collins. Collins would have six divisions and almost 100,000 men for the attack. The plan hinged on a concentrated strike by heavy bombers to destroy a significant portion of the German lines. After the bombardment, an overwhelming ground attack by the U.S. 9th, 4th, and 30th Infantry Divisions would penetrate the disrupted German defenses and hold open a corridor for the exploiting mobile divisions. Opposing Collins was German Lieutenant General Dietrich Choltitz's LXXXIV Corps, which had experienced heavy fighting and had many understrength units, such as the Panzer Lehr Division, which could muster only 3,200 troops along a three-mile front.

In order to overcome the obstacle of the hedgerows, a majority of the U.S. M-4 Sherman and M5A1 Stuart tanks and M10 tank destroyers (known to the British as Wolverines) taking part in COBRA were fitted with steel projections welded to their fronts that enabled them to burst through the hedgerows rather than ride up and over them (when their main guns would be skyward and their undersides vulnerable to German antitank weapons). To preserve operational security, Bradley forbade use of the "Rhinos"—so named because their front projections resembled tusks—until COBRA was actually launched. The Rhinos proved extremely effective, and both Bradley and Eisenhower later paid their inventor, Sergeant Curtis Culin, great credit.

A key element in the COBRA plan was to locate a point of penetration where there were sufficient parallel roads in the direction of the attack to allow follow-on forces into the breach. The most controversial aspect of the operation was carpet bombing by heavy bombers. Bradley designated a rectangular target box 2,500 yards wide and more than 7,000 yards long, and his IX Tactical Air Command commander, Major General Elwood "Pete" Quesada, met with Air Chief Marshal Sir Trafford Leigh-Mallory to coordinate the air attack. However, the competing needs for dropping maximum bomb tonnage, maintaining tactical positions for the infantry, and placing 1,500 bombers in the mile-wide corridor in a single hour could not be entirely reconciled.

Although the British launched GOODWOOD on schedule on July 18, supported by Operation ATLANTIC (July 18–21), an effort by the Canadians to secure Verrières Ridge dominating the Caen–Falaise road, the same start date for COBRA of July 18 was not met. It was rescheduled for July 24, but overcast skies led Leigh-Mallory to call off the carpet bombing. Unfortunately, U.S. Eighth Air Force bombers were already in flight, and they approached the target from a perpendicular direction, causing bombs to fall short of the target and into the 30th Infantry Division, killing 25 and wounding 131. With the attack postponed and the surprise lost, an infuriated Bradley was told that another attack would follow the next day.

COBRA began at 9:38 a.m. on July 25. During the course of an hour 550 fighter bombers, 389 medium bombers, and 1,500 heavy bombers of the U.S. Eighth Air Force dropped some 4,400 tons of high explosives and napalm on German-held land in the Saint-Lô area in front of the American lines. The Germans, alerted by the previous attack, had dug in. Despite this, the Panzer Lehr Division was left in shambles, with 70 percent of its soldiers suffering from shock and several battalion command posts destroyed. In order to minimize casualties from "shorts" (bombs that fell short of their targets, landing on friendly forces), Bradley had specified that the bombers approach from the east, out of the sun and parallel to the Saint-Lô–Periers road, but instead the bombers came from the north, perpendicular to the front line. In fact, Bradley's request was not possible due to constraints of time and space. The U.S. troops were largely exposed, ready to move forward, and inaccurate bombing again brought U.S. casualties, with another 111 men killed, almost 500 wounded, and psychological trauma for 200 more. Among the dead was Lieutenant General Lesley J. McNair, commander of Army Ground Forces, who was visiting the front to observe the attack and was killed by a direct hit, his body hurled some 60 feet and unrecognizable from the blast except for the three stars on his collar. McNair was the highest-ranking U.S. soldier to be killed in the European theater during the war.

At 11:00 a.m. VII Corps moved forward. Strong pockets of German resistance limited the advance to only a mile or two, but the defenses had been pierced in a number of places, opening the Germans to flanking attacks. The U.S. forces had a considerable edge in resources. COBRA ultimately pitted eight infantry divisions, three armor divisions, and 2,451 tanks and tank destroyers against two German infantry divisions, a parachute infantry division, four under-strength panzer divisions, a *Panzergrenadier* division, and an estimated 190 tanks and assault guns.

At the same time COBRA was launched, the Canadian II Corps commanded by Lieutenant General Guy Simonds mounted Operation SPRING in the British Second Army sector. Again, the chief goal was to hold in place German units that might otherwise be sent to the American sector to deal with COBRA. In bloody fighting, two German divisions prevented the Canadians from securing their secondary goal of Verrières Ridge and indeed drove the Canadians back to their start point. Nonetheless, SPRING achieved its principal goal, as the German armor remained in place rather than being shifted to deal with COBRA.

The next day, July 26, Collins made the bold decision to commit his armored and motorized forces, even though no U.S. unit had reached its planned objectives. The disrupted German command-and-control network failed to react when U.S. armored divisions sliced through the lines. The next day, July 27, Collins's mobile units exploited their success deeper into the German rear areas, having advanced in some areas up to 15 miles from the starting point. This led Bradley to order VIII Corps through the breach to seize Avranches.

According to the plan, once forces moved toward Brittany, the U.S. Third Army, commanded by Lieutenant General George S. Patton Jr., would be activated. To facilitate this transition, Bradley gave Patton immediate command of VIII Corps, which

A French woman watching a column of U.S. troops of the 4th Infantry Division in front of her house in La Basset, Normandy, on July 23, 1944, during Operation COBRA. (Galerie Bilderwelt/Getty Images)

he drove hard to capture Avranches, taken by Major General John S. Wood's 4th Armored Division on July 31, marking the end of CO-BRA. In just six days the entire German front collapsed, enabling the Allies to carry out their own operational blitzkrieg deep into France. In COBRA, U.S. forces sustained some 1,800 casualties. German losses are unknown.

Steven J. Rauch and Spencer C. Tucker

Further Reading

Blumenson, Martin. *The U.S. Army in World War II, European Theater of Operations: Breakout and Pursuit.* Washington, DC: U.S. Army, Office of the Chief of Military History, 1961.

Carafano, James J. *After D-Day: Operation Cobra and the Normandy Breakout.* Boulder, CO: Lynne Rienner, 2000.

Cole, Robert George (1915–1944)

U.S. Army soldier awarded the Medal of Honor for his role in the Normandy campaign. Robert George Cole was born at Fort Sam Houston, San Antonio, Texas, on March 19, 1915, the son of an army doctor. He graduated from Thomas Jefferson High School in San Antonio in 1933 and joined the army in July 1934 but was honorably discharged in 1935 to accept an appointment to the U.S. Military Academy, West Point.

Graduating from West Point in 1939, Cole was commissioned a second lieutenant in the 15th Infantry Regiment at Fort Lewis, Washington. He then transferred to the 501st Parachute Infantry Regiment at Fort Benning, Georgia, and in March 1941 he received his jump wings. D-Day, June 6, 1944, found Cole a lieutenant colonel commanding the 3rd Battalion of the 502nd Parachute Infantry Regiment.

After being in division reserve, Cole's battalion was assigned to guard the right flank of the 101st Airborne during the attempt to take Carentan and link up with the 29th Infantry Division advancing from Omaha Beach. On the afternoon of June 10, Cole led his battalion single file down a long causeway (later known as Purple Heart Lane) with marshes on either side. The Germans were dug in behind a hedgerow on the right. At the far end of the causeway was the last of four bridges spanning the Douve River floodplain. Carentan lay just beyond.

Suddenly Cole's unit was pinned down by withering German rifle, machine-gun, mortar, and artillery fire that prevented any movement and inflicted numerous casualties. Several attempts to force the German position proved fruitless, and the battalion took up defensive positions for the night.

At dawn the next morning after having taken more casualties from mortar fire and a strafing attack by two German aircraft, Cole called for artillery support, which, however, failed to dislodge the Germans. Cole then called for smoke on the dug-in Germans and ordered his men to fix bayonets. With utter disregard for his own safety and completely ignoring enemy fire, Cole rose to his feet in front of his battalion and, with drawn pistol, shouted to his men to follow him in the assault. Taking a fallen man's rifle and bayonet, Cole charged on and led what remained of his battalion against the German position. Close-in and even hand-to-hand fighting followed as the Germans were driven from their positions.

The assault, which came to be known as Cole's Charge, proved costly, as 130 of Cole's 265 men were casualties. With his battalion exhausted, Cole called for the 1st Battalion to pass through his lines and continue the attack. However, its ranks were also severely depleted from German mortar fire while crossing the fourth bridge, and the men took up positions with the 3rd Battalion rather than proceeding. Concentrated American artillery fire ended strong counterattacks by the German 6th Parachute Regiment that evening.

Cole was recommended for a Medal of Honor for his actions that day but did not live to receive it. He was shot and killed by a German sniper on September 18, 1944, during Operation MARKET GARDEN. Cole's widow accepted his Medal of Honor at a presentation ceremony at Fort Sam Houston on October 30, 1944. She was accompanied by Cole's two-year-old son, whom he had never seen in person. Lieutenant Colonel Cole is buried at the Netherlands American Cemetery and Memorial at Margraten in the Netherlands. Robert G. Cole High School at Fort Sam Houston is named for him.

Jason M. Sokiera

Further Reading

Ambrose, Stephen E. *Citizen Soldiers.* New York: Simon and Schuster, 1997.

Murphy, Edward F. *Heroes of World War II.* Novato, CA: Presidio, 1990.

Ryan, Cornelius. *A Bridge Too Far.* New York: Simon and Schuster, 1974.

Ryan, Cornelius. *The Longest Day.* New York: Simon and Schuster, 1959.

U.S. Senate, Committee on Veterans Affairs. *Medal of Honor Recipients, 1863–1973.*

Washington, DC: U.S. Government Printing Office, 1973.

Collins, Joseph Lawton "Lightning Joe" (1896–1987)

U.S. Army general. Born on May 1, 1896, in New Orleans, Louisiana, Joseph Lawton Collins was the brother of James Lawton Collins, another future U.S. Army general. Joseph Collins attended Louisiana State University during 1912–1913, then went on to the United States Military Academy at West Point, where he graduated in 1917, was commissioned a second lieutenant, and assigned to the 22nd Infantry. Although he did not take part in combat in World War I, he was promoted to captain in 1919 and served with U.S. occupation forces in Germany (1919–1921).

Collins was an instructor at West Point (1921–1925). He graduated from the Infantry School at Fort Benning, Georgia, in 1925 and then was an instructor there (1925–1931). Promoted to major in 1932, he was a student at the Command and General Staff School, Fort Leavenworth, Kansas (1932–1933), and then served in the Philippines (1933–1935). Collins attended the Army Industrial College (1936–1937) and the Army War College (1937–1938) before serving as an instructor at the latter (1938–1941). He was then chief of staff of VI Corps in Alabama (1941). Shortly after the Japanese attack on Pearl Harbor (December 7, 1941), Colonel Collins was named chief of staff of the Hawaiian Department. He was promoted to brigadier general in February 1942 and to major general that May, taking command of the 25th Infantry Division.

The 25th Infantry Division relieved the 1st Marine Division on Guadalcanal in December 1942. Collins earned the nickname "Lightning Joe" for his aggressiveness in this campaign, defeating the Japanese there in February 1943. He then led the 25th Infantry Division during the successful operations on New Georgia (June 30–August 25, 1943).

Transferring to the European theater in January 1944, Collins assumed command of VII Corps, the post he held for the remainder of the war. On D-Day (June 6, 1944), spearheaded by its 4th Division, VII Corps landed on Utah Beach. It then seized the vital port of Cherbourg (June 27). VII Corps is probably best remembered, however, for Operation COBRA (June 25–31), the breakout from the Normandy beachhead at Saint-Lô (July 25), an operation largely planned by Lieutenant General Omar N. Bradley but executed by Collins. VII Corps then repelled the German counterattack at Mortain (August 7–13), which led to the creation of the Falaise–Argentan pocket.

Collins led VII Corps during the disastrous Battle of Hürtgen Forest (September 19, 1944–February 10, 1945); at the Ardennes Offensive (Battle of the Bulge, December 16, 1944–January 16, 1945), where the corps held the northern shoulder of the bulge; at Köln (Cologne, February 1945); in the reduction of the Ruhr pocket (March–April); and, as the war ended, in the Harz Mountains. In April 1945, he was promoted to lieutenant general.

Following the war, Collins served as director of information for the War Department (December 1945–September 1947). He then served as vice chief of staff of the army (1947–1949). Promoted to full general (January 1948), he was then chief of staff of the army (August 1949–August 1953). Collins is credited with full racial integration of the army during the Korean War (1950–1953), in accordance with President Harry S. Truman's 1948 executive order.

Collins then served as U.S. representative to the North Atlantic Treaty Organization Military Committee and Standing Group. Following the 1954 Geneva Accords, the Dwight D. Eisenhower administration dispatched Collins to the State of Vietnam (later the Republic of Vietnam, or South Vietnam) as special envoy with the rank of ambassador (1954–1955). Although Collins did not think that Ngo Dinh Diem was capable of leading South Vietnam, he followed his instructions of supporting the Diem government by helping it establish a military training program and agrarian reforms. Collins retired from the army in March 1956. After serving as vice chairman of the President's Committee for Hungarian Refugee Relief, he entered private business. Collins died in Washington, D.C., on September 12, 1987.

Thomas D. Veve

Further Reading

Collins, J. Lawton. *Lightning Joe: An Autobiography.* Baton Rouge: Louisiana State University Press, 1979.

Weigley, Russell F. *Eisenhower's Lieutenants.* Bloomington: Indiana University Press, 1981.

Command Structure, Allied

As opposed to the German side, the Allies from the very start of Operation OVERLORD had both a joint and a combined command and staff structure. A joint command is one in which a single commander controls two or all of the service components, land, naval, and air. Under a combined command that same commander also controls the forces of two or more nations, and the headquarters staff supporting that commander is also combined. The nominal German commander in chief in France, Field Marshal Gerd von Rundstedt, was not such a commander in either sense, joint or combined. His Allied opposite number, General Dwight D. Eisenhower, was. The fully integrated military and political coalition between the United States and the United Kingdom was the most successful in history to that time and the model for the post–World War II North Atlantic Treaty Organization (NATO).

As the supreme Allied commander, Europe (SACEUR), Eisenhower answered to the Combined Chiefs of Staff, consisting of representatives from both the U.S. and the British Chiefs of Staff. The senior member of the U.S. Chiefs of Staff was General George C. Marshall, chief of staff of the U.S. Army. The senior member of the British Chiefs of Staff was Field Marshal Sir Alan F. Brooke (later Lord Alanbrooke), chief of the Imperial General Staff.

Eisenhower's deputy SACEUR was British air chief marshal Sir Arthur Tedder. The chief of the Combined Staff was U.S. major general Walter Bedell Smith. General Smith's deputy was British lieutenant general Sir Frederick E. Morgan, who had been in charge of planning Operation OVERLORD since March 1943. Much of the success of the D-Day landings was the result of his extensive and detailed staff work and planning. Under Smith and Morgan each of the principal staff sections of the Supreme Headquarters, Allied Expeditionary Force (SHAEF), had either a British principal and an American deputy or vice versa. The British and the Americans at that time had completely different staff structure organizations, but for SHAEF they adopted the American system—G-1, Personnel and Administration; G-2, Intelligence; G-3, Operations; and G-4, Logistics. NATO staffs are organized on that model to this day. The British also converted to that model following World War II.

All of the service component commanders on D-Day were British. British admiral Sir Bertram Ramsay was the commander in chief of Allied Naval Forces. The Western Task Force, supporting the American landings, was commanded by U.S. rear admiral Alan G. Kirk. The Eastern Task Force, supporting the British landings, was commanded by British rear admiral Sir Philip L. Vian. Air Marshal Sir Trafford Leigh-Mallory was the commander in chief of the Allied Expeditionary Air Forces. Directly under him were Lieutenant General Lewis H. Brereton, commander of the U.S. Ninth Air Force, and Air Marshal Sir Arthur Coningham, commander of the British Second Tactical Air Force. Also supporting the initial phases of the landings were the Allied strategic air forces, Royal Air Force Bomber Command, under Air Chief Marshal Sir Arthur Harris, and the U.S. Eighth Air Force, commanded by Lieutenant General James H. Doolittle.

The overall ground forces commander on D-Day was British general Sir Bernard Montgomery, commander of the 21st Army Group. Under him Lieutenant General Omar Bradley commanded the U.S. First Army, and Lieutenant General Sir Miles Dempsey commanded the British Second Army. As Allied forces poured ashore in the weeks following the landings, Bradley assumed command of the 12th Army Group, with Lieutenant General Courtney Hodges commanding the U.S. First Army and Lieutenant General George S. Patton Jr. commanding the U.S. Third Army. As the British forces built up, Montgomery's 21st Army Group included the British Second Army and the Canadian First Army, under Lieutenant General Henry Crear. At various times the 12th Army Group included Free French units, and the 21st Army Group included Free Polish units.

Montgomery remained dual-hatted as 21st Army Group commander and overall Allied ground commander until September 1, 1944, when Eisenhower himself assumed direct command of the ground forces. Fifteen days later, U.S. lieutenant general Jacob Devers's 6th Army Group, which had landed in southern France on August 15 and had been advancing steadily north, made contact with the U.S. Third Army. At that point control of the 6th Army Group passed from the Mediterranean theater of operations to the European theater of operations, hence under Eisenhower. The 6th Army Group consisted of the U.S. Seventh Army, under Lieutenant General Alexander M. Patch, and the French First Army, under General Jean de Lattre de Tassigny.

Eisenhower's absolute control of all the Allied military forces in Northwestern Europe gave him a distinct advantage over the Germans. Unlike Rundstedt and his successors, Eisenhower was not micromanaged on the battlefield by his political superiors. German chancellor Adolf Hitler, on the other hand, often meddled in the movements of individual divisions. The Allied command structure was more flexible than that of the Germans, and the Allies could respond much faster.

This caused Hitler to vastly underestimate his enemy's capability to react to the German offensive in the Ardennes in December 1944. Hitler and Colonel General Alfred Jodl, chief of the Oberkommando der Wehrmacht Operations Staff in Berlin, assumed that once the Germans attacked, Eisenhower would not be able to react effectively for up to two weeks while he awaited specific instructions from Washington and London. They were wrong. The Germans simply could not conceive that Eisenhower had the personal authority to order an immediate counterattack just three days after the start of the German offensive on December 16, 1944. Three days after Eisenhower gave the order, the U.S. Third Army counterattacked into the southern shoulder of the Bulge. It was the Allied command and staff structure that made such an operation possible.

David T. Zabecki

Further Reading

Atkinson, Rick. *The Guns at Last Light: The War in Western Europe, 1944–1945.* New York: Henry Holt, 2013.

D'Este, Carlo. *Decision in Normandy.* New York: E. P. Dutton, 1983.

Eisenhower, Dwight D. *The Crusade in Europe.* London: William Heinemann, 1948.

Ellis, L. F. *Victory in the West,* Vol. 1. United Kingdom Military Series. London: HMSO, 1962.

Harrison, Gordon A. *Cross-Channel Attack: U.S. Army in World War II.* Washington, DC: Center for Military History, 1951.

Morgan, Frederick. *Overture to Overlord.* Garden City, NY: Doubleday, 1950.

Command Structure, German

Germany has a near-legendary reputation for military efficiency and sure-handed command and control. In 1944, however, the reality was something quite different, especially in France as the Allies prepared to invade the European continent. Germany's command structure in Northwestern Europe was a self-inflicted liability. Unlike Allied supreme commander General Dwight Eisenhower, the German commander in chief, West (Oberbefehlshaber-West), Field

Field Marshal Karl Rudolf Gerd von Rundstedt, commander of German forces in France. When the Normandy invasion began on June 6, 1944, he immediately requested permission to send two of the panzer divisions stationed near Paris 120 miles north to the invasion beaches but Adolf Hitler delayed two hours, which meant that the panzers had to move in full daylight under Allied air attack. Following the successful Allied landings, Rundstedt urged Hitler to make peace, whereupon Hitler removed him from command. (Library of Congress)

Marshal Gerd von Rundstedt, had anything but complete military authority in his theater of operations.

Rundstedt had almost no direct control over most of Germany's key air force and navy elements in France. The Third Air Fleet, which included all the air defense artillery units in France, reported directly to the German Air Force High Command (Oberkommando der Luftwaffe) in Berlin. Naval Group West, which included the naval coastal artillery units and all ships operating off the coast, reported directly to the German Navy High Command (Oberkommando der Kriegsmarine), also in Berlin. Rundstedt himself reported to Adolf Hitler through the Armed Forces High Command (Oberkommando der Wehrmacht, OKW). The German Army High Command (Oberkommando des Heeres, OKH) meanwhile had no control over the war in the west, even though it had to provide the ground forces and support. The OKH focused strictly on the war in Russia, while the OKW ran the war in all the other theaters. The OKW was headed by Field Marshal Wilhelm Keitel, chief of the OKW, and Colonel General Alfred Jodl, chief of the OKW Operations Staff. Neither officer had served in combat since World War I. Jodl was the real power at the OKW, while Keitel was little more than a figurehead.

Rundstedt's First and Nineteenth Armies in southern France came under Army Task Group G, commanded by Colonel General Johannes Blaskowitz. The Seventh and Fifteenth Armies in northern France came under Army Group B, commanded by Field Marshal Erwin Rommel. The Seventh Army's 15 divisions were deployed from the mouth of the Seine River to the mouth of the Loire River. That sector included the Normandy coast, the Cotentin Peninsula, and all of Brittany. The Fifteenth Army's 18 divisions were deployed from the Seine to the Belgian–Dutch border, including the Pas de Calais, the sector of the French coast closest to Britain.

Making Rundstedt's command problems even more complicated, he did not even have complete operational control over all of the German ground forces in France. The main Wehrmacht striking force in France was Panzer Group West, which had 10 panzer and *Panzergrenadier* divisions. But all the panzer units in Northwestern Europe belonged to Germany's strategic reserve, which could not be committed without the concurrence of the OKW in Berlin. Rundstedt did not even have the authority to shift Fifteenth Army units south to Normandy or Seventh Army units north to the Pas de Calais in response to any Allied landing. Only Hitler through the OKW could authorize any such moves.

The final disruptive element was Rommel's traditional privilege as a field marshal, giving him direct access to the head of state. Rommel used that license to go over Rundstedt's head to Hitler whenever the two field marshals disagreed. Earlier in the war when he was in North Africa, Rommel had done the same thing frequently to Field Marshal Albert Kesselring, commanding the Mediterranean theater.

The Germans anticipated the Allied invasion, but the exact point of the landings was a toss-up between Normandy and the Pas de Calais. The latter seemed the more likely because it offered the shorter and most direct invasion axis into the Ruhr region, Germany's industrial heartland. During the months leading up to D-Day the Allies' sophisticated FORTITUDE deception operation focused the German attention on the Pas de Calais. By early June 1944 Rommel, along with most of the German commanders in France, believed that the main Allied landings would be preceded by a diversionary assault somewhere else.

While all the German commanders agreed that the beach defenses along the coast had to be as strong as possible, there was some divergence of opinion on how the overall defense should be conducted. Rundstedt knew the importance of a robust beach defense to disrupt and slow down the Allies, but he likewise was certain that it would be almost impossible to halt the invasion at the shoreline. As the landings at Salerno in September 1943 had shown, Allied naval power was simply too overwhelming. Rundstedt concluded that the main body of the panzer forces should be held well inland. Once the Allied center of gravity was clearly identified, the panzers then could launch a powerful counterattack by executing a double envelopment against the Allied units ashore. The Wehrmacht's experiences in Russia showed clearly the efficacy of such tactics. Almost every senior panzer commander in the German Army agreed with the broad outlines of Rundstedt's assessment, including General Heinz Guderian and General Leo Geyr von Schweppenburg, commander of Panzer Group West.

Rommel had different ideas. Based on his experiences as the only senior German commander in France who had any experience fighting the British and Americans, he believed that absolute Allied air supremacy made it impossible for armored formations to maneuver without being destroyed. Thus, he argued that the invaders had to be stopped at the waterline and then pushed back into the sea with immediate and violent counterattacks. That strategy required the mass of the panzers to be positioned as far forward as possible, and Rommel wanted the authority to commit them as he saw necessary.

Since the end of World War II much ink has been spilled arguing that Rommel had been right and could have defeated the Allied invasion had he been given a free hand. Such arguments, however, ignore several key realities of modern ground combat. First, Rommel advocated a rigid forward defense rather than the flexible defense in depth of which the Germans were the masters. Military history shows that rigid forward defenses almost always fail. Second, the Germans were certainly severely handicapped by Allied airpower, but with the bulk of the German forces massed forward, they would have presented just that many more tightly packed targets for Allied aircraft. In addition, the massed forward forces would also be within range of powerful, accurate Allied naval gunfire. Rommel had no experience dealing with naval shore support. Third, by spreading the panzer units along the coast to be able to respond to a landing at any point, Rommel would have been dispersing rather than concentrating the panzers. This was the exact same mistake the Allies made with their tank forces during the Battle of France in June 1940. The piecemeal commitment of armored forces could only result in a battle of attrition, one that the Germans could never win. Finally, much of the forward-most terrain along the coast was very poor tank country. The ground behind the British beaches in Normandy was reasonably good tank ground, but the terrain behind Omaha and Utah Beaches was far more channelized and restricted.

With Rundstedt and Rommel at loggerheads, Rommel exercised his field marshal's prerogative and appealed directly to Hitler. Hitler initially sided with Rommel, until Rundstedt protested in writing. Hitler finally split the difference between the two strategies, thus making both courses of action nonviable. Army Task Group G in southern France was allocated three panzer divisions, Rommel's Army Group B was allocated three, and Panzer Group West retained one *Panzergrenadier* and three panzer divisions as the OKW reserve. But even though the frontline commanders now had the panzer divisions in their orders of battle, they still did not have the authority to commit or even move them without OKW permission. Hitler had completely tied the hands of his own commanders, while at the same time Ultra intelligence intercepts gave Allied commanders a fairly accurate picture of the German panzer reserve situation.

Did the Germans ever have a chance of winning the 1944 Battle of France? Probably not. But their own self-imposed command problems made their defeat that much quicker and more certain.

David T. Zabecki

Further Reading

Boog, Horst, Werner Rahn, Reinhard Stumpf, and Bernd Wegner. *Germany and the Second World War,* Vol. 6, *The Global War.* Oxford, UK: Clarendon, 2001.

Isby, David, ed. *The German Army at D-Day: Fighting the Invasion.* London: Greenhill Books, 2004.

Megargee, Geoffrey P. *Inside Hitler's High Command.* Lawrence: University Press of Kansas, 2000.

Speidel, Hans. *Invasion 1944.* Stuttgart: Rainer Wunderlich Verlag, 1949.

Coningham, Sir Arthur "Mary" (1895–1948)

Royal Air Force (RAF) air marshal and pioneer in the use of tactical air support. Born in Brisbane, Australia, on January 19, 1895, Arthur Coningham served in the New Zealand Army in World War I until discharged for health reasons in April 1916. He then joined the British Royal Flying Corps and became a pilot, acquiring the nickname "Mary," derived from "Maori." Following the war, Coningham remained in the newly formed RAF. He served in both Iraq and Egypt and taught at the RAF college, among other assignments.

At the beginning of World War II, Coningham was promoted to air commodore and given command of Number 4 Group, composed of long-range night bombers based in Yorkshire. He was convinced of the necessity of close air support, which he was able to demonstrate on his promotion in July 1941 to air vice marshal and assignment to North Africa as commander of the Western Desert Air Force. There he became one of the pioneers of tactical air support, which his units provided for the British Eighth Army on the ground. Coningham improved coordination between air and ground forces, and his aircraft played an important role in the British victory in the Battle of El Alamein (October 23–November 4, 1942). He was knighted in 1942 for his services.

Coningham was in charge of air support in other key Allied operations. He commanded the First Tactical Air Force during the invasion of Sicily (July 9–August 22, 1943) and subsequent action in Italy. Transferred to command of the Second Allied Tactical Air Force in January 1944, he worked to plan air support for the Normandy invasion that commenced on June 6. During the invasion and until the end of the war in Europe, he earned high praise from Allied ground commanders.

At the end of the war, Coningham commanded the RAF Flying Training Centre. Promoted to air marshal in 1946, he nonetheless was forced to retire in August 1947, having had little service with the air staff; he had spent his entire career as an active pilot. Coningham died on January 30, 1948, in the crash of a passenger plane in the Atlantic Ocean.

Harold Lee Wise

Further Reading

Orange, Vincent. *Coningham: A Biography of Air Marshal Sir Arthur Coningham.* Washington, DC: Center for Air Force History, 1992.

Richards, Denis, and Hilary S. Saunders. *Royal Air Force, 1939–1945; Official History.* 3 vols. London: HMSO, 1953–1954.

Terraine, John. *A Time for Courage: The Royal Air Force in the European War, 1939–1945.* New York: Macmillan, 1985.

Cota, Norman Daniel "Dutch" (1893–1971)

U.S. Army general. Born in Chelsea, Massachusetts, on May 30, 1893, Norman Daniel "Dutch" Cota graduated from the U.S. Military Academy at West Point in 1917 and was commissioned in the infantry with the 22nd Infantry Regiment. He was an instructor at West Point between 1918 and 1920. Cota transferred to the Finance Department in 1920 and was the finance officer of West Point until 1924, when he transferred back to the infantry. Cota graduated from the Infantry School at Fort Benning, Georgia, in 1925 and served in the Hawaiian Department. He graduated from the Command and General Staff School in 1931, was an instructor at the Infantry School in 1932 and 1933, graduated from the Army War College in 1936, and was an instructor at the Command and General Staff School from 1938 to 1940.

Cota was in charge of plans and training for the 1st Infantry Division from March 1941; he was its chief of staff from 1942 to February 1943, taking part in the capture of Oran during Operation TORCH, the invasion of French North Africa (November 8, 1942). Promoted to brigadier general in February 1943, he became U.S. adviser to the Combined Operations Branch of the European theater of operations. Later that year, he was assistant commander of the 29th Infantry Division.

On June 6, 1944, Cota landed with his division on Omaha Beach, Normandy. Several of the men in his landing craft (an LCVP, for "landing craft vehicle and personnel") were killed by German fire as soon as the ramp went down. Cota was the only general officer on Omaha Beach that day. With American forces almost pushed back into the sea, he was an inspiring presence. Realizing that the men were doomed if they remained on the beach, he exposed himself to German fire as he repeatedly led small parties forward. Many historians credit him with almost single-handedly preventing a disaster that day. Cota later received the Distinguished Service Cross for his actions. Wounded at the Battle of Saint-Lô (July 11–19, 1944), he spent two weeks in the division hospital.

On August 13, 1944, Cota took command of the 28th Infantry Division, which he led through Paris in a liberation parade in August 1944, part of a show of force in support of General Charles de Gaulle to prevent a possible communist takeover. Cota was promoted to major general in September 1944.

On November 2, the 28th Infantry Division began an attack to capture the town of Schmidt during the Hürtgen Forest campaign (September 12–December 16), which was intended to break the Siegfried Line. The plan of attack was a recipe for disaster, with all three regiments of the division attacking in diverging directions, and had been imposed on the division by staff officers at V Corps. Cota protested his orders to both V Corps commander Major General Leonard Gerow and First Army commander Lieutenant General Courtney Hodges but was ordered to execute the plan. During the next nine days, the 28th Infantry Division suffered more than 6,000 casualties. Near the end of the battle,

Cota collapsed under the pressure of what was happening to his division.

If not for his performance on Omaha Beach, Cota almost certainly would have been relieved of his command after this debacle; as it was, the events at Schmidt cast a long shadow over him. The 28th Infantry Division was pulled out of the line and sent south to a quiet sector in Belgium to reconstitute. On December 16, it was manning the sector of the line known as Skyline Drive when the Germans launched their Ardennes Offensive (Battle of the Bulge, December 16, 1944–January 16, 1945). Although the already weak 28th Infantry Division was mauled during the German attack, it did not break. Rather, it conducted a tenacious and effective fighting withdrawal that contributed in no small part to disrupting the German timetable for the offensive. Cota returned to the United States in August 1945 to prepare for the anticipated invasion of Japan.

Cota retired from the army as a major general in 1946. He died in Wichita, Kansas, on October 4, 1971.

David T. Zabecki

Further Reading

Ambrose, Stephen E. *D-Day, June 6, 1944: The Climactic Battle of World War II.* New York: Simon and Schuster, 1994.

MacDonald, Charles B. *A Time for Trumpets: The Untold Story of the Battle of the Bulge.* New York: William Morrow, 1985.

Miller, Robert A. *Division Commander: A Biography of Major General Norman D. Cota.* Spartanburg, SC: Reprint Publishers, 1989.

Cotentin (Cherbourg) Peninsula

A peninsula located in Lower Normandy, which lies entirely within the Department of the Manche (named for the English Channel, known to the French as La Manche). Known also as the Cherbourg Peninsula, for the city of the same name, the Cotentin Peninsula is situated on the northwestern coast of France and extends into the English Channel along a north-to-northwest axis. To its immediate west are the British-controlled Channel Islands; to the southwest lies the Brittany Peninsula. Utah Beach, one of the American landing zones during the Normandy (D-Day) invasion, is situated on the peninsula's southeastern coast. After the June 6, 1944, landing, Allied forces first took Sainte-Mère-Église, located just a few miles inland, before battling for control of the entire peninsula and ultimately its chief city and seaport of Cherbourg.

The Cotentin Peninsula is divided into three separate geographical areas: La Hague (a headland), Cotentin Pass (a plain), and the Saire River Valley (Val de Saire). The southern portion of the peninsula features a broad area of marshlands (le Marais) that extends from east to west. The peninsula's western shoreline (Côtes des Îles) faces the Channel Islands.

Like much of Normandy, the Cotentin Peninsula is chiefly agricultural, with dairy farming the principal activity. It is also known for its seafood (especially oysters) as well as apple and pear production. It is not highly forested, as its predominant landscape features open fields and orchards sometimes surrounded by thick hedgerows, which presented significant challenges to Allied troops during World War II.

During the 9th and 10th centuries, Vikings began to settle on the Cotentin Peninsula; they were followed by Anglo-Danish and Anglo-Norse peoples, who began to cultivate crops. Because of the peninsula's relative isolation, vestiges of the Norman language can still be heard in the area; this is known as the Cotentinais dialect, which incorporates a number of Norse words into the French language.

Cherbourg is located near the northernmost portion of the peninsula. It is the region's only deepwater port, and thus securing it was a key goal for Allied forces. It was taken on June 29, and the entire peninsula was taken a day later. The peninsula's other population centers include Bricquebec, Barfleur, La Haye du Puits, Les Pieux, Montebourg, and Valognes.

Tourists can visit Utah Beach and its environs, which have remained little changed over the last seven decades. The village of Sainte-Mère-Église is home to a military museum commemorating the contributions of the U.S. Army 82nd and 101st Airborne Divisions, which played a major role in the battle for control of the Cotentin Peninsula.

Paul G. Pierpaoli Jr.

Further Reading

Breuer, William B. *Hitler's Fortress Cherbourg: The Conquest of a Bastion.* New York: Stein and Day, 1984.

Unwin, Peter. *The Narrow Sea: Barrier, Bridge, and Gateway to the World: The History of the English Channel.* London: Headline, 2004.

Crerar, Henry Duncan Graham (1888–1965)

Canadian Army general. Born on April 28, 1888, in Hamilton, Ontario, Henry Crerar served with distinction in the artillery during World War I, ending the war as a counterbattery staff officer for the Canadian Corps. During the interwar years, he remained in the small Permanent Force (regular army), primarily in staff appointments, and attended both the British Staff College (1923–1924) and the Imperial Defence College (1934–1935).

A brigadier at the onset of World War II, Crerar was promoted to major general in January 1940 and appointed chief of the Canadian General Staff six months later. In that capacity, he played a central role in dispatching two ill-trained Canadian battalions to Hong Kong—and Japanese captivity—in 1941, but he also built up a solid training establishment. Crerar, promoted to lieutenant general in November 1941, was ambitious, ruthless, and jealous of rivals. Posted overseas to command the I Canadian Corps that year, he spent much of his time intriguing against Lieutenant General Andrew McNaughton and had a major role in planning the disastrous Dieppe Raid (August 19, 1942). Crerar subsequently commanded the I Canadian Corps in Italy from November 1943 until he was recalled to England in March 1944 to lead the Canadian First Army in the Normandy invasion. With that appointment, Crerar had reached the pinnacle for a Canadian officer. He was promoted to general in November 1944.

Although historians have acknowledged his obvious administrative abilities, the excessively cautious and uninspiring Crerar was at best a pedestrian field commander. Field Marshal Bernard Montgomery, under whose command Crerar served in the campaign in Northwestern Europe, had little confidence in him. Crerar's bitter rivalry with the abler Lieutenant General Guy Simonds was unjustified on any military grounds, and there is little doubt, for this and other reasons, that the latter would have replaced him had the war continued much longer. Operation VERITABLE, the assault on the Reichswald region in Germany in February 1945, was an unmitigated disaster. Crerar accumulated vast resources, but his rigid planning forced them into a narrow bottleneck and produced massive casualties.

Crerar nevertheless deserves much credit for effectively representing Canadian interests in Allied councils and for building an overseas headquarters. He retired from the army in 1946 and died in Ottawa on April 1, 1965.

Patrick H. Brennan

Further Reading

English, J. A. *Failure in High Command: The Canadian Army and the Normandy Campaign.* Ottawa: Golden Dog, 1995.

Granatstein, J. L. *The Generals: The Canadian Army's Senior Commanders in the Second World War.* Toronto: Stoddart, 1993.

Crocker, Sir John Treddinick (1896–1963)

British Army officer who commanded I Corps during Operation OVERLORD. John Treddinick Crocker was born in London on January 4, 1896, into a middle-class family. He was a young boy when his father died, and a chronic respiratory illness prevented him from attending regular school classes. In 1915 during World War I, Crocker joined the British Army as a private in the cavalry. He performed splendidly as a soldier and was commissioned a second lieutenant in January 1917. He was awarded the Military Cross in April 1918 and the Distinguished Service Order that July.

In 1919, Crocker left the army and briefly studied for the law. By 1921, however, he had rejoined the army and was attached to the Royal Tank Corps. Promoted to captain in 1939, in 1934 he was made brigade major in the experimental Armored Brigade. In 1938 he was promoted to full colonel.

As a brigadier general, Crocker commanded the 3rd Armored Brigade beginning in April 1940 and saw much action during the May 10–June 24, 1940, Battle of France. In September 1940, now as acting major general, Crocker assumed command of the 6th Armored Division. In March 1942, he took command of XI Corps as acting lieutenant general. That September Crocker assumed command of IX Corps and saw action during the Tunisia campaign (November 17, 1942–May 13, 1943).

After being wounded in a training mishap, in August 1943 Crocker took command of I Corps, which he led during the Normandy invasion and campaign. On D-Day, his corps went ashore on Gold Beach. After driving the Germans to the Seine, I Corps carried out mopping-up operations in northeastern France and Belgium.

In October 1945 Crocker was promoted to the permanent rank of lieutenant general. He remained in the army until 1953 after serving as adjutant general to the forces, the second-highest post on the Army Council.

After retirement, Crocker served as vice chairman of the Imperial War Graves Commission. He was also ennobled as lord lieutenant of Middlesex. Crocker died at Middlesex, now part of London, on March 9, 1963.

Paul G. Pierpaoli Jr.

Further Reading

Delaney, Douglas E. *Corps Commanders: Five British and Canadian Generals at War, 1939–1945.* Vancouver: University of British Columbia Press, 2011.

Mead, Richard. *Churchill's Lions: A Biographical Guide to the Key British Generals of World War II.* Stroud, Gloucestershire, UK: Spellmount, 2007.

Culin, Curtis Grubb, III (1915–1963)

U.S. Army sergeant who invented the plow device that enabled tanks to overcome the hedgerows of Normandy. Curtis Grubb Culin III was born on February 15, 1915, in Cranford, New Jersey. He joined the New Jersey National Guard in 1940 and was a tanker with the 102nd Cavalry Reconnaissance Squadron (the "Essex Troop"), which became part of the U.S. Army 2nd Armored Division in World War II.

Culin took part in the Normandy invasion of June 6, 1944, but the Allied forces that came ashore soon found themselves dealing with the so-called *bocage* of Normandy. *Bocage* (believed to derive from the French word *bois,* meaning "wood") refers to a terrain of mixed woodland and fields separated by small, winding dirt lanes sunken through long use and located between narrow low ridges and banks topped by tall, thick hedgerows. Formed over centuries, the hedgerows were an ideal defensive barrier. Tanks plowing into the hedgerows could ride up over them but in so doing were lifted up, exposing their own thinly armored undersides to German antitank weapons, while at the same time their main guns pointed skyward and could thus not be brought to bear. The Allied advance now stalled.

In mid-July Culin came up with the idea of welding a steel bar to the front of an M-4 Sherman tank with four tusklike steel bars extending forward that worked as a sort of plow to enable the tank to burst through a hedgerow. The steel was readily available in the form of the chevaux-de-frise barriers that the Germans had erected on the invasion beaches.

The prototype worked well and ultimately was demonstrated before commander of U.S. ground forces in Normandy Lieutenant General Omar N. Bradley, who recalled in *A Soldier's Story* that Major General Leonard Gerow invited him to a test demonstration to see something that "will knock your eyes out." A tank fitted with Culin's device "backed off and ran head-on toward a hedgerow at ten miles an hour. Its tusks bored into the wall, pinned down the belly, and the tank broke through under a canopy of dirt." A second similarly equipped M-4 Sherman duplicated the performance. The fitting came to be known as "Culin's Cutter," and tanks so equipped were called "Rhinos." Bradley ordered that as many tanks as possible be equipped with the device, and by the time of the American breakout in Operation COBRA on July 25 a majority had the cutters.

Culin was subsequently awarded the Legion of Merit for his work. General Dwight D. Eisenhower, at the time supreme commander of the Allied Expeditionary Force, said after the war that "Culin's contributions to success in the Normandy Breakout reflected Yankee ingenuity at its best."

In November 1944, Curtis lost a leg to a land mine in the Battle of the Hürtgen Forest (September 19, 1944–February 10, 1945). When he returned to the United States and mustered out of the army, he resumed his prewar career as a salesman. Culin died in Cranford on November 20, 1963.

Spencer C. Tucker

Further Reading

Bradley, Omar N. *A Soldier's Story.* New York: Holt, 1951.

Carafano, James Jay. *GI Ingenuity: Improvisation, Technology, and Winning World War II.* Westport, CT: Praeger Security International, 2006.

Daugherty, Leo J. *The Battle of the Hedgerows: Bradley's First Army in Normandy, June–July 1944.* Shepperton, Surrey, UK: Ian Allan, 2001.

Hastings, Max. *Overlord: D-Day and the Battle for Normandy.* New York: Simon and Schuster, 1984.

Prados, John. *Normandy Crucible: The Decisive Battle That Shaped World War II in Europe.* New York: NAL Caliber, 2011.

D

de Gaulle, Charles (1890–1970)

French Army general, leader of Free French Forces, and the president of France. Born on November 22, 1890, in Lille, Charles de Gaulle demonstrated from an early age a keen interest in the military. He graduated from the French Military Academy at Saint-Cyr in 1913 and was commissioned a lieutenant.

De Gaulle's first posting was with Colonel Henri P. Pétain's 33rd Infantry Regiment. During World War I de Gaulle was promoted to captain, exhibiting a high degree of leadership and courage. Wounded twice, he was captured by the Germans at Verdun in March 1916 after being wounded a third time. Later he received the Legion of Honor for this action. Despite five escape attempts, he remained a prisoner of war until the end of the war.

After the war de Gaulle returned to teach history at Saint-Cyr, and in 1920 he was part of the French military mission to Poland. He returned to France to study and teach at the École de Guerre. De Gaulle then served as an aide to French Army commander Marshal Pétain, but the two had a falling-out, apparently because Pétain wanted de Gaulle to ghostwrite his memoirs. De Gaulle also became an important proponent of the new theories of high-speed warfare centered on tanks. In his 1934 book *Vers l'armée de métier* (published in English as *The Army of the Future*), de Gaulle proposed the formation of six completely mechanized and motorized divisions with their own organic artillery and air support. Another book, *Le fil de l'epée* (The Edge of the Sword) revealed much about de Gaulle's concept of leadership and his belief that a true leader should follow his conscience regardless of the circumstances.

Promoted to major and then to lieutenant colonel, de Gaulle served in the Rhineland occupation forces, in the Middle East, and on the National Defense Council. Although he was promoted to colonel in 1937 and had important political friends such as future premier Paul Reynaud, de Gaulle's views placed him very much on the outside of the military establishment.

When World War II began, de Gaulle commanded a tank brigade. His warnings about the German use of tanks in Poland fell on deaf ears in the French High Command. De Gaulle commanded the French 4th Armored Division in the 1940 Battle of France. Although the division was still in formation, he secured one of the few French successes of that campaign. Promoted to general of brigade on June 1, 1940, five days later de Gaulle was appointed undersecretary of defense in the Reynaud government. De Gaulle urged Reynaud to fight on, even in a redoubt in the Brittany Peninsula or removing the armed forces to North Africa. De Gaulle's resolve won the enthusiastic support of British prime minister Winston L. S. Churchill.

De Gaulle and Jean Monnet visited London and suggested to Churchill a plan for an indissoluble Anglo-French union that the French government had rejected. Returning to Bordeaux from the mission to London, de Gaulle learned that the defeatists had won, and France would sue for peace. On June 17, he departed France on a British aircraft bound for England. The next day, this youngest general in the French Army appealed to his countrymen over the British Broadcasting Corporation to continue the fight against Germany.

From this point forward, de Gaulle was the key figure in the French Resistance. With Churchill's support and because no prominent French politician had escaped abroad, de Gaulle set up a French government-in-exile in London and began organizing armed forces—the Free French—to fight for the liberation of his country. The Pétain government at Vichy declared de Gaulle a traitor and condemned him to death in absentia.

Initially, de Gaulle's position was at best tenuous. Most French citizens did not recognize his legitimacy, and relations with the British and Americans were at times difficult. De Gaulle insisted on being treated as the head of state of a major power, whereas American leaders, especially President Franklin D. Roosevelt, and even Churchill persisted in treating him as an auxiliary and often did not consult him on major decisions.

The British attack on the French fleet at Mers-el-Kébir (July 3, 1940) further undermined de Gaulle's credibility. Relations with the United States were not helped by a Free French effort to secure Saint-Pierre and Miquelon off Canada. The U.S. government recognized the Vichy government and continued to pursue a two-France policy even after the United States entered the war in December 1941.

With time, de Gaulle solidified his position as leader of the Resistance in France. Bitter over British moves in Syria and Lebanon and not informed in advance of the U.S.-British invasion of French North Africa, he established his headquarters in Algiers in 1943, where he beat back a U.S.-British effort to replace him with General Henri Giraud. De Gaulle's agent, Jean Moulin, secured the fusion of Resistance groups within France.

De Gaulle was not consulted regarding plans for the invasion of Normandy. Indeed, Roosevelt insisted that Churchill not provide de Gaulle with details of the invasion because he did not trust de Gaulle to keep the information secret. The British and Americans also placed little stock in the codes employed by the French, who refused to use those of the Americans and British. Relations remained tense because Roosevelt

General Charles de Gaulle escaped to London following the German victory in the Battle for France and became the key figure in the French Resistance as head of the Free French. However, the Americans and British distrusted him, and they did not consult him regarding their plans for the invasion of France. (Library of Congress)

continued to refuse to recognize de Gaulle as head of the French government. Only on the eve of the invasion did Churchill decide to share the news. On June 2 he sent two passenger aircraft to Algiers to bring de Gaulle and his entourage back to Britain. De Gaulle initially refused because of Roosevelt's intention to install a provisional Allied military government in France pending elections but then relented and flew to Britain on June 4. De Gaulle held to the position that an Allied military government would anger the French people and enhance the chances of the communists seizing power.

De Gaulle also at first rejected the request that he make a radio address to the French people after the invasion of France had occurred. A sticking point was the Allied intention to introduce military script as currency that made no mention of the legitimacy of de Gaulle's government. He did, however, record an address to the French people at noon on June 6 that was broadcast that evening, and several million leaflets bearing its text were dropped over France on the night of June 7–8.

De Gaulle returned to France on June 14 and proclaimed Bayeux the temporary French capital. On June 16 he flew to Algiers, then traveled to Rome to meet with the pope and the new Italian government. In early July he at last visited Washington, where he received the 17-gun salute of a senior military leader rather than the 21 guns of a visiting head of state. This did not sit well, and the meeting with Roosevelt was described as correct but was devoid of trust on both sides.

After the liberation of Paris in August, de Gaulle established a provisional government there. Full U.S. diplomatic recognition came only with the creation of the new government. Free French forces played a key role in the invasion of southern France (Operation DRAGOON) on August 15 and in the liberation of the rest of France.

De Gaulle secured for France an occupation zone in Germany and a key role in postwar Europe. But with the return of peace, the former political parties reappeared, and hopes for a fresh beginning faded. De Gaulle's calls for a new constitutional arrangement with a strong presidency were rejected, and he resigned in January 1946 to write his memoirs.

A revolt among European settlers and the French army in Algeria, who feared a sellout there to the Algerian nationalists, brought de Gaulle back to power in 1958. A new constitution tailor-made for de Gaulle established the Fifth Republic. De Gaulle's preservation of democracy was his greatest service to his country, but he also brought an end to the Algerian War and worked out a close entente with Konrad Adenauer's Federal Republic of Germany (West Germany). De Gaulle was also controversial, removing France from the North Atlantic Treaty Organization's military command, creating an independent nuclear strike force, encouraging Quebec to secede from Canada, and lecturing the United States on a wide variety of issues. He remained president until 1969, when he again resigned to write a new set of memoirs. Unarguably France's greatest 20th-century statesman, Charles de Gaulle died at his estate of Colombey-les-Deux-Églises on November 9, 1970.

Tom Lansford and Spencer C. Tucker

Further Reading

Berthon, Simon. *Allies at War: The Bitter Rivalry among Churchill, Roosevelt, and de Gaulle.* New York: Carroll and Graf, 2001.

Cook, Don. *Charles de Gaulle: A Biography.* New York: Putnam, 1983.

De Gaulle, Charles. *The Complete War Memories of Charles de Gaulle.* Translated by

Jonathan Griffin and Richard Howard. New York: Simon and Schuster, 1969.

Kersaudy, François. *Churchill and de Gaulle.* New York: Atheneum, 1982.

Lacouture, Jean. *De Gaulle: The Rebel, 1890–1944.* Translated by Patrick O'Brian. New York: Norton, 1990.

Ledwidge, Bernard. *De Gaulle.* New York: St. Martin's, 1982.

Dempsey, Miles Christopher (1896–1969)

British Army general. Born in New Brighton, Cheshire, on December 15, 1896, Miles Christopher Dempsey graduated from the Royal Military College, Sandhurst, in 1915. He saw action on the Western Front and in Iraq in World War I. Dempsey served at Sandhurst from 1923 to 1927 and was on the staff of the War Office from 1932 to 1934 and at Aldershot from 1934 to 1936. He was promoted to lieutenant colonel in 1938.

In 1940, Dempsey commanded the 13th Infantry Brigade (Royal Berkshires) in France as an acting brigadier, leading it with distinction during the retreat to and evacuation from Dunkerque (Dunkirk, May 26–June 4). Dempsey then helped train new British forces, was promoted to major general in January 1941, and was assigned command of the 42nd Armoured Division. In December 1942 at the request of Lieutenant General Bernard Montgomery, Dempsey took command of XIII Corps of the British Eighth Army and was promoted to lieutenant general. Dempsey helped plan the invasion of Sicily (Operation HUSKY, July 9–August 22, 1943) and then commanded his corps in the assault. He also directed the assault crossing to Italy of the Canadian 1st Infantry and 5th Armoured Divisions.

By January 1944 Dempsey had returned to Britain to command the British Second Army, and with his staff he helped develop the OVERLORD plan for the invasion of northern France. Dempsey is credited with the decision for and planning of Operation GOODWOOD (July 18–20, 1944). In the fall of 1944 the Second Army participated in the breakout from the Normandy beachhead and the campaigns for France and Belgium, liberated Brussels and Antwerp, and penetrated into Holland in Operation MARKET GARDEN (September 17–26), which was a failure. Dempsey had opposed the Eindhoven–Arnhem route, preferring instead an offensive closer to the U.S. First Army near Aachen. He was created Knight Commander of the Bath in June 1944 and Knight Commander of the British Empire in July 1945. In March 1945, the Second Army crossed the Rhine and then pushed to the Baltic. Dempsey personally took the surrender of Hamburg on May 3, 1945.

Dempsey kept close control of his subordinates, often placing his tactical headquarters close to theirs and keeping reserves under his own control in the early phases of a battle. He sought to avoid high casualties, arranging the maximum fire support and emphasizing the use of tactical airpower. Many scholars consider Dempsey's influence in the war to be minimal, dismissing him as Montgomery's cipher. Dempsey's introverted nature and his shunning of both publicity and self-promotion aided this impression. The close working relationship between Montgomery and Dempsey obscures the latter's authorship of operational decisions, as does their shared tendency to rely on verbal orders. They worked together for so long that they thought along similar lines and anticipated each other's reactions and decisions.

In August 1945, Dempsey succeeded General Sir William Slim as commander of the Fourteenth Army for the reoccupation of Singapore and Malaya. He followed Slim again as commander in chief of Allied Land Forces in Southeast Asia. Dempsey was promoted to full general on leaving that post and was commander in chief in the Middle East during 1946–1947. He retired at his own request in July 1947 and entered the private sector. Dempsey died in Yattendon, Berkshire, on June 5, 1969.

Britton W. MacDonald

Further Reading

De Guingand, Francis W. *Generals at War.* London: Hodder and Stoughton, 1964.

Hart, Stephen Ashley. *Montgomery and "Colossal Cracks": The 21st Army Group in Northwest Europe, 1944–1945.* Westport, CT: Praeger, 2000.

Montgomery, Bernard L. *Memoirs.* London: Collins, 1958.

Dieppe Raid. *See* JUBILEE, Operation

Dietrich, Josef "Sepp" (1892–1966)

German Schutzstaffel (SS) general and commander of Leibstandarte, a bodyguard unit responsible for Chancellor Adolf Hitler's personal safety. Born on May 28, 1892, in Hawangen, Bavaria, Josef Dietrich volunteered for the army in 1914 and became a crewman in one of Germany's first tanks. After the war he was active in the Freikorps before joining the National Socialist Party and the SS in 1928. Dietrich was selected as one of Hitler's bodyguards and was in charge of the buildup of the Leibstandarte. In the Blood Purge of July 1934, Dietrich led an execution squad in the elimination of the Sturmabteilung (Storm Troopers) leadership.

In early 1940, Dietrich was assigned command of the Leibstandarte SS Adolf Hitler, which became a *Panzergrenadier* division in 1942. With it he took part in the invasions of France, Greece, and the Soviet Union. When the Western Allies landed in Normandy on June 6, 1944, Dietrich commanded I SS Panzer Corps, and in September Hitler gave him command of the Sixth Panzer Army. Dietrich was awarded the Reich's highest decoration, the Oak Leaves, Swords, and Diamonds to the Knight's Cross of the Iron Cross, and in August 1944 he was promoted to the rank of Oberstgruppenführer. His Sixth Panzer Army was the designated main effort in the December 16, 1944–January 16, 1945, Ardennes Offensive (Battle of the Bulge) but was unable to realize Hitler's far-reaching expectations.

Dietrich then fought on the Eastern Front. His last operation, in Hungary during March 1945, failed. To that point the prototype of the National Socialist soldier, Dietrich lost Hitler's confidence because he questioned Hitler's directives and ordered the retreat of his exhausted troops.

After the war, Dietrich was found guilty of being responsible for the execution of U.S. prisoners of war (the December 17, 1944, Malmédy Massacre) and was sentenced to 25 years' imprisonment. He served only 10 years, but he was later arrested again and charged for murders committed in 1934. He was sentenced to only 18 months in prison. Dietrich died in Ludwigsburg, Bavaria, on April 21, 1966.

Martin Moll

Further Reading

Messenger, Charles. *Hitler's Gladiator: The Life and Times of Oberstgruppenführer and Panzergeneraloberst der Waffen-SS Sepp Dietrich.* London: Brassey's Defence Publishers, 1988.

Weingartner, James J. *Hitler's Guard: The Story of the Leibstandarte SS Adolf Hitler, 1933–1945.* Nashville: Battery Press, 1989.

Dollman, Friedrich (1882–1944)

German Army general. Born on February 2, 1882, at Würzburg, Bavaria, Friedrich Dollman joined the Bavarian Army as an officer candidate in 1899, and in 1901 he was commissioned a second lieutenant in the 7th Field Artillery Regiment. During World War I, he served as a captain on the General Staff. Dollman continued in the Reichswehr after the war, and between 1932 and 1936 he rose from colonel to general of artillery. In late August 1939 he took command of the Seventh Army, a post he held until his death.

The Seventh Army did not participate in the 1939 campaign against Poland and played only a minor role in the Battle of France (May 10–June 25, 1940). Nevertheless, Dollman was promoted to colonel general. The Seventh Army occupied France from 1940 to 1944.

Dollman did not get along with Field Marshal Erwin Rommel, who had charge of the defenses against an Allied invasion of France. In early June 1944, both men expected that poor weather conditions would postpone the Allied invasion of France. Dollman was at Rennes; he had ordered a map exercise there and required all divisional and regimental commanders to attend. Rommel was also away when the Allies invaded Normandy on June 6.

With the Allied invasion, Dollman unwisely ordered the Panzer Lehr and 12th SS Panzer Divisions to the front in broad daylight. This exposed them to relentless Allied air attack and delayed any effective German armored counterattack until June 9.

On June 26 Dollman learned that Allied forces had penetrated Seventh Army defenses at Saint-Lô. Dollman was far to the rear in a château at Le Mans. In a panic, he ordered II SS Panzer Corps commander SS-Obergruppenführer Paul Hausser to launch an immediate counterattack. Hausser asked for time to prepare, but Dollman refused the request. Dollman died on June 29, 1944, either of a heart attack or of self-inflicted poison. Hausser succeeded him in command of the Seventh Army.

Brandon S. Boor

Further Reading

Ambrose, Stephen E. *D-Day, June 6, 1944: The Climactic Battle of World War II.* New York: Simon and Schuster, 1994.

D'Este, Carlo. *Decision in Normandy.* New York: E. P. Dutton, 1983.

Doohan, James Montgomery (1920–2005)

Canadian-born actor and Canadian Army officer who was shot six times by friendly fire during the Normandy invasion on June 6, 1944. James Montgomery Doohan was born on March 3, 1920, in Vancouver, British Columbia, Canada. At age 19 he enlisted in the Royal Canadian Artillery. In 1940, he went to Great Britain for training. Eventually Doohan was commissioned a second lieutenant in the 13th Field Artillery Regiment of the 3rd Canadian Infantry Division, although his first combat mission would not occur until the D-Day invasion.

On June 6, 1944, Doohan landed on Juno Beach with his unit. While leading his men inland, he shot two German snipers, maneuvered his way through an antitank minefield, and dug in on higher ground after sunset. At approximately 11:30 that night as Doohan returned to his position from a nearby command post, he came under fire from an overzealous Canadian sentry with a light machine gun. Doohan was hit six times, receiving four bullets in a leg, one in his right hand, and one in his chest. The chest wound was not fatal only because a silver-plated cigarette case in his breast pocket deflected the bullet. Doohan eventually recovered from his wounds, although the middle finger of his right hand had to be amputated.

Toward the end of the war, Doohan trained to fly artillery observation aircraft. After the war was over he returned to Canada, where he became an actor on Canadian radio. Later he went to New York City and formally studied drama. During the late 1950s and early 1960s Doohan played a number of supporting roles on various American television shows, but it was his role as Montgomery "Scotty" Scott in the iconic 1966–1969 *Star Trek* series that made him a bona fide television star. After that series he did voice-over work, appeared on a soap opera, and was featured in a number of big-screen adaptations of *Star Trek* from the late 1970s into the early 1990s.

Doohan died on July 20, 2005, in Redmond, Washington.

Paul G. Pierpaoli Jr.

Further Reading

"Actor James Doohan, 85, Dies; Played 'Scotty' on Star Trek." *Washington Post,* July 21, 2005.

Doohan, James, with Peter David. *Beam Me Up, Scotty.* New York: Pocket Books, 1996.

Double-Cross System

The Abwehr, the German military intelligence service, had its successes. Thus, before the war the Germans were able to map British airfields and installations (producing an accurate target list for the 1940 Battle of Britain), but it was a different story after 1939 when all German spies in England were either interned, executed, or turned as double agents. The British, who have proven to be masters at this sort of enterprise, actually ran and controlled the entire German espionage system in the United Kingdom.

Early on the morning of June 6, 1944, as the largest invasion force in history made its way from England to the French coast, a radio message was flashed from London to Madrid warning the Germans of the assault and providing identification of some of the units taking part. This information—too late to alter German defensive dispositions—was supplied by "Cato," German chancellor Adolf Hitler's master spy in Britain, who by early 1944 had established a network of 24 subagents. In the days that followed, Cato warned the Germans that the Normandy invasion was merely a feint and that the main Allied attack would soon be delivered to the northeast in the Pas de Calais area by an invasion force commanded by Lieutenant General George S. Patton Jr.

Thus, Cato spearheaded the ingenious and complex apparatus code-named Operation FORTITUDE, which included the creation of a phantom army in southeastern England "commanded" by Patton and replete with dummy equipment and extensive signal nets providing false order of battle information, all of which conned the Abwehr and Hitler into confirming Hitler's own belief that the major Allied effort was yet to come and caused him to order the Fifteenth Panzer Army at Calais to remain in place and not to reinforce Field Marshal Erwin Rommel's Army Group B forces fighting to contain the Allies at the Normandy beachhead. For seven decisive weeks Hitler kept 19 of his best divisions awaiting an attack against northeastern France that never materialized. The infusion of the Fifteenth Army's panzers at Normandy could have been decisive by enabling the Germans to hurl back the Allied invasion.

Cato, who was awarded the Iron Cross in absentia by Hitler and was his favorite spy, was in reality a young Spaniard named Juan Pujol determined to overthrow fascism and working for Allied intelligence as a double agent. Pujol had come to believe that only the British could be counted on to uphold liberal principles in Europe. In 1940 in Madrid he offered to spy for the British but was turned down. He then approached the Germans, who accepted his services and gave him the code name "Cato." Cato then set himself up as a double agent in Lisbon, Portugal, a neutral country in the war. In 1942 the British finally agreed to take him on, and Cato moved to London with the British code name "Garbo."

Soon Cato, who had done the same while in Lisbon, established a substantial yet entirely fictional spy network. The whole was controlled by the British counterintelligence XX (Double Cross) Committee ("Twenty Committee" for the Roman numerals), headed by John Masterman, with the task of misleading the Germans about the Normandy invasion. The operation was amazingly clever. Spurious individuals were "selected" by Cato himself and then subjected to various tests, which they sometimes failed. Those "recruited" included a former Gibraltar waiter and a number of Welsh nationalists. All passed on little pieces of information, which Cato then sent by radio message to his German controller in Madrid, from whence it went to Berlin. The Abwehr then pieced together the smaller bits of information it had been fed to secure the larger picture. It was, in the words of British historian Sefton Delmer, who was involved in psychological warfare operations against the Germans, "the biggest and most decisive hoax of the war." Pujol is probably the only person in history to be awarded both the German Iron Cross and the British Member of the Most Excellent Order of the British Empire.

Spencer C. Tucker

Further Reading

Crowdy, Terry. *Deceiving Hitler: Double-Cross and Deception in World War II.* Oxford, UK: Osprey, 2008.

Delmer, Sefton. *The Counterfeit Spy.* New York: Harper and Row, 1971.

Masterman, J. C. *The Double-Cross System in the War of 1939–1945.* New Haven, CT: Yale University Press, 1972.

Ehlers, Walter David (1921–2014)

U.S. Army soldier awarded the Medal of Honor for his role in the Battle of Normandy. Walter David Ehlers was born in Junction City, Kansas, on May 7, 1921, and grew up on a farm in Manhattan. He and his brother Roland enlisted in the army at the outset of World War II in Europe.

The Ehlers brothers requested assignment to the same unit. At first in the 7th Infantry Division, they were then transferred to the 3rd Infantry Division. Following Operation TORCH, the Allied invasion of North Africa in November 1942, their company became part of the 18th Infantry Regiment, 1st Infantry Division. Roland was wounded during the July–August 1943 Sicily campaign. The 1st Infantry Division was then ordered to England to prepare for the cross–English Channel invasion of France. Roland rejoined his brother in England but was assigned to another company when the company commander determined that there was too great a possibility of the men both becoming casualties during the beach assault.

On June 6, both brothers took part in the 1st Division's assault on Omaha Beach. Unbeknownst to Walter, however, his brother was killed when his landing craft suffered a direct hit from a German mortar round (Walter did not learn of his brother's death until July 14).

June 9 found Staff Sergeant Ehlers leading his squad some eight miles inland. Near Goville, he led his unit in assaulting a German position blocking the advance. Despite heavy machine-gun fire, Ehlers and his squad eliminated a German mortar position, and Ehlers is credited with then singlehandedly knocking out the machine guns.

On June 10, Ehlers and his platoon found themselves far in advance of friendly units. Heavily engaged by the Germans from the front and flanks, the platoon was ordered to withdraw. Ehlers remained behind to cover the withdrawal, standing conspicuously to draw fire away from his men. When his squad's automatic rifleman was hit and wounded, Ehlers went to his assistance and carried him to safety, despite being shot in the torso himself. Ehlers then returned and, under German fire, recovered the Browning Automatic Rifle. After his wound was treated, Ehlers insisted on continuing to lead his unit rather than be evacuated.

Ehlers's heroic actions resulted in his receiving a battlefield commission as a second lieutenant and command of a platoon in Company C. Again wounded in subsequent fighting, he was evacuated but requested to return to his unit. Ehlers was awarded the Medal of Honor on December 19, 1944.

Ehlers survived the war. On his return home, he worked for the Veterans Administration and other veterans organizations for more than 37 years. Ehlers died in Long Beach, California, on February 20, 2014.

Edwin L. Kennedy Jr.

Further Reading

Collier, Peter, and Nick Del Calzo. *Medal of Honor: Portraits of Valor beyond the Call of Duty.* New York: Artisan, 2006.

Lang, George, Raymond L. Collins, and Gerard F. White. *Medal of Honor Recipients*

1863–1994, Vol. 2, *WWII to Somalia.* New York: Facts on File, 1995.

Phillips, James H., and John F. Kane, eds. *The Medal of Honor of the United States Army.* Washington, DC: U.S. Government Printing Office, 1948.

Eisenhower, Dwight David (1890–1969)

U.S. Army general; supreme commander, Allied Expeditionary Force, European theater of operations; and later president of the United States. Born in Denison, Texas, on October 14, 1890, Dwight David "Ike" Eisenhower grew up in Abilene, Kansas. Graduating from the U.S. Military Academy at West Point in 1915 as a member of the "class the stars fell on," he was commissioned a second lieutenant of infantry. His first posting was Fort Sam Houston, Texas.

Eisenhower commanded the fledgling tank corps training center at Camp Colt outside Gettysburg, Pennsylvania, during World War I. Following service in Panama, he graduated first in his class at the Command and General Staff School, Fort Leavenworth, Kansas, in 1926. He also graduated from the Army War College in 1928. During the interwar period Eisenhower served under a number of the army's finest officers, including Generals Fox Conner, John J. Pershing, and Douglas A. MacArthur. After Eisenhower returned from the Philippines in 1939, he served successively as chief of staff of the 3rd Infantry Division, IX Corps, and the Third Army, where he was promoted to temporary brigadier general in October 1941 and captured U.S. Army chief of staff General George C. Marshall's attention for his contributions to the Third Army's "victory" in the Texas-Louisiana war maneuvers of 1941.

Assigned to the War Department in the aftermath of the December 7, 1941, Japanese attack on Pearl Harbor, Eisenhower headed the War Plans Division and then the Operations Division of the General Staff before being promoted to major general in April 1942. Marshall then appointed Eisenhower commanding general of the European theater of operations in June 1942. Promotion to lieutenant general followed in July 1942. Eisenhower's appointment was met with great skepticism from senior British military officers because of his lack of both combat and command experience.

Eisenhower commanded Allied forces in Operation TORCH (the invasion of Northwest Africa) in November 8, 1942, and in Operation HUSKY (the invasion of Sicily) during July 9–August 22, 1943. In the interim, he was promoted to full general in February 1943. The efficient operation of his headquarters—Allied Forces Headquarters—became a model of Allied harmony and led to increased responsibilities in the Mediterranean theater of operations. In September 1943 his forces invaded the Italian mainland.

Eisenhower's generalship during this phase of the war has long been the subject of controversy, but his adept management of diverse personalities and his emphasis on Allied harmony led to his appointment as supreme commander, Allied Expeditionary Force, for the invasion of Northwestern Europe.

As commander of Operation OVERLORD, the Normandy invasion of June 6, 1944, Eisenhower headed the largest Allied force in history. When bad weather arrived over the English Channel area on June 4, Eisenhower took the difficult decision, based on information from his meteorologist that a break in the weather was pending, to proceed with the invasion. Success was not a

U.S. Army general Dwight D. Eisenhower commanded the Allied forces in the invasion of France and took the risky decision to proceed despite poor weather conditions. Here he is shown speaking with American paratroopers in England just before they boarded their planes to participate in the first assault of the Normandy invasion. (Library of Congress)

given, and Eisenhower had drawn up this statement in case of failure:

> Our landings in the Cherbourg-Harve area have failed to gain a satisfactory foothold and I have withdrawn the troops. My decision to attack at this time and place was based on the best information available. If any blame or fault attaches to this attempt, it is mine alone.

Following the expansion of the lodgment area, Eisenhower assumed direct command of the land battle on September 1, 1944. As the Allied forces advanced along a broad front toward the German border, he frequently encountered opposition from senior Allied generals over command arrangements and logistical support. He displayed increasing brilliance as a coalition commander, but his operational decisions remained controversial. His support of British field marshal Bernard L. Montgomery's abortive Operation MARKET GARDEN (September 17–26, 1944) is evidence of his unflinching emphasis on Allied harmony in the campaign in Northwestern Europe. In mid-December 1944, Eisenhower was promoted to general of the army as his forces stood poised to strike into the heartland of Germany.

When Adolf Hitler launched the Battle of the Bulge (Ardennes Offensive) on December 16, 1944, it was Eisenhower, among senior Allied commanders, who first recognized the scope and intensity of Germany's attack and also the key vulnerability in the German scheme of maneuver. Marshaling forces to stem the German advance, he defeated Hitler's last offensive in the west. By March 1945 Eisenhower's armies had crossed the Rhine River and encircled the Ruhr industrial area of Germany. As Soviet armies stood on the outskirts of Berlin, Eisenhower decided to seek the destruction of Germany's armed forces throughout southern Germany and not to launch a direct attack toward the German capital. On May 7, 1945, the mission of the Allied Expeditionary Force was fulfilled as he accepted the unconditional surrender of Germany's armed forces.

Following the war, Eisenhower succeeded General Marshall as chief of staff of the U.S. Army. In February 1948 Eisenhower retired from the military and assumed the presidency of Columbia University before being recalled to active duty by President Harry S. Truman in 1950 to become the first supreme Allied commander, Europe, in the newly formed North Atlantic Treaty Organization. In 1952, Eisenhower resigned from active military service and accepted the Republican Party's nomination for president.

Elected by a wide majority in 1952 and again in 1956, Eisenhower stressed fiscal restraint and nuclear over conventional forces, supported expanded U.S. military commitments overseas so long as they did not involve unilateral commitment of American forces, and warned of the dangers of a military-industrial complex. He left office in 1961 as one of the nation's most popular chief executives. His two administrations were marked by peace, although the U.S. economy suffered three recessions in less than eight years. After Eisenhower left the White House his successor, John F. Kennedy, restored him to the Army List as a five-star general. In 1961 Eisenhower retired to his farm in Gettysburg, Pennsylvania. He died in Washington, D.C., on March 28, 1969.

Cole C. Kingseed

Further Reading

Ambrose, Stephen E. *Eisenhower: Soldier, General of the Army, President-Elect.* New York: Simon and Schuster, 1983.

Chandler, Alfred D., et al., eds. *The Papers of Dwight David Eisenhower: The War Years,* Vols. 1–4. Baltimore: Johns Hopkins University Press, 1970.

D'Este, Carlo. *Eisenhower: A Soldier's Life.* New York: Henry Holt, 2002.

Eisenhower, David. *Eisenhower at War, 1943–1945.* New York: Random House, 1986.

Eisenhower, Dwight D. *Crusade in Europe.* New York: Doubleday, 1948.

English Channel

A shallow sea, part of the Atlantic Ocean, that separates France and Great Britain and connects the Atlantic with the North Sea. The French refer to the English Channel as La Manche (meaning "the sleeve"). The waterway is approximately 350 miles long. Its width varies from about 150 miles at its widest point to just 21 miles at the Strait of Dover, which separates Dover, England, from Calais, France. In all, the English Channel encompasses some 29,000 square miles.

The boundary of the channel begins at Land's End to the far west (southwestern England) and stretches to the Strait of Dover to the east. Water depth is relatively shallow, averaging about 350 feet. The deepest point is an underwater trough known as Hurds Deep, about 30 miles northwest of the Isle of Guernsey, where the water is approximately

600 feet deep. There are numerous islands located within the channel, the most significant of which are the Isle of Wight and the Channel Islands.

The English Channel is strategically significant because it controls ingress and egress to the North Sea and has long borders along southern England and northern France. Indeed, control of the English Channel could easily serve as a blockade of much of Western Europe.

Tides and currents within the English Channel can be treacherous and are subject to frequent changes of direction and intensity, depending on weather conditions. This makes the waterway a particularly challenging one to navigate. Tidal ranges between low and high tides can be extreme, as high as 42 feet in some locations during spring equinox. Westerly winds prevail, and gales—some of which rise suddenly and can be highly destructive—are frequent occurrences, particularly from October to February. The frequency of gales is at its low ebb during May to July, which explains in part why the Allies chose to launch the 1944 Normandy invasion on June 6. Some of these storms and squalls can reach the intensity of low-level hurricanes.

The English Channel played a pivotal role in World War II. It saw numerous attacks on ports along the channel as well as German attacks on civilian shipping. German submarine activity remained high, and for much of the conflict the waterway proved too dangerous for surface ships. Realizing that the Allies would have to mount an invasion of France via the English Channel to dislodge them from French soil, the Germans erected stout defenses along France's northern and western coasts. During most of the war the Germans occupied the Channel Islands, the only part of the British Commonwealth to be controlled by Germany. In June 1944 the Allies launched Operation OVERLORD—the invasion of Normandy via the English Channel. Today, France and England are connected via tunnels under the channel that link Folkestone and Calais.

Paul G. Pierpaoli Jr.

Further Reading

Ambrose, Stephen E. *D-Day: June 6, 1944: The Climactic Battle of World War II.* New York: Simon and Schuster, 1994.

Smith, Peter C. *Hold the Narrow Sea: Naval Warfare in the English Channel 1939–1945.* Annapolis, MD: Naval Institute Press, 1984.

Unwin, Peter. *The Narrow Sea: Barrier, Bridge, and Gateway to the World: The History of the English Channel.* London: Headline, 2004.

F

Falaise–Argentan Pocket (August 12–24, 1944)

Failed attempt of Allied forces in France to trap a significant portion of German forces withdrawing eastward with their defeat in Normandy. The U.S. breakout of U.S. Operation COBRA (July 25–31, 1944) ended the monthlong stalemate in Normandy and shattered the German defensive lines, creating a war of movement. Third Army commander Lieutenant General George S. Patton Jr. envisioned a drive on the Seine River and the liberation of Paris, but a politically less dramatic and strategically more important opportunity soon developed: trapping German forces west of the Seine. If this could be accomplished, the Allied advance east to Germany would be greatly eased, and the war would be shortened.

On August 7, 1944, in Operation LÜTTICH, German forces counterattacked with four panzer divisions at the express order of Chancellor Adolf Hitler and against the recommendation of Field Marshal Günther Hans von Kluge, commander of Army Group B and commander in chief, West. Kluge was convinced that the attack was doomed from the start and would drive German forces into the heart of the planned Allied envelopment. Unfortunately for the Allies, it did slow the Canadian push to Falaise.

At this point, however, Allied planning began to break down. Patton suggested a deeper envelopment that would net all the Germans west of the Seine. However, his superior, Lieutenant General Omar N. Bradley, commander of 12th Army Group, rejected this and insisted on a shorter hook. On August 10 Patton then turned units north from Le Mans, and by August 12 he had taken Alençon. The speed of Patton's movements surprised all concerned. The opportunity to close the Falaise pocket seemed in the offing.

Excluding forces remaining in the Brittany Peninsula, there were then some 350,000 German troops west of the Seine. About half were caught in the Falaise pocket, their only route of escape the 15-mile-wide Falaise gap. If Allied forces could close this, the envelopment would be complete. With success apparently in hand, the cautious Bradley ordered Patton to hold at Argentan. Officially, this was to avoid a chance head-on meeting between the two converging Allied armies. But Bradley was clearly concerned about Patton's willingness to leave his flanks open. Patton regarded the risk as both limited and worth taking. Continued slow movement by British and Canadian forces from the north left the pocket open. Allied ineptness, more than German courage and skill, was the primary reason the trap was not closed in time.

Primary responsibility for this failure rests with Bradley, 21st Army Group commander General Bernard L. Montgomery, and supreme commander, Allied Expeditionary Force, General Dwight D. Eisenhower. Bradley wanted to take no chances, and Eisenhower preferred to let his subordinates work out operational and tactical decisions on their own. Eisenhower failed to step in and bring the three competing generals—Montgomery,

Bradley, and Patton—to consensus or to order a common plan. Montgomery failed to push his subordinate commanders hard enough, but there were also logistical problems. Other Allied military leaders, including commander of the British Second Army Lieutenant General Sir Miles Dempsey, Canadian First Army commander Lieutenant General Henry Crerar, and Free French 2nd Armored Division commander Major General Jacques Leclerc, contributed to the disjointed nature of the Allied operation. A subsequent proposal by Patton to turn from his drive to the east and make a deeper envelopment was slow to reach Bradley, who ultimately rejected it.

In the Falaise pocket, the Germans lost approximately 200 tanks, 300 heavy guns, 700 artillery pieces, 5,000 vehicles, and a great many carts and horses. But German personnel losses were considerably less than hoped for—no more than 10,000 killed and 50,000 captured. Some 115,000 well-trained German troops escaped the pocket. More important, almost all of the key higher-level staff managed to get out, which made it possible for the Germans to reconstitute their devastated units faster than the Allies believed possible.

In all, 240,000 German soldiers crossed the Seine in the last week of August and then established a solid defensive line protecting the western approaches to Germany. Operation MARKET GARDEN (September 17–26), the Allied combined-arms assault to cross the lower Rhine River into Germany, was stymied by German units that had escaped from Normandy.

Fred R. van Hartesveldt and Spencer C. Tucker

Further Reading

Blumenson, Martin. *The Battle of the Generals: The Untold Story of the Falaise Pocket; The Campaign That Should Have Won World War II.* New York: William Morrow, 1993.

Hamilton, Nigel. *Monty: The Battles of Field Marshal Bernard Montgomery.* New York: Random House, 1994.

Keegan, John. *Six Armies in Normandy: From D-Day to the Liberation of Paris.* London: Jonathan Cape, 1982.

Lucas, James, and James Barker. *The Killing Ground: The Battle of the Falaise Gap, August 1944.* London: Batsford, 1978.

Ludewig, Joachim. *Rückzug: The German Retreat from France, 1944.* Lexington: University Press of Kentucky, 2012.

Whitaker, W. Denis. *Victory at Falaise: The Soldiers' Story.* Toronto: HarperCollins, 2000.

Festung Europa

"Festung Europa" is German for "Fortress Europe," the generic term for the fortifications ringing German-occupied Europe, especially the massive defenses erected on the Atlantic coast from Norway to Spain, the so-called Atlantic Wall. Designed to guard against the possibility of an Allied amphibious invasion, these static defenses stretched from Norwegian outposts on the Arctic Ocean all the way to the more integrated beach and harbor defenses along the Bay of Biscay. In modern military terms, this series of engineering works was an exercise in force multiplication in that by constructing strong defensive works, the Germans expected to be able to use inferior military units to man them, freeing up more capable troops for open warfare elsewhere.

The Germans built the defenses largely by forced and conscripted labor. Under the control and direction of Fritz Todt, German minister of armaments and munitions (and Albert Speer, Todt's successor after February 1942), hundreds of thousands of workers labored to build the fortified positions. The work began slowly, however, only gaining momentum after the tide of war had definitively shifted against the Germans. The plans originated at the direction of Adolf Hitler, who ordered the construction of some 15,000 defensive positions to be defended by 300,000 men.

Although Hitler's construction objective was never reached, the numbers were nonetheless impressive. By the time of the Allied invasion of Normandy on June 6, 1944, the Germans had placed 6.5 million mines, erected 500,000 beach obstacles, and expended 1.2 million tons of steel to reinforce 13.3 million tons of concrete in the thousands of positions that were completed.

When Field Marshal Erwin Rommel was assigned to command the likely invasion area, however, he decried the state of the defenses as he found them. Doubling and tripling the workload, he greatly strengthened the defenses. Nevertheless, his professional opinion was that these works would never be sufficient to keep the Allies off the beaches. He believed that if the Allies came ashore and could establish a lodgment, there would be no way to defeat them. Recognizing the threat not only of amphibious assault but also of parachute and glider-borne attacks, Rommel seeded the open fields and meadows behind the beaches that the Allies might use as landing zones with stout iron bars linked with barbed wire. These obstacles became known as "Rommel's asparagus." In the end, the static defenses erected by the Germans proved to be no more effective than the French Maginot Line had been four years earlier.

Robert L. Bateman

Further Reading

Harrison, Gordon A. *United States Army in World War II: The European Theater of Operations; Cross-Channel Attack.* Washington, DC: Center of Military History, 1951.

Kaufman, J. E., and R. M. Jurga. *Fortress Europe.* Conshohocken, PA: Combined Publishing, 1999.

Liddell Hart, Basil H., ed. *The Rommel Papers.* New York: Harcourt Brace, 1953.

Films Treating the Normandy Invasion

The Normandy invasion has been the main subject—or the background—for numerous film productions. It is not difficult to understand why the event has caught the attention of so many screenwriters, producers, and directors. D-Day was one of the climactic turning points of World War II. It led to the liberation of France and the eventual defeat of Nazi Germany some 11 months later. The perilous journey across a storm-tossed English Channel and the largest amphibious landing in military history were juxtaposed against the stark reality of the beach landings in northern France, where Allied troops encountered stout German resistance and man-made and natural obstacles that included 200-foot cliffs only yards from the water's edge. The more notable D-Day films are discussed below.

The Longest Day (1962) is perhaps the most famous and well known of the early major films dealing with D-Day. With an all-star cast that includes John Wayne, Richard Burton, Robert Mitchum, Henry Fonda, Sean Connery, and Eddie Albert, among others, *The Longest Day* was based on a 1959 best-selling book of the same name by Cornelius Ryan. D-Day is depicted from a wide variety of perspectives, including that of the Germans. The landings themselves do not occur until the third hour of a three-hour movie. At the time, the combat scenes were considered quite accurate and realistic. Produced by Darryl F. Zanuck, *The Longest Day* cost $10 million to make, making it the most expensive black-and-white movie made to that point. The film's themes of moral absolutism and patriotic duty seemed entirely right for the era. Indeed, it was released several years before the divisive and ambiguous Vietnam War and amid a perilous period in the Cold War. Nominated for five Academy Awards, *The Longest Day* won two Oscars—one for cinematography and another for best special effects.

The Americanization of Emily (1964), directed by Arthur Hiller and starring James Garner and Julie Andrews, is as much a war film as a comedy-drama. The film depicts a U.S. Navy officer, Charlie Madison (played by Garner), who claims to be a "practicing coward" and who falls in love with a British war widow, Emily (Julie Andrews), who despite her reservations finds Madison irresistible. The movie is set mainly in London in the weeks prior to the D-Day landings. Despite his considerable fear of combat, Madison is compelled to go ashore at Omaha Beach on June 6, 1944, and is reported as killed in action. Emily is crushed at having lost another loved one to the war. Nevertheless, Madison is soon found to be alive and in a British hospital. Emily, elated at the news, convinces Madison that he should accept his role as a "war hero" and not mention his prior misgivings.

Where Eagles Dare (1968), starring Richard Burton and Clint Eastwood, begins just prior to D-Day, when German operatives kidnap a U.S. general involved with the planning of the Normandy invasion. In response, a team of American and British commandos are tasked with carrying out a dangerous rescue mission. Their task, however, is complicated when they discover a German spy among them. This thriller was filmed on location in Austria and Bavaria and features a series of mind-bending plot twists and electrifying cinematography and special effects. In the end, the general is rescued from a castle high in the Alps.

The film *Overlord* (1975) is a black-and-white portrayal of the actual combat on the Normandy beaches, shot in documentary-like fashion. Billed at the time as the "most haunting and hypnotic film to have been made about the war," the film juxtaposes the beach landings with close-ups of soldiers' anxious faces as they leave their landing craft and wade ashore.

The 1980 film *The Big Red One,* starring Lee Marvin and Mark Hamill, follows the exploits of a U.S. Army sergeant (played by Marvin) in the 1st Infantry Division (the Big Red One) from World War I through the end of World War II in 1945. Included among the combat scenes is a relatively brief but fierce re-creation of the Allied landings at Omaha Beach. The film is also known for following the exploits of a rabidly loyal German Army sergeant, who is seen as a sort of distorted mirror image of Marvin's character.

Eye of the Needle (1981), which stars Donald Sutherland and Kate Nelligan, is based on the novel *Storm Island,* by Ken Follett. Sutherland plays a cunning German spy (the "Needle") who infiltrates the planning for the Normandy invasion and is then tasked with making his way back to Germany to report what he has learned to Adolf Hitler. However, en route the Needle is marooned on Storm Island off Scotland and befriended by a local husband-and-wife couple who soon discover his mission. In the end, the wife kills the spy just as he is about to be picked up by a German U-boat.

Perhaps the most celebrated film treating D-Day is *Saving Private Ryan* (1998), directed by Steven Spielberg and starring Tom Hanks and Matt Damon. The movie garnered five Academy Awards and is considered by many—including a number of D-Day veterans—to be the most compelling and lifelike depiction of the beach landings of any film ever made. *Saving Private Ryan* is a movie that treats the time-honored themes of courage, loyalty, and self-sacrifice. In the midst of the Omaha Beach carnage, Captain John Miller (portrayed by Hanks) and a small squad of men are dispatched to locate Private James F. Ryan (portrayed by Damon), whose four brothers have been recently killed in action. The U.S. Army wants to send Ryan, now his family's only son, home. Miller's unit braves great danger to carry out the mission, in the process questioning the wisdom and usefulness of its orders. The film clearly indicates the moral ambiguity of war in the post–Vietnam War era.

Although not a big-screen film, the HBO miniseries *Band of Brothers,* which began airing two days before the September 11, 2001, terror attacks, bears examination as well. Based on a book by historian Stephen Ambrose, the show (in 10 parts) was produced by Tom Hanks and Steven Spielberg. *Band of Brothers* details the experiences of a fictional Army Airborne company from its precombat training through its jump behind enemy lines just prior to the D-Day landings at Normandy in June 1944. Riveting and extremely accurate in its depictions, the series is based on the actual history of E (Easy) Company, 506th Parachute Infantry Regiment of the 82nd Airborne Division. *Band of Brothers* won seven Emmy Awards and a Golden Globe Award.

Other noteworthy film depictions of D-Day and the subsequent Normandy campaign include the French-language films *Le Bataillon du ciel* (The Sky Battalion, 1947) and *Un Jour avant l'aube* (One Day before Dawn, 1994) and the English-language film *Ike: Countdown to D-Day* (2004).

Paul G. Pierpaoli Jr.

Further Reading

Chambers, John Whiteclay, II, and David Culbert, eds. *World War II: Film and History.* New York: Oxford University Press, 1996.

Milberg, Doris. *World War II on the Big Screen: 450+ Films, 1938–2008.* Jefferson, NC: McFarland, 2010.

Nowell-Smith, Geoffrey, ed. *The Oxford History of World Cinema.* Oxford: Oxford University Press, 1996.

FORTITUDE, Operation (1944)

Deception operations in support of Operation OVERLORD, the Allied invasion of Normandy that began on June 6, 1944. Operation OVERLORD was a vast operation that was impossible to conceal, as it involved more than 150,000 troops and 5,000 ships. Operation FORTITUDE was the elaborate deception plan designed to mislead the German defenders as to the timing and location of the Allied invasion.

Operation FORTITUDE had two components: FORTITUDE NORTH and FORTITUDE SOUTH. Operation FORTITUDE NORTH was designed to convince the Germans that the Allies planned to invade Norway in cooperation with a Soviet offensive designed to drive Finland from the war. It also tried to deceive the Germans into thinking that the Norwegian invasion would take place prior to an invasion in France. The intent was to cause the Germans to shift divisions from France to Norway or to have these forces in transit so they could not take part in the battle. To achieve this, the British in Scotland employed dummy vehicles, inflatable tanks and aircraft, fake radio transmissions, and dummy subordinate headquarters simulating the Fourth Army Group in "preparations" for an invasion of Norway. German reconnaissance aircraft were allowed to fly over the "assembly points" and report this information to Berlin. Operation FORTITUDE NORTH worked, as the Germans actually reinforced Norway.

As the time for Operation OVERLORD approached, the second component of the deception plan, Operation FORTITUDE SOUTH, became critical. Knowing that the Allied buildup in southern England could not be kept hidden, the British and Americans planned to persuade the Germans that the chief Allied assault would fall in the Pas de Calais (across the English Channel from Dover) rather than in Normandy (the actual landing area). The Pas de Calais was the most obvious choice for a major amphibious operation. It was the closest point on the French coast to England and would minimize the length of Allied supply lines as well as offer an extensive road network that could be exploited in follow-on attacks through the Low Countries toward Germany once the beaches were taken.

The first step was to leak plans of the sham invasion of Calais. This was done, as during Operation FORTITUDE NORTH, through the British secret services, which planted stories and documents with double agents. Incredibly, the British seem to have identified or turned (recruited as a double agent) every German agent in Britain during the war. Double agents were particularly useful for providing small bits of information, which the Germans could then piece together. The British also arranged to leak sham information through neutral diplomats with Axis sympathies.

To build the desired perception on the part of German intelligence, a fictitious First U.S. Army Group (FUSAG) was portrayed directly across from Calais in Kent and Sussex. Lieutenant General George S. Patton, whose reputation as a hard-driving army leader was well known by the Germans, was repeatedly identified as FUSAG's commander. This fictitious force was composed of the U.S. Fourteenth Army and the British Fourth Army. With the exception of three real British divisions included in the fictitious British army, all of these formations were bogus. The ghost divisions had elaborate stories woven around them to make their existence more believable. The Allies even created shoulder patches for the nonexistent FUSAG and its subordinate divisions. In addition, the Allies had real soldiers wear the ghost division patches in case enemy agents were in a position to report their existence.

Special Allied signal units were used to transmit false radio transmissions from FUSAG and to simulate division, corps, and other army-level communications; these were transmitted in easily breakable ciphers so the Germans could decode the messages. In addition, false references to the fake headquarters were mentioned in bona fide messages.

As in Operation FORTITUDE NORTH, dummy tanks and airplanes built of inflatable rubber were placed in realistic-looking "camps" where German aerial reconnaissance was bound to see them. The deception was made even more believable by FUSAG troop movements in southeastern England. Some were elaborate hoaxes, but in most cases they corresponded to actual preinvasion movements by real British and Canadian divisions. Even though the real movements were being made to support the Normandy invasion, they were close enough to the FUSAG area to convince German aerial photo interpreters that they were seeing the imminent invasion of Calais.

A fleet of landing craft deemed unseaworthy but still usable bobbed in British ports across from Calais. Instructions for acts of sabotage were radioed to the French Resistance in the Calais area. In addition, to reinforce the notion that FUSAG would debark on the short route to Calais, the Allied air forces in their program of bombardment prior to OVERLORD dropped three times the tonnage east of the Seine as they did to the west.

In all of these activities, Allied intelligence, knowing what picture it wanted the Germans to see, had carefully taken apart FUSAG and sent bits and pieces about it where they knew the German intelligence services would pick them up. The Allies relied on the Germans to put the pieces of the puzzle together for themselves.

Soon it became apparent that the deception was bearing fruit. Ultra signals intercepts of German classified message traffic made reference to FUSAG. This was the proof the FORTITUDE operators needed. They could not expect to fool the Germans forever, but they hoped to minimize German anticipation of a Normandy landing until it was actually under way—and thereafter to keep alive anxiety that the "real" invasion would follow in the Pas de Calais at a later stage.

German intelligence arrived at the desired conclusion. German Army maps captured following the Normandy invasion indicated the presence of FUSAG in southeastern England. Division areas and corps headquarters corresponded almost exactly with the areas indicated by the Allied deception plan. However, Adolf Hitler was only partly deluded. On March 4, March 20, and April 6, he alluded to the likelihood of a Normandy landing in messages to his senior commanders. Still, apart from allocating Panzer Lehr and 116th Panzer Divisions to Normandy in the early spring, he made no decisive alteration of German defensive dispositions. Indeed, until he allowed divisions to cross the Seine into Normandy from the Pas de Calais at the very end of July, he himself remained prisoner to the delusion of a second "main" invasion in the Calais area throughout the critical weeks following the initial landings at Normandy.

James H. Willbanks

Further Reading

Barbier, Mary Kathryn. *D-Day Deception: Operation Fortitude and the Normandy Invasion.* Westport, CT: Praeger Security International, 2007.

Brown, Anthony Cave. *Bodyguard of Lies.* New York: Harper and Row, 1975.

Cruickshank, Charles. *Deception in World War II.* New York: Oxford University Press, 1980.

Hesketh, Roger. *Fortitude: The D-Day Deception Campaign.* London: St. Ermin's, 1999.

Kneece, Jack. *Ghost Army of World War II.* Gretna, LA: Pelican, 2001.

France, Campaign (June 6–September 15, 1944)

Allied campaign to liberate France from Axis control. The campaign to drive the Germans out of Western Europe began with the June 6, 1944, Allied landing in Normandy, the largest amphibious operation in history. U.S. general Dwight D. Eisenhower had overall command; British general Bernard L. Montgomery commanded the landing force of the 21st Army Group, which consisted of Lieutenant General Miles Dempsey's British Second Army and Lieutenant General Omar N. Bradley's American First Army.

Even with stiff resistance by German defenders, especially the German 352nd Infantry Division at Omaha Beach, Allied forces expanded the beachhead from 5 to 20 miles inland and joined all five beaches into a single continuous front by June 12. French Resistance forces supported the Allied effort by providing intelligence, sabotaging bridges and railways, and conducting harassment operations. Dempsey's Second Army began the drive toward Caen but met heavy resistance from German forces, including two panzer divisions. Meanwhile, Bradley's First Army moved up the Cotentin Peninsula toward the important port city of Cherbourg. Units of the U.S. VII Corps assaulted Fort du Roule and, guided by the French Resistance, scaled the cliffs. By June 27 Cherbourg was secure, but the Germans had heavily damaged the port facilities there, and they were unusable for more than a month.

By the beginning of July, Allied progress in Normandy had been slowed by the hedgerows of the *bocage* country, strong German positions at Caen, and the logistical challenges of supplying the Allied forces over the beaches. Enjoying the advantage of overwhelming air superiority, the eight corps of 21st Army Group pushed south, seizing Caen on July 10 and Saint-Lô on July 18. The capture of these two important cities set the stage for the Allied breakout west into the Brittany Peninsula and east toward Paris.

The slow pace of their advance in France concerned Allied commanders who feared that fighting would bog down, resulting in trench warfare resembling World War I. Bradley believed that the weak link in the German Army's defenses was General Paul Hausser's Seventh Army, south of Saint-Lô. Bradley's breakout plan, code-named Operation COBRA (July 25–31), was temporarily put on hold so that vital supplies could be sent to support the British Second Army's July 18–20 Operation GOODWOOD, an attempt to penetrate German lines outside of Caen. Although GOODWOOD did not achieve a breakout, it assisted COBRA by holding two German panzer divisions in place and preventing their redeployment to the Saint-Lô area.

Heavy saturation bombing along a four-mile corridor preceded COBRA as elements of Major General J. Lawton Collins's VII Corps attacked west of Saint-Lô on July 25. Concurrently, Major General Troy H. Middleton's VIII Corps, located west of VII Corps, struck toward Countances. Within two days VII Corps had pushed the German defenders back 10 miles, and on July 28 elements of the 4th Armored Division secured Countances. Sensing that the breakthrough was decisive, Bradley ordered Collins to continue the drive south toward the strategic city of Avranches. By the end of July it too was in Allied hands, and the German Seventh Army was in a precarious position, with its left flank exposed.

The capture of Avranches opened the Brittany Peninsula to the Allies. Meanwhile, Lieutenant General George S. Patton's U.S. Third Army became operational on August 1 as part of an overall restructuring of the Allied command. Montgomery's 21st Army Group was now composed of the British Second Army and Lieutenant General Henry Crerar's Canadian First Army. Bradley assumed command of the new 12th Army Group, composed of the American First and Third Armies. Patton's Third Army gained the greatest success, and Patton was certainly the outstanding general of the campaign for France.

The Third Army displayed instant efficiency and turned Operation COBRA, a local breakthrough, into a theater-wide breakout. The Third Army immediately exploited the opening at Avranches: Patton sent his VIII Corps to clear the Brittany Peninsula and also sent XX Corps and XII Corps south to the Loire River and XV Corps east toward Le Mans. These objectives were secured by August 13.

While the Third Army moved against limited opposition, the German Seventh Army hastily reorganized to launch a counterattack toward Avranches, hoping to cut off the Third Army. Not only did this attack fail, it also put the Seventh Army in a position where it might be surrounded by the Allies. To accomplish this, Montgomery, who was still overall ground commander, ordered the Canadian II Corps to attack south as Patton's XV Corps drove north.

The objective for both corps was the town of Argentan. Major General Wade Haislip's XV Corps reached Argentan on August 13, but the Canadian II Corps progressed slowly and was more than 20 miles from the objective. Patton pleaded with Bradley to allow XV Corps to press northward, but the 12th Army Group commander refused, fearing that XV Corps might be cut off or that excessive casualties from friendly fire might result from XV Corps moving into a zone reserved for the Canadian II Corps.

Even though the gap between the towns of Falaise and Argentan was not closed until August 19, the area was turned into a killing ground by constant Allied air attack, artillery bombardment, and direct ground fire from armored and infantry units. Although the German Seventh Army was savaged in these attacks, a great many German soldiers escaped. Failure to close the gap was one of the major mistakes of the war. Had the gap been sealed and the Seventh Army annihilated, the Western Allies would have faced far less resistance as they pushed east toward Germany. Operations following COBRA were so successful that most German forces in northwestern France had to retreat to the Seine River. Paris was liberated on August 25.

German garrisons doggedly held out in the northern port cities of Saint-Malo, Brest, Lorient, and Saint-Nazaire. Combat

American infantrymen entering Argentan, France, on August 14, 1944. (Photo12/UIG/Getty Images)

commands from the 4th and 6th Armored Divisions were insufficient to secure these heavily fortified ports quickly. Repeated assaults supported by air attacks and naval bombardments failed to dislodge the defenders. Saint-Malo was not taken until September 2, and Brest fell on September 19. In both cases, the Germans had demolished their port facilities. On the basis of these experiences, Supreme Headquarters, Allied Expeditionary Force, canceled planned assaults on Lorient and Saint-Nazaire, and German garrisons there held out until the end of the war.

The Western Allies addressed concern about the exposed southern flank of their armies, the need to secure a large functioning port, and interest in cutting off what German forces remained in southern France in Operation DRAGOON, the invasion of southern France. British prime minister Winston L. S. Churchill strongly opposed the plan because Operation COBRA had proven such a huge success, but Eisenhower prevailed, and DRAGOON commenced on August 15.

Lieutenant General Alexander Patch's American Seventh Army landed in southern France just east of Toulon. Major General Lucian Truscott's VI Corps spearheaded the landing and by August 17 had established a 20-mile beachhead. The French II Corps followed with the task of driving west to secure Toulon and Marseille, which it accomplished by August 28.

VI Corps moved rapidly west and then north up the east side of the Rhône River except for an armored group, Task Force Butler, which moved east of the Rhône River Valley in an effort to envelop German forces gathering at Montelimar. By this time the German Nineteenth Army, led by General of Infantry Friedrich Wiese, was pulling out of southern France. Truscott's corps inflicted severe material damage on the retreating Germans, however, capturing 57,000 of them and liberating Montelimar by August 28.

By September 3, the Seventh Army had driven north almost 250 miles up the Rhône River. The 1st Airborne Task Force was used to seal the Swiss border; the French I Corps took up a position to the right of Truscott's VI Corps, and the French II Corps flanked the left. On September 14 Patch's Seventh Army linked up with Patton's Third Army, sealing the open southern flank. On September 15 the 6th Army Group was formed, with Lieutenant General Jacob Devers commanding. It was composed of the American Seventh Army and General Jean de Lattre de Tassigny's French First Army. Besides securing the Allied southern flank, DRAGOON greatly aided the logistical situation by making available the large port at Marseille. Finally, southern France was cleared of German forces.

By the middle of September 1944 France had been liberated, and German forces had withdrawn into the Netherlands and to the West Wall, along the western German border. Although it had been severely bloodied, the German army in the west was not annihilated but was reorganizing and entrenching for a long fight. Unfortunately, the Allied drive east was so fast that lines of communication and supply could not keep up with the tactical advance. With insufficient supplies to advance all his army groups at once, Eisenhower now decided to support Montgomery's plan to cross the lower Rhine into Germany, Operation MARKET GARDEN (September 17–26).

Robert W. Duvall

Further Reading

Ambrose, Stephen. *Citizen Soldiers*. New York: Simon and Schuster, 1997.

Blumenson, Martin. *United States Army in World War II: The European Theater of*

Operations; Breakout and Pursuit. Washington, DC: Center of Military History, 1961.

Boog, Horst, Gerhard Krebs, and Detlef Vogel. *Germany and the Second World War,* Vol. 7, *The Strategic Air War in Europe and the War in the West and East Asia, 1943–1944/5.* Oxford, UK: Clarendon, 2006.

Breuer, William B. *Operation Dragoon: The Allied Invasion of the South of France.* Novato, CA: Presidio, 1987.

Guderian, Heinz G. *From Normandy to the Ruhr: With the 116th Panzer Division in WWII.* Edited by Keith E. Bonn, translated by Mary Harris. Bedford, PA: Aberjona, 2001.

Ludewig, Joachim. *Rückzug: The German Retreat from France, 1944.* Lexington: University Press of Kentucky, 2012.

Mitcham, Samuel W., Jr. *Retreat to the Reich: The German Defeat in France, 1944.* Westport, CT: Praeger, 2000.

Wilt, Alan F. *The French Riviera Campaign of August 1944.* Carbondale: Southern Illinois University Press, 1981.

Wood, James A. ed. *Army of the West: The Weekly Reports of German Army Group B from Normandy to the West Wall.* Harrisburg, PA: Stackpole, 2007.

Zaloga, Steven J. *Operation Cobra 1944: Breakout from Normandy.* Oxford, UK: Osprey, 2001.

French Resistance

Alongside Vichy France, the government headed by Marshal Henri Philippe Pétain that signed the armistice with Germany and to some degree cooperated with it during World War II, there was another France, that committed to see the fight through until Nazi Germany had been defeated. In June 1940 it took unusual clairvoyance and sangfroid to see the possibility of that in June 1940, but there were Frenchmen and Frenchwomen who embraced the challenge and dangers this represented.

No major political or military figure escaped from France in June 1940, and Charles de Gaulle, the youngest brigadier general in the French Army, stepped into the void. On June 18, 1940, from London, he called on Frenchmen to join him in continuing the fight. De Gaulle secured the support of British prime minister Winston Churchill and created the Free French, with its own military establishment. De Gaulle also worked to bring about a fusion of the resistance groups in France that were already organizing. De Gaulle representative Jean Moulin finally accomplished this in May 1943 in the formation of the National Resistance Council (CNR). Moulin's triumph was brief. The next month he was betrayed to the Gestapo and took his own life rather than risk revealing secrets under torture.

Underground paramilitary forces were organized as the French Forces of the Interior (FFI). The communists formed the largest single resistance group. Established only after the German invasion of the Soviet Union in June 1941, their National Front remained outside the CNR. The communists were the only ones who did not hesitate to execute captured German officers and soldiers. This brought savage German reprisals in the form of the execution of French hostages, rounded up at random by the Germans—first at a rate of 5 to 1, then 10 to 1, and finally 25 to 1 or more.

Members of the Resistance included both men and women, and they came from all walks of life. A number were members of the clergy. Resistance losses were also extraordinarily high.

Resistance activities took many forms. They included the publication of underground newspapers; providing intelligence on German troop dispositions, fortifications, and plans; sabotage; and aiding downed Allied aircrew or Jews in escaping France through Spain or across the English Channel. The British Special Operations Executive orchestrated a massive sabotage campaign, implemented by the French Resistance.

De Gaulle was not an easy ally. He insisted on being treated as a head of state, and he and Churchill were often at odds. U.S. president Franklin Roosevelt developed a profound dislike for the general, but efforts by the British and especially the Americans to replace him came to naught. Still, the United States only recognized his government in August 1944. The British and Americans rarely communicated their plans to de Gaulle, and the general was furious over Allied interference in French affairs, including British activities in Syria and Lebanon and the failure to notify him of their invasion of French North Africa until it was in progress. It should be noted here, however, that supreme commander of Allied forces in Western Europe General Dwight D. Eisenhower respected de Gaulle both as a soldier and a man and communicated with him regarding the Normandy invasion just before it occurred.

Before the Normandy invasion, the Resistance provided highly important information on the location and composition of German shore artillery batteries, order of battle, troop dispositions, and plans. The British and Americans developed a series of operations for the Resistance to execute on D-Day and thereafter and notified it by coded radio messages sent over the British Broadcasting Corporation. These activities included the sabotage of the French rail system and the destruction of bridges that the Germans might use in reinforcing Normandy as well as cutting telephone lines and destroying electrical facilities.

Such activities were highly important in the Allied victory in Normandy. The Resistance has been credited with the destruction on June 6 of more than 50 train locomotives and, in the month of June, making more than 800 cuts in rail lines, immobilizing some 200 trains. Normandy was for all practical purposes isolated as of June 7. One estimate holds that the French Resistance killed some 2,000 German soldiers in June alone. By the time of the American breakthrough of Operation COBRA on July 25, the 20,000 members of the Breton FFI had secured control of all of central Brittany. When the U.S. Third Army moved on Rennes, members of the FFI acted as auxiliaries and flank guards. Although there is still debate among scholars as to its size and effectiveness, Eisenhower wrote after the war that the French Resistance was worth some 10–15 divisions to the Allies during the Normandy invasion.

The French Resistance also played a significant role in facilitating the Allies' rapid advance through France following the invasion of Normandy and the lesser-known invasion of southern France (Operation ANVIL) on August 15. Ultimately 28 of France's 90 departments were liberated by the French themselves. By the end of the war France had fielded an army of 1.2 million men, making it the fourth-largest army in the European theater.

Although its numbers were quite small in terms of the total French population, the Resistance was also politically and morally important in providing an example of patriotism in a country that had been shattered by the stunning German defeat of 1940 and the travails of the German occupation. It also helped counter collaborationist France and those French citizens who had joined the pro-Nazi Milice and the Waffen-SS.

Spencer C. Tucker

Further Reading

Christofferson, Thomas, and Michael Christofferson. *France during World War II: From Defeat to Liberation.* New York: Fordham University Press, 2006.

Cointet, Jean-Paul. *Dictionnaire historique de la France sous l'occupation.* Paris: Tallandier, 2000.

Crowdy, Terry. *French Resistance Fighter: France's Secret Army.* Oxford, UK: Osprey, 2007.

Eisenhower, Dwight D. *Crusade in Europe: Report on Operations in Northwest Europe, June 6, 1944–May 8, 1945.* New York: Doubleday, 1997.

Schoenbrun, David. *Soldiers of the Night: The Story of the French Resistance.* New York: Dutton, 1980.

G

Gale, Sir Richard Nelson (1896–1982)

British Army officer who commanded the 6th Airborne Division during the Normandy invasion. Richard Nelson "Windy" Gale was born in London on July 25, 1896. After attending secondary schools he sought entrance into the British Army, but a lackluster academic record initially prevented this. After briefly working as an insurance agent, he finally gained admittance to the Royal Military Academy at Sandhurst in 1915. Commissioned a second lieutenant by year's end, he joined the Worcestershire Regiment in the fighting in France, where he won the Military Cross.

Gale remained in the British Army after the war and was stationed in India, where he studied at the Staff College at Quetta. Promoted to captain in 1930, he returned to England in early 1936, and in 1937 he became a staff officer in the War Office. Promoted to major in December 1938, Gale joined the General Staff as a planning officer.

A lieutenant colonel by early 1941, Gale commanded a battalion in the 46th Division. In the late summer of 1941 Gale, now a brigadier, received command of the new 1st Parachute Brigade. Highly praised for his work in training the brigade, he was assigned to the War Office in 1942, where he held, consecutively, the posts of deputy director of staff duties and director of air operations.

In May 1943, Gale was promoted to major general and took command of the newly organized 6th Airborne Division. Initially undermanned, the division was augmented by components from other British airborne units and a Canadian parachute battalion.

Gale accompanied his men in the British airborne operation, code-named TONGA (June 5–7), landing in France by glider. TONGA's mission was to support the invading Allied ground troops, sow confusion among the German defenders, and sever bridges and other routes inland. TONGA was successful, and Gale was awarded the Distinguished Service Award for his role.

On September 5, the 6th Airborne Division was rotated back to Britain for rest and recuperation. In the closing months of World War II, Gale commanded the I Airborne Corps. Known for his bluntness and boisterous leadership style, he was also admired as a pioneering strategist and tactician. He was a staunch proponent of employing elite forces as shock troops and constantly preached the need for flexibility and mobility. Gale was also a firm believer in the need for superlative troop training, the use of new technology, and firm but personal leadership.

After the war, Gale held a number of field and staff commands and was promoted to lieutenant general in 1947. He retired from the army in 1957, but less than a year later in 1958 he was called back to service as the North Atlantic Treaty Organization's deputy supreme Allied commander, Europe, a post he held until 1960, when he retired a final time. Gale was honored with the Knight Grand Cross (Order of Bath). He died in London on July 29, 1982.

Paul G. Pierpaoli Jr.

Further Reading

Gale, Sir Richard Nelson. *Call to Arms: An Autobiography.* London: Hutchinson, 1968.

Gale, Sir Richard Nelson. *With the 6th Airborne Division in Normandy.* London: Smason Law, Marston, 1948.

Mead, Richard. *Churchill's Lions: A Biographical Guide to the Key British Generals of World War II.* Stroud, Gloucestershire, UK: Spellmount, 2007.

Shannon, Kevin, and Stephen Wright. *One Night in June: The Story of Operation Tonga, the Initial Phase of the Invasion of Normandy, 1944.* Shrewsbury, UK: Airlife, 1994.

Gerhardt, Charles Hunter (1895–1976)

U.S. Army officer who commanded the 29th Infantry Division during the June 6, 1944, Normandy invasion. Charles Hunter Gerhardt was born in Richmond, Virginia, on June 6, 1895, the son of a career army officer. Hunter entered the U.S. Military Academy, West Point, where he proved to be a gifted athlete and graduated in 1917. Commissioned a second lieutenant that same year, he served with the 89th Infantry Division in France in World War I. Thereafter, Gerhardt held a variety of posts with the 8th, 11th, and 14th Cavalry Regiments.

Promoted to lieutenant colonel in July 1940 and to brigadier general in July 1941, Gerhardt took command of the 91st Infantry Division based at Camp White (Oregon). By then, he had earned a reputation as an idiosyncratic and often prickly leader who tended to obsess over protocol minutiae and small, inconsequential infractions. His personality and record as a commander meant that he had as many detractors as he had supporters. Nevertheless, in June 1942 Gerhardt was promoted to major general; the following year he assumed command of the 29th Infantry Division.

The 29th landed on Omaha Beach on June 6, 1944, and then engaged in a hard-fought battle that resulted in the taking of Saint-Lô the following month. Following a campaign across France, Gerhardt's division reached the Elbe River in Germany by late April. Following the German surrender in May, the 29th remained in western Germany for a brief time as an occupation force.

Gerhardt's command of the 29th, along with the campaign in France and Germany, proved controversial. The 29th sustained slightly more than 20,000 casualties in fewer than 10 months, an astronomically high attrition rate. Only the 1st Infantry Division, which unlike the 29th had also fought in North Africa and Italy, suffered a higher casualty rate during the war. Gerhardt's tactics were called into question by his superiors, as was his overall judgment as a commander. Indeed, Gerhardt reportedly acquiesced to the establishment of a de facto brothel for his men in northern France, which outraged General Omar N. Bradley, who promptly shut the operation down. By 1945, a morbid joke about Gerhardt's command suggested that he actually commanded three divisions—one on the battlefield, one in the hospital, and another in the cemetery.

After the war ended, the army investigated Gerhardt's decisions during 1944 and 1945 and concluded that he had been too cavalier with the lives of his soldiers and took the unusual decision to demote him to colonel on April 30, 1946. Nevertheless, Gerhardt remained in the army, serving as defense attaché to Brazil and holding a staff position at Fort Meade, Maryland. He eventually regained the rank of brigadier general and was permitted to retire in 1952 as a major general.

Gerhardt died on October 6, 1976, in Winter Haven, Florida.

Paul G. Pierpaoli Jr.

Further Reading

Balkoski, Joseph. *Beyond the Beachhead: The 29th Infantry Division in Normandy.* Mechanicsburg, PA: Stackpole Books, 2005.

Ewing, Joseph. *29, Let's Go! A History of the 29th Infantry Division in World War II.* New York: Battery Press, 1986.

Gerow, Leonard Townsend (1888–1972)

U.S. Army general. Born in Petersburg, Virginia, on July 13, 1888, Leonard Townsend Gerow graduated from the Virginia Military Institute in 1911 and was commissioned a second lieutenant of infantry. He took part in the 1914 occupation of Veracruz, Mexico. Following U.S. entry into World War I, Gerow served in France from April 1918 with the Signal Corps, fighting in the Second Battle of the Marne and in the Saint-Mihiel and Meuse-Argonne Offensives.

After the war, Gerow served on the staff of the Signal Corps in France (1918–1920). He was promoted to permanent major in June 1920 and alternated staff assignments in Washington, tours in Shanghai and the Philippines, and training courses at Fort Benning, Georgia, and Fort Leavenworth, Kansas, where he excelled. From 1935 onward, Gerow served in the War Department's War Plans Division. Promoted to brigadier general in October 1940, he became chief of the War Plans Division in December 1940. From December 1941, he served simultaneously as assistant chief of staff.

In February 1942 Gerow was promoted to major general and took command of the 29th Infantry Division, which began advanced training in Britain the following October. Gerow was a leading member of the talented group of top American officers whom General Dwight D. Eisenhower gathered around himself after he was appointed supreme commander in Europe. In July 1943 Gerow assumed command of V Corps in what became Lieutenant General Omar N. Bradley's First Army, which experienced heavy fighting in the Normandy campaign commencing with the invasion of June 6, 1944.

On August 25, 1944, Gerow was the first Allied general to enter Paris. He then led V Corps in campaigns through northern France and the Rhineland. In January 1945 Gerow was promoted to lieutenant general and took command of the new Fifteenth Army, which secured the western French coast, taking the ports of Saint-Nazaire and Lorient. The area was also a staging ground for training and equipping units to join the 12th Army Group, which carried the battle into Germany.

From October 1945 to January 1948, Gerow was commandant of the Command and General Staff College. He then commanded the Second Army at Fort Meade, Maryland, retiring in July 1950. A special act of Congress promoted Gerow to general on July 19, 1954. He died in Petersburg, Virginia, on October 12, 1972.

Priscilla Roberts

Further Reading

Ewing, Joseph. *29, Let's Go! A History of the 29th Infantry Division in World War II.* Washington, DC: Infantry Journal Press, 1948.

Roy, Claude. *Eight Days That Freed Paris.* London: Pilot Press, 1945.

Weigley, Russell F. *Eisenhower's Lieutenants: The Campaigns of France and Germany, 1944–1945.* Bloomington: Indiana University Press, 1981.

Geyr von Schweppenburg, Leo Dietrich Franz Freiherr (1886–1974)

German Army general. Leo Dietrich Franz Freiherr Geyr von Schweppenburg was born in Potsdam, Germany, on March 2, 1886. He joined the German Army in 1904 and during World War I fought on a number of fronts, ending the war as a captain.

Remaining in the army, Geyr was promoted to colonel in 1935 and to major general in 1935. During 1935–1937 he was military attaché to the United Kingdom, the Netherlands, and Belgium. Returning to Germany from London, he was promoted to lieutenant general in 1937 on assuming command of the 3rd Panzer Division.

Geyr distinguished himself in the German invasion of Poland in September 1939 that began World War II and won personal commendation from German chancellor Adolf Hitler. Promoted to general of cavalry in February 1940, Geyr commanded the XXIV Panzer Corps, which he led in the May 1940 invasion of France and then in the June 1941 invasion of the Soviet Union. Made general of panzer troops in July, he assumed command of the XL Panzer Corps in the invasion of the Caucasus.

In early 1943 Geyr was transferred west to France and ordered to organize new units there to meet the expected invasion of France by the Western Allies. Toward this end, commander of German forces in the West Field Marshal Gerd von Rundstedt ordered Geyr to form 10 panzer and motorized divisions. In November 1943 Geyr's command was formally established as Panzer Group West, the chief concentration of German armor in France.

When the anticipated Allied invasion of the northern coast of France occurred on June 6, 1944, Geyr's forces, assembled near Mailly-le-Camp in the Aube department of north-central France, were to advance northward, meet the Allies, and drive them into the sea. German field marshal Erwin Rommel, charged with the actual German coastal defenses, wanted Geyr's tanks to be in close proximity to the coast so they could react quickly and not be savaged by Allied airpower as they made their way northward. Rommel, who had experienced the full might of Allied airpower firsthand in North Africa, understood the damage that overwhelming numbers of Allied ground-attack aircraft would inflict on German armor. Hitler, Rundstedt, and Geyr did not; indeed, Hitler welcomed the prospect of an invasion as a means to get at the Western Allied forces and destroy them. All three men wanted the German tanks held back in order to defeat the invaders in a land campaign of maneuver. Rommel understood that Allied airpower ensured that once the Allies had established a firm lodgment ashore, there would be no stopping them.

Rundstedt retained control of German armor in France. Anticipating an Allied effort to try to destroy as many of the tanks as possible before any invasion, he ordered them dispersed. This proved prescient in that the massive Allied bombing raid of May 3–4 on Mailly-le-Camp by 346 British Avro Lancaster heavy bombers and 14 de Havilland Mosquitoes was largely a failure, with 42 Lancasters shot down.

Following the June 6, 1944, Allied invasion, Geyr rushed three panzer divisions northward and was able to prevent the loss of Caen to the advancing British and Canadian forces. He was planning a major counterattack when he was wounded in a Royal Air Force attack on his headquarters at La Caine on June 10, whereupon the counterattack was canceled. Although Geyr's forces held the British and Canadians at bay during the next weeks, Geyr was relieved of his command when he supported Rundstedt's request that Hitler authorize a withdrawal from Caen. Geyr was then assigned to an administrative post as inspector general of armored troops.

Captured by U.S. forces at the end of the war, Geyr was held until 1947. He then published his memoirs, translated into English as *The Critical Years* (1952). He also advised the Federal Republic of Germany on the structure of the new German military. Geyr died in Irschenhausen near Munich on January 27, 1974.

Spencer C. Tucker

Further Reading

Beevor, Antony. *D-Day: The Battle for Normandy.* New York: Viking, 2009.

D'Este, Carlo. *Decision in Normandy.* New York: E. P. Dutton, 1983.

Ford, Ken, and Howard Gerrard. *Caen 1944.* Oxford, UK: Osprey, 2004.

Geyr von Schweppenburg. *The Critical Years.* London: A. Wingate, 1952.

Trew, Simon, and Stephen Badsey. *Battle for Caen.* Stroud, UK: Sutton, 2004.

Gold Beach. *See* Terrain and Tactical Problems on D-Day

GOODWOOD, Operation (July 18–20, 1944). *See* Caen, Battle to Secure

H

Hand Grenades

Hand grenades are small bombs thrown by hand. Numerous types of hand grenades were employed during World War II. The U.S. military used offensive, defensive, and special-use grenades. The MkIII A1, a can-shaped grenade filled with eight ounces of flaked TNT, was used for offensive purposes because no fragmentation took place after the initial explosion. The MkII "pineapple" grenade was for defensive use and was based on the old British Mills Bomb design. Troops could not assault forward because of the fragmentation of its serrated shell, which created a 10-yard killing radius. The M15 white phosphorous (WP) "Willie Pete" grenade, used for smoke generation and the assaulting of caves and pillboxes, saw limited use. In tight quarters, the almost two-pound M15 WP created severe eye, respiratory, and skin injuries.

The standard hand grenade for British forces was the revised M36 Mills Bomb. It had a serrated cast-iron body filled with TNT and was used defensively. Of note was the screw-in fuze, which was put in place prior to combat. To use the grenade, the user pulled the pin and then threw the grenade. When the grenade left the user's hand, the spring-loaded lever was released, activating the fusing sequence. A more specialized grenade was the Gammon Bomb (No. 82), a 20-ounce cloth bag filled with plastic explosive. It had an attached screw-off metal cap that was removed to arm the device. The Gammon Bomb was effective against pillboxes and bunkers.

The standard German hand grenades were the high-explosive stick grenade (Stielhandgranate 24) and the high-explosive hand grenade (Eierhandgranate 39). The offensive Stiel. 24, universally known as the "potato masher" grenade, contained a bursting TNT charge and could be fitted with a fragmentation sleeve for defensive use. The igniter was activated by pulling the porcelain bead found in the handle behind the metal cap. A heavier Stiel. 43 variant existed; it contained almost twice the TNT charge and could also be fitted with a fragmentation sleeve. The offensive Eier. 39 was egg-shaped, and its older and newer designs differed slightly. The TNT filler was initiated by a detonator and friction igniter. More specialized German grenades were the offensive wooden and concrete improvised hand grenades (Behelfshandgranate-Holz and -Beton) and numerous forms of smoke grenades (Nebelhandgranate) based on stick, conventional, egg, and glass body designs.

Robert J. Bunker

Further Reading

U.S. Department of the Army. *Hand and Rifle Grenades: FM 23–30.* Washington, DC: U.S. Government Printing Office, 1949.

U.S. War Department. *Handbook on German Military Forces.* 1945; reprint, Baton Rouge: Louisiana State University Press, 1995.

Higgins, Andrew Jackson (1886–1952)

U.S. businessman and naval constructor. Born on August 28, 1886, in Columbus,

Nebraska, Andrew Jackson Higgins moved to Alabama in 1906, where he worked in the timber industry, becoming familiar with shallow-draft boats. In 1923, he started Higgins Lumber and Export Company in New Orleans. By 1926, Higgins had moved away from timber and was focused on manufacturing boats.

During the 1930s, Higgins Industries built a variety of shallow-water boats. Higgins sold vessels to the Coast Guard and the Army Corps of Engineers, and in 1939 he received contracts to build a boat for amphibious operations and to manufacture fast patrol torpedo boats.

Higgins Industries designed and manufactured for the U.S. armed forces in World War II the LCP (landing craft, personnel), LCPL (landing craft personnel, large), LCVP (landing craft vehicle, personnel), and LCM (landing craft, mechanized). Higgins also oversaw the construction of other products, including an airborne droppable lifeboat and secretly manufactured items required by the Manhattan Project. During the war, Higgins Industries expanded to eight plants around New Orleans. The firm built more than 20,000 vessels for the Allies. General Dwight D. Eisenhower, supreme commander of Allied forces in Western Europe, said of Higgins, "He is the man who won the war for us."

Following the war Higgins's company experienced financial difficulties, but during the 1950–1953 Korean War, the company again thrived. Andrew Higgins died in New Orleans on August 1, 1952.

R. Kyle Schlafer

Further Reading

Lorelli, John A. *To Foreign Shores: U.S. Amphibious Operations in World War II.* Annapolis, MD: Naval Institute Press, 1995.

Strahan, Jerry E. *Andrew Jackson Higgins and the Boats That Won World War II.* Baton Rouge: Louisiana State University Press, 1994.

Hitler, Adolf (1889–1945)

Leader (führer) of Germany. Born on April 20, 1889, in Braunau am Inn, Austria, Adolf Hitler had a troubled childhood. He was educated at primary school and Realschule in Linz, but he dropped out at age 16. Hitler aspired to become an artist, and on the death of his mother Klara in 1907 (his father Alois had died in 1903), he moved to Vienna. He attempted to enroll at the Viennese Academy of Fine Arts but was unsuccessful. Hitler lived in flophouses and made some money selling small paintings of Vienna scenes to frame shops. It was in Vienna that Hitler developed his hatred of Jews, who had assimilated into Viennese society. But he also developed an aversion to internationalism, capitalism, and socialism. He developed an intense sense of nationalism and expressed pride in being of German descent.

Probably to avoid compulsory military service, Hitler left Austria in May 1913 and settled in the south German state of Bavaria. On the outbreak of World War I in 1914, he enlisted in the Bavarian Army and served with distinction. There he found the sense of purpose he had previously lacked. He saw extensive military action, was wounded, and served in the dangerous position of Meldegänger (dispatch runner). Temporarily blinded in a British gas attack, Hitler ended the war in a military hospital. He had risen to the rank of lance corporal and won the Iron Cross First Class, an unusual distinction for someone of his rank.

After the war, Hitler returned to Munich and remained in the military as a counterintelligence agent, reporting on political groups, and he then became involved in politics full-time. In the summer of 1919 and on the order of his commanding officer, Hitler joined the Deutsche Arbeiterpartei (German Worker's Party), later known as the Nationalsozialistische Deutsche Arbeiterpartei (National Socialist German Worker's Party, or Nazi Party). His oratorical skills, combined with generous financial support from the German Army, soon made him one of its leaders. Disgruntled by Germany's loss in the war, Hitler became the voice of the dispossessed and angry. He blamed Germany's defeat on the "November criminals"—the communists, the Jews, and the Weimar Republic.

Taking a cue from Benito Mussolini's march on Rome the previous year, on November 8, 1923, Hitler and his followers attempted to seize power in Bavaria as a step toward controlling Germany. This Beer Hall Putsch was put down by the authorities with some bloodshed. Hitler was then arrested and brought to trial for attempting to overthrow the state. He used his trial to become a national political figure in Germany. Sentenced to prison, he served only nine months (1923–1924). While at the Landsberg Fortress, he dictated his stream-of-consciousness memoir, *Mein Kampf* (My Struggle). Later when he was in power, royalties on sales of the book and his images made him immensely wealthy, a fact he deliberately concealed from the German people.

Hitler formed few female attachments during his life. He was involved with his niece, Geli Raubal, who committed suicide in 1931, and later with Eva Braun, whom he hid from the public. Deeply distrustful of people, Hitler was a vegetarian who loved animals and especially doted on his dogs. He was also a severe hypochondriac, suffering from myriad real and imagined illnesses.

Hitler restructured the Nazi Party, and by 1929 it had emerged as a political force in Germany, winning representation in the Reichstag. In April 1932, Hitler ran against Field Marshal Paul von Hindenburg for the presidency of Germany. Hitler railed against the Weimar Republic for the Versailles Treaty at the end of World War I, the catastrophic inflation of 1923, the alleged threat posed by the communists, and the effects of the Great Depression. Hindenburg won, but Hitler received 13 million votes in a completely free election, and by June 1932 the Nazis were the largest political party in the Reichstag.

On January 30, 1933, Hindenburg appointed Hitler chancellor. Hitler quickly acted against any political adversaries. Fresh elections under Nazi auspices gave the Nazis in coalition with the Nationalists a majority in the Reichstag. The Enabling Act of March 1933 gave Hitler dictatorial powers. On the death of Hindenburg in August 1934, Hitler amalgamated the office of president and chancellor, with the combined title of führer. He also took direct control of the armed forces. In the Night of the Long Knives of July 1934, Hitler purged the party and especially the Sturmabteilung (Storm Troopers) and removed several political opponents. He also reorganized Germany administratively, dissolving political parties and labor unions and making Germany a one-party state.

Opposition to the Nazis soon was crushed, and many dissidents were sent to concentration camps. The ubiquitous Gestapo kept tabs on the civilian population, but the state was not characterized solely by repression by any means. In the first several years Hitler was carried forward on a wave of disillusionment with the Weimar Republic, and a plebiscite showed that a solid majority of Germans approved of his actions.

On assuming political power, Hitler initiated actions against and introduced legislation to isolate the Jews. They were turned into a race of "untouchables" within their own state, unable to pursue higher education, certain careers, or a full public life. The Nuremberg Laws of 1935 defined as Jewish anyone with at least one Jewish grandparent and classified them as noncitizens, without rights. Hitler remarked that war in Europe would lead to the "extinction of the Jewish race in Europe."

In 1934, Hitler took Germany out of the League of Nations and the Geneva disarmament conference. Germans were put back to work, and rearmament, albeit at first secret (it was announced in 1935), began. Hitler's most daring gamble was in March 1936, when he marched German troops into the Rhineland and remilitarized it. He sent German forces to aid the Nationalist insurgency in Spain during 1936–1939 and formed an alliance with Mussolini's fascist Italy. In November 1937, Hitler announced plans to his top advisers and generals for an aggressive foreign policy and war, and in March 1938 he began his march of conquest with the Anschluss (joining) with Austria. That fall he secured the Sudetenland of Czechoslovakia, and in March 1939 he took over the remainder of Czechoslovakia. Poland was the next pressure point. To secure his eastern flank, in August 1939 Hitler concluded a nonaggression pact with the Soviet Union (the Molotov-Ribbentrop Pact). On September 1, 1939, German forces invaded Poland, touching off World War II in Europe.

Applying new tactics of close cooperation between air and ground elements centered in a war of movement that came to be known as blitzkrieg (lightning war), the German military enjoyed early success on the battlefield. Poland was taken within one month. When Britain and France, which had gone to war with Germany on the invasion of Poland, rejected peace on a forgive-and-forget basis, Hitler invaded the west. Norway and Denmark were taken beginning in April 1940. France and the Low Countries fell in May and June. Hitler's first rebuff came in the July 10–September 30, 1940, Battle of Britain, when the Luftwaffe failed to drive the Royal Air Force from the skies, a necessary precursor to a seaborne invasion. After next securing his southern flank in the Balkans by invading and conquering Greece and Yugoslavia in April 1941, Hitler invaded the Soviet Union on June 22, 1941. When the United States entered the war against Japan in December 1941, Hitler declared war on the United States, in keeping with agreements he had made with Japan.

Increasingly, Germany suffered the consequences of strategic overreach: German troops not only had to garrison much of Europe but also were sent to North Africa. Hitler's constant meddling in military matters, his changes of plans, and his divide-and-rule concept of administration all worked to the detriment of Germany's cause. On Hitler's express (but rarely written) orders, millions of people, mainly Jews, were rounded up and systematically slaughtered.

Hitler welcomed the invasion of France by the Western Allies as an opportunity to get at and defeat them. "Let them come," he said, "we will give them the thrashing of their lives." Hitler was, however, deceived by the Allied deception effort preceding the Normandy invasion, believing that the D-Day landing of June 6, 1944, was merely a feint, with the main Allied effort to come in the Pas de Calais region. He refused to allow his commanders in France, Field Marshals Gerd von Rundstedt and Erwin Rommel, discretion in the allocation of resources and delayed by several hours action on the request by his commander in the West, Field Marshal Gerd von Rundstedt, to release two panzer divisions stationed near Paris, meaning that they had to move northward in full daylight. He then withheld most of the remaining panzer divisions until too late and then only committed them piecemeal, when much of their strength was destroyed by overwhelming Allied airpower.

On July 20, 1944, Colonel Claus von Stauffenberg, a leader of the German opposition to Hitler, placed a bomb in the Wolfsschanze, Hitler's headquarters in East Prussia. Although Hitler survived the blast, he was thereafter a physical and psychological wreck.

From mid-January 1945, Hitler took up residence in Berlin. He refused negotiation to the end, preferring to see Germany destroyed and claiming that the German people did not deserve to continue. He married Eva Braun on April 29, 1945, and rather than be taken by the Russians, who were closing in on Berlin, he and his new wife committed suicide in the bunker of the Chancellery on April 30, 1945. After the fall of the Soviet Union in 1991, the Russians confirmed that they had Hitler's remains, ending myths that he had escaped to South America.

Wendy A. Maier-Sarti

Further Reading

Bracher, Karl Dietrich. *The German Dictatorship: The Origins, Structure, and Effects of National Socialism.* New York: Praeger, 1970.

Bullock, Alan. *Hitler: A Study in Tyranny.* New York: Harper, 1952.

Burleigh, Michael. *The Third Reich: A New History.* New York: Hill and Wang, 2000.

Fest, Joachim C. *Hitler.* Translated by Richard and Clara Winston. New York: Harcourt Brace Jovanovich, 1974.

Flood, Charles Bracelen. *Hitler: The Path to Power.* Boston: Houghton Mifflin, 1989.

Gordon, Sarah. *Hitler, Germans, and the Jewish Question.* Princeton, NJ: Princeton University Press, 1988.

Hitler, Adolf. *Mein Kampf.* New York: Houghton Mifflin, 1999.

Jones, J. Sydney. *Hitler in Vienna, 1907–1913: Clues to the Future.* New York: Stein and Day, 1983.

Kershaw, Ian. *Hitler.* 2 vols. New York: Norton, 1999–2000.

Shirer, William L. *Berlin Diary, 1934–1941.* London: Sphere, 1970.

Hobart, Sir Percy Cleghorn Stanley (1885–1957)

British Army general. Born in Naini, India, on June 14, 1885, Percy Cleghorn Stanley Hobart excelled in studies at Clifton College and then graduated from the Royal Military Academy at Woolwich. He was commissioned in the engineers in 1904 and posted to India in 1906, where he distinguished himself. Sent to France with the Indian Expeditionary Force during World War I in January 1915, Hobart fought on the Western Front and in Mesopotamia, where he was wounded in April 1916. By the end of the war, he was a major. After the war Hobart graduated from the Staff College, Camberley, and then returned to India in 1921.

Convinced that the future of ground warfare lay in tanks, Hobart joined the Royal Tank Corps in 1923. An instructor at the Staff College at Quetta from 1923 to 1927, he was brevetted lieutenant colonel in 1922 and colonel in 1928. In 1927 and 1928 he was second-in-command of 4th Battalion, and in 1931 and 1932 he commanded the 2nd Battalion of the Tank Corps. First inspector and then commander of the corps in 1933 and 1934, Hobart raised the 1st Tank Brigade and commanded it during 1934–1937. Promoted to major general and assigned to head military training in 1938, he went to Egypt to raise what became the 7th Armoured Division, championing its use apart from infantry formations.

Hobart retired from the army in 1939, largely because of his outspoken nature and zealous championing of tanks in armored doctrine and tactics. Early in World War II he was serving as a colonel in the Home Guard when Prime Minister Winston L. S. Churchill recalled him to active duty to command first the 11th Armoured Division in England in 1941 and 1942 and then the 79th Armoured Division, with its unique engineering equipment. These assignments gave Hobart the opportunity to showcase his innovative talents. Equipment included forerunners to the modern combat engineer vehicle, specialized vehicles for laying and clearing mines, an amphibious tank, and a flamethrower tank (the Crocodile). Such special tanks were known as "Hobart's Funnies" or "Hobo's Funnies," playing on Hobart's nickname "Old Hobo."

Hobart commanded his division in the 21st Army Group through the campaign in Northern Europe to the end of the war. He retired for a second time in 1946 but served as lieutenant governor of the Royal Hospital, Chelsea, during 1948–1953. Hobart died at Farnham, Surrey, on February 19, 1957.

Robert L. Bateman and Spencer C. Tucker

Further Reading

Futter, Geoffrey W. *The Funnies: The 79th Armored Division and Its Specialized Equipment.* Hemel Hempstead, UK: Model and Allied Publications, 1974.

Hart, Russell A. *Clash of Arms: How the Allies Won in Normandy.* Boulder, CO: Lynne Rienner, 2001.

Macksey, Kenneth. *Armored Crusader: A Biography of Major-General Sir Percy Hobart.* London: Hutchinson, 1967.

Howard, John (1912–1999)

British Army officer who spearheaded the successful effort to secure two key bridges in Normandy, France, on June 6, 1944, just before the Allied amphibious assault. John Howard was born in London on December 8, 1912, and entered the British Army as a private in 1932. In 1938, he left the army as a noncommissioned officer and secured a position as a police officer in Oxford. Soon after World War II began in September 1939, Howard was recalled to military service. Completing an officer training course in 1940, he was commissioned a second lieutenant. By May 1942, he was a major in command of D Company, 2nd Battalion, Oxfordshire and Buckinghamshire Light Infantry.

As part of the planning for the invasion of France, Howard's unit was chosen to execute a risky mission to immediately precede the amphibious assault. The operation was to secure two key bridges on the eastern flank of the invasion zone—one spanning the Caen Canal and another traversing the Orne River, which flows parallel to the canal. At the time, German forces controlled the bridges. Howard helped plan the operation and spent months training his men for it.

Seizing the bridges was critically important to the Normandy landings. If the bridges were not immediately taken, the Germans would be able to move men and armor toward the beaches, imperiling the thousands of infantrymen coming ashore. Or, the Germans could subsequently blow up the bridges in a withdrawal, cutting off a crucial Allied resupply route.

Shortly before midnight on June 5, 1944, several British Handley Page heavy bombers towed six Horsa gliders south over the English Channel toward the northern French coast. The gliders carried 181 men, including Howard. Let loose not far from the landing zone, the lead glider piloted by Howard landed at 12:16 a.m. The landing was rough, but the glider came to rest just 50 yards from the Caen Canal Bridge. In less than a half hour, Howard and his men had subdued the defenders and secured the span. Not long after, Howard's men also secured the bridge crossing the Orne. Throughout the early morning hours of June 6, Howard's detachment was steadily reinforced by British commandos and paratroopers, permitting the British to advance toward Caen. Howard's daring operation resulted in 16 British casualties—2 killed and 14 others wounded.

Howard's unit continued in action as an infantry company for the next three months in the subsequent France campaign, but in September 1944 Howard was ordered back to Great Britain to restructure his unit. That November he was seriously injured in a vehicular accident, and he never again saw action. In 1946, he left the army as a major and subsequently had a lengthy career as a civil servant.

For his war efforts, Howard was awarded the British Distinguished Service Order, second in importance only to the Victoria Cross, and the French Croix de Guerre avec Palme. France renamed the Caen Canal Bridge Pegasus Bridge (the Pegasus, or flying horse, is the official symbol of British airborne units). Later, the road leading to the bridge was renamed Esplanade Major John Howard. In 1962, Howard served as an adviser for the Hollywood film *The Longest Day,* which depicted his unit's exploits on June 6, 1944.

Howard died in Surrey, England, on May 5, 1999.

Paul G. Pierpaoli Jr.

Further Reading

Ambrose, Stephen E. *Pegasus Bridge.* New York: Simon and Schuster, 1985.

Howard, John, and Penny Bates. *The Pegasus Diaries: The Private Papers of Major John Howard, DSO.* Barnsley, South Yorkshire, UK: Pen and Sword, 2009.

Huebner, Clarence Ralph (1888–1972)

U.S. Army general. Born in Bushton, Kansas, on November 24, 1888, Clarence Ralph Huebner enlisted in the army as a private in 1910. He earned a commission by examination, and by the time the United States entered World War I in 1917, he was a captain commanding a company of the 28th Infantry Regiment. Huebner distinguished himself in fighting in France during World War I, was wounded, and ended the war as a lieutenant colonel in command of the 28th Regiment in the Meuse-Argonne Offensive. He then served in occupation forces in Germany after the armistice. Returning to the United States in 1919, Huebner reverted to his permanent rank of captain.

With U.S. entry into World War II, Huebner was promoted to brigadier general in February 1942 and to major general in March 1943. He became deputy chief of staff to British general Sir Harold Alexander in North Africa and in August 1943 replaced Major General Terry de la Mesa Allen in command of the 1st Infantry Division. Huebner led the division, nicknamed the "Big Red One," in the Normandy invasion on June 6, 1944. When the war ended in Europe, he was commander of V Corps. Lieutenant General Huebner retired in November 1950 and died in Washington, D.C., on September 23, 1972.

John F. Votaw

Further Reading

Blumenson, Martin, and James L. Stokesbury. *Masters of the Art of Command.* Boston: Houghton Mifflin, 1975.

Society of the First [Infantry] Division. *Danger Forward: The Story of the First Division in World War II.* Washington, DC: Society of the First Division, 1947.

J

Jodl, Alfred (1890–1946)

German Army general and chief of the armed forces operations staff during World War II. Born on May 10, 1890, in Würzburg, Germany, Alfred Jodl joined a Bavarian field artillery regiment in 1910 and served in World War I, finishing the war as a general staff officer. His superior performance secured him a position in the postwar Reichswehr.

Serving primarily in staff positions during the interwar years, Jodl was assigned in 1939 as a general major to the Oberkommando der Wehrmacht (Armed Forces High Command, OKW) as chief of the Wehrmachtführungsamt (Armed Forces Operations Office, renamed in 1940 Wehrmachtführungsstab, or Armed Forces Operations Staff). Promoted to general der artillerie in 1940, he held his OKW position until the German surrender in May 1945.

Despite his position as chief of operations, Jodl had little direct influence on the planning and execution of Germany's military campaigns. This was primarily a result of German chancellor Adolf Hitler's unwillingness to delegate authority. Jodl was an admirer of the führer's successes in 1939 and 1940 but was not slavish in his devotion to Hitler. After investigating Army Group A's lack of progress during the Caucasus campaign of 1942, Jodl returned to endorse the commander's actions, thus contradicting Hitler. In the inevitable tirade that followed Jodl stood his ground, reportedly giving as good as he got. Even though he was disillusioned with his commander in chief and with the conduct of the war, Jodl held true to his belief in obedience and duty and remained at his post for the rest of the war. He was promoted to colonel general in January 1944.

Brought before the International Military Tribunal at Nuremberg after the war, Jodl was tried as a war criminal. Found guilty, he was condemned to death and hanged in Nuremberg on October 16, 1946.

David M. Toczek

Further Reading

Görlitz, Walter. "Keitel, Jodl, and Warlimont." In *Hitler's Generals,* edited by Correlli Barnett, 139–169. New York: William Morrow, 1989.

Megargee, Geoffrey P. *Inside Hitler's High Command.* Lawrence: University of Kansas Press, 2000.

Warlimont, Walter. *Inside Hitler's Headquarters.* Translated by R. H. Barry. New York: Praeger, 1964.

JUBILEE, Operation (Dieppe Raid, August 19, 1942)

Abortive World War II Allied raid against the northern French port of Dieppe. From a British perspective, there were good reasons for such a raid. In early 1942 Prime Minister Winston Churchill was under heavy political pressure as a result of a series of major military reverses. Churchill hoped that such a raid might provide a convincing military success and blunt Soviet and U.S. criticism of the failure to open a second front in Europe. Soviet leader Joseph Stalin had dropped not-so-subtle hints that his country might leave the war, and German chancellor Adolf Hitler was certain that Churchill would try to bolster Stalin's resolve by attempting a raid against the northern coast of France. The range of British fighter aircraft determined the likely point of attack.

Dieppe was strongly defended. German colonel general Kurt Hesse was in overall command, and Dieppe was held essentially by the 57th Infantry Regiment. While this was not a top unit, its men nonetheless took full advantage of the terrain.

In planning the operation, chief of combined operations Vice Admiral Louis Mountbatten modified it without formal approval from Churchill and the British Chiefs of Staff. Later Mountbatten was able to mask his personal responsibility in the disaster.

Minesweepers cleared a path across the English Channel for the sizable naval forces committed to the operation. Commanded by Captain J. Hughes-Hallett, it consisted of 237 vessels of all types, 179 of them landing craft. These transported some 6,100 Allied troops (4,963 Canadians, about 1,075 British Army commandos, and 50 U.S. Army rangers). Some 730 aircraft, the majority of them Spitfire fighters, provided air cover and ground support.

Just before dawn on August 19, 1942, the troops came ashore. Code-named JUBILEE, the operation may have been the largest raid in history. The initial landing began at 4:50 a.m., and the attackers withdrew by 2:00 p.m. Some German coastal guns were destroyed but at prohibitive cost. The Allies suffered 3,367 casualties, including 1,946 captured

The aftermath of the Allied raid on Dieppe on August 19, 1942. This costly attack against the German-held French port on the English Channel was highly controversial but it did provide the Allies useful lessons for the future. (Corel)

and 907 killed. German losses were 314 killed and 294 wounded. The Canadians suffered the worst. Their high casualty rate led to much bitterness afterward. Overall, casualties were the highest in the war for any major offensive involving all three services. In addition to vehicles and tanks destroyed, the Allies lost 98 aircraft; Luftwaffe losses totaled 48. The Royal Navy also lost 34 vessels: 33 landing craft and the destroyer *Berkeley*, which was scuttled to prevent it from being taken by the Germans.

The Dieppe Raid led to bitter recriminations between Britain and Canada and further strained relations with the United States and the Soviet Union. The raid also produced its share of historical controversies and myths, including the belief, since disproved, that the Germans were aware of it in advance.

One of the chief mysteries surrounding Dieppe is why the raid was even attempted. The evidence that it had virtually no hope of success was subsequently concealed under the patent lie that it provided vital future lessons. The raid did serve to convince even diehards among the Americans that the Western Allies were not ready to assault Festung Europa (Fortress Europe) in 1942 and demonstrated the need for strong naval and air preliminary bombardment along with thorough training of assault forces. It also demonstrated the difficulty of attacking ports and led to the decision to develop artificial harbors (Mulberries) for the eventual cross-channel invasion (Operation NEPTUNE). Even today, the Dieppe Raid remains a useful lesson on how not to conduct military planning.

Spencer C. Tucker

Further Reading

Atkin, Ronald. *Dieppe 1942: The Jubilee Disaster.* London: Macmillan, 1980.

Ford, Ken. *Dieppe 1942: Prelude to D-Day.* London: Osprey, 2003.

Robertson, Terence. *Dieppe: The Shame and the Glory.* Boston: Little, Brown, 1962.

Villa, Brian Loring. *Unauthorized Action: Mountbatten and the Dieppe Raid.* New York: Oxford University Press, 1990.

Whitehead, William. *Dieppe, 1942: Echoes of Disaster.* Toronto: Personal Library, 1979.

Juno Beach. *See* Terrain and Tactical Problems on D-Day

Kirk, Alan Goodrich (1888–1963)

U.S. Navy admiral. Born in Philadelphia, Pennsylvania, on October 30, 1888, Alan Goodrich Kirk graduated from the U.S. Naval Academy at Annapolis in 1909, then specialized in gunnery and served in the Asiatic Fleet. During the period of U.S. involvement in World War I, Kirk was stationed at the Naval Proving Ground, Dahlgren, Virginia.

In the 1920s Kirk was executive officer of the presidential yacht and served as presidential naval aide. He was then gunnery officer for the battleship *Maryland*. Kirk graduated from the Naval War College in 1929 and then was an instructor there for two years. In 1931 he assumed his first command, a destroyer, and during 1933–1936 he served in the Office of the Chief of Naval Operations. He was then executive officer of the battleship *West Virginia* before taking command of the light cruiser *Milwaukee* and serving as operations officer to the commander of the U.S. Fleet.

In 1939 Kirk became an American naval attaché in London, where he familiarized himself thoroughly with Royal Navy procedures, which he strongly admired even though British condescension occasionally irked him. Kirk's forceful advocacy of greater Anglo-American cooperation and urgent warnings in 1940 of Britain's extreme danger helped persuade President Franklin D. Roosevelt and his administration to assist Britain with measures potentially liable to precipitate conflict with Germany.

In March 1941 Kirk became director of naval intelligence, but fierce bureaucratic infighting with the War Plans Division was one reason why, despite clues that Japan planned to attack American forces, his office failed to produce any specific warnings of Japanese intentions. In October 1941 Kirk returned to sea duty as commander of a division of destroyer escorts in the Atlantic Fleet, fortuitously escaping responsibility for the failure to predict the Pearl Harbor raid.

Promoted to rear admiral in November 1941, in March 1942 Kirk became chief of staff to Admiral Harold Stark, commander of American naval forces in Europe. In London, Kirk contributed substantially to Allied strategic planning. In February 1943 he took command of Amphibious Force, Atlantic Fleet, and that July he led an amphibious naval task force in the Sicily landings (July 9, 1943). Kirk's outstanding success in the face of unexpectedly difficult conditions brought him command of all U.S. naval forces for the June 6, 1944, Normandy landings, embarked in the heavy cruiser *Augusta* (CA-31). He then commanded all U.S. naval forces in France. Kirk was promoted to vice admiral in May 1945.

Kirk retired with the rank of admiral in March 1946. He then served as ambassador to Belgium and minister to Luxembourg until 1949 and spent a further two years as ambassador to the Soviet Union (April 1949–October 1951) and the Republic of China (May 1962–April 1963). Kirk died in New York City on October 15, 1963.

Priscilla Roberts

Further Reading

Dorwart, Jeffery. *Conflict of Duty: The U.S. Navy's Intelligence Dilemma, 1919–1945.*

Annapolis, MD: Naval Institute Press, 1983.

Leutze, James R. *Bargaining for Supremacy: Anglo-American Naval Collaboration, 1937–1941.* Chapel Hill: University of North Carolina Press, 1977.

Morison, Samuel Eliot. *History of United States Naval Operations in World War II,* Vol. 11, *The Invasion of France and Germany, 1944–1945.* Boston: Little, Brown, 1957.

Kluge, Günther Adolf Ferdinand von (1882–1944)

German Army field marshal. Born in Posen, Prussia (now Poznan, Poland), into an old aristocratic family on October 30, 1882, Günther Adolf Ferdinand von Kluge joined the army as an artillery officer in 1901. During World War I he served on the General Staff (1916–1918) and was wounded in fighting at Verdun in 1918.

Selected to continue in the Reichswehr after the war, Kluge was promoted to major general in February 1933 and named inspector of Signal Troops. He became a lieutenant general in April 1934 and commanded the 6th Division in Münster. With German chancellor Adolf Hitler's expansion of the army, Kluge commanded VI Corps in 1936. In 1938 Hitler purged Kluge, along with other German generals, for supporting General Werner von Fritsch, who had opposed Hitler's plans for war.

With war looming, Hitler recalled Kluge from retirement in October 1938 and gave him command of the newly established 6th Army Group. Later, the unit was redesignated the Fourth Army. Kluge led it during the invasion of Poland in September 1939. An innovative commander, he won Hitler's admiration and promotion to colonel general.

Kluge led the Fourth Army against France and the Low Countries in May 1940. Promoted to field marshal in July, he went on to command the Fourth Army in the invasion of the Soviet Union on June 22, 1941, and Army Group Center from December 1941 to October 1943, again proving himself to be an effective field commander.

Injured in a car accident in October 1943, Kluge went on prolonged medical leave. On July 5, 1944, however, he replaced Field Marshal Karl Gerd von Rundstedt as commander in chief, West, and commander of Army Group B in Normandy. Kluge was aware of the plot to assassinate Hitler but wavered in his support and finally declined to participate. He also failed to report it. Following the bomb attempt on Hitler's life on July 20, 1944, Kluge came under increased suspicion.

Kluge led Operation LÜTTICH (known to the Western Allies as the Mortain Counteroffensive), the German counteroffensive during August 7–13, 1944, designed to throw back the gains made by the U.S. First Army in its Normandy breakout and cut off the U.S. Third Army, which had advanced into Brittany. On its failure, Kluge was relieved of command on August 17 and replaced by Field Marshal Walther Model.

Kluge wrote to Hitler urging him to make peace and end the suffering for the German people. Aware that he would be implicated in the conspiracy against Hitler and depressed by the military situation, Kluge committed suicide at Valmy, France, on August 19, 1944.

Spencer C. Tucker

Further Reading

Lamb, Richard. "Field-Marshal Günther von Kluge." In *Hitler's Generals,* edited by Correlli Barnett, 395–409. New York: Grove Weidenfeld, 1989.

Mitcham, Samuel W., Jr. *Hitler's Field Marshals and Their Battles.* Chelsea, MI: Scarborough House, 1988.

Krancke, Theodor (1893–1973)

German Navy admiral. Theodor Krancke was born in Magdeburg, Germany, on March 30, 1893. He joined the German Navy as a cadet in 1912 and during World War I served in the torpedo boat flotilla with the Grand Fleet. Remaining in the greatly downsized German Navy after the war, Krancke was promoted to captain in October 1937. In November 1939 he assumed command of the heavy cruiser (also known as a pocket battleship) *Admiral Scheer.* Krancke planned the naval phase of Operation WESERÜBUNG, the German invasion of Norway and Denmark in April 1940. During October 23, 1940–April 1, 1941, he took the *Admiral Scheer* into the Atlantic to attack merchant shipping, during which his ship sank 13 merchant ships and the armed British merchant cruiser *Jervis Bay* and also captured 3 merchant ships—a total of 115,195 tons of Allied and neutral shipping. Krancke was promoted to rear admiral in April 1941 and to vice admiral in April 1942.

Appointed commander in chief of German Navy Group Command West, headquartered in Paris, in April 1943, Krancke had charge of all German naval vessels based in French ports as well as the various land-based naval units and the naval coastal artillery and antiaircraft batteries along the French Atlantic coast. After German radar detected the Allied invasion fleet at 3:09 a.m. on June 6, 1944, Krancke ordered the shore batteries to prepare to fire and his naval assets to attack the Allied ships. Krancke had scant resources available, however. These consisted chiefly of torpedo boats. Although they attacked the invasion fleet, they could in no way prevent the invasion.

In April 1945, Krancke was appointed commander of German naval forces in Norway. He remained in command there after the war for several months to supervise the removal of German minefields and the demilitarization of German shore facilities. Made a prisoner in November, he was held until October 1947. Krancke subsequently published an account of his cruise in the *Admiral Scheer,* which appeared in English as *Pocket Battleship: The Story of the Admiral Scheer* (1958). Krancke died at Wentorf bei Hamburgon, Germany, on June 18, 1973.

Spencer C. Tucker

Further Reading

Bekker, Cajus. *Hitler's Naval War.* Garden City, NY: Doubleday, 1974.

Krancke, Theodor. *Pocket Battleship: The Story of the Admiral Scheer.* New York: Norton, 1958.

Schofield, Brian Betham. *Operation Neptune.* London: Ian Allan, 1974.

L

La Fière Causeway, Battle of the (June 6–9, 1944)

The Battle of the La Fière Causeway near the town of Sainte-Mère-Église was one of the most fiercely fought small-unit actions of the Normandy campaign. It cost the 82nd Airborne Division more than 500 casualties, while the success of U.S. VII Corps' landings in Normandy hung in the balance.

The area bounded by the town of Sainte-Marie-du-Mont, close to Utah Beach, and Sainte-Mère-Église, farther inland, was a piece of relatively high and dry ground. It was bounded on one side by the tidal salt marshes just a few hundred yards inland from the shoreline and on the other three sides by the swampy floodplains of the rivers around Sainte-Mère-Église.

The two critical missions for VII Corps once it gained the shore were to move inland as fast and as far as possible while blocking German reinforcements that were expected to move into the area in an effort to cut off the beachhead. The key to accomplishing both of those tasks was to secure control of one or both of the only two usable bridges over the Merdert River, one at Chef-du-Pont, southwest of Sainte-Mère-Église, and the other at La Fière, two miles west of the town. The ancient stone bridge at La Fière was close to the east bank of the river, but then the unpaved road from the bridge followed along the top of a very narrow elevated causeway, running through the river's west-bank floodplain for some 500 yards to a small group of buildings on the firmer ground at Cauquigny.

Seizing both bridges and securing the exits from the bridgeheads was entrusted to the 82nd Airborne Division, commanded by Major General Matthew Ridgway, with Brigadier General James Gavin as assistant division commander. The best way to take a bridge is both ends simultaneously. According to the operations plan, the 507th and 508th Parachute Infantry Regiments (PIR) jumped into drop zones west of the Merdert, beyond the flooded area. The 505th PIR dropped on the east bank, between the river and Sainte-Mère-Église. Its mission was to capture the town, secure the eastern ends of both bridgeheads, and then link up with the 507th and 508th.

The weather was poor in the early morning hours of June 6. Low cloud cover and heavy German antiaircraft fire broke up the formations of Douglas C-47 transports carrying the 507th and 508th PIRs, who were therefore scattered over a wide area. Indeed, many of the paratroopers landed east of the river.

The 505th PIR was lucky enough to make a relatively tight drop. Half of the regiment landed within a mile of the designated drop zones. The 3rd Battalion of the 505th secured Sainte-Mère-Église by 4:30 a.m. The 1st Battalion meanwhile captured Manoir de la Fière, a small group of stone farm buildings close to the east end of the bridge. About the time the manor was secured, a small element from the 507th occupied the group of buildings at Cauquigny. The 82nd held the bridge and both ends of the causeway, at least for the moment.

As always, the Germans reacted quickly. At 5:30 a.m. a company from the 91st Air

Landing Division's 1057th Grenadier Regiment, reinforced with four tanks from the 100th Panzer Training and Replacement Battalion, attacked Cauquigny. Pushing the Americans out, the Germans then attacked straight down the causeway toward La Fière. Fierce fighting followed, but the 505th PIR managed to stop the Germans and knock out two of the tanks. But at the end of June 6, the western end of the causeway was still in German hands.

On June 7 the Germans again attacked, this time supported by artillery and mortar fire. The battle raged back and forth all day as the Americans held on grimly. Early that morning the 82nd's 325th Glider Infantry Regiment landed. Later in the day troops of its 1st Battalion waded across the inundated floodplain north of La Fière and attempted to flank the Germans at Cauguigny. But the glider men encountered a large German force and were pinned down. The Germans still held Cauguigny.

After the 325th's attack failed, Ridgway ordered Gavin to launch a frontal assault straight down the causeway. Gavin designated the 3rd Battalion of the 325th as the spearhead, with a scratch company from the 507th PIR in reserve. Supported by 155mm howitzers from the 90th Infantry Division's 345th Field Artillery Battalion, which had moved up from the beach, the assault started at 10:30 a.m. on June 9. The point elements made it across the causeway and reached Cauguigny, but there the attack faltered under the press of mounting casualties. Gavin then committed his small reserve of 507th paratroopers commanded by Captain Robert Rae. That last desperate push tipped the balance. By the end of June 9 the men of the 90th Infantry Division were passing over the causeway and fanning out into the Cotentin Peninsula beyond. The Utah Beach landings had been secured.

David T. Zabecki

Further Reading

Crookenden, Napier. *Drop Zone Normandy.* New York: Macmillan, 1976.

Harrison, Gordon A. *United States Army in World War II: The European Theater of Operations; Cross Channel Attack.* Washington, DC: U.S. Army, Office of the Chief of Military History, 1951.

Marshall, S. L. A. *Night Drop: The American Airborne Invasion of Normandy.* Boston: Little, Brown, 1962.

Nordyke, Phil. *All American, All the Way: The Combat History of the 82nd Airborne Division in World War II.* New York: Zenith, 2005.

Ryan, Cornelius. *The Longest Day.* New York: Simon and Schuster, 1959.

Landing Craft

Both sides utilized amphibious warfare during World War II. Early landing craft were usually improvised from conventional vessels such as barges and ferries, but purpose-built craft were developed to land troops and equipment on hostile shores. Such specialized vessels allowed an attacker to land a larger number of men and their equipment and do so faster and in a smaller area than would otherwise be possible. Modified craft continued to be used during the war, however, notably by General Douglas MacArthur's forces in the Southwest Pacific.

Although before the war the U.S. Marine Corps had embraced amphibious warfare as its raison d'être, it took the practical demands of World War II to force mass production of landing craft and amphibious tractors. Only the United States built large numbers of amphibious wheeled and tracked vehicles that allowed the transport of men and equipment from ship to shore and then inland.

Landing craft came in a wide variety of forms. They were armored and unarmored and were designed to transport both personnel and vehicles. Some had bow ramps, and others had a fixed-bow configuration. Most landing craft, however, had a blunt bow, were powered by diesel engines acting on twin screws, were anchored at the stern, and had a shallow draft forward, a flat bottom, and a bow ramp. This ramp allowed the rapid unloading of men or cargo.

The Western Allies and especially the United States built by far the largest number of landing craft during the war to meet needs in both the European and Pacific theaters. Allied troops had to invade and secure areas in the Mediterranean and then invade Northwestern Europe, and in the Pacific they had to recapture the various islands held by the Japanese.

Many Allied landing craft were quite large and transported smaller landing craft. The craft were identified not by name but instead by numbers appended to the general designation. Landing craft also had a wide number of specialist variants. The most common types of British and U.S. landing craft employed in the Normandy invasion are as follows:

Great Britain

LCA (landing craft assault). The chief purpose of the LCA was to move troops from transport ships to a hostile enemy shore. The equivalent of the U.S. LCVP (landing craft vehicle and personnel), it was made of plywood and had a flat-bottom hull. Armored plates could be added to provide some protection. Slow speed and heavy weight were the LCA's chief drawbacks.

The LCA had a crew of 4 and could carry 36 troops or 8,000 pounds of cargo. It had a bow ramp, displaced 9 tons, and was 41 feet 6 inches in length and 10 feet in beam. Loaded draft was 1 feet 9 inches forward and 2 feet 3 inches aft. Propelled by two 65-horsepower Ford V-8 gasoline engines, it had a range of 50–80 miles and a rated loaded speed of 6 knots. It was armed with one .30-caliber light machine gun and two .303 Lewis guns.

Used in virtually all theaters of the war, LCAs on June 6, 1944, landed troops on the three British invasion beaches of Juno, Gold, and Sword. They also put ashore the U.S. infantry on the two flanks of the U.S. Omaha Beach and the rangers who assaulted Pointe du Hoc and served during the westernmost landings on Utah Beach as well as the predawn landing on Îles Saint-Marcouf. LCAs were manufactured beginning in 1939, and something fewer than 2,000 were produced.

LCT (landing craft tank Mk4). The LCT was the largest British landing vessel of the war and the equivalent of the U.S. LST. First built in 1941, the LCT was produced in six different models (Mk1–Mk6) during the war.

The LCT Mk4 had a crew of 13 and could transport 3 light tanks or 356 tons of cargo. It had a bow ramp and displaced 595 tons. It was 187 feet 3 inches in length, with a beam of 38 feet 9 inches. Draft was 3 feet 8 inches forward. Its two 460-horsepower Paxman diesel engines gave it a rated speed of 8 knots and a range of some 1,100 miles. It could transport 356 tons of cargo. Armament consisted of two 20mm cannon or two Bofers 40mm guns.

LCTs were employed by the Americans as well as the British and saw wide service during the Normandy campaign. Some even served in the Korean War and the Vietnam War. A total of 2,633 LCTs were produced during World War II, of which 865 were Mk4s.

LCT-R (landing craft tank–rocket). The LCT-R was developed from the LCT Mk3 and was designed to provide withering artillery fire just in advance of a shore assault.

The landing ramp was welded shut, and a second deck was added to accommodate installation of the rocket launch tubes. This necessitated a higher bridge aft. The LCT-R mounted 1,044 3-inch RP-3 rockets, while the lower deck provided storage for up to 5,000 additional rockets. Firing occurred in 24 successive bursts of 39–42 rockets each. The rockets had a range of some 1,000 yards. The LCT-R had a speed of some 9 knots.

United States
LCVP (landing craft vehicle, personnel, also known as the Higgins Boat). Designed by entrepreneur Andrew J. Higgins and with a plywood hull, the LCVP was inspired by watercraft specifically constructed for use in swamps and marshes. The LCVP displaced some 9 tons. It had a crew of 4 and could carry 36 troops, a jeep, and 12 infantrymen or 8,000 pounds of cargo.

The LCVP was 36 feet 3 inches in length and 10 feet 10 inches in beam. It had a draft of 2 feet 2 inches forward and 3 feet aft. Powered by a 225-horsepower Gray Marine diesel engine or a 250-horsepower Hall-Scott gasoline engine, at 12 knots the LCVP had greater speed than its British counterpart. Armament was provided by two .30-caliber Browning machine guns. First produced in 1941, 23,358 LCVPs were manufactured.

LCI (landing craft infantry). The LCI was designed to land infantry and was developed in response to a request from the British for a craft capable of landing many more men than the small LCA. The result was a small steel ship capable of landing some 200 men.

The LCI entered service in 1943. It had a crew of 24 officers and men and could carry 180 troops, later 210. It displaced 238 tons and was 158 feet 6 inches in length with a beam of 23 feet 3 inches. It had a draft of 5 feet 4 inches forward and 5 feet 11 inches aft. Powered by eight GM diesel engines on two shafts (four engines per shaft), with 1,600 horsepower, the LCI could reach a speed of 16 knots and had a range of 4,603 miles. Armament consisted of four Oerlikon 20mm cannon. Some LCIs were used to lay a smoke screen in a landing, while others provided close-in gunfire support to troops already ashore. A total of 923 LCIs were manufactured by a wide range of builders.

LCM (landing craft mechanized). The LCM was a landing craft designed primarily to land vehicles. It had a crew of four. The LCM-3 version, produced by Higgins Industries, had a displacement of 52 tons loaded. It was 50 feet in length and 14 feet in beam, with a draft of 3 feet forward and 4 feet aft. Propelled by two 110-horsepower diesel engines, it was capable of eight knots loaded. It could transport a 30-ton tank (e.g., the M4 Sherman), 60 fully equipped troops (twice the number of a LCVP), or 30 tons of cargo. Armament was two Browning .50-caliber machine guns.

LST (landing ship tank). Its crews said that "LST" stood for "long slow target," but the LST was a very successful vessel type intended to be seagoing craft to deliver vehicles and bulk supplies directly to the shore. The United States altered the original British design and produced them for both nations. The British later modified some of the designs for their own use.

The LST was undoubtedly the most widely known larger landing vessel of the war and a staple of the later landings in the Pacific theater. The common LST crew complement was some 110 men. Produced in a number of different classes, the most common LST, the Mk2, was 327 feet 9 inches in overall length, with a beam of 50 feet and displacement of 1,809 tons (3,942 tons fully loaded). Draft when loaded was 8 feet 2

Jeeps of the U.S. Army 5th Engineer Special Brigade debark from a Landing Ship Tank (LST) at Fox Green, Omaha Beach, Normandy, June 12, 1944. (MPI/Getty Images)

inches forward and 14 feet 1 inches aft. Powered by two General Motors 12–567 diesel engines on two shafts and fitted with twin rudders, LSTs were capable of 12 knots.

The bow of the ship opened, allowing the front ramp to drop and the crew to land cargo directly on a shore. LSTs could carry 2,100 tons of material or 20 tanks or 400 troops. The LST could carry smaller landing craft and was configured with davits to lower the personnel-carrying LCVPs over the sides. Some LSTs carried only two LCVPs in this fashion, while others carried six. LSTs were armed with one 3-inch gun, six 40mm and six 20mm antiaircraft guns, and two .50-caliber and four .30-caliber machine guns.

LSTs proved to be remarkably versatile. During the Normandy invasion 38 were converted into small hospital ships. Through September 28, 1944, LSTs had transported 41,035 wounded men back to England from Normandy. Some LSTs, fitted with extra cranes, were employed as ammunition ships. Some 1,000 LSTs were manufactured in the United States during the war. Requisitioned from the Japanese, LSTs saw important service in the Korean War, notably in the Inchon Landing of September 1950.

DUKW. The Allies also developed true amphibians capable of transporting men and equipment from ship to shore and then inland. Of these the best known is undoubtedly the DUKW (an administrative code for a 1942 model amphibious four-wheel-drive truck). Manufactured by the General Motors Corporation, the DUKW was powered by a GMC six-cylinder 94-horsepower engine and had both a propeller and wheels that moved it at 5.5 knots in the water and up to 50 miles per hour on land. It had an operational range of about 400 miles on land. It weighed 6.5 tons and was 32 feet in length and 8 feet 4 inches in width. The DUKW had a crew of 1 and carried 12 troops or 5,000 pounds of cargo. It was particularly useful for transporting litters of wounded.

All DUKWs were fitted with a ring mount, and perhaps a quarter were armed with a single .50-caliber machine gun. A total of 21,147 DUKWs were built. A number of these popular amphibians remain in service today as tourist attractions.

Landing craft were immensely important to the Allies throughout the war, so much so that U.S. Army chief of staff George C. Marshall stated in 1943 that "Prior to the present war I never heard of landing craft except as a rubber boat. Now I think of nothing else." The availability of landing craft dictated timetables for Allied amphibious actions, and the shortage of them precluded simultaneous landings in northern France (in the June 6, 1944, Operation OVERLORD) and southern France (in the August 15, 1944, Operation ANVIL-DRAGOON). Some historians have argued that U.S. chief of naval operations Admiral Ernest J. King placed too many landing craft in the Pacific, thus hindering Allied efforts in Europe. Current scholarship has concluded that the major problem was overcommitment within the European theater itself.

Far less glamorous than combatant vessels, landing craft were nonetheless an essential element in the Allied victory in World War II, just as they continue to be an integral part of naval operations today.

Spencer C. Tucker

Further Reading

Baker, A. D., III. *Allied Landing Craft of World War Two*. Annapolis, MD: Naval Institute Press, 1985.

Bartlett, Merrill L., ed. *Assault from the Sea: Essays on the History of Amphibious Warfare*. Annapolis, MD: Naval Institute Press, 1983.

Chesneau, Roger, ed. *Conway's All the World's Fighting Ships, 1922–1946*. London: Conway Maritime, 1980.

Coakley, Robert W., and Richard M. Leighton. *Global Logistics and Strategy*. Washington, DC: Office of the Chief of Military History, Department of the Army, 1968.

Morison, Samuel Eliot. *The Two-Ocean War*. New York: Galahad Books, 1963.

Lee, John Clifford Hodges (1887–1958)

U.S. Army lieutenant general. Born in Junction City, Kansas, on August 1, 1887, John Clifford Hodges Lee graduated from the U.S. Military Academy at West Point in 1909 and was commissioned in the Corps of Engineers. During World War I he served as aide to Major General Leonard Wood, commanding general of the 89th Division, then as chief of staff of the 89th Division. Lee graduated from the Army General Staff Training Course at Langres in 1918 and was actively involved with the planning of the Saint-Mihiel and Meuse-Argonne Offensives. He ended the war as a temporary colonel.

During the interwar years, Lee graduated from the Army War College (1932) and the Army Industrial College (1933). He oversaw numerous harbor and river projects and commanded the San Francisco Port of Embarkation (1940). Promoted to brigadier general in October 1940, the arrogant Lee, whose initials were J. C. H., came to be known as "Jesus Christ Himself." In November 1941 he assumed command of the 2nd Infantry Division, and in February 1942 he was promoted to major general.

That May, Lee took command of the Services of Supply (SOS) in the United

Kingdom to oversee the greatest engineering project of the war: the massive buildup of men and supplies for the invasion of occupied Europe, code-named BOLERO. In addition to commanding the SOS (designated the Communications Zone [COMMZ] on June 7, 1944) and acting as the G-4 (assistant chief of staff for logistics) for the European theater of operations, U.S. Army Headquarters, Lee served as deputy theater commander, with special responsibility for administration and supply, from January to July 1944. He was promoted to lieutenant general in February 1944.

With the dissolution of the COMMZ at the end of the war, Lee took charge of the successor command—Theater Service Forces, European theater. In January 1946, he was assigned as commanding general of the Mediterranean theater and deputy supreme commander of Allied Forces, Mediterranean. Lee retired from the army in December 1947 and died in York, Pennsylvania, on August 30, 1958.

Steve R. Waddell

Further Reading

Ruppenthal, Roland G. *The U.S. Army in World War II: The European Theater of Operations; Logistical Support of the Armies.* 2 vols. Washington, DC: Center of Military History, 1953, 1959.

Waddell, Steve R. *U.S. Army Logistics: The Normandy Campaign, 1944.* Westport, CT: Greenwood, 1994.

Leigh-Mallory, Sir Trafford (1892–1944)

British air chief marshal. Born in Mobberley, Cheshire, England, on July 11, 1892, Trafford Leigh-Mallory graduated with honors from Cambridge University. He served in the British Army in the infantry during World War I but transferred to the Royal Flying Corps in 1916. By war's end, he commanded a fighter squadron.

Leigh-Mallory remained with the Royal Air Force (RAF) after the war and graduated from both the RAF Staff College and the Imperial Defence College. He also taught at the Army Staff College. He was promoted to air commodore in 1936 and to air vice marshal in 1938.

In 1937 Leigh-Mallory assumed command of the Number 12 Fighter Group, a post he held when the war started. During the July 10–September 30, 1940, Battle of Britain, his primary responsibility was defense of the Midlands industrial area and reinforcing the Number 11 Fighter Group over southeastern England. He disagreed with his counterpart at Number 11, Air Vice Marshal Keith Park, and with the head of Fighter Command, Air Chief Marshal Hugh Dowding, concerning which fighter tactics best opposed the Luftwaffe.

Leigh-Mallory favored the so-called Big Wing tactic involving multiple squadrons striking the attacking Luftwaffe with all available air assets at once, which because of the assembly required meant that the defenders were sometimes slow to respond. Park and Dowding supported repeated single-squadron attacks with quicker response times. In actions that bordered on insubordination, Leigh-Mallory boasted that he would secure Dowding's removal. That prediction became reality when Air Chief Marshal Sir Charles Portal backed Leigh-Mallory, which led to Dowding's dismissal in November 1940 and Park's transfer the next month. Air Marshal William Sholto Douglas, the new Fighter Command chief, named Leigh-Mallory to command the Number 11 Fighter Group.

Under his command, the Number 11 Group instituted his Big Wing tactics but with only marginally greater success than previously experienced. Leigh-Mallory began offensive air operations against Luftwaffe airfields in France, and he commanded the air support for the ill-fated August 19, 1942, Dieppe Raid. In November 1942 he assumed leadership of the RAF Fighter Command. Leigh-Mallory emphasized operations known as "rhubarbs," "circuses," and "beehives"—hunter-killer flights of hundreds of fighter aircraft, often combined with bombers, that flew at low level over France in search of Luftwaffe targets of opportunity. Such operations were considered ineffective by many and incurred grievous losses.

In November 1943, the Combined Chiefs of Staff named Leigh-Mallory commander of the Allied Expeditionary Air Forces for Operation OVERLORD, the invasion of Normandy on June 6, 1944. Promoted to air chief marshal in December 1943, Leigh-Mallory directed Allied fighter attacks in his "Transportation Plan" against railroad marshaling yards in an effort to disrupt German reinforcement efforts against the Normandy beachhead. On D-Day he commanded 9,000 aircraft, and his pilots swept the skies over the beaches to clear them of German fighters.

Leigh-Mallory's job of coordinating Allied tactical air forces was largely completed by October 1944, when he was named to command all Allied air forces in the Far East. En route to his new post, he and his wife were both killed when the airplane in which they were passengers crashed near Grenoble, France, on November 14, 1944.

Thomas D. Veve

Further Reading

Bungay, Stephen. *The Most Dangerous Enemy: A History of the Battle of Britain*. London: Aurum, 2000.

Johnson, David Alan. *The Battle of Britain*. Conshohocken, PA: Combined Publishing, 1998.

Newton Dunn, Bill. *Big Wing: The Biography of Air Chief Marshal Sir Trafford Leigh-Mallory*. Shrewsbury, UK: Airlife, 1992.

Townsend, Peter. *Duel of Eagles*. London: Orion, 2000.

LÜTTICH, Operation (Mortain Counteroffensive, August 7–13, 1944)

Named for a German victory in Belgium early in World War I, Operation LÜTTICH (known to the British and Americans as the Mortain Counteroffensive or the Battle of Mortain) was the German effort to wipe out the gains made by the U.S. First Army in Operation COBRA and ultimately drive the Allied armies from Normandy. The fighting occurred in the vicinity of Mortain, Normandy, during August 7–13, 1944.

Following the success of COBRA, on August 2 Adolf Hitler ordered Field Marshal Günther von Kluge, German commander in the West and, after Rommel was injured on July 17, commander of Army Group B confronting the Allied forces in Normandy, to mount a counteroffensive with the goal of driving back the U.S. First Army and reaching the coast of the Cotentin Peninsula in the vicinity of Avranches, thereby cutting off the U.S. Third Army, which had moved into Brittany. Hitler demanded that the attack include "all available panzer units, regardless of their present commitment." Hitler's decision changed the course of the campaign for France and decided the Normandy campaign.

The attack orders went out to the German units involved on the night of August 6. Some accounts hold that Ultra, the Allied code-breaking operation, revealed the German plans and gave the Americans time to prepare. This is not true. Ultra intelligence did not reach the units involved until midnight on August 6, and the German attack occurred so soon thereafter that there was no time to change troop dispositions to meet it.

The attack was to occur through Mortain, which had already fallen to the Americans. Kluge had at his disposal the newly formed XLVII Panzer Corps of four panzer divisions (two of them SS), along with two infantry divisions and five battle groups. Opposing them was the U.S. VII Corps, commanded by Major General J. Lawton Collins, of five infantry divisions and three armored combat commands.

Major General Leland S. Hobbs's 30th Infantry Division absorbed the bulk of the German attack, and the division's stubborn resistance repulsed the German thrust. The key role on the ground was played by the 2nd Battalion of the 120th Infantry Regiment occupying Hill 317, the dominant terrain feature near Mortain. Supported by tactical air strikes and sustained by supply drops, the battalion held off the 2nd Panzer Division until it was relieved by the U.S. 35th Division on August 12. Of some 700 men in the battalion, more than 300 died in the battle.

Airpower was decisive. Daylight on August 7 saw the German forces under savage air attack. German commanders had warned Hitler that a concentrated armor thrust could not succeed against the overwhelming strength of Allied tactical airpower, and this proved correct. Aircraft of the U.S. Army Air Forces IX Tactical Air Command and the Royal Air Force (RAF) Second Tactical Air Force savaged the attacking German tanks and infantry. RAF rocket-firing Hawker Typhoon ground-attack aircraft were particularly effective against the German armor. So many Typhoons were involved on August 7 that there were actually several air collisions. From morning to late afternoon, Typhoons flew 294 sorties over the battlefield. Supreme commander of the Allied Expeditionary Force General Dwight D. Eisenhower credited the Typhoons with having been decisive in the battle's outcome.

Within a day the Americans had regained the initiative. The Germans foolishly continued their attacks, however, allowing VII Corps to attack from the flanks. In the fighting, VII Corps sustained some 2,000–3,000 killed. German personnel losses are unknown, but reportedly Germany lost some 150 tanks, half of its attacking force. As Hitler had put it on August 2, "The outcome of the whole campaign in France depends on the success of this attack." In effect, in ordering the attack he had merely speeded up the German defeat in northwestern France and set the stage for the next great Allied air-land victory.

As early as August 8, U.S. ground forces commander Lieutenant General Omar N. Bradley was confident that the Mortain counterattack had been contained and that there was now opportunity for an encirclement from north and south. In the presence of General Eisenhower, then at his headquarters, Bradley telephoned British ground forces commander General Bernard Montgomery and secured approval for a bold course of action designed to encircle the German forces west of Argentan and Falaise. This turned into the great killing ground of the Falaise–Argentan pocket (August 12–21).

Spencer C. Tucker

Further Reading

Buisson, Jules, and Gilles Buisson. *Mortain et sa bataille, 2–13 août 1944.* Paris: Le Livre d'Histoire, 2004.

D'Este, Carlo. *Decision in Normandy.* New York: E. P. Dutton, 1983.

Fey, William. *Armor Battles of the Waffen-SS.* Lancaster, PA: Stackpole Books, 2003.

Gooderson, Ian. *Air Power at the Battlefront: Allied Close Air Support in Europe, 1943–45.* London: Frank Cass, 1997.

Hallion, Richard P. *The U.S. Army Air Forces in World War II: D-Day 1944, Air Power over the Normandy Beaches and Beyond.* Washington, DC: U.S. Air Force History and Museum Program, 1994.

Lewin, Ronald. *Ultra Goes to War.* New York: McGraw-Hill, 1978.

Van Der Vat, Dan. *D-Day: The Greatest Invasion; A People's History.* New York: Bloomsbury, 2003.

Lyme Bay, Battle of (April 28, 1944)

In preparation for their invasion of Normandy, some 30,000 U.S. troops were to participate in Exercise TIGER, consisting of practice landings at Slapton Beach on the coast of Devon in southeastern England. The area had been selected for its resemblance to the designated invasion site of Utah Beach on France's Normandy coast. Exercise TIGER was to last from April 22 to April 30, 1944.

The first practice assault, on April 27, 1944, proceeded smoothly, but the next, on the morning of April 28, became a nightmare for those involved. The troops were embarked on nine tank landing ships (LSTs), which were to have been protected by a Royal Navy force of the destroyer *Scimitar,* the Flower-class corvette *Azalea,* three motor torpedo boats, and two motor gunboats patrolling the entrance to Lyme Bay, where the exercise was to occur. In addition, other motor torpedo boats were to have under surveillance the French port of Cherbourg, where German motor torpedo boats (S-boats) were based. However, the *Scimitar* had been rammed the previous day and was at Portsmouth for repairs, and its replacement did not sail because of a mix-up in the shore command. The U.S. commander, Read Admiral Don Pardee Moon, learned of this only after the operation was under way.

On the morning of April 28, nine German S-boats of the 9th Flotilla (*S-100, S-130, S-136, S-138, S-140, S-142, S-143, S-145,* and *S-150*) that had departed on patrol from Cherbourg crossed the channel. They were engaged by British destroyers, and the *Azalea*'s commander received an enemy alert shortly after midnight. However, he continued to lead the LSTs in a straight-line formation, making them an easy target, and did not attempt to warn the U.S. vessels.

The German S-boats spotted the convoy of LSTs in Lyme Bay and, after tracking it for a half hour, attacked it with torpedoes, hitting *LST-507* at 2:03 a.m. A large fire broke out and quickly spread amid the stored vehicles and ammunition, forcing the embarked soldiers and crew to abandon ship. Many soldiers panicked, put on their life belts incorrectly, and were drowned in the frigid 42-degree water. More than 260 of the vessel's crew and passengers perished.

At 2:17 a.m., *LST-531,* in the middle of the U.S. column, exploded under the impact of two torpedoes. It sank within six minutes, with the loss of 467 men. A torpedo also hit *LST-289,* but it remained afloat and lost only 13 men in the explosion. Friendly fire damaged *LST-511.*

The escort HMS *Azalea* returned up the column after the first explosion, but its crew could not determine the source of the attack. The corvette's crew was unable to seek information because, owing to a typographical error in their orders, the U.S. and British were using different radio frequencies and could not communicate.

After the Germans had expended their torpedoes, several LSTs returned and rescued survivors. They were joined by HMS *Saladin,* the relief escort for the *Scimitar.* Eyewitnesses reported that sections of the sea were covered with corpses. Although figures vary, deaths caused by the German attack probably totaled 198 sailors and 551 soldiers. Another 200 personnel were wounded. The German S-boats returned to Cherbourg unscathed.

Official embarrassment and concern that disclosure might compromise the Normandy landings led to the order that the events of April 28 be kept secret. Indeed, 10 officers killed in the action had detailed knowledge of the forthcoming invasion that they could have revealed had they been captured, and the invasion was on hold until their bodies were located and identified. Exercise TIGER did not become public until after the end of the war. Even today, there is little documentation available about events on April 28. The events of that day did lead to better coordination, more extensive training in life belt use, and the inclusion of more small craft in the actual Normandy landings in order to pick up men in the water.

Spencer C. Tucker

Further Reading

Garn, Kenneth H. *The Secret D-Day.* Bowie, MD: Heritage Books, 1994.

Lewis, Nigel. *Exercise Tiger: The Dramatic True Story of a Hidden Tragedy of World War.* Upper Saddle River, NJ: Prentice Hall, 1990.

Small, Ken, and Mark Rogerson. *The Forgotten Dead: Why 946 American Servicemen Died off the Coast of Devon in 1944—and the Man Who Discovered Their True Story.* London: Bloomsbury, 1988.

Tent, James Foster. *E-Boat Alert: Defending the Normandy Invasion Fleet.* Annapolis, MD: Naval Institute Press, 1996.

M

Machine Guns

Machine guns are relatively small-caliber, automatic-fire, crew-served weapons. The machine gun of World War II was a weapon class in itself. In World War I, machine guns were mainly heavy, water-cooled, belt-fed weapons mounted on heavy tripods and used for trench defense or for long-range suppressive fire. The need for machine guns in aircraft and the invention of the British Lewis gun during World War I, however, created a new form of machine gun.

Germany and the United States were the first nations to develop the light machine gun (LMG) for infantry assault use. The Germans stripped down their Machinengewehr 08/15 (MG-08/15), fitted it with a bipod and a rudimentary stock, and reduced the operational weight to 28 pounds. The resulting MG-34, with its 75-round drum magazine, could be carried by a man on the battlefield. It was produced in large numbers throughout the war. In 1942, the Germans introduced the MG-42.

Machine guns of the period operated either by recoil or by gas. Recoil-operated machine guns, such as the German MG-34 and MG-42, often had high rates of fire. When the cartridge was fired, the recoil was used to eject the spent cartridge by pushing the breechblock rearward against a spring, after a safety delay. The spring then forced the breechblock forward again and in so doing reloaded the weapon, which fired as soon as the breech was locked. Gas-operated weapons used gas from the cartridge discharge, which was bled off from a gas port in the barrel. This operated a gas piston, which interacted with the breechblock to extract and reload the weapon.

After World War I, machine guns were classified as either heavy or light. The heavy versions were still mounted on tripods, equipped with both direct and indirect sighting methods, and used for direct shooting and long-range interdictory fire. The LMGs, however, were the weapons used prolifically by the infantry. These weapons were often but not always fed by magazines or cartridge strips. They were fitted with bipod legs and could be carried in battle by one man. Because of the high rate of ammunition expenditure, one other man or two other men normally accompanied the light machine-gunner, carrying spare ammunition and sometimes spare barrels.

Ammunition for the machine gun was supplied in various ways. One method was the strip, in which a number of rounds were held on a metal base that was fed through the gun and then reloaded when empty. Another method was the magazine, which was a spring-loaded box or drum fitted to the gun that could be replaced when empty. Magazines held about 30 rounds of ammunition, and weapons so fitted included the British Bren.

Belt feeds, which allowed sustained long-range fire, were found, for example, on the Browning M-1917AI and M-1919A4 .30-caliber machine guns, the German MG-34 and MG-42 guns, and the British Besa 7.92mm gun (mainly used as coaxial tank armament).

The LMG was issued on the basis of one weapon to every 7 to 10 men, meaning that every infantry platoon had three or four of them, though this varied from army to army; U.S. infantry platoons, for instance, were armed only with the Browning Automatic Rifle and not LMGs. Infantry usually could also call on support from the heavy machine guns if needed. World War II infantry tactics were based on fire and movement, with the LMG firing and the riflemen of a section moving or vice versa. In the British Army the LMG was considered a support weapon, allowing the riflemen to close on the enemy and attack with the bayonet. The Germans saw the LMG as the main weapon with which to win a firefight with the enemy, who was then to be rolled up by the infantrymen in the section.

U.S. Army infantry companies were equipped with LMGs. The M-1917 series water-cooled, .30-caliber Browning LMG was used by U.S. units throughout the war. It was belt-fed and could be carried in the company as well as fitted to just about every vehicle in or near the front line. It led to the M-1919 series of .30-caliber air-cooled machine guns that were the principal U.S. machine guns of the war. They were only moderately accurate, as they had no butt stock to allow effective fire control but instead were fired with a pistol grip at the rear of the gun body. The M-1919A6, based on the same receiver, did have a butt stock and was fired from a bipod.

Backing up these weapons was the .50-caliber Browning. The M-1921 series was originally a water-cooled weapon developed to attack aircraft and observation balloons. Its air-cooled offspring, the M-2 series ("Ma Deuce"), was used by every U.S. branch in every environment and theater of the war. It could be fired from a tripod mount or fixed on vehicles and could be set for single-shot fire, although it was not intended for use against personnel. The M-2 .50-caliber

U.S. soldiers manning a Browning M-2 .50 caliber machine gun in their armored vehicle in England shortly before departing for France in the Normandy invasion. (Galerie Bilderwelt/ Getty Images)

gun was also fitted in a number of aircraft, equipped with a lighter barrel and often with a solenoid firing mechanism. It is still in service in many armies today, including the U.S. Army.

The Lewis gun, employed by British infantry initially, was soon replaced by the Enfield version of an LMG produced on license from the Brno arms firm of Czechoslovakia. Known as the Bren gun, it was regarded by many as the finest LMG ever made. The Bren was a .303-caliber, detachable-box, magazine-fed, gas-operated weapon with a rate of fire of 450 to 540 rounds per minute. It was accurate and had a quick barrel-change system that coped with rapid firing. The Bren gun served throughout World War II and was well respected, although its rate of fire and the tactical restrictions placed on it meant that it was no match in a firefight with its German equivalent. The British also used the famous Vickers .303 machine gun in a support role.

Machine guns were used not only by the infantry, however. They were also mounted in tanks for protection against infantry and for air defense. Most tanks had a coaxial rifle-caliber machine gun fitted in the turret and another in the hull, the latter operated by the driver, the codriver, or the radio operator. These machine guns were of great value in suppressing enemy machine guns and artillery when use of the main armament was ineffective or impossible.

The Americans and Germans also linked two or more machine guns for antiaircraft use. U.S. tanks were equipped with .50-caliber machine guns for antiaircraft defense, the gun being fitted above the commander's cupola on the tank and capable of a 360-degree traverse and a 90-degree elevation. Although the .50-caliber machine gun was a formidable weapon, it had few antiaircraft successes and was more often used in the ground role for attacking soft-skinned vehicles and buildings.

Aircraft were also fitted with machine guns. The British Spitfire, for example, carried eight .303-caliber machine guns, but these were short-range guns and were relatively ineffective against German aircraft. The British also employed the .303-caliber machine gun for bomber defense. The Americans entered the war with the .50-caliber weapon in their aircraft, which could inflict great damage on German and Japanese fighter aircraft. The Germans, however, were using 20mm and 30mm cannon from the start, and they soon learned that one hit from such a weapon was worth more than any number of .303 rounds and better than a burst of .50-caliber (roughly 12.7mm) ammunition.

The British turned to the 20mm cannon for later versions of their fighter aircraft, and the weapon proved singularly effective. The smaller caliber also meant that more ammunition could be carried per gun as compared with the German 30mm cannon, but the Germans turned to another air weapon: the antiaircraft rocket. American fighter aircraft, however, continued to utilize the .50-caliber gun.

Naval use of machine guns was limited, although early World War II warships carried some machine guns for local protection. It was soon found, however, that much heavier weapons were needed for antiaircraft protection, and in most cases the light and heavy machine guns went into lockers. Naval aircraft reflected their ground-based counterparts in terms of the weapons fitted on them.

David Westwood

Further Reading

Allen, W. G. B. *Pistols, Rifles and Machine Guns.* London: EUP, 1953.

Daniker, Gustav. *Die Maschinenwaffen im Rahmen der Taktik.* Berlin: E. S. Mittler and Sohn, 1942.

Smith, W. H. B., and Joseph Edward Smith. *Small Arms of the World: A Basic Manual of Small Arms.* 9th ed. Harrisburg, PA: Stackpole Books, 1969.

Marshall, George Catlett (1880–1959)

U.S. Army general, chief of staff of the army, secretary of state (1947–1949), and secretary of defense (1950–1951). Born in Uniontown, Pennsylvania, on December 31, 1880, George Catlett Marshall graduated from the Virginia Military Institute in 1901. Commissioned in the infantry in 1902, he then held a variety of assignments, including in the Philippines. He attended the Infantry and Cavalry School, Fort Leavenworth, in 1907 and was an instructor at the Staff College between 1907 and 1908.

After the United States entered World War I, Marshall went to France with the American Expeditionary Forces as training officer to the 1st Division in June 1917. Promoted to lieutenant colonel in 1918, he became chief of operations of the U.S. First Army, winning admiration for his logistical skills in directing the repositioning of hundreds of thousands of men quickly across the battlefront for the Meuse-Argonne Offensive. After working on occupation plans for Germany, Marshall became aide to General John J. Pershing, who was named chief of staff of the army in 1921.

Beginning in 1924, Marshall spent three years in Tianjin (Tientsin), China, with the 15th Infantry Regiment, then five years as assistant commandant in charge of instruction at the Infantry School, Fort Benning, Georgia, where he helped to train numerous future U.S. generals. He was promoted to colonel in 1932, holding assorted command posts in the continental United States. He was promoted to brigadier general in 1936.

In 1938 Marshall became head of the War Plans Division in Washington, then deputy chief of staff with promotion to major general that July. President Franklin D. Roosevelt promoted Marshall over many more senior officers to appoint him chief of staff of the army as a temporary general on September 1, 1939, the day that German armies invaded Poland. As war began in Europe, Marshall worked to revitalize the American defense establishment. Supported by pro-Allied civilians such as Secretary of War Henry L. Stimson, Marshall instituted and lobbied for programs to recruit and train new troops; expedite munitions production; assist Great Britain, China, and the Soviet Union in resisting the Axis powers; and coordinate British and American strategy. After the United States entered the war in December 1941, Marshall presided over an increase in the U.S. Army from a mere 200,000 men to a wartime maximum of 8 million men and women. For this he became known as the "Organizer of Victory."

Marshall was a strong supporter of opening a second front in Europe, a campaign ultimately deferred until June 1944. Between 1941 and 1945 he attended all the major wartime strategic conferences, including those at Washington, D.C., as well as Placentia Bay, Quebec, Cairo, Tehran, Malta, Yalta, and Potsdam. Marshall was the first to be promoted to the newly authorized five-star rank of general of the army in December 1944. Perhaps his greatest disappointment was that he did not exercise field command, especially command of the European invasion forces. Roosevelt and the other wartime chiefs wanted him to remain in Washington, and Marshall bowed to their wishes. He was a major supporter of the Army Air Forces, and in 1945 he advocated use of the atomic bomb against Japan.

On the urging of President Harry S. Truman, Marshall agreed to serve as special envoy to China (1945–1947). As secretary of state, he advanced the Marshall Plan to rebuild Europe, and he then served as president of the American Red Cross (1949–1950). Truman persuaded him to return to government service as secretary of defense in September 1950. In that capacity, Marshall worked to repair relations with the other agencies of government that had become frayed under his predecessor and to build up the U.S. military to meet the needs of the Korean War and commitments in Europe while at the same time maintaining an adequate reserve. Marshall opposed General

Douglas MacArthur's efforts for a widened war with China and supported Truman in his decisions to fight a "limited war" and to remove MacArthur as commander of United Nations forces.

Marshall resigned in September 1951, ending 50 years of dedicated government service. Awarded the Nobel Peace Prize in 1953 for the Marshall Plan, he was the first soldier so honored. He was certainly one of the nation's greatest military leaders and one of the most influential figures of the 20th century. Marshall died in Washington, D.C., on October 16, 1959.

Spencer C. Tucker

Further Reading

Cray, Ed. *General of the Army: George C. Marshall, Soldier and Statesman.* New York: Norton, 1990.

Marshall, George C. *The Papers of George Catlett Marshall.* 4 vols. to date. Edited by Larry I. Bland. Baltimore: Johns Hopkins University Press, 1981–.

Pogue, Forrest C. *George C. Marshall.* 4 vols. New York: Viking, 1963–1987.

Stoler, Mark A. *Allies and Adversaries: The Joint Chiefs of Staff, the Grand Alliance, and U.S. Strategy in World War II.* Chapel Hill: University of North Carolina Press, 2000.

Stoler, Mark A. *George C. Marshall: Soldier-Statesman of the American Century.* Boston: Twayne, 1989.

Millin, William "Piper Bill" (1922–2010)

Scottish bagpiper who served as personal piper to Brigadier General Simon Fraser, 15th Lord Lovat, during World War II. William Millin, known popularly for decades as "Piper Bill," was born in Regina, Saskatchewan, Canada, on July 14, 1922, the son of a Scottish immigrant family. When he was a young boy his family moved back to Scotland, where he eventually joined the Territorial Army. A gifted bagpiper, Millin played with the Highland Light Infantry pipe band as well as the Queen's Own Cameron Highlanders band.

In 1943, Millin volunteered to join the 1 Special Service Brigade (1 SSB), commanded by Lord Lovat. Almost immediately, Lovat made Millin his personal piper. As Lovat's brigade readied itself for the D-Day landing, Lovat instructed Millin to play his bagpipes during the landing at Sword Beach and the ensuing fighting. When Millin reminded him that British Army regulations forbade the use of bagpipes during battle, Lovat replied, "Ah, but that's the English War Office. You and I are Scottish, and that doesn't apply." When 1 SSB went ashore on June 6, Millin was the only soldier to wear a kilt, which he later recalled had "floated" as he waded, unarmed, toward the beach. Upon reaching knee-deep water, he commenced playing the pipes and did so throughout the ensuing hard fighting.

Millin accompanied Lord Lovat to the Caen Canal Bridge (Pegasus Bridge), just outside Caen, France, toward the end of the first day of operations. That bridge had been secured by British airborne troops in the early morning hours of June 6.

After the Normandy campaign, Millin accompanied Lovat's brigade during fighting in the Netherlands and Germany. Millin's D-Day exploits were made famous in the 1962 Hollywood film *The Longest Day.*

After the war, Millin worked for a time on Lord Lovat's Scottish Highland estate and then became a psychiatric nurse, retiring in 1988. Millin died in Torbay, England, on July 17, 2010.

Paul G. Pierpaoli Jr.

British Army piper Bill Millin is best remembered for playing the bagpipes while under fire during the D-Day landing in Normandy. Millin later talked to captured German snipers who claimed they did not shoot at him because they thought he was crazy. (Galerie Bilderwelt/Getty Images)

Further Reading

Ambrose, Stephen E. *D-Day, June 6, 1944: The Climactic Battle of World War II.* New York: Simon and Schuster, 1994.

Burns, John F. "Bill Millin, Scottish D-Day Piper, Dies at 88." *New York Times,* August 19, 2010, http://www.nytimes.com/2010/08/20/world/europe/20millin.html?_r=0.

Montgomery, Sir Bernard Law (First Viscount Montgomery of Alamein) (1887–1976)

British army field marshal. Whether considered a latter-day Marlborough or Wellington or the most overrated general of World War II, Bernard Law Montgomery remains the most controversial senior Allied commander of World War II. Montgomery was born in Kennington, London, on November 17, 1887. He entered the Royal Military College, Sandhurst, in 1907 and the next year was commissioned into the Royal Warwickshire Regiment. Montgomery served in India, and in World War I he fought on the Western Front, where he was wounded. He ended the war as a division staff officer.

Following occupation duty in Germany after the war, Montgomery graduated from the Staff College at Camberley in 1921 and returned there as an instructor five years later. In 1929, he rewrote the infantry training manual. He then served in the Middle East, commanded a regiment, and was chief instructor at the Quetta Staff College from 1934 to 1937. Between 1937 and 1938, he commanded the 1st Brigade.

Montgomery then took command of the 3rd Infantry Division, which he led in France as part of the British Expeditionary Force after the start of World War II. He distinguished himself in the British retreat to Dunkerque (May 26–June 4, 1940), and in

July he took command of V Corps in Britain, protecting the English southern coast.

In April 1941 Montgomery assumed command of XII Corps, which held the crucial Kent area in England. He established himself as a thoroughly professional soldier; he was also very much the maverick. Montgomery helped plan the disastrous Dieppe Raid (August 19, 1942), but left to command the First Army in the planned Allied invasion of North Africa. On August 13 following the death of General William Henry Ewart Gott, Montgomery took command of the Eighth Army in Egypt, repulsing Field Marshal Erwin Rommel's attack at Alam Halfa (August 13–September 7, 1942).

Montgomery rebuilt the Eighth Army's morale. Known for his concern for his men's welfare, he was also deliberate as a commander. In the Battle of El Alamein (October 23–November 4, 1942), his superior forces defeated and drove westward German and Italian forces under Rommel. Montgomery's less than rapid advance, however, allowed the bulk of the Axis forces to escape. Montgomery was promoted to full general that November.

Following the Axis surrender in the May 3–13, 1943, Battle of Tunis, Montgomery played an active role in the July 9–August 22 invasion of Sicily, and he led the Eighth Army in Italy in September, where his forces again carried out what has been characterized as a leisurely advance, this time north to Naples.

Montgomery returned to Britain in January 1944 to assist in planning for Operation OVERLORD, the Allied invasion of Normandy, under the overall direction of the supreme commander, Allied Expeditionary Force, U.S. Army general Dwight D. Eisenhower. Montgomery received command of all the Allied ground forces for invasion, which made up the 21st Army Group. He foresaw a 90-day battle, ending with Allied forces reaching the Seine River. Montgomery planned on an immediate breakout from the invasion beaches to secure Caen. British and Canadian armies would then form a shoulder to attract and defeat the main German counterattacks, while U.S. armies secured the Cotentin Peninsula and Brittany.

Montgomery has been much criticized for his role in the hard-fought Battle of Normandy of two and a half months that followed. Bad weather certainly played a factor in dashing Allied plans, disrupting essential resupply from Britain, as did the Norman *bocage* countryside, but Montgomery was also conscious of the need to minimize casualties, for as British prime minister Winston Churchill stressed, Britain's manpower resources were fast drying up, and with this came diminished influence vis-à-vis the Americans and Soviets. Casualties were to be minimized and the British Army's strength preserved. Montgomery sought to fight a campaign that would minimize weaknesses and take maximum advantage of Allied firepower.

The capture of Caen was critical to Montgomery's plan, but as the fighting progressed, he altered the initial plan of taking Caen by assault and switched to flanking efforts to force a German withdrawal. Delays in these, however, led to a strategy of attracting and holding German counterattacks north of Caen, while U.S. forces to westward took Cherbourg. Caen was still in German hands in mid-July, even though Rommel focused his own resources on preventing the anticipated American breakout. The Americans achieved the planned breakout in Operation COBRA (July 25–31), then turned back the German counteroffensive of Operation LÜTTICH (August 7–13). Montgomery's diversionary Operation GOODWOOD came at high cost, and he failed to press his subordinates sufficiently to close the Falaise–Argentan pocket (August 12–24) in time to trap the majority of German forces withdrawing from France. British casualties in the Normandy campaign had been heavy, however.

In September Eisenhower moved his headquarters to France, and Montgomery, promoted to field marshal that same month, then commanded the British and Canadian 21st Army Group. His effort to end the war by the end of the year with a daring invasion of Germany across the Rhine at Arnhem in Operation MARKET GARDEN (September 17–26) was a surprise from the conservative Montgomery. Eisenhower went along, but the plan failed.

Montgomery's forces defended the north shoulder in the German Ardennes Offensive (December 16, 1944–January 16, 1945). His claim in a press conference that British troops had in effect rescued the Americans caused considerable acrimony. Montgomery then directed the drive into northern Germany.

Following the war, Montgomery commanded British occupation troops in Germany between May 1945 and June 1946. From 1946 to 1948, he was chief of the Imperial General Staff. He next served as chairman of the West European commanders in chief from 1948 to 1951 and as commander of North Atlantic Treaty Organization forces in Europe and deputy supreme commander between 1951 and 1958. He retired in September 1958. A prolific writer, he drafted his memoirs that same year. Montgomery died at Isington Mill, Hampshire, England, on March 24, 1976.

Colin F. Baxter and Spencer C. Tucker

Further Reading

Baxter, Colin F. *Field Marshal Bernard Law Montgomery, 1887–1976.* Westport, CT: Greenwood, 1999.

Hamilton, Nigel. *Monty.* 3 vols. New York: McGraw-Hill, 1981–1986.

Lewin, Ronald. *Montgomery as a Military Commander.* New York: Stein and Day, 1972.

Montgomery, Bernard L. *The Memoirs of Field-Marshal the Viscount Montgomery of Alamein, K.G.* London: Collins, 1958.

Moon, Don Pardee (1894–1944)

U.S. Navy admiral. Born in Kokomo, Indiana, on April 18, 1894, Don Pardee Moon graduated from the U.S. Naval Academy at Annapolis in 1916. Assigned to the battleship *Arizona,* he became a specialist in naval gunnery and invented several devices credited with improving its accuracy. He subsequently served aboard the battleships *Colorado* and *Nevada* before being assigned to shore duty in 1926.

In 1934 Moon took command of the destroyer *John D. Ford* in the Asiatic Squadron. Commander Moon then had charge of a destroyer division in 1941 and was promoted to captain the next year. He took part in the Allied invasion of North Africa (Operation TORCH) in November 1942. Promoted to rear admiral in 1944, he commanded Exercise TIGER, a rehearsal for the Normandy invasion on the English coast near Slapton Sands, during which in the Battle of Lyme Bay (April 28, 1944) German E-boats attacked and sank three LSTs, with considerable loss of life.

During the June 6 Normandy invasion, Moon had charge of the American landings at Utah Beach, commanding from the attack transport *Bayfield.* The *Bayfield* remained in position off the coast with its crew on four-hour shifts for the next three weeks before being ordered to the Mediterranean to take part in the invasion of southern France. On

August 4, 1944, Moon committed suicide aboard the *Bayfield* at Naples, Italy. His death was attributed to battle fatigue.

Spencer C. Tucker

Further Reading

Alter, Jonathan P., and Daniel Crouch. *My Dear Moon, Rear Admiral Don Pardee Moon: A Literary Collection; Life, Death and the Untold Story.* Charleston, SC: BookSurge, 2005.

Morison, Samuel Eliot. *History of United States Naval Operations in World War II*, Vol. 11, *The Invasion of France and Germany, 1944–1945.* Boston: Little, Brown, 1957.

Schofield, B. B. *Operation Neptune.* London: Ian Allan, 1974.

Morgan, Frederick Edgeworth (1894–1967)

British Army general. Born on February 5, 1894, in Paddockwood, Kent, England, Frederick Morgan graduated from the Royal Military Academy, Woolwich, in 1913 with a commission in the artillery. He served with the Canadian Corps in World War I, in India from 1919 to 1935, and later in the War Office. A logistician, Morgan commanded support forces for the 1st Armoured Division beginning in 1938, and he fought with that division in the Battle of France (May 10–June 25, 1940). He then commanded the 55th Division and I Corps.

Morgan next held various staff positions, including that of assistant to U.S. Army lieutenant general Dwight D. Eisenhower in planning the November 8, 1942, invasion of North Africa (Operation TORCH). Promoted to temporary lieutenant general in 1942, Morgan was named chief of staff to the supreme Allied commander (COSSAC) in March 1943 and charged with developing the plans for the invasion of Normandy across the English Channel.

The most significant aspect of Morgan's assignment was that the supreme Allied commander would not be appointed for another nine months. Working without standard command guidance, Morgan and his staff planned a three-division initial landing and the use of artificial harbors (Mulberries). In 1944 when U.S. general Dwight D. Eisenhower was designated supreme Allied commander and British general Bernard Montgomery was designated land forces commander, Montgomery criticized the landing plan as too narrow, and Eisenhower agreed. The plan was then expanded to a five-division front. It was possible to do so in a relatively short period because Morgan and his staff had done most of the detailed staff work on the potential lateral landing beaches. It was one of the most brilliant pieces of operational staff work in all military history.

Eisenhower nonetheless insisted on bringing along his existing chief of staff, Major General Walter Bedell Smith. Morgan agreed to step down and serve as Bedell Smith's deputy chief of staff, a post he filled effectively until the end of the war. His unselfish action made it possible for the COSSAC staff to accept the changes and then complete the necessary staff work on time.

Morgan retired in 1946. He served briefly as head of the United Nations Relief and Recovery Administration in Germany. Between 1951 and 1956, he played an important role in the development of British atomic energy. Morgan died in Northwood, Middlesex, England, on March 19, 1967.

John F. Votaw and David T. Zabecki

Further Reading

Green, Phillip. "Frederick Morgan." In *Chief of Staff: The Principal Officers behind*

History's Great Commanders, Vol. 2, *World War II to Korea and Vietnam,* edited by David T. Zabecki, 103–116. Annapolis, MD: U.S. Naval Institute Press, 2008.

Harrison, Gordon A. *Cross-Channel Attack: The European Theater of Operations, United States Army in World War II.* Washington, DC: Center of Military History, U.S. Army, 1989.

Morgan, Sir Frederick. *Overture to Overlord.* Garden City, NY: Doubleday, 1950.

Pogue, Forrest C. *United States Army in World War II: The European Theater of Operations; The Supreme Command.* Washington, DC: Office of the Chief of Military History, Department of the Army, 1954.

Mortain, Battle of. *See* LÜTTICH, Operation

Mulberries

Mulberries were the artificial harbors constructed to support the Allied invasion of France in June 1944. Early invasion planning for the Allied assault on occupied Europe quickly revealed the need for securing a major port to support the invasion forces and ensure the operation's success. The Dieppe Raid of August 19, 1942, by British and Canadian forces demonstrated to the Allied planners that ports were too difficult to assault directly. It also validated fears that German defenders would be able to destroy vital facilities before a port could be captured.

If the Allies could not capture a major port, they would have to bring their own with them. The British War Office began the planning and construction of two artificial anchorages and ports to support the upcoming Allied invasion of France. The Combined Chiefs of Staff officially approved the artificial port concept at Quebec in August 1943. The project was code-named MULBERRY. The Allies would fabricate the two artificial ports in England, tow them across the English Channel, and establish them off the French coast. Mulberry A would support the U.S. invasion beaches, and Mulberry B would support the British beaches.

The prefabricated ports incorporated numerous components that had code names of their own. The first step in the process involved the creation of artificial anchorages known as Gooseberries. Engineers accomplished this feat by positioning and sinking a number of block ships on D-Day, June 6, 1944, to create Gooseberries. Five such anchorages were created, two off Omaha Beach for the Americans and three off the British and Canadian beaches. The ships utilized were obsolete U.S., British, Dutch, and French warships and merchant vessels.

Two of the anchorages served as the foundation for the two Mulberries. The outermost breakwater consisted of bombardons, large floating constructions that were 200 feet in length and 25 feet across and weighed 1,500 tons. These were located approximately 5,000 feet out from the high-water line. They enclosed an outer harbor, and 1,000 to 1,500 yards closer to shore a row of sunken ships known as Corncobs and large concrete caissons known as Phoenixes created another breakwater to shelter the inner harbor. The floating and sunken breakwaters protected a series of piers, pier heads, and moorings for large vessels, such as Liberty ships, and smaller landing craft.

Plans called for Mulberry A to have three pier heads, two pontoon causeways, and moorings for seven Liberty ships and five large and seven medium coasters. It was to have a capacity of 5,000 tons of cargo and 1,400 vehicles per day. Construction began on June 7, 1944, with a planned completion date of June 24. On June 10, the engineers

With the Germans controlling all the French ports, the British built and then towed across the English Channel two artificial harbors, known as Mulberries. Although Mulberry A was destroyed in the great storm of June 18, it and Mulberry B proved invaluable in getting large quantities of supplies to the Allied forces ashore. (Photo12/UIG/Getty Images)

completed the Omaha Beach Gooseberry, followed on June 13 by the Utah Beach Gooseberry.

On June 16, the first LST (tank landing ship) pier went into operation at Omaha, with one vehicle landing every 1.6 minutes. By midnight on June 17, U.S. Navy engineers working on Mulberry A had placed all 24 bombardons and 32 of 52 phoenixes, along with mooring facilities for two Liberty ships. They also had completed the western LST pier, with work on the eastern pier under way.

As that work progressed, construction on pontoon causeways at both beaches continued. The first and second pontoon causeways at Omaha entered service on June 10 and 20, respectively. At Utah, the first opened on June 13, and a second opened on June 16. The initial concept of the artificial port appeared to be proving its worth. Work on the British Mulberry B proceeded at a similar pace.

Unfortunately for the Allies, the worst storm in the English Channel in half a century hit the Normandy coast on June 18, halting all landing operations for three days and, more important, destroying Mulberry A and forcing the Americans to abandon the artificial port. This made capture of the port of Cherbourg all the more important. As feared, however, the German defenders put up a stiff resistance, and the port did not fall until June 27 and only after it had been effectively destroyed. The first Allied cargo did not arrive through Cherbourg until July 16, and even then only in small amounts. By the end of July, cargo arriving in Cherbourg constituted only 25 percent of the total arriving over the beaches at Omaha and Utah.

The great storm also seriously damaged Mulberry B off the British beaches, but it could be repaired. General Dwight D. Eisenhower, commander of the Allied Expeditionary Force, ordered that Mulberry A not be rebuilt and that parts from it be used to complete Mulberry B to the original specifications. When completed, Mulberry B became known as the Harbor at Arromanches. By October, the port enclosed two square miles of water and could berth 7 Liberty ships and 23 coasters at the same time. Intended for use only until French ports were repaired and put back into operation, the artificial harbor remained in service until November 19. By the end of December, disassembly had begun.

While the contribution of the Mulberries did not meet preinvasion expectations because of the storm destruction, the artificial harbors proved invaluable in the Allied supply effort. Fortunately for the Allies, DUKW amphibious trucks and LSTs proved more effective in moving supplies over the beaches than expected and were able to compensate for the shortfalls from the Mulberries. The combination of tonnage delivered over the beaches, through the Mulberries, and through captured French ports enabled Operation OVERLORD to succeed, leading to the victory in France.

Steve R. Waddell

Further Reading

Bykofsky, J., and H. Larson. *The U.S. Army in World War II: Transportation Corps Operations Overseas.* Washington, DC: Center of Military History, 1957.

Hartcup, Guy. *Code Name Mulberry: The Planning, Building and Operation of the Normandy Harbours.* New York: Hippocrene Books, 1977.

Ruppenthal, Roland G. *The U.S. Army in World War II: The European Theater of Operations; Logistical Support of the Armies.* 2 vols. Washington, DC: Center of Military History, 1953, 1959.

N

NEPTUNE, Operation (June 6–July 3, 1944)

Operation NEPTUNE was the assault phase of Operation OVERLORD, the Allied cross–English Channel invasion of France. The stated objective drawn up by his staff and presented on July 27, 1943, to General Dwight Eisenhower, who would have overall responsibility, was "to carry out an operation from the United Kingdom to secure a lodgment on the Continent from which further offensive operations can be developed. This lodgment area must contain sufficient port facilities to maintain a force of 26 to 30 divisions and to enable this force to be augmented by follow-up formations at the rate of from three to five divisions a month."

The mammoth cross-channel attack, codenamed OVERLORD, was no doubt the most elaborately planned operation in military history. The Western Allies planned to land on the Cotentin Peninsula in Normandy. Meanwhile, U.S. and British aircraft worked to soften the German defenses and isolate the beachheads. Between April 1 and June 5, 1944, Allied aircraft flew 200,000 sorties and dropped 195,000 tons of bombs. The Allies lost 2,000 aircraft in the process, but by D-Day they had largely isolated the landing areas and had achieved virtually total air supremacy.

British admiral Bertram H. Ramsay had overall command of NEPTUNE. He had been flag officer at Dover during the Dunkerque (Dunkirk) Evacuation four years before. He had also had charge of the naval planning of the invasion of North Africa in November 1942 and commanded one of the two fleets carrying troops for the invasion of Sicily in July 1943. The invading naval force was organized as two task forces. Rear Admiral Alan Goodrich Kirk commanded the Western Task Force supporting the American sectors in the invasion, while the Eastern Task Force under Admiral Sir Philip Vian supported the British and Canadian sectors.

The invasion fleet itself was drawn from eight different navies, comprising 6,939 vessels: 1,213 warships, 4,126 landing craft of various types, 736 ancillary craft, and 864 merchant vessels. Great Britain provided the majority of these. Of the 1,213 warships, 893 (74 percent) were British and 200 were American. Canada also made a significant contribution. The remainder of the warships were Dutch, French, Greek, Norwegian, and Polish. The British also provided 3,261 of the landing craft. In all, the landing involved 195,700 naval personnel.

The warships included 6 battleships, 2 monitors, 23 cruisers (5 heavy and 18 light), and 105 destroyers and destroyer escorts. Of the warships, 138 were assigned to shore bombardment.

Paratroopers and gliders would land in France proceeding the landing in a nighttime operation. Three airborne divisions were involved: the U.S. 82nd and 101st and the British 6th. The lightly armed paratroopers, operating in conjunction with the French Resistance, had the vital task of securing the flanks of the assault area and destroying key transportation choke points to prevent the Germans from reinforcing their beach defenses. Two German panzer divisions were stationed just outside Caen. If they were permitted to reach the beaches in time, they could strike the amphibious forces from the flank and roll them up. Transporting the Allied airborne forces alone required 1,340 C-47 transports and 2,500 gliders. Ten thousand aircraft would secure control of the skies.

Only 10 days each month would be suitable for the invasion, as it required a date near the full moon to provide some illumination at night to aid in navigation, and the spring tide would expose German defensive obstacles and mines seaward of the beaches. A full moon would occur on June 6, and Allied Expeditionary Force supreme commander U.S. general Dwight D. Eisenhower had selected June 5 for the assault. While the weather was fine during most of May, it sharply deteriorated early in June. Indeed, June 4 saw fierce winds and high seas that would make it impossible to launch the landing craft from the larger ships at sea, while low cloud cover prevented aircrews from locating targets on land. Allied troopships already at sea in preparation for the landing were obliged to take shelter along the southern coast of England that night. The next suitable landing period would be nearly a month hence, but follow-up operations were already under way, with the reinforcing units moving into the embarkation points vacated by the assault forces.

Early in June, Eisenhower's chief meteorologist, British Group Captain J. M. Stagg, forecast a brief improvement for June 6. Eisenhower faced a difficult decision and decided to proceed. This irrevocable decision, taken at 4:00 a.m. on June 5, ultimately worked to the Allies' advantage, for the Germans did not expect a landing in such poor weather. Indeed, confident that there would be no landing for several days, German field marshal Erwin Rommel, who had assumed command of Army Group B and the coastal defenses in November 1943, set out for Germany on June 5 to confer with Adolf Hitler.

The French Resistance was informed by radio messages in code, and the airborne forces took off on schedule the night of June 5–6, but thick cloud banks, German antiaircraft fire, jumpy flight crews, and Pathfinders that were immediately engaged in firefights on the ground, with their crews unable to set up their beacons, all led to premature drops and to paratroopers and gliders being scattered all over the peninsula and in the English Channel. This was an advantage in that the wide dispersion of forces caused confusion among the defenders as to the precise Allied plans. Smaller groups linked up, and most objectives were secured.

The Germans were well aware of the Allied intention to invade Northwestern Europe, and beginning in mid-1942 the Todt Organization had begun erecting fortifications along the coasts of Holland, Belgium, and France. Altogether the Germans expended some 17.3 million cubic yards of concrete and 1.2 million tons of steel. By June 1944 the Atlantic coastline bristled with perhaps half a million foreshore obstacles and 4 million mines. Rommel disagreed with German commander in chief, West, Field Marshal Gerd von Rundstedt and Chancellor Hitler on the necessity of repelling the invasion on the beaches. Rommel was well aware from the campaign in North Africa of the consequences of Allied domination of the air. Once the Allied forces got ashore, it would be too late. If the Allies were to be stopped, it would have to be done on the beaches. Rundstedt and Hitler disagreed. They believed that a large mobile armor reserve would defeat the Allies in maneuver warfare once the invaders were ashore. Indeed, Hitler welcomed the invasion as a chance to engage and destroy the British and U.S. forces. "Let them come," he said. "They will get the thrashing of their lives."

Rommel had in the Fifteenth Army in northern France and the Seventh Army in Normandy a total of 68 divisions: 25 static coastal, 16 infantry and parachute, 20 armored and mechanized, and 7 reserve. The Germans were weak in the air and at sea, however. The Third Air Fleet in France deployed only 329 aircraft on D-Day. The German Navy focused on expanding coastal artillery and laying mine barriers. German naval forces between Cherbourg and Ostend included 5 fleet torpedo boats and 4 motor torpedo boat (S-boot) flotillas. Germany also deployed 4 destroyers on the Biscay coast and 36 motor torpedo boats. Some 36 German submarines, most operating from French ports, were also deployed during the campaign.

The Germans had greatly strengthened the defenses of the channel ports, which Hitler ordered turned into fortresses in order to deny their use to the Allies. All of this was for naught, because the Allies came over the beaches and brought their own ports with them. In one of the greatest military engineering achievements in history, thousands of men labored in Britain for months to build two large artificial harbors known as Mulberries. After the initial Allied landings, these were to be hauled across the channel and sunk in place.

The only possibility of German success was for the defenders to rapidly introduce panzer reserves, but this step was fatally delayed by two factors. The first was Allied naval gunfire support and air superiority of some 30 to 1 over Normandy itself. The second factor was Hitler's failure to immediately commit resources available elsewhere. An elaborate Allied deception convinced him that the invasion at Normandy was merely a feint and that the main thrust would come in the Pas de Calais. The British controlled the entire German spy network in the United Kingdom and used it to feed disinformation to the Germans, while Operation FORTITUDE NORTH caused Hitler to believe that the Allies intended to invade Norway from Scotland, leading him to maintain and even reinforce the substantial German forces stationed there, and FORTITUDE SOUTH led Hitler to believe that the main Allied effort in France would come in the form of a subsequent landing in the Pas de Calais, the narrowest point of the English Channel, and that the lodgment in Normandy was only a feint. In effect, the deception totally immobilized 19 German divisions east of the Seine. Although units of the Fifteenth Army were ultimately moved west to Normandy, this was done piecemeal, and hence they were much easier for the Allies to defeat.

Early on June 6, the Normandy invasion began. In the days before the invasion, ships had taken aboard 130,000 troops, 2,000 tanks, 12,000 other vehicles, and 10,000 tons of supplies. Two American and two British divisions and one Canadian division were to be put ashore. British general Bernard Montgomery had overall command of the land forces in the operation. The American divisions came under the U.S. First Army commanded by Lieutenant General Omar N. Bradley, while the Anglo-Canadian formations were under British Second Army commander Lieutenant General Miles C. Dempsey. The amphibious assault would occur early in the morning after the airborne assault, with five infantry divisions coming ashore along the 50-mile stretch of coast, divided into five sectors. The designated landing sites were, from west to east, the U.S. 4th Infantry Division (Utah), the U.S. 1st Infantry (Omaha), the British 50th Infantry

(Gold), the Canadian 3rd Infantry (Juno), and the British 3rd Infantry (Sword).

Admiral Ramsay had overall command at sea, with responsibility devolved between the Western Naval Task Force, under U.S. rear admiral Alan G. Kirk, and the Eastern Naval Task Force, under British rear admiral Sir Philip L. Vian. The assault convoys included some 16 transports, 106 LSTs, 2 other landing ships, 867 landing craft, and 72 landing craft in the fire-support role in the American sector and 130 LSTs, 40 other landing ships, 1,300 landing craft, and 242 landing craft in the fire-support role in the British and Canadian sector.

At about 5:30 a.m. on June 6, 1944, the bombardment ships opened up against the 50-mile-long invasion front, engaging the German shore batteries. The first U.S. assault troops landed 30 to 40 minutes later, and the British landing craft were ashore two hours later.

The landing was in jeopardy only on Omaha Beach, where because of rough seas only 5 of 32 amphibious duplex-drive tanks reached the shore. Support artillery was also lost when DUKW amphibious trucks were swamped by the waves. A number of landing craft were hit and destroyed, and those troops of the 1st Infantry Division who gained the beach were soon pinned down by a withering German fire. Bradley even considered withdrawal. At 9:50 a.m., however, the gunfire support ships opened up against the German shore batteries. Destroyers repeatedly risked running aground to provide close-in gunnery to assist the troops ashore; indeed, several destroyers actually scraped bottom. By noon the German defenders were giving way.

Landings on the other beaches were much easier. Overall, for the first day the Allies put ashore 75,215 British and Canadian troops and 57,500 U.S. forces on D-Day. These sustained some 10,300 casualties—4,300 British and Canadian and 6,000 U.S. A recent study suggests that a nighttime landing would have produced fewer casualties; still, the losses were comparatively light. Now the task was to expand the toehold by moving inland.

In the weeks following the initial landings, other infantry and armored divisions landed; a total of some 1 million men were ashore within a month. Admiral Ramsay also had responsibility for the movement of the 146 pieces of the Mulberry harbors across the channel by tugs. While the two Mulberries were indeed put in place, unfortunately for the Allies during June 19–23 a force 6–7 storm destroyed Mulberry A in the American sector. The storm also sank or drove ashore merchant ships and a great many small craft, bringing to a halt the discharge of supplies. Vital ammunition stocks had to be flown in. Mulberry A was abandoned, but a strengthened Mulberry B then provided supplies to both armies. At the same time, on June 15 the Allies had begun Operation PLUTO, the laying of a cross-channel oil pipeline for the vehicles in France.

On June 25 the British Admiralty resumed operational control of the English Channel, through the normal chain of command. Operation NEPTUNE, the assault phase, officially ended on July 3.

Spencer C. Tucker

Further Reading
Ambrose, Stephen E. *D-Day: June 6, 1944: The Climactic Battle of World War II.* New York: Simon and Schuster, 1994.

D'Este, Carlo. *Decision in Normandy.* New York: E. P. Dutton, 1983.

Hartcup, Guy. *Code Name Mulberry: The Planning, Building and Operation of the Normandy Harbours.* London: David and Charles, 1977.

Hastings, Max. *Overlord: D-Day, June 6, 1944.* New York: Simon and Schuster, 1984.

Hesketh, Roger. *Fortitude: The D-Day Deception Campaign.* New York: Overlook, 2000.

Lewis, Adrian R. *Omaha Beach: A Flawed Victory.* Chapel Hill: University of North Carolina Press, 2001.

Roskill, Stephen W. *The War at Sea, 1939–1945: Official History,* Vol. 3, Part 2. London: HMSO, 1961.

Schofield, B. B. *Operation Neptune.* London: Ian Allan, 1974.

Normandy

Normandy is a region in coastal north-central France that borders the English Channel. It was here that the Allies launched Operation OVERLORD on June 6, 1944 (D-Day), establishing five principal beachheads between Cherbourg to the west and Le Havre to the east. The subsequent Normandy campaign resulted in the liberation of Paris in August and set the stage for the eventual offensive into Germany the following year. At the time of the invasion, the region had been under German occupation for four years.

Normandy encompasses approximately 11,825 square miles and has historically been lightly populated. In 1944, the population was believed to have been about 1.35 million. Then as now, Normandy is a rich agricultural region, producing cattle, milk, cheese, butter, seafood, and apples. Upper Normandy, in the east, has traditionally been the most industrialized part of the region. Normandy's principal cities include Rouen and the three port cities of Caen, Le Havre, and Cherbourg.

Normandy is topographically divided into two areas—the Armorican Massif in the west, which includes high granite cliffs along part of the shoreline, and the Paris Basin in the east, which features coastal limestone cliffs. The Seine River flows through Normandy and empties into the English Channel at Le Havre. In addition to the Seine, Normandy is home to five separate tributaries of the Seine and nine different coastal rivers, some of which form estuaries. Because the area is heavily agricultural, only 10–15 percent of the land is forested. In the region's western areas particularly, many small farms and plots of land are separated by thick hedgerows bordering sunken lanes; in France this is known as the *bocage*. The hedgerows provided the Germans with excellent defensive positions once the invasion began and posed a distinct challenge for Allied forces moving inland.

In the third century CE barbarian invaders laid waste to much of Normandy, which had heretofore been part of the Roman Empire. In 406, the first Germanic tribes began invasions from the east. Toward the middle of the ninth century, the Vikings began raiding into the upper Seine Valley and eventually took control of most of northern France. Normandy then became a personal fiefdom of the Viking/Norwegian leader known as Robert of Normandy (Rollo). He and his descendants gradually adopted the local language, and the Vikings intermarried with the indigenous peoples of the region. Over time, the population became known as the Normans; in 1066 William, Duke of Normandy, became king of England after the pivotal Battle of Hastings. Thereafter, the English and French Normans competed with each other for control of Normandy, and during the Hundred Years' War the English occupied the region for a number of years (1345–1360 and 1415–1450).

After the Napoleonic Wars ended in 1815, Normandy experienced the Industrial Revolution, and its ports became busy centers of commerce, with goods moving through from interior France and on to foreign ports. The 19th century also saw the rise of coastal tourism and beach resorts. After the June 22, 1940, armistice between France and Germany, Normandy became part of occupied France.

The topography and geography of Normandy presented Allied forces with major obstacles in 1944. Even before Allied troops could make it inland, they had to contend with extreme tides in the English Channel (varying as much as 42 feet between high and low tides), dangerous and unpredictable currents, and inclement weather. Furthermore, high cliffs and high ground on some beaches made an amphibious landing perilous at best.

Omaha Beach, one of the five beachheads established in June 1944, was perhaps the most dangerous. There U.S. forces contended with granite cliffs nearly 200 feet high, which gave the Germans a great defensive advantage. The Americans encountered unanticipated fierce resistance and obstacles littering the beach, including minefields. Utah Beach, the westernmost landing zone located on the Cotentin Peninsula, had fewer steep cliffs but nevertheless presented daunting challenges to the American invaders. Mainly British forces landed at Gold Beach, which was in the center of the five landing zones. The landing zone there was comparably flat. Juno Beach, to the east of Gold Beach, saw chiefly British and Canadian forces landing on relatively flat and level beaches. The British landing force at Sword Beach, the easternmost of the beachheads, initially suffered relatively low casualties, but heavy resistance not far inland soon reversed that trend.

Today, tourists from all over the world travel to see Normandy's various monuments and battle sites. These include the beaches at the five landing zones, the Caen War Memorial, and the Montormel Memorial. Tourists can also visit the Omaha Beach Museum and the Atlantic Wall Museum in Ouistreham. Perhaps the most sobering place of remembrance is the American Cemetery overlooking Omaha Beach, where 9,387 Americans killed in action are buried.

Paul G. Pierpaoli Jr.

Further Reading

Ambrose, Stephen E. *D-Day, June 6, 1944: The Climactic Battle of World War II.* New York: Simon and Schuster, 1994.

Marriott, Leo, and Simon Forty. *The Normandy Battlefields and the Bridgehead.* Philadelphia: Casemate, 2014.

Unwin, Peter. *The Narrow Sea: Barrier, Bridge, and Gateway to the World; The History of the English Channel.* London: Headline, 2004.

Omaha Beach. *See* Terrain and Tactical Problems on D-Day

OVERLORD, Operation, Planning for

Operation OVERLORD, the invasion of Normandy, France, on June 6, 1944, was the Western Allies' greatest operation of World War II and the finest hour of Anglo-American cooperation. Only the United States and the British Empire could have successfully undertaken the largest and most dangerous amphibious assault in history. The operation was so complicated that U.S. Army chief of staff General George C. Marshall said that it almost defies description.

The Allies assembled 2 million troops of numerous nationalities, nearly 5,000 ships, and 11,000 aircraft without the Germans knowing where or when the invasion would take place. British prime minister Winston L. S. Churchill, already thinking offensively, established the Office of Combined Operations to plan raids on Nazi-occupied Europe. A cross–English Channel invasion became likely after the December 1941–January 1942 Arcadia Conference in Washington, which reaffirmed British-U.S. determination to defeat Germany first. Marshall flew to Britain in April to propose an early opening of the second front (code-named SLEDGEHAMMER), and although he returned to Washington in the belief that an invasion of the continent would take place within a year, the British sent Vice Admiral Lord Louis Mountbatten, head of Combined Operations, to Washington in June to tell the Americans that a cross-channel invasion was not possible in 1942. This was confirmed in the disastrous Allied Dieppe Raid of August 19, 1942.

At the January 1943 Casablanca Conference, where U.S. president Franklin D. Roosevelt and Churchill agreed to exploit Allied success in North Africa, they also stipulated that preparations for a cross-channel attack should continue. Shortly after Casablanca, General Frederick E. Morgan was appointed chief of staff to the supreme Allied commander (designated COSSAC), and a small Anglo-American planning group began work in Norfolk House, St. James's Square, London, on what would become the greatest military operation in history. Its objective was to mount an invasion with a target date of May 1, 1944, to secure a lodgment on the European continent from which further offensive operations could be carried out.

By the end of July 1943, the Anglo-American COSSAC staff had produced a 113-page plan for OVERLORD. Limited by a lack of amphibious landing craft, the initial plan called for a three-division assault along a 30-mile front. After a weekend conference at Largs in Scotland, planners selected the Normandy coast as offering the best chance for success. An invasion there would be most likely to surprise the Germans, who would expect it to occur in the closest point to Britain, the Pas de Calais, and who concentrated their defenses on that stretch of the French coast. Normandy was within the maximum range of Allied air cover. The Allies hoped that it would result in the early capture of the port of Cherbourg. The disastrous failure of the Dieppe Raid, in which the attacking Canadians suffered 60 percent casualties, appeared to rule out a direct attempt to seize a major port. The Allied answer was to build, tow across the channel, and assemble their own artificial harbors, known as Mulberries.

COSSAC planners examined meticulously the requirements necessary for successful invasion. These included such variables as weather, tide and moon conditions, and sand on the landing-site beaches. All were designed to produce a solution to the ultimate question of where and how a cross-channel invasion could be launched.

An essential part of planning for OVERLORD included an elaborate deception plan, the largest of the war by either side. Originally the brainchild of COSSAC staff, the operation, code-named FORTITUDE, involved a massive effort to deceive Germany about the date and place of the invasion. The operation saw the creation of a nonexistent U.S. army to mislead the Germans into believing that the Normandy landings were merely a feint and that the main landing would be under the command of Lieutenant General George S. Patton in the Pas de Calais. The ruse reinforced the already existing German conviction that the main landing would indeed take place in that part of France closest to Britain. Another part of FORTITUDE was to draw off resources from France by convincing the Germans that the Allies also intended to invade Norway. Both aspects of FORTITUDE worked to perfection.

On December 6, 1943, Roosevelt named General Dwight D. Eisenhower as the

Senior British and American commanders (L–R) General Omar Bradley, Admiral Sir Bertram Ramsey, Air Chief Marshal Sir Arthur Tedder, General Dwight D. Eisenhower, General Sir Bernard Montgomery, Air Chief Marshal Sir Trafford Leigh-Mallory, and General Walter Bedell Smith are shown discussing preparations for the D-Day invasion in February 1944. (Popperfoto/Getty Images)

commander of Supreme Headquarters, Allied Expeditionary Force (SHAEF), which replaced COSSAC. Morgan continued on as deputy chief of staff, SHAEF. Both Eisenhower and British general Bernard L. Montgomery, who was designated ground forces commander for D-Day, argued for a month's delay of the invasion until June in order to obtain another month's production of the critically important landing craft. Acquisition of these was necessary to increase from three to five the number of divisions in the initial assault. The delay would also allow for increasing the number of airborne divisions to protect the flanks of the 50-mile beachhead from two to three.

The scale of preparations for OVERLORD is staggering. In the four months before D-Day, plans poured forth from SHAEF and Allied armies. The U.S. First Army, in coordination with the Western Naval Task Force and the Ninth Tactical Air Force, planned the landings on Omaha and Utah Beaches. The British Second Army, in coordination with the Eastern Naval Task Force and the British Second Tactical Air Force, planned the landings on Sword, Juno, and Gold Beaches. The Ninth Air Force's plan for the invasion alone ran 847,500 words in 1,376 pages and weighed more than 10 pounds.

By June 1944 there were 1,536,965 U.S. troops in Britain. Stockpiles of equipment for the invasion came to 2.5 million tons and included everything from artillery and bulldozers to dental chairs and tanks. Wags remarked that only the barrage balloons overhead kept the British Isles from sinking under the weight of men and equipment. Administrators required each unit landing in France to carry a 30-day supply of blank forms and stationery. Approximately 7 million tons of oil were stored in the United Kingdom.

On the eve of D-Day, 2,700 vessels (not counting the 1,897 smaller landing craft carried in the landing ships) were steaming toward Normandy. No fewer than 195,000 sailors manned the invasion fleet, carrying 130,000 troops, 12,000 vehicles, 2,000 tanks, and nearly 10,000 tons of stores. Overhead, thousands of Allied fighters provided a protective umbrella for the invasion force.

Fortunately, OVERLORD planners had the invasions of North Africa, Sicily, and Italy as well as amphibious operations in the Pacific as guides for their D-Day planning. Allied planning for OVERLORD, based on honest debate, cooperation, and teamwork, laid the groundwork for the massive defeat of the German Army in the Battle of Normandy.

Colin F. Baxter

Further Reading

Baxter, Colin F. *The Normandy Campaign, 1944: A Selected Bibliography.* New York: Greenwood, 1992.

D'Este, Carlo. *Eisenhower: A Soldier's Life.* New York: Henry Holt, 2002.

Harrison, Gordon A. *United States Army in World War II: The European Theater of Operations; Cross-Channel Attack.* Washington, DC: U.S. Government Printing Office, 1951.

Morgan, General Sir Frederick E. *Overture to Overlord.* New York: Doubleday, 1950.

P

Patton, George Smith, Jr. (1885–1945)

U.S. Army general. Born on November 11, 1885, in San Gabriel, California, George Patton Jr. attended the Virginia Military Institute for a year before graduating from the U.S. Military Academy at West Point in 1909. An accomplished horseman, he competed in the 1912 Stockholm Olympic Games. He also participated in the 1916–1917 Punitive Expedition into Mexico.

On U.S. entry into World War I, Patton deployed to France as an aide to American Expeditionary Forces commander General John J. Pershing but transferred to the Tank Corps and, as a temporary major, commanded the first U.S. Army tank school at Langres, France. Patton then commanded the 304th Tank Brigade as a temporary lieutenant colonel. Wounded in the Saint-Mihiel Offensive, he was promoted to temporary colonel and took part in the Meuse-Argonne Offensive.

After the war, Patton remained an ardent champion of tank warfare. He graduated from the Cavalry School in 1923, the Command and General Staff School in 1924, and the Army War College in 1932. Returning to armor, Patton was promoted to temporary brigadier general in October 1940 and to temporary major general in April 1941, when he took command of the newly formed 2nd Armored Division. Popularly known as "Old Blood and Guts" for his colorful speeches to inspire the men, Patton commanded I Corps and the Desert Training Center, where he prepared U.S. forces for the invasion of North Africa.

In November 1942 Patton commanded the Western Task Force in the landing at Casablanca, Morocco, part of Operation TORCH. Following the U.S. defeat in the Battle of the Kasserine Pass (February 14–22, 1943), in March he was promoted to lieutenant general and assumed command of II Corps. He quickly restored order and morale and took the offensive against the Axis forces.

In April, Patton assumed command of the Seventh Army for the invasion of Sicily in July 1943. He employed a series of costly flanking maneuvers along the northern coast of the island to reach Messina ahead of the British Eighth Army on the eastern side. Patton, however, ran afoul of the press and his superiors when he struck two soldiers who suffered from battle fatigue in August. Relieved of his command, he was then used as a Trojan horse to disguise the objective of Operation OVERLORD, the cross–English Channel invasion of France (June 6, 1944). The Germans assumed that Patton would command any such invasion, but he actually remained in Britain in command of the Third Army while appearing to be in command of the fictional 1st U.S. Army Group, a successful ruse to trick the Germans into believing that the invasion would occur in the Pas de Calais area.

Following the Normandy invasion, Patton was at last unleashed in August when his Third Army arrived in France and spearheaded a breakout at Saint-Lô, beginning on July 11–19, and campaigned brilliantly across northern France. Moving swiftly, his forces swung west to clear the Brittany

Peninsula and then headed east, although he was frustrated by the failure of General Omar Bradley and supreme commander General Dwight D. Eisenhower to recognize the importance of sealing the Falaise–Argentan gap. Patton's forces crossed the Meuse River in late August to confront German defenses at Metz, where the Germans held the Americans until December. During the German Ardennes Offensive (Battle of the Bulge, December 16, 1944–January 16, 1945), Patton executed a brilliant repositioning movement and came to the relief of the hard-pressed American forces at Bastogne.

By the end of January Patton began another offensive, piercing the Siegfried Line between Saarlautern (Saar Louis) and Saarbrücken. On March 22, the Third Army crossed the Rhine at Oppenheim. Patton continued his drive into Germany and eventually crossed into Czechoslovakia. By the end of the war, his men had covered more ground (600 miles) and liberated more territory (nearly 82,000 square miles) than any other Allied force.

Promoted to temporary general, Patton became military governor of Bavaria. He soon found himself again in trouble for remarks in which he criticized de-Nazification and argued that the Soviet Union was the real enemy. Relieved of his post, he assumed command of the Fifteenth Army, a force that existed largely on paper. Patton suffered a broken neck in an automobile accident near Mannheim and died in Heidelberg on December 21, 1945.

T. Jason Soderstrum and Spencer C. Tucker

Further Reading

Blumenson, Martin. *Patton: The Man behind the Legend, 1885–1945.* New York: William Morrow, 1985.

D'Este, Carlo. *Patton: A Genius for War.* New York: HarperCollins, 1995.

Hirshson, Stanley P. *General Patton: A Soldier's Life.* New York: HarperCollins, 2002.

Hogg, Ian V. *The Biography of General George S. Patton.* London: Hamlyn, 1982.

Pegasus and Horsa Bridges, Battle for (June 6, 1944)

The first battle of D-Day began at 16 minutes after midnight on June 6, 1944. The lead of six Allied gliders landed in France carrying an assault force with the mission of seizing and holding the two bridges over the Caen Canal and the Orne River. The capture of what later became known as Pegasus and Horsa Bridges was one of the two great special operations missions of Operation OVERLORD. Commanded by Major John Howard, the force of 181 men from two companies of the 2nd Oxfordshire and Buckinghamshire Light Infantry vectored in three gliders on each bridge.

The mission of what was designated Operation DEADSTICK was to secure the flank of the drop and landing zones of the British 6th Airborne Division on the east side of the canal and river. Those two waterways ran roughly parallel only several hundred yards apart, from the city of Caen north to the coast. Control of both bridges was essential to block tanks of the 21st Panzer Division from moving against the lightly armed British airborne troops. The bridges would also serve as the main supply link between the drop zones and the British landing force at Sword Beach, which ran immediately to the west of the mouth of the Orne River.

Prior to the landing, the members of the assault force had spent months training and rehearsing for the mission. The landings were one of the most impressive feats of precision flying during World War II. The three huge Horsa gliders carrying the Caen Canal

(Pegasus) Bridge assault force landed within 40 meters of their pinpoint targets on the east side of the canal. The lead glider, however, made a rough landing, and the two pilots and many of the troopers, including Howard, careered out through the nose of the cockpit. Many were knocked unconscious temporarily but recovered quickly. They formed up according to plan and then raced out onto the bridge, firing on the German strongpoint on the opposite bank. They also attacked and neutralized a German bunker and an antitank gun on the near side.

As Howard's coup de main force fought its way across the bridge, the leader of the 1st Platoon, Lieutenant Herbert "Den" Brotheridge, was shot and critically wounded. The platoon's backup medic, Private Leslie Chamberlain, carried Brotheridge off the bridge and into the roadside café immediately on the west side of the canal. Chamberlain worked frantically to keep the severely wounded officer alive but to no avail. Brotheridge was the first Allied fatality of D-Day.

The café, which became Howard's command post, was owned by Georges and Therese Condrée, who lived on the upper floor. They were active members of the Resistance, and much of the key intelligence reporting on the bridge and its defenses had come from them. As the fighting raged for control of the bridge and the strongpoints, the Condrées' three young daughters huddled in the basement, where Brotheridge lay dying.

Several hundred yards to the east, only two of the three gliders of the Orne River (Horsa) Bridge element landed on target. The third mistakenly landed at the Dives River, some seven miles away. Fortunately, Horsa Bridge was less heavily defended than Pegasus Bridge. The British commandos were able to secure and hold it with little difficulty. As soon as the bridges were secure, Howard's radio operator transmitted the pre-determined code message "Ham and Jam," the former indicating Pegasus and the later indicating Horsa.

Forty minutes after Howard's force landed, the paratroopers of the 6th Airborne Division began dropping. The 2nd Ox & Bucks held both bridges against sporadic German counterattacks for another two hours until reinforced by paratroopers from the 7th Somerset Light Infantry Battalion. One of the first 7th Somerset officers to reach Pegasus Bridge was Lieutenant Richard Todd, who had been an actor before joining the army. Todd returned to acting after the war, and he later played Howard in *The Longest Day*, the classic 1962 war movie about D-Day.

After the war both bridges were officially named Pegasus and Horsa Bridges—Pegasus from the shoulder patch of the British Airborne Forces and Horsa after the glider.

David T. Zabecki

Further Reading

Ambrose, Stephen. *Pegasus Bridge.* New York: Simon and Schuster, 1986.

Crookenden, Napier. *Drop Zone Normandy.* New York: Macmillan, 1976.

Ellis, L. F. *Victory in the West,* Vol. 1. United Kingdom Military Series. London: HMSO, 1962.

Harrison, Gordon A. *United States Army in World War II: The European Theater of Operations; Cross Channel Attack.* Washington, DC: U.S. Army, Office of the Chief of Military History, 1951.

Ryan, Cornelius. *The Longest Day.* New York; Simon and Schuster, 1959.

PLUTO

PLUTO was the acronym/code word for "Pipeline under the Ocean" or "Pipeline

Underwater Transport of Oil." It was designed to supply petroleum to France following the Normandy invasion of June 6, 1944. A sustainable and considerable supply of petroleum was essential to maintain the highly mechanized and motorized Allied forces in their drive across France, and General Dwight D. Eisenhower identified PLUTO as second in importance only to the Mulberry artificial harbors for the success of the invasion and subsequent liberation of France.

A network of high-pressure pipelines, PLUTO carried vital petroleum products. The three-inch pipelines were of two types. The HAIS pipe was of lead with an outer steel winding, and the HAMEL pipe was of steel. Each mile of HAIS pipe incorporated 24 tons of lead, 7.5 tons of steel tape, and 15 tons of steel outer armor, in addition to other materials such as cotton tape and jute serving. In all, PLUTO incorporated nearly 800 miles of pipes, the vast majority of which came from British manufacturers. PLUTO pumping stations were carefully disguised as buildings and gravel pits and even as an ice cream shop.

The pipe was laid from large floating steel bobbins known as "conundrums," for cone-ended drum. Each weighed 1,600 tons and carried 60 miles of pipeline. The first pipe-laying ship was the converted coastal freighter HMS *Holdfast.* As it and the other three pipe-laying ships towed one of the five conundrums across the channel, the cable unrolled from its bobbin and sank to the seabed. In all, a total of 34 pipe-laying ships and

Logistical preparations for the Allied invasion of France were extensive and even included an oil pipeline (PLUTO: Pipeline under the Ocean) that ran under the English Channel from England to France. Here, engineers are shown dismantling it in December 1945. (AP Photo)

600 officers and men were involved in the operation.

The two principal pipelines were "Bambi," from the Isle of Wight to Cherbourg, and "Dumbo," from Dungeness in Kent to Boulogne. Bambi ultimately had 4 lines totaling 280 miles, while Dumbo numbered 17 lines totaling 500 miles of pipeline capable of pumping 1.35 million gallons a day. Supplementing these were Tambola ship-to-shore pipelines.

Although Bambi and Dumbo were ready by D-Day, the pipeline operation was delayed by the prolonged German defense of Cherbourg and mining of that port. In the meantime, oil went ashore to the Normandy beaches directly from tankers via minipipelines.

By September 18 when both pipelines were working, Allied forces had already retaken Paris and broken the German army in France. Bambi closed on October 4 (U.S. tankers were then directly delivering fuel to Cherbourg and Le Havre), and Dumbo then supplied all the cross–English Channel pumping.

PLUTO made it possible to dispense with a large number of tankers and removed them as possible targets. It also sharply reduced congestion at Mulberry B and the French ports once the latter were back in operation. By the end of the war in Europe, PLUTO had delivered 172 million gallons of petroleum to France.

The vast majority of the PLUTO pipelines were salvaged during the period 1946–1949. Some of the pipe missed by the salvage operation can be seen in the Isle of Wight Shipwreck Centre and Maritime Museum at Arreton.

Spencer C. Tucker

Further Reading

Knight, Bob, Harry Smith, and Barry Barnett. *PLUTO: World War II's Best-Kept Secret.* Bexley, UK: Bexley Council, 1998.

Searle, Adrian. *Pipe-Line under the Ocean.* Isle of Wight, UK: Shanklin Chine, n.d.

Pointe du Hoc, Seizure of (June 6, 1944)

Pointe du Hoc is a prominent terrain feature on the Normandy coast. Its 100-foot cliffs jut out into the English Channel and overlook beaches to either side. Part of the German West Wall, on June 6, 1944, Pointe du Hoc was an important German observation point that provided full view of the two American invasion sites of Utah Beach to the west and Omaha Beach to the east. From Pointe du Hoc, German artillery observers could radio or telephone via buried wire firing instructions to artillery located inland.

Pointe du Hoc received its initial armament in 1943 in the form of six captured French 155mm guns in open concrete gun pits, manned by men of the 2nd Battery of the 1260th Army Coastal Artillery Regiment. In order to protect the artillerymen, elements of the 352nd Infantry Division were stationed there also. In the spring of 1944 when the likelihood of a cross-channel attack sharply increased, the Germans began installing enclosed concrete casements, although only four of the planned six casements had been completed by June 6. The casements were built over and in front of the circular gun pits housing the artillery. The Germans also built a concrete observation bunker and installed mounts for 20mm Flak 30 antiaircraft guns. Following an Allied bomber raid on Pointe du Hoc in April 1944, however, the Germans removed its 155mm guns.

During the planning for Operation OVERLORD, securing Pointe du Hoc was considered an important objective simply to prevent German observers there from calling in accurate artillery fire on the invasion beaches.

A group of U.S. Army Rangers demonstrating on June 13, 1944, how they climbed a rope ladder up the cliff face at Pointe du Hoc a week earlier to surprise a Nazi gun position overseeing Omaha Beach. (Bettmann/Getty Images)

The task of taking it was assigned to the U.S. Army 2nd and 5th Ranger Battalions. Lieutenant Colonel James Earl Rudder, commander of the 2nd Ranger Battalion, had command.

Three companies of rangers were to be landed by sea at the foot of the cliffs and then were to scale them using ropes, ladders, and grapples, all while under enemy fire. The operation was to be carried out just in advance of the main landings. In preparation for the operation, British commandos trained the rangers on the Isle of Wight.

The assault force was transported by the British in 10 LCA (landing craft assault) landing craft; two other landing craft carried supplies, while four DUKW amphibious trucks transported 100-foot scaling ladders secured from the London Fire Brigade. At 6:30 a.m. on June 6 as Rudder's lead LCA approached the beach, he discovered that the coxswain was heading the craft toward Pointe de la Percée rather than Pointe du Hoc. Rudder then ordered a course correction, but the mistake proved costly, as the LCAs now had to fight the tidal current, slowing their movement as they ran parallel to the coast. German fire also exacted a toll. One landing craft carrying men sank, with all but one of its occupants drowned; another LCA swamped. One supply craft also sank, and the crew of the other jettisoned the stores aboard to stay afloat. German fire also sank one of the DUKWs. When they reached the landing site, the rangers were already some 40 minutes late.

The landing craft had been fitted with rocket launchers to fire grapnels and ropes up the cliffs. As the rangers scaled the cliffs, the U.S. Navy destroyer *Satterlee* and the Royal Navy destroyer *Talybont* provided critical fire support, pinning down the German defenders. The cliffs, however, proved to be higher than the scaling ladders could reach, and the primary means up them was by rope.

The plan had called for eight companies (A and B of the 2nd Ranger Battalion and the entire 5th Ranger Battalion) to follow the initial assault, if successful. Flares from the cliff top would signal the second wave to join the attack, but because of the delayed landing the signal came too late, and the other rangers came ashore at their secondary landing site of Omaha Beach instead of Pointe du Hoc. It has been suggested, however, that the added impetus provided by these 500-plus rangers on the stalled Omaha Beach landing may have averted disaster, as the troops sought to push inland.

It took the rangers at Pointe du Hoc some 90 minutes to reach the top. There they confirmed earlier reports from the French Resistance that the German artillery pieces had been relocated. A ranger patrol located five of the six guns nearby and used thermite grenades to disable them.

The rangers, however, were isolated from the other Allied forces, and the most costly part of the battle for Pointe du Hoc now occurred as soldiers of the German 914th Grenadier Regiment mounted several counterattacks, pushing the rangers back to a small perimeter. The rangers were able to hold there, however, thanks in part to naval gunfire support.

The Germans withdrew on the evening of June 7. At noon on June 8, the 116th Infantry Regiment and the 5th Ranger Battalion linked up at Pointe du Hoc with the survivors of the 2nd Ranger Battalion. By that time, the initial ranger assault force of some 255 men had been reduced to only about 90 still capable of combat.

Today Pointe du Hoc is covered with shell and bomb craters, but the concrete observation post remains intact and is a prime tourist destination.

Spencer C. Tucker

Further Reading

Black, Robert W. *The Battalion: The Dramatic Story of the 2nd Ranger Battalion in World War II.* Mechanicsburg, PA: Stackpole Books, 2006.

Black, Robert W. *Rangers in World War II.* New York: Ivy Books, 1992.

Brinkley, Douglas. *The Boys of Pointe du Hoc: Ronald Reagan, D-Day, and the U.S. Army 2nd Ranger Battalion.* New York: W. Morrow, 2006.

Hatfield, Thomas M. *Rudder: From Leader to Legend.* College Station: Texas A&M University Press, 2011.

Quesada, Elwood Richard "Pete" (1904–1993)

U.S. Army Air Forces general. Born in Washington, D.C., on April 13, 1904, Elwood Richard "Pete" Quesada attended the University of Maryland and Georgetown University. He enlisted in the U.S. Army Air Corps in September 1924 as a flying cadet and earned his wings and a commission in the Air Reserve in 1925. He briefly played professional baseball before going on active duty in September 1927. Quesada flew as a crew member of the *Question Mark,* a modified Fokker C-2A trimotor monoplane that set a world record for airborne endurance in 1929.

Quesada served in the 1930s as assistant military attaché to Cuba, personal pilot to the assistant secretary of war for air during an expedition to collect African wildlife, and technical adviser to the Argentine Air Force. Stints at the Air Corps Tactical School and the U.S. Army's Command and General Staff College led him to consider the problem of air-to-ground coordination.

After commanding the 33rd Pursuit Group at Mitchel Field, New York, in 1941, Quesada was promoted to brigadier general in December 1942 and deployed to North Africa. Taking command of the XII Fighter Command, he served as deputy commanding general of the Northwest African Coastal Air Force. There he learned the tactical air doctrine developed by British air marshal Sir Arthur Coningham, which used air liaison officers (ALOs) to coordinate air-to-ground operations, colocated air and army command centers, and streamlined command-and-control procedures between ground units and supporting tactical air. Quesada adopted and improved upon all of these techniques in 1944.

Promoted to major general, Quesada commanded the IX Tactical Air Command in Europe for Operation OVERLORD on June 6, 1944. The next day found Quesada directing some 1,500 from his headquarters at a new airstrip created just above Utah Beach. His subsequent support of Major General J. Lawton Collins's VII Corps demonstrated brilliant innovative tactics. Recognizing that close air support was a key Allied force multiplier, Quesada installed VHF air force radios in tanks to enable ALOs in armored assaults to talk directly to pilots overhead. Deviating from accepted doctrine that air units sacrificed effectiveness if distributed in "penny packets," he allocated fighter-bombers in four-ship formations to provide constant reconnaissance and close air support to Collins's armored columns. Quesada also placed pilots in tanks to serve as forward air observers. Quesada's tactics proved crucial to the success of COBRA (July 25–31), the Allied Normandy breakout in July.

Throughout 1944, Quesada continued to innovate. During the Ardennes Offensive (December 16, 1944–January 16, 1945), he used radar to provide close air support in poor weather. Using modified Norden bombsights combined with radar, he enhanced navigation and bombing accuracy.

During 1946–1947 Quesada commanded the Third Air Force, and in 1947–1948 he commanded the Tactical Air Command. However, Quesada was marginalized within the newly independent U.S. Air Force, which stressed strategic nuclear bombing. After commanding Joint Task Force Three at Eniwetok (1948–1951), Quesada retired as a lieutenant general. Entering private industry, he served as the first head of the Federal Aviation Agency during 1958–1961. Quesada died in Washington, D.C., on February 9, 1993.

William J. Astore

Further Reading

Hallion, Richard P. *Strike from the Sky: The History of Battlefield Air Attack, 1911–1945*. Washington, DC: Smithsonian Institution Press, 1989.

Hughes, Thomas Alexander. OVERLORD: *General Pete Quesada and the Triumph of Tactical Air Power in World War II*. New York: Free Press, 1995.

Kohn, Richard H., and Joseph P. Harahan, eds. *Air Superiority in World War II and Korea: An Interview with Gen. James Ferguson, Gen. Robert M. Lee, Gen. William Momyer, and Lt. Gen. Elwood R. Quesada*. Washington, DC: Office of Air Force History, 1983.

R

Ramsay, Sir Bertram Home (1883–1945)

Royal Navy admiral. Born at Hampton Court Palace in England on January 20, 1883, Bertram Home Ramsay joined the Royal Navy aboard HMS *Britannia* in 1898 and served on the North American and Red Sea stations and on Home Fleet destroyers before World War I. During that war, he held commands with the Grand Fleet and the Dover Patrol. Following World War I Ramsay commanded cruisers and a battleship, and as a rear admiral he was naval aide to King George V and Home Fleet chief of staff. Ramsay retired in December 1938 at the age of 55, his career apparently over.

When World War II began, Ramsay returned to active duty and was assigned to command the port of Dover. Following the German invasion of France on May 10, 1940, he organized and executed Operation DYNAMO, the successful evacuation of the British Expeditionary Force from Dunkerque (Dunkirk, May 26–June 4, 1940), for which he was knighted. Ramsay, now with the rank of acting admiral, was assigned to planning for Operation TORCH, the Allied invasion of North Africa, and he directed the landings at Algiers and Oran on November 8, 1942. After the Axis collapse in North Africa, he planned the invasion of Sicily and commanded the Eastern Task Force for the landings that began on July 9, 1943. Reinstated on the active list, he was appointed commander of British naval forces in the Mediterranean.

On December 29, 1943, Ramsay was appointed Allied naval commander in chief for the upcoming Allied invasion of Normandy (June 6, 1944). He planned and executed this huge undertaking, code-named Operation NEPTUNE, that involved more than 2,700 warships and well over 4,000 minor vessels supporting the initial landing of troops on five beaches, plus subsequent landings of troops and armor. Ramsay was criticized on occasion for his insistence on detailed planning, but he contended that it was necessary given the complexity of the task, and the outcome certainly justified this assessment. For his efforts, he was promoted to full admiral on the active list in June 1944.

Ramsay turned over to the U.S. Navy control of the French ports from Le Havre southward as they were captured while retaining responsibility for those to the north and east. He later directed amphibious operations to clear the South Beveland Peninsula and Walcheren Island in October and November 1944 that opened the port of Antwerp.

Ramsay died on January 2, 1945, when his plane crashed on takeoff from the airfield at Toussus-le-Noble, near his headquarters at Saint-Germain-en-Laye, France.

Paul E. Fontenoy

Further Reading

Chalmers, W. S. *Full Cycle: The Biography of Admiral Sir Bertram Ramsay.* London: Hodder and Stoughton, 1959.

Love, Robert W., Jr., and John Major, eds. *The Year of D-Day: The 1944 Diary of Admiral Sir Bertram Ramsay.* Hull, UK: University of Hull Press, 1994.

Stephen, Martin. *The Fighting Admirals: British Admirals of the Second World War.* Annapolis, MD: Naval Institute Press, 1991.

Ridgway, Matthew Bunker (1895–1993)

U.S. Army general. Born on March 3, 1895, in Fort Monroe, Virginia, Matthew Bunker Ridgway graduated from the U.S. Military Academy at West Point in 1917 and was commissioned in the infantry and assigned to the border post of Eagle Pass, Texas. Promoted to captain, he returned to West Point and served as an instructor there from 1918 to 1924. In 1925, he graduated from the Infantry School at Fort Benning, Georgia. He then held a variety of overseas assignments. In 1932, he was promoted to major.

Ridgway graduated from the Command and General Staff School at Fort Leavenworth, Kansas, in 1935 and from the Army War College in 1937. Between 1939 and 1942, he was in the War Plans Division of the War Department's General Staff.

A protégé of U.S. Army chief of staff General George C. Marshall, Ridgway was promoted to lieutenant colonel in July 1940, to colonel in December 1941, and to temporary brigadier general in January 1942. He was then assigned as assistant division commander of the 82nd Infantry Division assembling at Camp Claiborne, Louisiana, under Major General Omar N. Bradley. In June 1942, Ridgway assumed command of the 82nd, reorganizing it in August into an airborne division when he was promoted to temporary major general.

Ridgway commanded the 82nd in Sicily in July and August 1943 and in Italy from September to November 1943, during which time the unit captured Naples and fought in the drive to the Volturno River before returning to England to prepare for the Normandy invasion. He made his only combat jump with his division on June 6, 1944, and he fought with the 82nd throughout the Normandy campaign. In August 1944, he turned over command of the division to Brigadier General James Gavin and subsequently took command of the newly formed XVIII Airborne Corps, leading it in Operation MARKET GARDEN (September 17–26, 1944), during the Ardennes Offensive (December 16, 1944– January 16, 1945), and throughout the drive into Germany.

Promoted to lieutenant general in June 1945, Ridgway briefly commanded the Mediterranean theater. From 1946 to 1948, he was U.S. representative to the United Nations Military Staff Committee, and from 1948 to 1949 he headed the Caribbean Defense Command. Appointed deputy chief of staff of the army in August 1949, Ridgway took command of the Eighth Army in Korea on the death of Lieutenant General Walton Walker in December 1950. In that post, Ridgway stopped its retreat before Chinese forces, restored its morale, and returned it to the offensive. He subsequently succeeded General of the Army Douglas MacArthur as United Nations commander in April 1951. Appointed supreme Allied commander, Europe, of the North Atlantic Treaty Organization in May 1952, Ridgway was promoted to full general. In August 1953, he was appointed army chief of staff.

Declining to serve his full four-year term because of his disagreement with some of President Dwight D. Eisenhower's defense policies that slighted conventional in favor of nuclear forces, Ridgway retired in June 1955. He then wrote his memoirs and served on various corporate boards. Ridgway died in Fox Chapel, Pennsylvania, on July 26, 1993.

Guy A. Lofaro

Further Reading

Blair, Clay. *Ridgway's Paratroopers: The American Airborne in World War II*. New York: Simon and Schuster, 1985.

Ridgway, Matthew B. *Soldier: The Memoirs of Matthew B. Ridgway, as Told to Harold H. Martin.* New York: Harper, 1996.

Soffer, Jonathan N. *General Matthew B. Ridgway: From Progressivism to Reaganism, 1895–1993.* Westport, CT: Praeger, 1998.

Rifles

The nations that went to war in 1939 were all armed with rifles from World War I, although some modifications had been made during the 1919–1939 period.

Great Britain

The British were initially armed with the World War I modified Rifle No. 1, Short, Magazine, Lee Enfield, in Marks III to V. The Mark VI had also appeared and was the forerunner of the weapon introduced after the outbreak of war, the Rifle No. 4, Mark I, and its subsequent derivatives. It fired the .303 (inch) Mark VI, Mark VII, and Mark VIII cartridges. Wartime shortages caused Great Britain to import many rifles from Canada and the United States, but these were issued to the Home Guard, not to regular troops. The British experimented with semi-automatic and self-loading rifles but did not bring any into service.

United States

In 1936, the U.S. Army adopted John Garand's new rifle as the Rifle, Semi-Automatic, M1, replacing the Springfield Cal .30-06 M-1903A3 rifle. Indeed, the United States became the only country in World War II to have a semiautomatic rifle as a standard infantry weapon. The rugged Garand weighed

An infantryman training with his 9-short semi-automatic .30-06 Garand rifle, the standard U.S. Army infantry weapon of the Normandy invasion. (Library of Congress)

9 pounds 8 ounces (unloaded) and was a gas-operated, clip-fed, air-cooled, semiautomatic shoulder weapon that fired .30-06-caliber ammunition from an eight-round clip. It had an effective range of 440 yards and a maximum range of 3,200 yards. The M1 was the standard U.S. infantry firearm from 1936 to 1957. The one problem with this weapon was that it had an unpleasant recoil because it fired the same cartridge as the Springfield.

The United States also produced the only true carbine of the war, the U.S. Carbine Cal .30 M1. It fired a shortened .30-caliber cartridge, which was designed by Winchester and adopted in October 1941. The weapon was seen as a medium-range, medium-velocity arm, designed for use by junior officers and men who had heavy loads to carry. More accurate than the M-1911 pistol, it nevertheless was considered too light in firepower. Nonetheless, it was used widely and was even equipped with the first infrared sighting equipment to be fitted to a weapon (the M3). The Carbine was also issued in a fully automatic version (the M2), which was not widely used, and it had a paratroop version with a folding stock. Basically, the weapon did not have the killing power needed in a military weapon, and although it was a good design, it was not as valuable as a good submachine gun.

Germany

Germany commenced the war with a shortened, lightened version of the Gewehr 98, which had become the Kar(abine) 98k(urz). It fired the 7.92mm s.S.Patrone (*schweres Spitzgeschoss,* heavy-pointed bullet) cartridge.

During the war the Soviets placed increased emphasis on the submachine gun, and the Germans also made great strides in developing their own semiautomatic assault rifles. This new genre in the rifle world was intended to provide increased firepower without sacrificing range. Submachine guns are excellent weapons at short (pistol) ranges of up to 50 yards, but beyond that there is a need for accurate and effective fire out to 300 yards. Machine guns were the mainstay of the German Army's infantry tactics, but the sheer weight of numbers in Soviet attacks made it imperative that every German infantryman be able to put down effective defensive fire.

Mauser (the main German small-arms manufacturer) had been looking into semiautomatic rifles since the 19th century, but technical problems had ruled out its designs until the German Army began to collect Russian Tokarev semiautomatic rifles on the battlefield. The Germans then went ahead wholeheartedly, utilizing the Soviet innovations. The first rifle in the new range was the Gewehr 41 W. Gases trapped in the muzzle operated the action by means of a rod that extended to the rear to the breech mechanism. At the same time, the Germans "borrowed" the Russian Degtyarev machine-gun locking system to close the bolt firmly for firing.

The U.S. Garand system worked by means of a gas port tapped into the barrel that allowed gases in the barrel to operate a rod, which in turn forced the bolt back against a spring. The first German system was much less sophisticated. The next German design was similar to the Garand but was imported from the Soviets. Now there was a gas port some 12 inches along the barrel, allowing gas energy to operate the reloading mechanism. This system was seen in the Gewehr 43.

The Germans also fielded a revolutionary weapon, the Fallschirmjäger Gewehr 42. This paratroop weapon had a folding bipod, and it was gas-operated and fired from a closed bolt when in single-round mode, which increased accuracy. In automatic mode (for it really was a light machine gun), it fired from an open bolt, allowing better cooling but making it far more dangerous to handle. This system was first seen in the U.S. Johnson light machine gun.

The modern assault rifle had its genesis in the German Sturmgewehr rifles from 1943 onward. In 1938, development of the short 7.92mm cartridge began, and by 1942 test weapons were in production. In 1943 the first were submitted for troop testing, and in 1944 the Sturmgewehr 44 was on limited issue to troops. This weapon was the first true assault rifle and eventually led to the design of the Soviet AK-47 and the Czech Model 58.

Demands from the field led to the adaptation of many standard service rifles for sniping use. The No. 4 British rifle became the No. 4 Mark I(T) and was equipped with a No. 32 telescope. The German Kar 98k was also fitted with a telescopic sight, as was the Soviet M-1891/30. The United States issued the M-1903 in an A4 version, made by Remington. The M-1C and M-1D versions of the Garand were the sniper models but were issued only in limited numbers from 1944 on.

Rifles were adapted to fire rifle grenades. The Germans developed their grenade attachment to fit the Kar 98k and fired high-explosive and smoke grenades as well as indicator bombs. The Americans fitted the Garand with the Grenade Launcher M-7, used with a gas propellant cartridge that was loaded with black powder (the M3 cartridge).

World War II saw a number of extremely effective designs in service, but the days of the bolt action were ending, and the influence of the Sturmgewehr range of rifles in particular caused all nations to look to semiautomatic and assault rifle design. Since 1945, the gas-operated semiautomatic (and even fully automatic) rifle has taken over on the battlefield.

David Westwood

Further Reading

Hogg, Ian. *Military Small Arms Data Book.* London: Greenhill/Stackpole, 1999.

Huon, Jean. *Military Rifle and Machine Gun Cartridges.* Alexandria, VA: Ironside International, 1988.

Smith, W. H. B. *Small Arms of the World.* 7th ed. Harrisburg, PA: Stackpole, 1962.

Walter, John. *Dictionary of Guns and Gunmakers.* Philadelphia: Greenhill/Stackpole, 2001.

Rommel, Erwin Johannes Eugen (1891–1944)

German Army field marshal. Born in Heidenheim, Württemberg, Germany, on November 15, 1891, Erwin Johannes Eugen Rommel joined the German Army in 1910 as an officer candidate. He then attended the officers' training school at Danzig (present-day Gdansk, Poland) and was commissioned in January 1912.

During World War I, Rommel was wounded while fighting in France in September 1914. On his recovery, he won renown in service on the Italian and Romanian fronts. At Caporetto, he and his men took 9,000 Italian prisoners and captured 81 guns. Promoted to captain, Rommel was also awarded the Pour le Mérite.

Rommel remained in the Reichswehr after the war and took charge of security at Friedrichshafen in 1919. In January 1921 he was posted to Stuttgart, where he commanded an infantry regiment, and then he was assigned to Dresden in 1929, where he was an instructor at the Infantry School until 1933. There he wrote *Infantry Attacks,* a textbook on infantry tactics. In 1935, Rommel received command of a battalion of the 17th Infantry Regiment. He taught briefly at the Kriegsakademie (War Academy) in 1938 and then commanded Adolf Hitler's army security detachment.

In 1940, Rommel used his access to Hitler to secure command of the 7th Panzer Division and led it in spectacular fashion in the invasion of France. Promoted to lieutenant general in February 1941, he assumed command of the Afrika Korps, German forces in Libya. An aggressive, bold commander who led from the front, Rommel employed daring attacks and was tenacious in battle. His skill as a field commander earned him the sobriquet "Desert Fox." He was promoted to general of panzer troops in July 1941, to colonel general in January 1942, and to field marshal in June 1942.

Rommel was defeated in the October 23–November 4, 1942, Battle of El Alamein, but he conducted a skillful withdrawal west into Tunisia. After returning to Germany for reasons of health, he was assigned as commander of Army Group B with responsibility for northern Italy. In November 1943, he became inspector general of coastal defense in France and worked to strengthen the so-called Atlantic Wall.

On January 1, 1944, Rommel became head of Army Group B in France, subordinate to German commander in chief, West (Oberbefehlshaber West), Field Marshal Karl Rudolf Gerd von Rundstedt. Based on his experiences in North Africa, Rommel believed that if an Allied invasion was to be stopped, it would have to be at the beaches. Rundstedt and Hitler, however, envisioned a cordon on the shoreline and large mobile German forces inland that would destroy the Allies once they landed. Rommel believed that Allied air supremacy would render that outcome impossible.

Rommel did what he could to improve the coastal defenses, but when the invasion occurred he was in Germany. He had left France on June 5, assuming that the Allies would not attempt a landing owing to marginal weather conditions and hoping to meet with Hitler and persuade him to move one of the panzer divisions to the Saint-Lô–Carantan area, where it could act immediately to confront an invasion. Returning to France thereafter, Rommel personally oversaw the German defense of Caen, but on July 17, 1944, he was badly wounded in an air attack that caught his staff car on the road near Sainte-Foy-de-Montgommery.

Rommel, never a fanatic Nazi, grew despondent over Hitler's estrangement from reality but failed in his efforts to convince the German leader that the war was lost. When approached about participating in a plot to overthrow Hitler, Rommel refused to join in but also failed to inform the authorities. In the aftermath of the unsuccessful attempt on Hitler's life, Rommel was given the choice of a trial for treason or suicide. He chose the latter. Rommel died of a cyanide capsule on October 14, 1944, near Ulm and was accorded a state funeral. His death was officially announced as a heart attack brought on by his wounds.

Annette Richardson

Further Reading

Fraser, David. *Knight's Cross: A Life of Field Marshal Erwin Rommel.* New York: HarperCollins, 1994.

Heckmann, Wolf. *Rommel's War in Africa.* Translated by Stephen Seago. Garden City, NY: Doubleday, 1981.

Liddell Hart, Basel H., ed. *The Rommel Papers.* New York: Da Capo, 1953.

Mellenthin, F. W. *German Generals of World War II: As I Saw Them.* Norman: University of Oklahoma Press, 1977.

Rommel, Erwin. *Infantry Attacks.* Mechanicsburg, PA: Stackpole, 1994.

Rutherford, Ward. *The Biography of Field Marshal Erwin Rommel.* London: Hamlyn, 1981.

Roosevelt, Franklin D. (1882–1945)

U.S. politician and president from 1933 to 1945. Born on January 30, 1882, at his family's Hyde Park estate in Dutchess County, New York, Franklin Delano Roosevelt was educated at home until age 14. He then attended Groton Preparatory School, Harvard University, and Columbia University Law School. In 1905 Roosevelt married his fifth cousin Eleanor Roosevelt, President Theodore Roosevelt's niece.

After passing the bar examination, Franklin Roosevelt joined the law firm of Carter, Ledyard and Milburn. In 1910 he won a seat in the New York Senate, where he served two terms and was a strong advocate of progressive reform. In 1913 he was appointed assistant secretary of the navy and worked diligently and effectively in that post. A strong advocate of intervention on the Allied side and military preparedness, he helped prepare the navy for its role in World War I.

In 1920, Roosevelt ran unsuccessfully as the vice presidential candidate of the Democratic Party on the ticket headed by James M. Cox. During the campaign, Roosevelt advocated U.S. entry into the League of Nations. In 1921 he was stricken with polio. Although his suffering was acute and left him permanently disabled, he remained intensely interested in politics. In 1924 he attended the Democratic Convention and nominated Alfred E. Smith, governor of New York, for president. Four years later, Roosevelt was elected governor of New York. His efforts in seeking relief for suffering New Yorkers following the 1929 stock market crash and the onset of the Great Depression led to his reelection in 1930.

In November 1932 Roosevelt was elected president of the United States on the Democratic ticket, triumphing over incumbent president Herbert Hoover. Roosevelt promised the American people a "New Deal" and began regular radio broadcasts to the American people, the first U.S. president to do so. Known as Fireside Chats, these addresses were designed to restore morale. Legislative products of his first frenzied 100 days in office included banking reform, the Agricultural Adjustment Act, and the National Industrial Recovery Act (NIRA). Congress allocated more than $3 billion under the NIRA for the Public Works Administration. The National Recovery Administration set minimum wages and limited hours for employees. The Federal Emergency Relief Administration provided funds to relief agencies run by the state, and the new Civilian Conservation Corps employed thousands of young men to replant forests, build parks, and work on flood-control projects. During this time, Roosevelt also established the Securities and Exchange Commission to oversee stock trading.

In the second phase of the New Deal the Works Progress Administration was established, extending employment to more than 2 million workers to construct bridges, roads, and buildings. Another measure, the 1935 Social Security Act, provided disability insurance as well as pensions for the aged. The American people welcomed Roosevelt's programs, and in 1936 they overwhelmingly reelected him to office. While Roosevelt's New Deal clearly helped mitigate the effects of the Great Depression and served as a considerable morale booster, in the end it failed to achieve a sustained or robust economic recovery; indeed, the American economy would not completely right itself until rearmament for World War II was under way.

With the beginning of World War II in Europe in September 1939, Roosevelt increasingly turned his attention to foreign affairs and military preparedness, despite strong isolationist sentiments in Congress and among many American voters. On September 8, 1939, he proclaimed a limited national emergency, which allowed expansion of the army from 135,000 men to 227,000. Believing that the security of the United States demanded the defeat of the Axis powers and sensing that Adolf Hitler was a mortal threat to the world, Roosevelt gradually moved the United States from its isolationist stance. Later in September he called on Congress to amend one of the Neutrality Acts, which it did the next month, allowing the Allies to purchase arms in the United States on a cash-and-carry basis.

Following the defeat of France in June 1940, Roosevelt pledged to support Britain in every manner short of declaring war. In September, he concluded an agreement with Britain whereby that country would receive 50 World War I–vintage destroyers in return for granting the United States rights to bases located in British territory in the Western Hemisphere, chiefly the Caribbean. He also initiated a major rearmament program in the United States and secured passage of the Selective Service Act, the first peacetime draft in the nation's history.

By early 1941, Roosevelt and British prime minister Winston L. S. Churchill were coordinating their nations' policies regarding the Axis powers. In the spring of 1941, Roosevelt ordered U.S. destroyers to provide protection as far as Iceland for the North Atlantic convoys bound for Britain. In March 1941, on his urging, Congress passed the Lend-Lease Act, which extended U.S. aid to countries fighting the Axis powers.

Roosevelt also began pressuring Japan to leave China, which the Japanese had invaded in 1937. When Japanese troops occupied southern Indochina in the spring of 1941, he embargoed scrap metal and oil shipments to Japan. Roosevelt also ordered the Pacific Fleet from San Diego to Honolulu, Hawaii, in order to intimidate Japan, but the embargo caused Japanese leaders to opt for war with the United States. On December 7, 1941, Japanese aircraft attacked the U.S. Pacific Fleet at Pearl Harbor, Hawaii. The following day Roosevelt called for a declaration of war on Japan, referring to the Japanese attack as "a day that will live in infamy." No reliable evidence exists to substantiate persistent allegations that the president set up the fleet at Pearl Harbor in order to bring about U.S. entry in the war.

From 1941 to 1945, Roosevelt skillfully guided the United States through the war and worked to ensure a secure postwar world. He established a close relationship with Churchill and strongly pushed a "Germany first" strategy. During the course of the war, the United States fielded not only a navy larger than all the other navies of the world combined but also the largest air force and best-armed and most mobile and heavily mechanized army in world history. The United States also provided in Lend-Lease the machines of war, raw materials, and food that enabled other nations to continue fighting the Axis powers. Amid these circumstances, full economic recovery was achieved in the United States.

Roosevelt strongly advocated opening a second front against Germany and, when an invasion of France in 1942 proved unfeasible, pushed for Operation TORCH, the U.S. and British invasion of North Africa. He appointed General Dwight D. Eisenhower to command the invasion of Western Europe, and the Normandy invasion of June 6, 1944, was the culmination of Roosevelt's Grand Strategy and especially his insistence—in the face of Churchill's oft-stated preference for a peripheral strategy in the Mediterranean—that the invasion of France occur in 1944.

In 1944, Roosevelt ran successfully for an unprecedented fourth presidential term against Republican candidate Thomas Dewey. In February 1945 Roosevelt met Churchill and Soviet dictator Joseph Stalin at Yalta in the Crimea. The Yalta Conference built on decisions already reached at the prior Tehran Conference and was an effort to secure a stable postwar world. Roosevelt gambled that with his considerable charm, he could convince Stalin that he had nothing to fear from the United States and that Britain, the Soviet Union, China, and the United States could cooperate to secure a peaceful postwar world. Although accused of making unnecessary concessions to the Soviet Union at Yalta, Roosevelt really had little choice in these, as the Red Army already occupied much of Eastern Europe, and the U.S. military wished to induce the Soviets to enter the war against Japan.

At Yalta Roosevelt was already gravely ill, and shortly afterward he sought rest at his second home in Warm Springs, Georgia. He died there of a massive cerebral hemorrhage on April 12, 1945. Vice President Harry S. Truman succeeded him as president. Franklin Roosevelt, one of the best-loved presidents in U.S. history, had successfully led the nation through two of its greatest trials—the Great Depression and World War II.

Kathleen G. Hitt and Spencer C. Tucker

Further Reading

Cashman, Sean Dennis. *America, Roosevelt, and World War II.* New York: New York University Press, 1989.

Collier, Peter, and David Horowitz. *The Roosevelts: An American Saga.* New York: Touchstone, 1995.

Dallek, Robert. *Franklin D. Roosevelt and American Foreign Policy, 1932–1945.* New York: Oxford University Press, 1995.

Dawes, Kenneth S. *FDR: Into the Storm, 1937–1940; A History.* New York: Random House, 1993.

Dawes, Kenneth S. *FDR: The War President, 1940–1943; A History.* New York: Random House, 2000.

Freidel, Frank. *Roosevelt: A Rendezvous with Destiny.* New York: Little, Brown, 1990.

Goodwin, Doris Kearns. *No Ordinary Time: Franklin and Eleanor Roosevelt; The Home Front in World War II.* New York: Simon and Schuster, 1994.

Hamilton, Nigel. *The Mantle of Command: FDR at War, 1941–1943.* Boston: Houghton Mifflin Harcourt, 2014.

Hanby, Alonzo L. *For the Survival of Democracy: Franklin Roosevelt and the World Crisis of the 1930s.* New York: Simon and Schuster, 2004.

Kaiser, David. *No End Save Victory: How FDR Led the Nation into War.* New York: Basic Books, 2014.

Larrabee, Eric. *Commander in Chief: Franklin Delano Roosevelt; His Lieutenants and Their War.* New York: Simon and Schuster, 1987.

Roosevelt, Theodore, Jr. (1887–1944)

U.S. Army general. Born in Oyster Bay, New York, on September 13, 1887, Theodore Roosevelt Jr. was the son of President Theodore Roosevelt and graduated from Harvard University in 1908. Roosevelt Jr. worked with his father in the preparedness campaign prior to World War I. When the United States entered the war, he served in the army and rose to the rank of lieutenant colonel in command of the 26th Regiment of the 1st Division. He was wounded in action and awarded the Distinguished Service Cross.

Following the war, Roosevelt helped organize what became the American Legion. He transferred to the Army Reserve as a colonel and was elected to the New York legislature. Roosevelt was assistant secretary of the navy from 1921 and ran unsuccessfully for governor of New York state in 1924. In that year, he became the chairman of American Express. Roosevelt served as governor of Puerto Rico during 1929–1932 and governor-general of the Philippines from 1932 to 1933. He became an editor at Doubleday, Doran and Company in 1935 and wrote or coauthored eight books.

Roosevelt returned to active military duty in April 1941, this time as commander of the 26th Infantry Regiment of the 1st Infantry Division, the same unit he had led in World War I. He served in North Africa and Sicily and became assistant division commander of "the Big Red One" under Major General Terry de la Mesa Allen. In Sicily, II Corps commander Major General Omar Bradley relieved both Allen and Roosevelt because of the division's sluggish advance across central Sicily and the undisciplined conduct of many of its soldiers.

Roosevelt then served as a liaison officer for the U.S. Fifth Army. In 1944, he was assigned as assistant division commander of the 4th Infantry Division for the Normandy landings. On several occasions he requested permission to go ashore with the first assault wave, but Major General Raymond O. Barton, the division commander, repeatedly refused because Roosevelt, who had a severe case of arthritis, limped and walked with a cane. Roosevelt finally prevailed when he threatened to put his request in writing and send it up the chain of command.

Roosevelt was not only the sole general officer to land on Utah Beach on D-Day (June 6) but was also the only general officer on any beach to land in the first wave, and at age 57 he was one of the oldest soldiers there. His son Quentin II also landed on one of the beaches, making them the only father and son pair that day.

Drifting tides caused the Utah Beach assault force to land in the wrong place, which proved fortunate for the Americans because the spot where they did land was far less well defended. Once on the beach, Roosevelt made the tactically correct decision not to try to shift to the planned landing point and instead to direct the follow-on waves to the new landing points. He is reported to have stated, "We'll start the war from right here." Roosevelt repeatedly led small groups across the beach and established them inland, and he was under constant enemy fire the entire day. Lieutenant General Bradley later said that Roosevelt's conduct on Utah Beach was the bravest act he had seen in more than 40 years of military service.

Roosevelt died in his sleep of a heart attack on July 12, 1944, most probably brought on in no small measure by the combat stress of D-Day. At the time, he had been selected for command of the 90th Infantry Division with promotion to major general. Roosevelt was awarded the Medal of Honor posthumously and was later buried at the World War II American Cemetery at Colleville-sur-Mer, Normandy. With the long-overdue award of the Medal of Honor to Theodore Roosevelt Sr. for his own actions in Cuba in 1898, the Roosevelts became only the second father-and-son pair to be Medal of Honor recipients, after Arthur and Douglas MacArthur.

David T. Zabecki

Further Reading

Jeffers, H. Paul. *Theodore Roosevelt, Jr.: The Life of a War Hero.* Novato, CA: Presidio, 2002.

Renehan, Edward J. *The Lion's Pride: Theodore Roosevelt and His Family in Peace and War.* New York: Oxford University Press, 1998.

ROUNDUP, Operation (1943)

Code name for a projected Allied cross–English Channel invasion of France in the spring of 1943. Following U.S. entry into World War II in December 1941, President Franklin D. Roosevelt agreed to concentrate U.S. military efforts on the defeat of Germany, the more formidable Axis power. The Arcadia Conference in Washington (December 22, 1941–January 14, 1942) confirmed this decision, with Roosevelt committing the United States to BOLERO, the rapid buildup of U.S. forces in Britain.

U.S. military planners and especially army chief of staff General George C. Marshall wanted an early U.S.-British invasion of France. They believed that a military diversion was necessary to keep the Soviet Union in the war and that the quickest way to end the war was to concentrate resources for a massive cross-channel invasion. Toward that end, American planners wanted the earliest possible date for action. British prime minister Winston L. S. Churchill, who feared a repetition of the bloody stalemate in Flanders during World War I, preferred a gradual, more opportunistic approach that would commit major Allied military assets in the Mediterranean theater. Chief of the Imperial General Staff General Sir Alan Brooke supported Churchill.

General Marshall directed Brigadier General Dwight D. Eisenhower and the War Plans Division to devise a cross-channel invasion plan. Presented to Roosevelt as the Marshall Memorandum in March 1942, it considered two options: SLEDGEHAMMER and ROUNDUP. SLEDGEHAMMER was originally a British contingency cross-channel invasion for late 1942, to be implemented only if the Soviet Union was in danger of collapsing or if German armies in the east were defeated and France became vulnerable. SLEDGEHAMMER would utilize whatever forces were available. ROUNDUP, another British plan, envisioned an invasion of France by 48 divisions.

It is not clear how seriously the planners regarded SLEDGEHAMMER, but ROUNDUP was actively considered. It called for 18 British and 30 U.S. divisions to invade the French coast somewhere between Le Havre and Calais in the spring of 1943. U.S. planners believed that 1943 was the earliest possible date for a large-scale invasion. They also thought that it might be the only time such an invasion was possible, as by 1944 the Soviet Union might either have been driven from the war or have been victorious and rendered unwilling to cooperate with an Allied invasion of France.

Under heavy U.S. pressure, Churchill agreed to carrying out ROUNDUP no later than April 1943. Privately, however, the British worked to scuttle the cross-channel plan by diverting resources to more modest and, according to them, more realistic objectives. In the summer of 1942, with Roosevelt unwilling to risk defeat in Europe, the Americans reluctantly agreed to Operation GYMNAST, a plan to invade French North Africa, supposedly without prejudice to the future of ROUNDUP. The Dieppe Raid of August 19, 1942, however, destroyed any illusions about ROUNDUP. The cross-channel invasion of France was postponed; its final incarnation, Operation OVERLORD, did not occur until June 6, 1944.

Spencer C. Tucker

Further Reading

D'Este, Carlo. *Decision in Normandy.* New York: E. P. Dutton, 1983.

Eisenhower, David. *Eisenhower at War, 1943–1945.* New York: Random House, 1986.

Stoler, Mark A. *Allies and Adversaries: The Joint Chiefs of Staff, the Grand Alliance, and U.S. Strategy in World War II.* Chapel Hill: University of North Carolina Press, 2000.

Stoler, Mark A. *The Politics of the Second Front: American Military Planning and Diplomacy in Coalition Warfare, 1941–1943.* Westport, CT: Greenwood, 1977.

Rudder, James Earl (1910–1970)

U.S. Army officer who commanded the D-Day operation to seize Pointe du Hoc in Normandy. James Earl Rudder was born in Eden, Texas, on May 6, 1910. Graduating from Texas A&M University in 1932, he became a high school teacher and football coach in Brady, Texas, and in 1938 he became football coach and teacher at Tarleton Agricultural College in Texas.

Rudder had been commissioned a 2nd lieutenant in the U.S. Army Reserve upon graduation from Texas A&M, and in 1941 he was called to active duty. After commanding an infantry company at Fort Sam Houston, Texas, he became a battalion executive officer in the 83rd Infantry Division at Camp Atterbury, Indiana. In June 1943, Rudder was ordered to organize and train the 2nd Ranger Battalion at Camp Forrest, Tennessee.

Rudder led the 2nd Ranger Battalion in the difficult but immensely important operation to seize the German-held key terrain feature of Pointe du Hoc that provided excellent observation of the American invasion beaches. Under German fire, Rudder's men scaled the 100-foot cliffs and, after having taken greater than 50 percent casualties, seized the German observation point. Rudder was himself wounded twice in the operation. He and his men then rebuffed German counterattacks during the next two days until relieved.

In January 1945 Rudder assumed command of the 109th Infantry Regiment, which fought in the Battle of the Bulge. A full colonel by the end of the war, he left the army afterward and returned to Texas and civilian life. He continued in the reserves, however, and was promoted to brigadier general in 1954 and to major general in 1957.

Subsequently mayor of Brady, Texas, Rudder became vice president of the Brady Aviation Company in 1953, and in 1955 he became Texas land commissioner. In 1958 he became vice president of Texas A&M University, and in 1959 he was its president. He was president of the entire A&M University system from 1965 until his death in Houston on March 23, 1970.

Spencer C. Tucker

Further Reading

Black, Robert W. *The Battalion: The Dramatic Story of the 2nd Ranger Battalion in World War II.* Mechanicsburg, PA: Stackpole Books, 2006.

Black, Robert W. *Rangers in World War II.* New York: Ivy Books, 1992.

Brinkley, Douglas. *The Boys of Pointe du Hoc: Ronald Reagan, D-Day, and the U.S. Army 2nd Ranger Battalion.* New York: W. Morrow, 2006.

Hatfield, Thomas M. *Rudder: From Leader to Legend.* College Station: Texas A&M University Press, 2011.

Rundstedt, Karl Rudolf Gerd von (1875–1953)

German field marshal. Born at Aschersleben, Germany, on December 12, 1875, Karl

Rudolf Gerd von Rundstedt joined the army in 1893 and served throughout World War I. Following the war, he rose steadily in the new Reichswehr. He was promoted to lieutenant colonel in October 1920 and colonel in February 1923. Rundstedt was then chief of staff of the 2nd Infantry Division. In March 1925 he assumed command of the 18th Infantry Regiment. In November 1927 he was promoted to major general and a year later he commanded the 2nd Cavalry Division.

Promoted to lieutenant general in March 1929, Rundstedt took command of the 3rd Infantry Division and then Group Command I. He was promoted to general of infantry in October 1932 and to colonel general in March 1938. Unhappy with Adolf Hitler's growing power, Rundstedt retired on October 31, 1938. He was recalled to duty at the age of 64, and in September 1939 he led Army Group South into Poland.

In the German invasion of France in May 1940, Rundstedt commanded Army Group A, composed of 45 divisions. By May 14, his tanks had opened up a broad gap in the Allied front. Rundstedt argued that his tanks should halt until infantry divisions could catch up. Hitler agreed but made the order a fast one, stopping General of Panzer Troops Heinz Guderian's panzer thrust that could have cut off the British escape from Dunkerque. Hitler promoted Rundstedt to field marshal on July 19, 1940. Later, Rundstedt took command of occupation forces and was given responsibility for coastal defenses in Holland, Belgium, and France.

Rundstedt participated in Operation BARBAROSSA, the June 22, 1941, invasion of the Soviet Union, as commander of Army Group South. His forces made slow progress during the first weeks, but in September 1941 he directed the capture of Kiev and 665,000 Soviet troops. Rundstedt strongly opposed continuing the advance into the Soviet Union during the winter and advised Hitler to call a halt, but his advice was rejected.

Rundstedt continued the advance and reached Rostov on November 21, but a Soviet counterattack forced his troops back. When Rundstedt called for withdrawal, Hitler replaced him with General Walther von Reichenau. After the führer recalled him to duty in March 1942, sending him to France as Oberbefehlshaber West (commander in chief, West), Rundstedt organized the construction of the fortifications known as the Atlantic Wall along 1,700 miles of coastline.

When the Normandy invasion began on June 6, 1944, Rundstedt immediately requested permission to send two of the panzer divisions stationed near Paris the 120 miles north to the invasion beaches, but Hitler delayed for two hours, which meant that the panzers had to move in full daylight.

Following the Normandy landings, Rundstedt urged Hitler to make peace. Hitler responded by replacing him with Field Marshal Günther von Kluge, but in September Rundstedt returned to his former post. Having been in command during the last major German offensive (Ardennes, Battle of the Bulge, December 16, 1944–January 16, 1945), he was sacked as Oberbefehlshaber West in March 1945.

Rundstedt was the prototype, if not the caricature, of the old-style Prussian officer, deeply attached to Germany's imperial traditions. He never failed to contradict Hitler with respect to military matters when he felt it necessary to do so, but he also never questioned his regime. Captured by the Western Allies on May 1, 1945, Rundstedt was released in May 1949 and lived in Hanover, Germany, until his death on February 24, 1953.

Martin Moll

Further Reading

Keegan, John. *Rundstedt.* New York: Ballantine Books, 1974.

Messenger, Charles. *The Last Prussian: Biography of Field Marshal Gerd von Rundstedt, 1875–1953.* Washington, DC: Brassey's Defence Publishers, 1991.

Ziemke, Earl F. "Field-Marshal Gerd von Rundstedt." In *Hitler's Generals,* edited by Correlli Barnett, 175–207. New York: Grove Weidenfeld, 1989.

S

Sainte-Mère-Église

Sainte-Mère-Église is a commune in the Cotentin Peninsula of the Manche department in Normandy. The town played an important role on D-Day as it stood astride Route N23, which the Germans would have to utilize in mounting any significant counterattack against the American Utah and Omaha beachheads.

At about 1:30 a.m. on June 6 well in advance of the amphibious landings, paratroopers of the U.S. 82nd and 101st Airborne Divisions dropped directly into Sainte-Mère-Église as part of Operation BOSTON. This proved costly because some of the town buildings were on fire, and this illuminated the descending paratroopers, making them easy targets for German ground fire. Other paratroopers were sucked into the flames, and still others landed in trees and were slain before they could cut themselves free.

The most famous incident of the operation involved Private John Steele of the 505th Parachute Infantry Regiment. His parachute caught on the spire of the church. Pretending to be dead, he hung there for two hours as the fighting went on below. Subsequently taken prisoner by the Germans, he escaped and rejoined his outfit after Lieutenant Colonel Edward C. Krause's 3rd Battalion of the 505th Regiment took control of the town at about 5:00 a.m., killing 30 German soldiers and capturing another 11. This gave Sainte-Mère-Église the claim of being the first French town liberated in the Allied invasion.

The Germans counterattacked late on June 6 and the next day, but the troopers held Sainte-Mère-Église until they were relieved by troops and tanks from Utah Beach on the afternoon of June 7.

Today a number of small museums in the area commemorate the events of D-Day, and a dummy paratrooper hangs from a parachute on the church spire. The coat of arms of Sainte-Mère-Église has a church in its center flanked by two white stars descending on parachutes.

Spencer C. Tucker

Further Reading

Harrison, Gordon A. *United States Army in World War II: The European Theater of Operations; Cross Channel Attack.* Washington, DC: U.S. Army, Office of the Chief of Military History, 1951.

Ryan, Cornelius. *The Longest Day: June 6, 1944.* New York: Simon and Schuster, 1959.

Saint-Lô, Battle of (July 11–19, 1944)

Key battle following the June 6, 1944, Normandy invasion. Saint-Lô was the hub of an extensive road net that allowed the Germans to rapidly shift men and weapons east and west to meet American attacks. Lieutenant General Omar N. Bradley, commanding the U.S. First Army, needed the road from Saint-Lô west to Périers as a line of departure for an offensive (code-named COBRA) to break out of the Normandy *bocage* of hedgerow country. The *bocage* consisted of small fields and orchards surrounded by

180 | **Saint-Lô, Battle of**

Captured and destroyed German tanks in a field northwest of Saint-Lô in Normandy, France, in August 1944 during World War II. Note the hedgerows dividing the fields and that proved formidable obstacles to the Allied advance. (AP Photo)

underbrush-covered earthen dikes three to five feet thick and six to nine feet high, with numerous narrow, sunken lanes. These brush-crowned embankments walled in the fields and provided excellent positions for the German defenders.

On July 11, Major General Charles H. Gerhardt's 29th Infantry Division began the attack to take Saint-Lô and the Martinsville Ridge to its east. The 35th Infantry Division attacked on its right, and the 2nd Infantry Division (V Corps) attacked on its left. Defending was the 3rd Parachute Division of General of Parachute Panzer Troops Eugen Meindl's II Parachute Corps plus badly battered Kampfgruppen (battle groups) of varying sizes from the 266th, 352nd, and 353rd Infantry Divisions under command of the 353rd.

The 116th Infantry Regiment attacked on the left and the 115th Infantry Regiment attacked on the right in the 29th Infantry Division's zone, using assault groups composed of infantry, tanks, and engineers to methodically attack and seize each field. Many tanks were equipped with steel prongs hastily welded to the front of their hulls to help them through hedgerows and to punch holes in which to place explosives. By the end of the day the 116th Infantry decisively penetrated German defenses, but heavier resistance stopped the 115th. However, the 2nd Infantry Division seized Hill 192, which overlooked the Saint-Lô area.

Attacking U.S. forces made little headway between July 12 and 14. On July 15, the Germans stopped both regiments. At 7:30 p.m., however, the 116th Infantry again began making headway, but it was halted for the night by higher headquarters. The 2nd Battalion failed to receive the order, and although it was cut off, it was not attacked. Meanwhile, that same day the 35th Infantry Division seized the north slope of Hill 122 about a mile north of Saint-Lô.

On July 16 the 115th Infantry was again thwarted, but the 116th Infantry defeated two German counterattacks. On July 17 the 115th continued attacking the high ground on the Martinville Ridge, commanding the German rear area. Major Thomas D. Howie's 3rd Battalion, 116th Infantry, attacked southwest, and by 6:00 a.m. it had taken the village of La Madeleine without opposition, relieving the regiment's 2nd Battalion. La Madeleine was about 500 yards from Saint-Lô itself.

The 2nd Battalion was supposed to attack into Saint-Lô but had suffered too many casualties to do this. Howie then took the mission. Shortly after he issued his orders Howie was killed, and his executive officer, Captain William H. Puntenney, assumed command. Heavy German artillery and mortar fire followed by a counterattack thwarted the attack plan. U.S. artillery and mortar fire and air strikes then defeated the German counterattack. Both the 2nd and 3rd Battalions of the 116th Infantry were now isolated from the remainder of the division. By the end of the day of July 17, however, the 29th Division was on the inner slopes of hills that led directly into Saint-Lô.

On the morning of July 18, the 35th Infantry Division reported that the Germans had pulled out everywhere in its sector. Task Force C, commanded by Brigadier General Norman D. Cota, assistant division commander of the 29th Infantry Division, and composed of reconnaissance tank, tank destroyer, and engineer units, was tapped to seize the town. Cota was to obtain infantry support from the nearest available infantry unit just before entering the town. That was the 1st Battalion, 115th Infantry (less one platoon designated to contain a small number of German holdouts). By 7:00 p.m., Saint-Lô had been secured. Major Howie's men carried his body into the town and placed it on the rubble surrounding what had been the Cathedral of Notre-Dame.

Pockets of resistance still remained, and the Germans poured in mortar and artillery fire. Cota was wounded and some 200 of the 600-man task force became casualties, but the capture of Saint-Lô and the adjacent high ground solidly protected the U.S. First Army's left flank as it penetrated the German lines and prepared the way for the breakout of Operation COBRA.

Uzal W. Ent

Further Reading

Boog, Horst, Gerhard Krebs, and Detlef Vogel. *Germany and the Second World War,* Vol. 7, *The Strategic Air War in Europe and the War in the West and East Asia 1943–1944/5.* Oxford, UK: Clarendon, 2006.

Carafano, James Jay. *After D-Day: Operation Cobra and the Normandy Breakout.* Boulder, CO: Lynne Rienner, 2000.

Johns, Glover S., Jr. *The Clay Pigeons of St. Lo.* Harrisburg, PA: Military Service Publishing, 1958.

Lodieu, Didier. *Dying for Saint-Lô: Hedgerow Hell, July 1944.* Paris: Histoire and Collections, 2007.

Mitcham, Samuel W., Jr. *Retreat to the Reich: The German Defeat in France, 1944.* Westport, CT: Praeger, 2000.

Weigley, Russell. *Eisenhower's Lieutenants: The Campaigns of France and Germany, 1944–1945.* Bloomington: Indiana University Press, 1981.

Simonds, Guy Granville (1903–1974)

Canadian Army general. Born on April 23, 1903, at Bury Saint Edmunds, England, the son of a British Army officer who brought his family to Canada, Guy Granville Simonds graduated from the Royal Military College of Canada, Kingston, Ontario, in 1925 and then served with the artillery in the small interwar Canadian Army, where he emerged as a rising star. A brilliant performance at the British Army Camberley Staff College in 1936–1937 confirmed this promise. During World War II, Simonds rose from major to brigadier in September 1942 and to major general in April 1943.

Simonds was naturally aggressive with an intuitive grasp of mobile, armored warfare. Field Marshal Sir Bernard Montgomery considered him a protégé and far superior to the plodding General Henry Crerar. Simonds cut his teeth commanding the Canadian 1st Division in Sicily with great success and then briefly the 5th Armoured Division in Italy. In January 1944 he was promoted to lieutenant general and given command of the Canadian II Corps, which he commanded in the June 6, 1944, Normandy invasion.

Simonds's battle plans in the assaults around Caen and particularly in the bloody attritional fighting to close the Falaise–Argentan gap from the north in August 1944 (Operations TOTALIZE and TRACTABLE) were operational masterpieces but were so complex that they often overmatched the abilities of his inexperienced army. Simonds's performance at Falaise remains controversial. Although he sacked subordinates with abandon and relentlessly pressed his exhausted soldiers forward, many historians have criticized him for showing insufficient "resolution." In fact, the task given to Simonds's corps was beyond its capacity—at least in the time allotted—not least because most units were well understrength.

The greatest achievement of Simonds and the Canadian First Army (he assumed command from an ailing Crerar in September 1944) was undoubtedly the clearance of the Scheldt estuary in the fall of 1944, which opened Antwerp to shipping and resolved the supply problem that had threatened to strangle Allied mobility. Fighting under the most appalling conditions and despite Montgomery's inexplicable refusal to allocate sufficient troops, at least until General Dwight D. Eisenhower finally intervened, the Canadians prevailed. Simonds displayed more innovation and flexibility, and both commander and men proved that they had absorbed the summer's hard lessons.

Simonds's career went into eclipse after the war. He lost out to the more politically astute Lieutenant General Charles Foulkes in running the postwar army and left little mark except as a critic of Canada's drift into the American military orbit. Simonds died on May 15, 1974, in Toronto.

Patrick H. Brennan

Further Reading

Graham, Dominic. *The Price of Command: A Biography of General Guy Simonds.* Toronto: Stoddart, 1993.

Jarymowycz, Roman. "General Guy Simonds: The Commander as Tragic Hero." In *Warrior Chiefs: Perspectives on Senior Canadian Military Leaders,* edited by B. Horn and S. Harris, 107–142. Toronto: Dundurn, 2001.

Slapton Sands, Battle of. *See* Lyme Bay, Battle of

SLEDGEHAMMER, Operation

Code name for an Allied contingency invasion of France. Following U.S. entry into World War II in December 1941, President Franklin D. Roosevelt decided that the United States would endeavor to contain Japanese expansion in the Pacific while first concentrating on the defeat of Germany. At the Arcadia Conference (December 22, 1941–January 15, 1942), Roosevelt committed the United States to Operation BOLERO, the rapid buildup of U.S. forces in Britain.

American planners, especially U.S. Army chief of staff General George C. Marshall, advocated a cross–English Channel invasion as the best means to end the war as quickly as possible. An invasion of France by the Western Allies would also relieve German pressure on the Soviet Union. British prime minister Winston L. S. Churchill, who feared a repetition of the bloody stalemate in Flanders during World War I, sought to commit major Allied military assets in the Mediterranean theater and involve the United States in efforts to contain Soviet power. Chief of the Imperial General Staff General Sir Alan Brooke supported Churchill's position.

Marshall directed Brigadier General Dwight D. Eisenhower of the War Plans Division to draw up a plan, which Marshall then presented to Roosevelt in March 1942, for a British-U.S. invasion of the French coast somewhere between Le Havre and Calais. Known as the Marshall Memorandum, it outlined two military options. The first of these was SLEDGEHAMMER. Originally conceived by the British as an emergency invasion of France to prevent a Soviet collapse (or to take advantage of the situation if German forces were defeated in the east and France become vulnerable to invasion), SLEDGEHAMMER was a high-risk operation. It is a matter of debate whether the War Department actually considered SLEDGEHAMMER viable. The second option, ROUNDUP, called for a 48-division invasion in early 1943.

Although the Marshall Memorandum emphasized that ROUNDUP was the preferred solution, it noted that even a failed small cross-channel invasion of France would be preferable to dispersing Allied military assets elsewhere. U.S. planners believed that the spring of 1943 was not only the earliest possible date for an all-out invasion of France but could also be the only date, as by 1944 the Soviet Union might have been driven from the war.

Churchill fought against SLEDGEHAMMER and ROUNDUP, believing that a cross-channel invasion, even in 1943, was too risky. He favored the Mediterranean strategy, known as GYMNAST, in which British and French forces would invade and conquer French North Africa, supposedly without prejudicing ROUNDUP.

The Dieppe Raid of August 19, 1942, destroyed any illusions about the possibility of an Allied invasion of France in 1942 or even 1943. The cross-channel invasion of France, Operation OVERLORD, did not occur until June 6, 1944.

Spencer C. Tucker

Further Reading

D'Este, Carlo. *Decision in Normandy.* New York: E. P. Dutton, 1983.

Eisenhower, David. *Eisenhower at War, 1943–1945.* New York: Random House, 1986.

Steele, Richard W. *The First Offensive 1942: Roosevelt, Marshall and the Making of American Strategy.* Bloomington: Indiana University Press, 1973.

Stoler, Mark A. *Allies and Adversaries: The Joint Chiefs of Staff, the Grand Alliance, and U.S. Strategy in World War II.* Chapel Hill: University of North Carolina Press, 2000.

Smith, Walter Bedell (1895–1961)

U.S. Army general. Born in Indianapolis, Indiana, on October 5, 1895, Walter Bedell Smith was nicknamed "Beetle." He joined the Indiana National Guard in 1910 and briefly attended Butler University. Smith then earned a commission in the National Guard and served with the 39th Infantry in France during World War I, where he was wounded in August 1918.

Smith remained in the army after the war and proved himself to be a capable administrator. Assignments included the Bureau of Military Intelligence, the Bureau of the Budget, and the Federal Liquidation Board. He was also a student and then an instructor at the Infantry School at Fort Benning, Georgia; the Command and General Staff School at Fort Leavenworth, Kansas; and the Army War College. His abilities were noted by General George C. Marshall, who became army chief of staff in September 1939. The following month Marshall named Smith assistant secretary of the General Staff and, in August 1941, secretary of the General Staff.

After the United States entered the war, Smith became the U.S. secretary to the Combined Chiefs of Staff in February 1942. Following heavy lobbying from European theater commander Lieutenant General Dwight D. Eisenhower, Marshall reluctantly ordered Smith to Europe in September 1942 to assume his most recognizable role as Eisenhower's chief of staff. Smith earned Eisenhower's trust to handle staff planning and administration, thus allowing his commander to spend more time on operational matters. In a post far less glamorous than battle command, Smith made decisions beyond staff direction, often issuing orders to field commanders in Eisenhower's name.

Eisenhower rejected any notion that Smith should be assigned anywhere but as his chief of staff. Entrusted by Eisenhower with the job of negotiating with Italian emissaries, Smith, through a combination of bluster and intimidation, secured the Italian surrender on September 3, 1943.

As planning for Operation OVERLORD began in earnest, Smith became chief of staff, Supreme Headquarters, Allied Expeditionary Force. The main body of the Operation OVERLORD plan, however, had been developed by British general Sir Frederick Morgan, who had been appointed chief of staff to the supreme Allied commander months before Eisenhower was assigned as that commander. When Eisenhower insisted on Smith being his chief of staff, Morgan loyally agreed to step down; Morgan served to the end of the war as Smith's deputy.

On June 5, 1944, when Eisenhower turned to Smith for advice on whether he should launch the Normandy landings, Smith urged that the attack proceed, calling it "the best possible gamble." The invasion began the following day. When the Third Reich collapsed, Eisenhower authorized Smith to accept the German surrender at Rheims on May 7, 1945.

In January 1946, Smith returned to Washington to be chief of the Operations and Planning Division of the Joint Chiefs of Staff. In March, President Harry S. Truman appointed him ambassador to the Soviet Union, where he remained until 1949. Smith was convinced that the United States should take a strong stand against Soviet expansion and that the Soviet Union would back down if confronted by American power. From 1950 to 1953, Smith served as the second director of the Central Intelligence Agency. He was promoted to full general on August 1, 1951. Smith retired from the Army on February 9, 1953. He also served as undersecretary of state in the Eisenhower administration.

Smith retired from government service on October 1, 1954. He then entered private business. Smith died in Washington, D.C., on August 9, 1961.

Thomas D. Veve

Further Reading

Crosswell, D. K. R. *Beetle: The Life of General Walter Bedell Smith.* Lexington: University Press of Kentucky, 2010.

Montague, Ludwell Lee. *General Walter Bedell Smith as Director of Central Intelligence, October 1950–February 1953.* University Park: Pennsylvania State University Press, 1992.

Smith, Walter Bedell. *Eisenhower's Six Great Decisions: Europe 1944–1945.* London: Longmans, Green, 1956.

Smith, Walter Bedell. *My Three Years in Moscow.* Philadelphia: Lippincott, 1949.

Stagg, James Martin (1900–1975)

Scottish-born meteorologist who headed the team of meteorologists advising General Dwight D. Eisenhower in the weeks leading up to the Normandy invasion of June 6, 1944. James Martin Stagg was born in Dalkeith, Midlothian, Scotland, on June 30, 1900. Graduating from the University of Edinburgh, in 1924 he secured a position in the British Meteorological Office. During 1932–1933 he led a British polar expedition to the Canadian Arctic, and in 1939 he became superintendent of the Kew Gardens Observatory. In 1943 Stagg, whom many described as morose and prickly, received a commission as a group captain in the Royal Air Force Volunteer Reserve. It was in this position that he became Eisenhower's chief meteorological adviser.

Eisenhower had scheduled the D-Day invasion to take place sometime between June 5 and June 7. However, the month began amid seemingly endless squalls, high winds, and treacherous seas in the English Channel. Early on June 4, Stagg recommended that Eisenhower not go forward with the invasion on June 5 owing to continuing stormy conditions and a low ceiling. The general heeded the advice and postponed the landings until at least June 6. Late in the evening of June 4, Stagg and his staff saw a potential window of opportunity opening up on June 6. Stagg advised Eisenhower of this, and the next morning the general gave the order for the invasion to begin early on June 6. Although conditions on that day were far from ideal, with stiff winds, rough seas, and occasional showers, the operation was a success. Furthermore, the Germans were taken somewhat by surprise, not believing that the Allies would attempt a huge amphibious operation in such conditions.

For his invaluable services leading up to D-Day, Stagg was made an officer of the U.S. Legion of Merit in 1945; that same year he was made an officer of the Order of the British Empire. Eight years later he was honored with an appointment as a companion of the Order of the Bath. Meanwhile, in 1951 he was elected as a fellow to the Royal Society of Edinburgh. Elected president of the Royal Meteorological Society in 1959, Stagg retired as head of the Meteorological Office in 1960.

Stagg died in England on June 23, 1975.

Paul G. Pierpaoli Jr.

Further Reading

Ross, John. *The Forecast for D-Day and the Weatherman behind Ike's Greatest Gamble.* Guilford, CT: Lyons, 2014.

Stagg, J. M. *Forecast for Overlord.* New York: Norton, 1971.

Steele, John Marvin (1912–1969)

U.S. Army paratrooper whose experience in the Normandy invasion made him well known. John M. Steele was born in Metropolis, Illinois, on November 29, 1912. After enlisting in the army in 1942, Steele trained as a paratrooper and joined the 82nd Airborne Division. Assigned to Company F of its Parachute Infantry Regiment, he arrived in North Africa in May 1943. On July 9, 1943, he parachuted into Gela, Sicily, but broke his leg during the jump. After recovering in a Tunisian hospital, he returned to Italy in September and saw combat that ranged from Salerno to Naples. In November 1943, he accompanied his unit when it was assigned to England to prepare for the invasion of France.

Late on June 5, 1944, elements of the 82nd Airborne, including Steele's company, parachuted into the vicinity of the town of Sainte-Mère-Église in Normandy. Casualties were heavy as German defenders shot at the paratroopers as they descended, illuminated by burning buildings. Several units, including Steele's, were inadvertently dropped directly into the village, which was stoutly defended. As Steele came down, he was wounded in the leg by flak. His chute then became hung up on a church bell tower at about 1:00 a.m. on June 6. As fighting raged around him, he was unable to free himself and then feigned death. Two German soldiers, however, took him prisoner. After three days in captivity, Steele managed to escape to Allied lines and was sent to a military hospital in England. He was awarded both a Bronze Star and a Purple Heart for his actions at Sainte-Mère-Église, the first French town liberated by the Allies.

Steele jumped again in Operation MARKET GARDEN (September 17–26, 1944) and fought in the German Ardennes Offensive (Battle of the Bulge, December 16, 1944–January 16, 1945). He mustered out of the army in September 1945. The 1962 Hollywood film *The Longest Day* saw Steele portrayed by Red Buttons. As a prominent tourist attraction, the church at Sainte-Mère-Église has a parachute and dummy paratrooper hanging from its spire.

Steele died of cancer on May 16, 1969, in Fayetteville, North Carolina.

Paul G. Pierpaoli Jr.

Further Reading

"John M. Steele, Ex-Paratrooper Who Landed on Steeple on D-Day, Dies." *New York Times,* May 17, 1969, http://query.nytimes.com/gst/abstract.html?res=9505EFD71F30EE3BBC4F52DFB3668382679EDE.

Ryan, Cornelius. *The Longest Day: The Classic Epic of D-Day.* New York: Simon and Schuster, 1994.

Sword Beach. *See* Terrain and Tactical Problems on D-Day

T

Tanks

Tanks are armored, tracked, armed vehicles originally developed in World War I. Improved in the years after the war, the tank came into its own as a weapon system in World War II. During the fighting in Normandy, German tanks and self-propelled guns, while fewer in number, were better armed. The German Panther and Tiger were also far better armored than the U.S. Sherman and British Cromwell tanks. Allied tank crews bemoaned their lack of protection and hitting power. In the Normandy fighting, the Allied tanks also proved highly vulnerable to well-concealed German antitank guns and infantry *Panzerfausts*.

Germany

Ironically, because France and Britain had led in the development of tanks in World War I, the German Army pioneered the development of panzer (armored) divisions, three of which were formed as early as 1935. Based on tanks, they also included motorized infantry, artillery, and other elements capable of keeping up with the tanks, which were to smash through weak points in enemy defenses and then exploit the breakthrough. Initially, the divisions were equipped with the specially developed light tanks PzKpfw I and II (PzKpfw is the abbreviation for *Panzerkampfwagen,* or "armored fighting vehicle"), while two larger designs, the PzKpfw III and IV, were being built. The PzKpfw IV became the backbone of German armor at the end of the war. The most important tank of the series, up-gunned and up-armored from earlier versions, it weighed 23.6 tons, carried a crew of five, and mounted a long-barreled 75mm main gun. Its 300-horsepower gasoline engine allowed a speed of 25 miles per hour. The main armament of the PzKpfw IV gave it parity in hitting power with later Soviet and American tanks.

When Germany invaded the Soviet Union on June 22, 1941, German armor encountered the Soviet T-34, whose superior firepower, speed, shape, suspension, armor, and maneuverability made all German tanks virtually obsolete. By March 1942, however, Germany had prototypes of the PzKpfw VI Tiger heavy tank. It had a five-man crew. The 700-horsepower gasoline engine could drive this 55-ton tank at 24 miles per hour. It was armed with a powerful 88mm (3.46-inch) gun. It had 100mm hull front armor and 120mm armor on the gun mantelet.

While the Tiger was not especially nimble or reliable and was better suited to defense than offense, its gun could destroy any other tank in the world, while it in turn could be destroyed only by the heaviest Allied antitank guns and then only at much shorter ranges than the Tiger's main gun.

In November 1942, the first production PzKpfw V Panther was delivered. A new tank designed to counter the T-34, it was Germany's best tank of the war. The 1944 version carried a crew of four and mounted a long-barreled 75mm gun. It also had two 7.92mm machine guns. The 44.8-ton vehicle was equipped with a 700-horsepower gasoline engine.

The Germans also manufactured increasing numbers of assault antitank guns and *jagdpanzers,* self-propelled guns that mounted the heaviest possible limited-traverse antitank gun on a tank chassis. Although these enjoyed success against the British and Americans, who lacked a heavy tank until late in the war, they were less successful against the Soviet Union's later T-34 medium tank with a 85mm gun and especially the IS-1 (JS-1) heavy tank that mounted a 100mm gun.

Great Britain
By World War II, the British Army had opted for two categories of tanks—high-speed cruiser tanks and heavily armored but slow infantry tanks. An emphasis on mobility and armor protection, at the expense of gun power, plagued British tanks throughout the war.

The A27 Centaur saw service in Normandy. The essential element of its design was the Merlin engine, designated the Meteor in its tank version. With the Merlin required for aircraft, Leyland was asked to come up with a design that would utilize the Liberty engine of the Crusader yet could be modified to take the Meteor when it became available. The design was known as the A27L (for "Liberty"). The first production models, designated the Cruiser Tank, Mk VIII, Centaur (A27L), began coming off the assembly lines in late 1942. Some 950 Centaurs were manufactured, including 80 that substituted a 95mm howitzer as the main gun for purposes of close infantry support. The Centaur weighed 63,500 pounds, had a five-man crew, was powered by a 395-horsepower Liberty engine that drove it at 27 miles per hour, and was armed with a 6-pounder (57mm) main gun and one machine gun. It had maximum 76mm armor protection.

The Royal Marines Armoured Support Group employed Centaurs in the Normandy invasion, using them to provide covering fire from LCTs (landing craft tanks) and then fire over the beaches. Centaurs saw extensive service throughout the remainder of the war in the fighting in Northern Europe. Some were later converted to Cromwells by the substitution of the new Meteor engine. Modifications included artillery outpost tanks, antiaircraft tanks, engineer tanks, and armored recovery vehicles. A few became armored personnel carriers and were known as Centaur Kangaroos.

The principal British manufactured tank in Normandy was the Mk4 Cromwell. The Cromwell was the A27 with the powerful 600-horsepower Meteor and designated the A27M. The new engine drove it at up to 40 miles per hour. Originally designated the Cromwell III, it entered production in January 1943 as the Cruiser Tank, Mk VIII, Cromwell (A27M). Fighting in North Africa had led to demand for a gun that could fire both high-explosive and armor-piercing shell, and the result was a British version of the U.S. 75mm gun, essentially a bored-up 6-pounder that could fire American 75mm ammunition. Problems with the new gun were not completely corrected until May 1944, however.

Numerically the Cromwell was the most important British heavy cruiser tank of the war, and it and the American-built M-4 Sherman were the principal armored fighting vehicle of the British armored divisions that fought across Northern Europe in 1944–1945. The Cromwell's 75mm gun, however, made it inferior to the German PzKpfw V and even late-model PzKpfw IVs. Its narrow hull, however, precluded up-gunning. It and the Centaur had the same boxlike turret construction.

The A22 Churchill was a more successful design. Originally produced in 1941, it was not truly successful until 1944, with the Churchill VII production. This 40-ton version had a crew of five and a 75mm main gun. Its 350-horsepower engine could drive it at 12.5 miles per hour. Variations were used for many purposes, for example, as engineer vehicles and for close support.

United States

The M4 Sherman medium was the standard U.S. tank of the Normandy fighting and the war in Europe. The M4A1 weighed 33.25 tons and had a crew of five and maximum 51mm armor. It mounted a 75mm main gun and had a .50-caliber antiaircraft gun and two .30-caliber machine guns. The Sherman had two great advantages over the German tanks: its powered turret enabled crews to react and fire more quickly, and it offered greater mechanical reliability and repairability. Rugged, simple in design, easy to maintain, and highly maneuverable, the M4 was consistently upgraded in main gun and armor during the course of the war. The M4A1 had a cast-iron hull; the M4A2, used only by the U.S. Marine Corps, had new engines; and the M4A4 and M4A6 had longer hulls and tracks. Some variants also employed improved appliqué armor.

Sherman variants performed a wide variety of roles, including but not limited to tank recovery, flamethrowers, mine clearing, and bridging. The Sherman chassis also provided the basis for the M7B1 howitzer motor carriage mounting a 105mm howitzer as its principal armament. The M4 chassis was also utilized in the M10 and M10A tank destroyers, essentially a gun motor carriage mounting a 3-inch gun, as well as the more satisfactory M36 series mounting a 90mm gun.

The M4 entered combat for the first time with the British Eighth Army in the October

U.S. Sherman M4 tanks fire their main 75mm guns on a firing range in England on May 9, 1944, in preparation for the invasion of France. The M4 served in a variety of roles, but as a medium tank it was at a disadvantage in dealing with much of the German armor. The M26 Pershing heavy tank did not appear until January 1945. (AP Photo)

1942 Battle of El Alamein. It saw service on virtually every fighting front of the war and had a long life thereafter. Indeed, M4s remained in service until only recently in the armies of a number of nations. In part because comparable British tanks, the Cromwell IV and VII, were not available until the end of 1943 and were not in wide use until the spring of 1944, the Sherman was probably the most important tank in British service and was more widely used than any of the British-designed or British-produced types during 1943–1945.

Initially the Sherman was a poor match for the most numerous German tank, the Pz-Kpfw Mark IV Panther. At a 1,000-yard range a Sherman's 75mm gun stood little chance of knocking out the Panther, while at the same range the Panther's high-velocity 75mm could indeed knock out the Sherman. The American tankers could only hope that they could use their powered turret to good advantage in order to lay the main gun quickly and get off several rounds before the Panther could fire.

German tanks had thicker frontal armor and a gun with a much higher velocity. The Tiger's 88mm and the same caliber *Panzerschreck* antitank weapon could easily knock out the Shermans, whereas the U.S. 2.36-inch Bazooka (copied from the *Panzerschreck*) was only effective against German side armor. Also, the Sherman track width was only 14 inches, while German tanks had a track 30–36-inch width and thus were not as easily bogged down. Indeed, U.S. tanker crews often added extensions to their tank tracks to rectify this situation.

Although the British utilized all models of the M4, the most numerous was the M4A4 type. The major British innovation regarding the Sherman was to replace its 75mm main gun with a 17-pounder (76.2mm). This up-gunned M4, known as the Sherman Firefly, was the most powerfully armed British tank of the entire war. Conversion began as a fallback position should the new Challenger tank encounter problems in testing. The Challenger indeed experienced difficulties, and in February 1944 conversion of the Shermans received priority. Because of delays in the Challenger program, that tank was not available for participation in the Normandy landings, and the Firefly was the only British tank capable of taking on and defeating the German Tiger and Panther tanks. Owing to a shortage in 17-pounder guns for tank use, the Firefly was initially supplied one per cavalry troop. Not until early 1945 was the up-gunned Firefly available in large numbers.

The British also developed a large number of Sherman variants. These included the Adder, Salamander, Crocodile, and Badger flamethrower tanks; the fascine carrier; the Twaby Ark, Octopus, and Plymouth bridging vehicles; rocket launchers; and the Scorpion, Lobster, and Crab flail antimine tanks.

In April 1943 the British also began experiments with a duplex drive (DD) on the Sherman. The DD had proven successful with their Vallentine tank, which by that date was obsolete. Sherman DD tanks were waterproofed and fitted with a collapsible canvas screen around the hull to provide flotation. Struts, erected by means of rubber tubing filled by compressed air, held the canvas in place. Two small propellers, folded away while on land, pushed the Sherman through the water at a speed of about four knots. Sherman DD tanks constituted an entire brigade of the 79th Armored Division in the Normandy landings and were the first British tanks to land, "swimming" ashore from LCTs. DD tanks, however, were easily swamped and required careful handling and the right conditions in which to operate.

The Sherman's great disadvantages were its engine and main gun. Its gasoline (vice diesel) engine led GIs to give it the nickname the "Ronson" after the Ronson cigarette lighter, sold with the slogan "lights first time every time." The Sherman was also consistently outgunned by the larger German tanks against which it had to fight. Its 75mm gun was relatively ineffective, but the replacement 76mm (17-pounder) gun with much higher muzzle velocity proved successful. After the British began mounting the 76mm on their Shermans, the Americans followed suit in February 1944. These appeared in the M4A1 through M4A3 models.

One of the major problems for the U.S. Army in the European theater was its lack of a heavy tank with which to deal with German tanks of thicker frontal armor and higher-velocity guns. In the course of 1944–1945 the 3rd Armored Division alone lost 648 Sherman tanks completely destroyed in combat and another 700 knocked out, repaired, and put back into operation. This represented a loss rate of 580 percent. In fact, the United States lost 6,000 tanks in Europe in World War II. The Germans never had more than half that total.

The answer to the German tanks was a heavy tank. The United States was slow to develop a heavy tank, largely the consequence of Lieutenant General George S. Patton's belief that tank destroyers rather than other tanks should deal with German armor. The heavy M-26 tank was standardized in January 1945, but only a few reached Europe before the end of the war there.

One of the myths of World War II is that the Germans enjoyed superiority in both numbers and quality of tanks. This is simply untrue. What the Germans possessed was a better mix of vehicles for the circumstances, a superior tactical doctrine for their employment, and more effective leadership.

In the end, better Allied equipment and above all superior numbers simply overwhelmed them.

Spencer C. Tucker

Further Reading

Chamberlain, Peter, and Chris Ellis. *British and American Tanks of World War Two.* London: Cassell, 1969.

Ellis, Chris. *Tanks of World War II.* London: Chancellor, 1997.

Jentz, Thomas L., and Hilary L. Doyle. *German Panzers in World War II: From Pz.Kpfw.I to Tiger II.* Atglen, PA: Schiffer Military History, 2001.

Tucker, Spencer C. *Tanks: An Illustrated History of Their Impact.* Santa Barbara, CA: ABC-CLIO, 2004.

Taylor, Maxwell Davenport (1901–1987)

U.S. Army general. Born in Keytesville, Missouri, on August 26, 1901, Maxwell Davenport Taylor graduated from the U.S. Military Academy at West Point in 1922 and was commissioned in the engineers. He attended the Engineer School at Fort Belvoir, Virginia, before being assigned to the 3rd Engineers in Hawaii. In 1926, Taylor transferred to field artillery. A talented linguist, he taught French and Spanish for five years at West Point; graduated from the Command and General Staff School, Fort Leavenworth, Kansas, in 1935; and was then an assistant military attaché in Japan.

In 1937, Taylor was assigned to Colonel Joseph W. Stilwell's staff. Following graduation from the Army War College in 1940, Taylor was appointed to the staff of U.S. Army chief of staff General George C. Marshall and promoted to lieutenant colonel. In July 1942 he became chief of staff of the 82nd Airborne Division as a colonel, and in December he was promoted to brigadier general as the divisional artillery commander.

Taylor joined the 82nd in Sicily after the July 9, 1943, Allied invasion, and on September 7 he volunteered for a secret mission behind enemy lines, going to Rome to determine if an airborne drop there was feasible. Meeting with Italian officials, he determined that the Germans had quickly secured both Rome and the facilities necessary for such an operation to succeed. On his recommendation, the mission was scrapped just as the first troop-laden aircraft became airborne. Taylor was then senior representative on the commission that convinced the new Italian government to declare war on Germany.

Taylor returned to the 82nd, and in March 1944 in the United Kingdom he took command of the 101st Airborne Division (the Screaming Eagles). Promoted to major general the same month, he jumped with the division during the June 6, 1944, Normandy invasion behind Utah Beach. After being rotated back to Britain after more than a month of combat, Taylor and his division next participated in Operation MARKET GARDEN (September 17–26). On September 17 the division seized Vechel, captured and held the Zon Bridge, and then took Sint Oedenrode and Eindhoven. Taylor was subsequently wounded and was out of action for two weeks. He rejoined his division on December 25 and fought with it for the remainder of the December 16, 1944–January 16, 1945, German Ardennes Offensive. The division then helped mop up pockets of resistance in the Ruhr before resuming the advance east. At the end of the war in Europe, the 101st helped seize Berchtesgaden.

In September 1945 Taylor became superintendent of West Point, where he initiated curriculum reforms. Between 1949 and 1951, he headed the Berlin Command. In 1951, he was promoted to lieutenant general and became the U.S. Army's deputy chief of staff for operations and training. In February 1953, Taylor took command of the Eighth Army in Korea as a full general at a time when an armistice was imminent. He was then commanding general, Army Forces Far East, in 1954 and commander in chief, Far East Command, in 1955.

Taylor served as the army chief of staff between 1955 and 1959, differing sharply with President Dwight D. Eisenhower's strategy of "massive retaliation." Taylor urged greater emphasis on conventional forces and the ability to fight limited wars, which later became known as "flexible response." Retiring in 1959, Taylor expressed his views publicly in his book *The Uncertain Trumpet,* which caught the attention of Senator John F. Kennedy. In 1961 as president, Kennedy brought Taylor out of retirement to serve as his military adviser during 1961 and 1962; thereafter Taylor was appointed chairman of the Joint Chiefs of Staff, serving in that post from 1962 to 1964. He opposed the commitment of U.S. ground troops to Vietnam but urged an escalation of the war through the bombing of North Vietnam. In 1964 and 1965 he was ambassador to South Vietnam. For the remainder of his life, he defended U.S. policies in Vietnam and blamed his country's defeat on the media. Taylor was president of the Institute for Defense Analysis between 1966 and 1969 and president of the Foreign Intelligence Advisory Board from 1965 to 1970. Taylor died in Washington, D.C., on April 19, 1987.

Uzal W. Ent and Spencer C. Tucker

Further Reading

Taylor, John M. *General Maxwell Taylor: The Sword and the Pen.* New York: Doubleday, 1989.

Taylor, Maxwell D. *The Uncertain Trumpet.* New York: Harper, 1960.

Tedder, Sir Arthur William (1st Baron Tedder) (1890–1967)

British marshal of the Royal Air Force (RAF). Born on July 11, 1890, at Glenguin, Scotland, Arthur William Tedder graduated from Magdalene College, Cambridge, in 1913. Commissioned in the British Army later that year, he served in France at the beginning of World War I but was posted to the Royal Flying Corps in 1916. He rose to command 70 Squadron and accepted a commission in the RAF in 1919.

From 1929 to 1931, Tedder was assistant commandant of the RAF Staff College. He then held administrative positions at the Air Armament School and the Air Ministry. He headed up training from 1934 to 1936, then was commander in the Far East. In 1937 he was promoted to air vice marshal. He returned to Britain to become director of research in the Air Ministry in 1938.

In the summer of 1940, Tedder was transferred to North Africa as deputy air commander. He became air commander in chief of the Middle East Air Force in June 1941, directing air operations against the Axis powers in North Africa. Tedder constantly struggled with a shortage of air assets. A forceful airpower advocate along with his subordinate, Air Vice Marshal Arthur Coningham, Tedder worked to combine and coordinate RAF activities with ground forces in innovative ways. In February 1943 as commander in chief of Allied air assets in the Mediterranean, Tedder was overall air commander for the 1943 Tunisia and Sicily campaigns.

In late 1943, Tedder used the experience gained in these operations to help plan air support for the June 6, 1944, Normandy invasion as deputy supreme commander, earning high praise from commander General Dwight D. Eisenhower. Tedder developed a detailed plan to use airpower to disrupt German communications and supply lines prior to the actual landings. In November 1944, he replaced Air Chief Marshal Trafford Leigh-Mallory as commander of tactical air forces. At the end of the war in Europe, Tedder signed the surrender agreement with Germany on behalf of Eisenhower.

On his return to Britain, Tedder was promoted to marshal of the RAF (five-star rank). In January 1946 he was made a baron and appointed chief of the air staff, a post he held until his retirement in 1950. From 1954 to 1960, he was chairman of the Standard Motor Company. Tedder died in Surrey, England, on June 3, 1967.

Harold Lee Wise

Further Reading

Orange, Vincent. *A Life of Marshal of the RAF Lord Tedder of Glenguin.* London: Frank Cass, 2002.

Tedder, Sir Arthur. *With Prejudice: The War Memoirs of Marshal of the Royal Air Force Lord Tedder G.C.B.* Boston: Little, Brown, 1967.

Terraine, John. *A Time for Courage: The Royal Air Force in the European War, 1939–1945.* New York: Macmillan, 1985.

Tehran Conference (November 28–December 1, 1943)

One of the most important Allied conferences during World War II. Usually overshadowed by the 1945 Yalta Conference, the meeting at Tehran was in fact equally as or more important than Yalta because of the decisions made there. Attending were the

"Big Three"—U.S. president Franklin D. Roosevelt, British prime minister Winston L. S. Churchill, and Soviet leader Joseph Stalin. The conference was also the first face-to-face meeting between Roosevelt and Stalin.

The Soviet leader claimed that his wartime responsibilities would not allow him to travel far, so the conference, code-named Eureka, took place at Tehran, Iran; the journey to Tehran was Stalin's first trip abroad since 1912. Held from November 28 to December 1, 1943, the conference was immediately preceded by a meeting at Cairo (code-named Sextant) that involved Chinese Nationalist leader Jiang Jieshi (Chiang Kai-shek) and featured a discussion of the Allied effort against Japan. Because the Soviet Union was not then at war with Japan, Stalin refused to attend that meeting, necessitating the Eureka Conference.

At the Tehran meeting, Roosevelt was convinced that he could win over Stalin and, toward that end, turned on his formidable charm to try to secure the Soviet leader's confidence. At Tehran and later at Yalta, Roosevelt deliberately distanced himself from Churchill, a serious mistake. The British prime minister could not believe that the democracies would take separate paths.

The Western leaders labored under a number of disadvantages at Tehran. The first involved the strategic military situation. British and U.S. troops were then fighting the Germans only in Italy with 14 divisions, whereas the Soviet Union had 178 divisions locked in combat. In addition, the Western leaders feared that Stalin might yet seek a diplomatic accommodation with Adolf Hitler, and Roosevelt was also anxious to secure Soviet assistance in the war against Japan.

At Tehran, Stalin pressured the West on an early date for an Allied invasion of France. The Soviet ambassador to London, Ivan Maisky, had counseled Stalin to press for an immediate second front, which he knew was impossible, in order to secure additional Lend-Lease aid. Stalin insisted on learning the name of the commander of Operation OVERLORD as proof that the Western Allies were indeed serious about a cross-channel invasion, and in a follow-up meeting in Cairo after Eureka, Roosevelt named General Dwight D. Eisenhower to the post. The three leaders also spent a great deal of time discussing Germany and its possible future division at Tehran. Roosevelt suggested splitting Germany into five states and internationalizing the Ruhr and other areas. Churchill, fearful of potential Soviet expansion into Europe, thought that Prussia might be detached from the rest of Germany.

Discussions over Poland were more controversial. All three leaders agreed on the Oder River as the future Polish-German boundary, but the Western leaders rejected the Soviet demand that a tributary of the Oder, the Western Neisse River, be the southern demarcation line. Nor did they sanction Poland securing the important port of Stettin on the west bank of the Oder. The three did concur that Poland would receive most of East Prussia, although the Soviet Union claimed the Baltic port of Königsberg (the future Kaliningrad) and land to the northeast. The Western leaders could hardly oppose the Curzon Line, established by the victorious Allies at the 1919 Paris Peace Conference following World War I, as the eastern boundary of Poland. The British did object, however, to the Soviet seizure of the predominantly Polish city of L'vov (L'viv).

Churchill pointed out to Stalin that Britain had gone to war over Poland, but Stalin insisted that the Red Army needed security in its rear areas and that a primary goal of the war was to protect the Soviet Union against future German attack. Obviously, a Poland that had been compensated for the loss of its eastern territory to the Soviet Union by receiving German territory in the west would necessarily have to look to the Soviet Union for security.

Churchill later had the difficult task of promoting all of these arrangements to the Polish government-in-exile in London; the large Polish community in the United States was also upset by the arrangements. Stalin refused normal diplomatic relations with the London Poles, charging that they were stirring up trouble for the Red Army. No independent Polish government would ever concede changes that put the country at the Soviet Union's mercy. Thus, a Polish government subservient to Moscow was probably inevitable.

Stalin also demanded that the Soviet Union be allowed to keep its 1939–1940 acquisitions of Bessarabia, the Karelian Isthmus, and the Baltic states. Although these acquisitions were clear violations of the Atlantic Charter, the Siege of Leningrad gave Stalin a strong argument for a security zone there. He also insisted that Finland cede its Arctic port of Petsamo, pay heavy reparations, and provide space for a base to protect sea approaches to Leningrad. In return he promised to respect Finland's independence, assuming that Finland behaved properly.

Stalin reassured Roosevelt that the Soviet Union would enter the war against Japan after the defeat of Germany. Stalin also stressed the importance of an Allied invasion of France to relieve pressure on the Red Army from German troops on the Eastern Front. Further, he expressed the view that a landing in southern France (the future Operation ANVIL) would be most helpful. Stalin was pleased when the Western leaders told him that the invasion of northern France (Operation OVERLORD) was scheduled for May 1944 and pledged to launch a Soviet ground offensive to coincide with it. The three leaders also agreed that after the war Iran, which was serving as a supply corridor to the Soviet Union and was occupied by Allied troops, would be restored to full territorial integrity and sovereignty and that all troops would be withdrawn.

Although the Tehran Conference served to dissipate tensions between the two Western leaders and Stalin, sharp differences on the conduct of the war and the composition of postwar Europe remained. These differences were very much in evidence at the February 1945 Yalta Conference.

Spencer C. Tucker

Further Reading

Dunn, Walter Scott. *Second Front Now, 1943.* Tuscaloosa: University of Alabama Press, 1980.

Edmonds, Robin. *The Big Three: Churchill, Roosevelt and Stalin in War and Peace.* New York: Norton, 1991.

Fischer, Louis. *The Road to Yalta: Soviet Relations, 1941–1945.* New York: Harper and Row, 1972.

Gardner, Lloyd C. *Spheres of Influence: The Great Powers Partition Europe, from Munich to Yalta.* Chicago: Ivan R. Dee, 1993.

Nadeau, Remi. *Stalin, Churchill and Roosevelt Divide Europe.* New York: Praeger, 1990.

Perlmutter, Amos. *FDR and Stalin: A Not So Grand Alliance, 1943–1945.* Columbia: University of Missouri Press, 1993.

Sainsbury, Keith. *The Turning Point: Roosevelt, Stalin, Churchill, and Chiang-Kai-shek, 1943; The Moscow, Cairo, and Teheran Conferences.* Oxford: Oxford University Press, 1985.

Terrain and Tactical Problems on D-Day

The immediate task for the Allies on June 6, 1944, was getting ashore at Normandy. Once the first wave accomplished this, the far greater tactical problem was getting off the beach and moving farther inland. Opposed landing beaches are almost always killing zones. The longer the initial waves stay on the beach, the greater the casualty rate and the probability that the assault will fail. The only solution to that tactical problem is to get off the beach and push inland as fast and as far as possible, thereby disrupting the enemy's defenses. The enemy, of course, will do everything to hold the attackers on vulnerable ground as long as possible.

Every landing is different, and the solution to the tactical problem is always a function of the terrain itself—the topography of the beach, the exits off the beach, and the ground immediately behind to the depth of at least artillery range. All of those factors were somewhat different for the five Operation OVERLORD beaches along some 45 miles of the Normandy coast. Gold, Juno, and Sword, the three British beaches, were roughly similar, bounded on the east by the Orne River and the Caen Canal. Omaha Beach, to the west of Gold Beach, was completely different, and Utah Beach, across the Vire and Douve Rivers and on the far west end of the landings, was different still. The Allies therefore faced and had to solve simultaneously three very different sets of terrain-tactical problems.

Arromanches, which sat to the western side of Gold Beach, marked the dividing line between two very different types of terrain. Immediately west of Arromanches high bluffs and rocky cliffs dominated the coastal terrain. For most of the first eight miles west of the town the rocky cliffs came right down to the water's edge, making the shoreline useless for landings. From east of Arromanches all the way to the Orne River the ground was more gently sloping as it approached the coast. The three British beaches were generally sandy except the Sword Beach sector; it had significant rocky clusters between the sand beach and the waterline. Overall, Juno, Sword, and the eastern half of Gold were good landing beaches.

While the Canadians on Juno Beach had the toughest fight in the British zone, the three eastern beaches were generally easier to get off of than the two American beaches in the west. The eastern exit routes were not as channelized, and the ground immediately inland was reasonably good tank country, rolling and fairly open. The Germans took advantage of the good tank ground and massed most of their panzer divisions in the area directly east of the British and Canadian landings. The British tactical imperative was to get as much of their own armor ashore as fast as possible to deal with the panzers as they moved forward. During the weeks immediately following the landings, almost all of the major armored battles occurred around the British beachhead.

The British 6th Airborne Division was dropped to the east of the Orne River in order to screen the Allied left flank. The line of the Orne River and the Caen Canal was the key to delaying the German reserves. The two parallel waterways ran northeasterly for almost eight miles from the city of Caen to the coast. Although the waterways were significant military obstacles, the British also had to take and hold the two key bridges across the channels halfway between the city and the coast. That mission was assigned to D Company, 2nd Battalion, Oxfordshire and Buckinghamshire Light Infantry Regiment, commanded by Major John Howard. The glider-borne assault on what later came to be called the Pegasus and Horsa Bridges was one of the most daring and successful special forces operations of the entire war.

The Omaha Beach sector started west of Arromanches, near the small waterfront town of Port-en-Bessin. The four-mile stretch of beaches from about two miles west of Port-en-Bessin to the town of Verville-sur-Mer was generally sandy and reached inland far enough to support the landing of a reinforced division. West of Verville-sur-Mer the coastline became rocky again, with high cliffs running right to the water's edge. One of the major problems on Omaha was the long and wide band of small flat rocks that ran parallel to the water, right down the middle of the Fox-Green and Easy-Red sectors. Called a "shingle," the band was not a major obstacle for soldiers on foot, but the slippery rocks were difficult for vehicles to cross, especially tracked vehicles.

Along the inland side of the sand beach the ground rises sharply into a long line of steep bluffs. Four large draws that run down to the beach were the only paths that vehicles could use to get on top of the bluffs and from there move inland. As masters of the tactical exploitation of terrain, the Germans had the draws mined and covered with interlocking machine-gun and mortar fire. Securing the draws required the American infantrymen to assault frontally up the face of the bluffs and then envelop the draws from the rear. It was a casualty-intensive operation for both attackers and defenders.

Omaha was the most difficult of all the D-Day beaches to secure and to get off of, especially the westernmost Dog-Red, Dog-White, and Dog-Green sectors. The terrain on top of the bluffs overlooking Omaha was completely different than the ground behind

The iconic image of American soldiers going ashore from an LCI (Landing Craft Infantry) at Normandy, while under heavy German fire, June 6, 1944. (Library of Congress)

the British beaches. It was Normandy *bocage* country, classic defender's ground. A *bocage* is a farm field usually having only one entrance and completely enclosed by an earthen berm up to six feet high, with dense shrubbery growing on top. Generally *bocage* fields were no larger than a football field. Most of the *bocage* fields in Normandy have been there since the Middles Ages. The network of the shrubs' roots penetrating deep into the earthen walls make them almost as dense and as strong as solid rock. Laid out like the squares on a chess board, each field is a ready-made fortress. The Germans defended almost every *bocage* field with mines, mortars, machine guns, and antitank weapons. A well-dug-in German platoon could hold up a much larger American force for days. Just before each position finally fell, the defenders would systematically withdraw to the next field to the rear, which had already been laid out for defensive purposes.

Once off the beach, the ground behind Omaha was also the hardest to fight through. The ground on the far western end of Omaha Beach consists of high cliffs right at the waterline. The extreme western flank drops almost straight down into the valley of the Vire River as it empties into the ocean. The Germans had a battery of captured long-range French 155mm guns near the western edge on a promontory called Pointe du Hoc. From there they could direct fire down on most of Omaha Beach and all of Utah Beach on the other side of the Vire. Although it was a terrible place to make a landing, the guns had to be neutralized as early in the invasion as possible. That was the mission of the 2nd Ranger Battalion, commanded by Lieutenant Colonel James Earl Rudder, the second great special forces operation of D-Day.

To reach the German guns, Rudder's Rangers had to approach the base of the cliffs in their landing craft and then climb straight up, under German fire. Initially proceeding to the wrong spot, their landing craft then had to relocate to the correct landing area. If a casual observer today stands on the cliffs at Pointe du Hoc or even looks at a 1:50,000 military scale map of the coast, it is hard to see how the rangers could have missed on their first attempt such an obvious dagger of rock, jutting straight out into the water. But from the vantage point of a small boat at water level several thousand meters out, the long cliff wall appears completely different. The cliffs seem to be one flat, massive wall, with Pointe du Hoc blending seamlessly into it.

The most western of the Allied landing sectors, Utah Beach, presented a significantly different set of terrain problems. The beach itself is ideal, flat and wide. The ground immediately inland, however, consists of saltwater marshes that are impossible even for soldiers on foot to move across. The exits from Utah are a series of four long and narrow causeways that run across the marshes to the higher ground about two miles inland. The exit problem for Utah was even more difficult than that for Omaha. On Omaha at least, the attacking infantrymen could work around the draws. Troops advancing inland from Utah had no alternative but to go straight down the causeways. Thus, the 101st Airborne Division dropped into the vicinity of Sainte-Marie-du-Mont with the mission of taking the causeways from the rear and holding them for the 4th Infantry Division to get across.

The higher ground directly southwest of Utah is like an island, almost completely surrounded by low, wet ground. Ten miles southwest of the beach the Merderet River runs southeast until it merges with the much larger Douve River, which then curves around to the northeast and empties into the sea at the western end of Utah. On military maps the Merderet does not appear to be a significant obstacle. The main stream is only a couple of yards wide and a few feet deep. The river, however, is flanked by a wide floodplain on both sides extending hundreds of meters. The entire area along the river can be turned into an impassable marsh by opening the tidal floodgates from the ocean. That is exactly what the German defenders did in the last days of May 1944.

The U.S. VII Corps had two critical operational tasks. In addition to pushing inland as far and as fast as possible, it also had to block German reinforcements that would try to move into the area to cut off the initially isolated Utah beachhead. The key to accomplishing both missions was the immediate seizure of the only two bridges over the Merderet, one at Chef-du-Pont, southwest of Sainte-Mère-Église, and the other at La Fière, two miles west of the town. Further complicating the tactical problem at La Fière, the very old stone bridge is close to the north bank of the river, but the then-unpaved road leading south from the bridge ran along the top of a very narrow elevated causeway through some 500 yards of the Merderet's south-bank floodplain. At the end of the causeway a small group of buildings stood on firmer ground at Cauquigny.

Seizing both Merderet bridges and establishing secure bridgeheads was the primary mission of the 82nd Airborne Division, which dropped in on both sides of the river near Sainte-Mère-Église. The battle to take the La Fière causeway was one of the fiercest fights in the days immediately following the landings.

Operation OVERLORD was both risky and complex. On June 6 alone the Allies suffered approximately 9,000 casualties. But OVERLORD succeeded. By June 12 the Allies linked up all five of the beachheads and were in France to stay. The main reason the operation succeeded was the skill and the determined fighting spirit of the Allied soldiers and their leaders. But the major supporting factor was the plan itself, which was a solid one. British and American operational planners, originally working under British lieutenant general Sir Frederick Morgan, spent months analyzing in excruciating detail the beaches and the ground inland. They then expertly matched the forces available with the scheme of maneuver to solve the terrain-tactical problem. Without such exacting and precise staff work and planning, the casualties undoubtedly would have been much higher, and Operation OVERLORD just might have failed.

David T. Zabecki

Further Reading

Boog, Horst, Werner Rahn, Reinhard Stumpf, and Bernd Wegner. *Germany and the Second World War,* Vol. 6, *The Global War.* Oxford, UK: Clarendon, 2001.

Ellis, L. F. *Victory in the West,* Vol. 1. United Kingdom Military Series. London: HMSO, 1962.

Harrison, Gordon A. *United States Army in World War II: The European Theater of Operations—Cross Channel Attack.* Washington, DC: U.S. Army, Office of the Chief of Military History, 1951.

Mann, John. *The D-Day Atlas.* New York: Facts on File, 1994.

Morgan, Frederick. *Overture to Overlord.* Garden City, NY: Doubleday, 1950.

TIGER, Exercise. *See* Lyme Bay, Battle of

Todt Organization

The Todt Organization (OT), named for German minister of arms and munitions Fritz

Todt, handled construction projects throughout territory occupied by the German Army during World War II. Formed in 1933 by Todt, then head of technology and road construction, the OT was at first chiefly identified with construction of the great autobahn road system in Germany that was the pride of the Third Reich. In 1938, German leader Adolf Hitler assigned the OT the task of quickly completing the West Wall (also known as the Siegfried Line), defenses in western Germany that were designed to hold back a French Army attack in order to allow Germany to concentrate its military resources in the east against Poland. Todt was an adroit manager, and in record time some 500,000 workers constructed 5,000 concrete bunkers.

With the beginning of World War II, the OT provided the German Army with engineers and construction specialists involved in the building and repair of bridges, dams, airfields, and fortifications as well as factories. In March 1940, Todt became the Reich's minister of arms and munitions. The OT was in fact the only organization in the Third Reich, apart from the Hitler Youth, that bore the name of a member of the governing elite.

Following the German invasion of the Balkans in the spring of 1941, the OT had charge of extracting minerals there and shipping them to the Reich. With the invasion of the Soviet Union, the OT took on the great responsibility of reconstructing and maintaining the Soviet transportation network. The OT also made use of vast numbers of conscript laborers throughout German-occupied Europe. In all, the OT mobilized some 1.4 million people, 80 percent of whom were non-Germans (many were prisoners of war).

The OT's most ambitious task was the construction of the Atlantic Wall, the German defenses against an invasion of France by the Western Allies; it ran from Norway to the Bay of Biscay. On this effort, the OT expended some 13.3 million tons of concrete and 1.2 million tons of steel in 3,000 fortifications. The ruins of many of these can still be seen today. The OT also built the submarine pens in France that proved so difficult for Allied aircraft to destroy.

Following Todt's death in an airplane crash in February 1942, his assistant, Albert Speer, took over the OT, and under him it reached its greatest extent. Increasingly, the OT was involved in cleaning up bomb damage from Allied air raids on Germany. In autumn 1944, the OT was renamed the Front-OT, when it was armed and enlisted in the defense of German territory.

Spencer C. Tucker

Further Reading

Seidler, Franz Wilhelm. *Die Organisation Todt: Bauen für Staat und Wehrmacht, 1938–1945.* Koblenz, Germany: Bernard and Graefe, 1987.

Taylor, Blaine. *Hitler's Engineers: Fritz Todt and Albert Speer, Master Builders of the Third Reich.* Philadelphia: Casemate Publishers, 2010.

TOTALIZE, Operation (August 7–13, 1944)

Operation TOTALIZE (also spelled TOTALISE) was the inaugural offensive by the First Canadian Army, which had been established only on July 23 and was commanded by Lieutenant General Harry Crerar. The operation took place during August 7–13, 1944, in the latter stage of the Battle of Normandy.

The U.S. Army breakout on the Allied western flank in Operation COBRA (July 25–31) had been a great success, ending with the capture of Avranches. TOTALIZE took place on the Allied eastern flank south of Caen with the goal of breaking through the German defenses there and securing the high ground north of the town of Falaise. Accomplishing this would enable the Western Allies to close off the Falaise pocket and prevent German forces there from escaping eastward. Canadian Army lieutenant general Guy Simonds, commander of II Corps, planned and had command of TOTALIZE. Simonds had previously directed Operations ATLANTIC (the Canadian part of Operation GOODWOOD, July 18–20) and SPRING (July 25–27).

German forces were well dug in on Verrières Ridge, with a number of antitank guns positioned farther back to prevent any Allied breakthrough along the Caen–Falaise road. The principal German defending units forward were the 85th and 89th Infantry Divisions and what remained of the 272nd Grenadier Infantry Division, which had been savaged in Operation SPRING. Farther to the rear were some 50 tanks of the 12th SS Panzer Division and an attached heavy tank battalion.

For TOTALIZE, Simonds had four infantry divisions (the 2nd and 3rd Canadian and the British 49th [West Riding] and 51st [Highland] divisions), two armored divisions (the 4th Canadian and the 1st Polish), and two armored brigades (the 2nd Canadian and the 33rd British). Simonds planned a night attack preceded by a raid by heavy bombers.

Simonds was well aware from previous British Second Army offensives of the effectiveness of German defenses in depth. Following the massive aerial bombing of Operation SPRING, the tanks had been able to break through, but the infantry had been unable to keep up and, separated from the tanks, had taken heavy casualties. To remedy this, Simonds ordered the creation of an improvised armored personnel carrier (APC), known as the Kangaroo, to enable the infantry to move with the tanks. These were converted armored vehicles. The first were some 72 105mm self-propelled M7 Priests with guns removed (known as "defrocked priests").

At 11:00 p.m. on August 7, Royal Air Force Bomber Command heavy bombers laid a carpet of bombs along a four-mile stretch on each side of the Caen–Falaise road. A half hour later, the two armored columns began their four-vehicle-wide advance along each side of the road: tanks, Kangaroo APCs, half-tracks, self-propelled antitank guns, and mine-flail tanks.

The first phase was successful. Problems developed in the second phase, however. Following a second bomber strike on suspected rearward German positions, the 4th Canadian Armoured Division was to penetrate the Germans' second position, closely followed by the 3rd Canadian Division to expand the penetration. The final phase would have the 1st Polish Armored Division push forward, with the infantry divisions following on to occupy the captured ground. The plan proved overly complicated for the inexperienced personnel of the 4th Canadian Armoured and 1st Polish Armored Divisions.

SS-Colonel Kurt Meyer, who now commanded the 12th SS Panzer Division, was able to bring forward reserves, mount counterattacks, and halt the Allied advance at some nine miles, seven miles short of Falaise. The attackers had suffered some 1,256 casualties and the loss of 146 tanks. The Germans sustained perhaps 3,000 casualties and lost 465 tanks.

The Canadian First Army then consolidated its gains and began preparations for a fresh attack, Operation TRACTABLE (August 14–21), also directed by Simonds.

Spencer C. Tucker

Further Reading

Bercuson, David. *Maple Leaf against the Axis: Canada's Second World War.* Toronto: Stoddart, 1995.

D'Este, Carlo. *Decision in Normandy: The Real Story of Montgomery and the Allied Campaign.* London: Penguin, 2004.

Ellis, Lionel F., G. W. G. Allen, A. E. Warhurst, and James Robb. *Victory in the West,* Vol. l, *The Battle of Normandy.* London: HMSO, 1962.

Graham, Dominic. *The Price of Command: A Biography of General Guy Simonds.* Toronto: Stoddart, 1993.

Hart, S. *Road to Falaise.* Stroud, UK: Sutton, 2004.

Perrun, Jody. "Best-Laid Plan: Guy Simonds and Operation Totalize, 7–10 August, 1944." *Journal of Military History* 67(1) (January 2003): 137–173.

Roy, Reginald H. *1944: The Canadians in Normandy.* Toronto: Macmillan of Canada in collaboration with the Canadian War Museum, 1984.

Tout, Ken. *Road to Falaise.* Stroud, UK: Sutton, 2002.

TRACTABLE, Operation (August 14–21, 1944)

Operation TRACTABLE was the final offensive by the First Canadian Army during the Battle of Normandy. Carried out during August 14–21, its goal was to seize Falaise and the smaller towns of Trun and Chambois in order to join with U.S. forces to move southward in order to close the Falaise gap, preventing sizable German forces trapped in the Falaise pocket from escaping eastward.

Canadian Army lieutenant general Guy Simonds, commander of II Corps, planned the operation. Simonds, who had also planned Operation TOTALIZE (August 7–13), sought to incorporate two successful tactics employed in it, namely an attack by heavy bombers just prior to the ground assault (although, unlike in TOTALIZE, this would occur in daylight) and the extensive use of improvised armored personnel carriers to permit the infantry to keep pace with the tanks.

TRACTABLE involved the 4th Canadian Armoured and 1st Polish Armored Divisions, the Canadian 2nd Armoured Brigade, and the Canadian 3rd Infantry Division, joined on the second day of the offensive by the Canadian 2nd Infantry Division. Opposing German forces under the command of SS-Colonel Kurt Meyer included the 12th SS Panzer Division and what remained of two infantry divisions. Allied ground forces commander General Bernard Montgomery hoped that the Canadians would be able to capture Falaise by midnight, after which, joined by the Polish 1st Armored Division, they would move against Trun, some 11 miles to the east. Linking up with the American Third Army would then be an easy matter, trapping some 350,000 German troops in the Falaise pocket.

Had the attackers achieved surprise, the offensive probably would have achieved its goals on time. Unfortunately for the Allies, however, a Canadian officer with a copy of the attack plan in his possession mistakenly drove his vehicle into German territory, where he was killed and the plan was discovered. Meyer was thus able to concentrate his 15 remaining tanks and 12 88mm antitank guns against the Allied approach route.

TRACTABLE began at 12:00 a.m. on August 14 with a raid by 800 Royal Air Force Bomber Command heavy bombers. Many of the bombs fell short, however, inflicting 400 casualties among the Poles and Canadians. The Canadian artillery then laid down a smoke screen cover, and the tanks and armored personnel carrier moved forward. The Germans nonetheless inflicted heavy casualties on the attackers, causing Simonds to commit the 2nd Canadian Infantry Division, which had been in reserve.

The going was slow. Men of the Canadian 2nd Infantry Division were not able to enter Falaise until August 16. Although the town was not finally cleared until August 18, Simonds was now able to reorganize his forces for the final drive on Turn and Chambois to close the pocket. This effort by the Canadian and Polish armored divisions began on August 16. Innovative tactics by 1st Polish Armored Division commander Major General Stanislaw Maczek brought the capture of Champeaux.

By August 19 the Poles were at Chambois and Mont Ormel (Hill 262), having closed the Falaise gap to only several hundred yards. The Poles took Mont Ormel in fierce fighting that same day. Two days of intense close-quarter fighting followed, with the Poles able to hold off counterattacks by German units seeking to escape the pocket.

Almost out of ammunition, the Poles were relieved by Canadian troops, who were then finally able to seal the gap and link up with the U.S. Third Army. TRACTABLE had claimed as many as 1,441 Polish casualties, a third of those lost by the Allied side in the operation.

By the evening of August 21, the vast majority of German forces unable to escape the pocket had surrendered. Total German losses in the Falaise pocket were probably on the order of 10,000 killed and 50,000 taken prisoner, but some 115,000 well-trained German troops had escaped to bolster the Reich's western defenses.

Spencer C. Tucker

Further Reading

Bercuson, David. *Maple Leaf against the Axis: Canada's Second World War.* Toronto: Stoddart, 1995.

D'Este, Carlo. *Decision in Normandy: The Real Story of Montgomery and the Allied Campaign.* London: Penguin, 2004.

Ellis, Lionel F., G. W. G. Allen, A. E. Warhurst, and James Robb. *Victory in the West,* Vol. 1, *The Battle of Normandy.* London: HMSO, 1962.

Graham, Dominic. *The Price of Command: A Biography of General Guy Simonds.* Toronto: Stoddart, 1993.

Hart, S. *Road to Falaise.* Stroud, UK: Sutton, 2004.

Roy, Reginald H. *1944: The Canadians in Normandy.* Toronto: Macmillan of Canada in collaboration with the Canadian War Museum, 1984.

Tout, Ken. *Road to Falaise.* Stroud, UK: Sutton, 2002.

U

Utah Beach. *See* Terrain and Tactical Problems on D-Day

Vian, Sir Philip Louis (1894–1968)

Royal Navy admiral of the fleet. Born in London on June 13, 1894, Philip Louis Vian entered the Royal Navy in 1910. Educated at the Hillside School and the Royal Naval colleges of Osborne and Dartmouth, he served in destroyers and cruisers during World War I and the interwar years.

At the beginning of World War II, Vian was commanding a reserve destroyer flotilla on Atlantic convoy duty. He soon distinguished himself as an aggressive and effective leader of light forces. As the commodore commanding the 4th Destroyer Flotilla of four modern Tribal-class destroyers and a cruiser, he seized the German Navy supply ship *Altmark* in Norwegian territorial waters on February 16, 1940, and freed 299 British prisoners held in it.

Vian also distinguished himself in the 1941 Norwegian campaign and in the chase of the German battleship *Bismarck,* which led to his early promotion to rear admiral that July. He then led Force K, a squadron of light cruisers, in offensive operations along the Norwegian coast until he was transferred to command Cruiser Squadron 15 in the Mediterranean in October 1941.

There, Vian further demonstrated his skill as his ships covered resupply convoys to Malta, most notably during the Second Battle of Sirte on March 22, 1942. In 1943, he commanded a squadron of five escort carriers charged with providing fighter cover and close air support for Operation AVALANCHE, the September 9, 1943, Salerno landings. Force V, operating in light winds and confined waters, provided more than half of all air support during the operation's first four days. This success was tempered, however, by Vian's inexperience in carrier operations, which showed in extraordinarily high operational losses.

Vian led the naval Eastern Task Force covering the June 6, 1944, Normandy invasion (Operation NEPTUNE) before taking command of the British carrier squadron destined for the Pacific. He was promoted to vice admiral in November 1944. After preliminary strikes against oil refineries in Sumatra, the carriers joined the U.S. Pacific Fleet at Okinawa in March 1945. After two months providing important air support to U.S. land operations on that island, the British Pacific Fleet withdrew to refit, then rejoined the U.S. Third Fleet for the final attack on the Japanese home islands. Vian's adaptability to carrier warfare requirements supported the integration of U.S. practice into the Royal Navy, and his drive was manifest in the fleet's accomplishments.

Following World War II, Vian served ashore and afloat until his retirement in 1952, when he was promoted to admiral of the fleet. Vian died at Ashford Hill, Berkshire, England, on May 27, 1968.

Paul E. Fontenoy

Further Reading

Brown, J. David. *Carrier Operations in World War II: The Royal Navy.* London: Ian Allan, 1968.

Brown, J. David, ed. *The British Pacific and East Indies Fleets.* Liverpool, UK: Brodie, 1995.

Smith, Peter C. *Task Force 57.* London: William Kimber, 1969.

Vian, Sir Philip. *Action This Day.* London: Mullee, 1960.

Warships, Allied

Nearly 7,000 ships, boats, and amphibious craft took part in Operation NEPTUNE, the naval part of the Normandy invasion. Of this number, 1,213 were warships. These included battleships, cruisers, and destroyers as well as specialized gunfire support ships and other vessels. The Royal Navy provided the bulk of these. Of the 1,213 warships, 893 were British and 200 were American, with the remainder provided by other nations. The British also furnished 3,261 landing craft.

Battleships

The largest and most powerful ships taking part in the Normandy invasion were the seven British and U.S. battleships. Battleships had long been regarded as the most powerful ships afloat, essential if a nation was to seek control of the seas. This place, however, was taken during World War II by the aircraft carrier, which could project potent firepower at far longer distances. Aircraft carriers did not take part in the Normandy invasion, however, because of the short distance across the English Channel for Allied aircraft.

Allied battleships taking part were, however, not the fast and more modern and powerful battleships then serving in the Pacific theater. Instead, the battleships supporting the Normandy invasion with long-range gunfire were among the oldest ships active in both the Royal Navy and the U.S. Navy; while all of these ships had gone through extensive refits, USS *Arkansas* and HMS *Warspite* had both been commissioned before World War I, in 1912 and 1913, respectively. The main armament of the seven battleships ranged from 12-inch to 16-inch guns. Four British and three American battleships were assigned to the landings, although HMS *Nelson* was held in reserve until June 10. The four British battleships with their dates of commissioning, tonnages, and main armaments were the *Nelson* (1925, 38,000 tons, 8 15-inch guns), the *Ramillies* (1915, 33,000 tons, 8 15-inch guns), the *Rodney* (1925, 38,000 tons, 9 16-inch guns), and the *Warspite* (1913, 35,000 tons, 6 15-inch guns). The three U.S. Navy battleships were the *Arkansas,* BB-33 (1912, 26,100 tons, 12 12-inch guns); *Nevada,* BB-36 (1916, 38,000 tons, 10 14-inch guns); and *Texas,* BB-35 (1914, 27,000 tons, 10 14-inch guns).

Monitors

Monitors were heavily armored shore bombardment vessels. Two British monitors took part in the Normandy invasion. They were the *Erebus* (1916, 8,000 tons, two 15-inch guns) and *Roberts* (1941, 8,100 tons, and two 15-inch guns).

Cruisers

Twenty-three cruisers took part. Cruisers were next to battleships in firepower but had traditionally been assigned an independent role as commerce destroyers. During World War II they fulfilled a variety of roles, including shore bombardment. The Washington Naval Treaty of 1922 had defined cruisers as warships of up to 10,000 tons

The old (commissioned in 1912) U.S. battleship *Arkansas* (BB-33) firing its main 12-inch guns in support of the Allied invasion of France. (Frank Scherschel/The LIFE Picture Collection/Getty Images)

displacement and mounting guns no larger than 8 inches. Generally speaking, the heavy cruisers had 8-inch guns, while light cruisers mounted 5.75-inch or 6-inch guns. Five heavy cruisers participated in the Normandy invasion: two from Britain and three from the United States. There were also 18 light cruisers: all were British except two from the Free French Navy and one from the Polish Navy.

Destroyers and Destroyer Escorts

Destroyers had been developed to combat the fast torpedo boat, the introduction of which threatened the capital ships. They were fast, light warships with the task of providing a protective screen for the battle fleet. During World War I they proved invaluable in protecting convoys of merchant ships, a service they replicated in World War II. The relatively shallow draft of the destroyers enabled them on occasion to provide valuable close-in naval gunfire support as they did in the Normandy invasion, indeed dangerously close to shore and on occasion scraping the sea bottom.

A total of 105 destroyers took part. Of this number, Britain provided 56 and the United States provided 34. Canada provided 7, Poland provided 4, Norway provided 3, and the Free French provided 1.

Rounding out the Allied warships were 3 gunboats, 14 sloops, 63 frigates and destroyer escorts, 71 corvettes, 98 fleet minesweepers, 189 other minesweepers, 18 patrol craft, 60 antisubmarine trawlers, 4 minelayers, 495 coastal craft of all types, 1 seaplane carrier, 2 midget submarines, and 58 antisubmarine groups.

Of the larger Allied warships, the Polish light cruiser *Dragon* sustained heavy damage from a German torpedo on July 7 and was then sunk as part of the Arromanches breakwater. Of destroyers and destroyer escorts, HMS *Glennon* was mined on June 8 and sunk by German artillery two days later, HMS *Boadicea* was torpedoed and sunk on June 13, and HMS *Fury* was mined on June 21 and not repaired. HMS *Swift* succumbed to a mine on June 24, and HMS *Wrestler* was damaged by a mine and not repaired. The United States lost the destroyer *Cory,* sunk by a mine on June 6, and the destroyer escort *Rich,* also lost to a mine on June 10. The Norwegians lost the *Svenner* to a German torpedo on June 6. Other Allied warships were also lost, and many Allied landing craft and amphibious vehicles were sunk in the landings.

Spencer C. Tucker

Further Reading

Morison, Samuel Eliot. *History of United States Naval Operations in World War II,* Vol. 11, *The Invasion of France and Germany, 1944–1945.* Boston: Little, Brown, 1957.

Roskill, Stephen W. *The War at Sea, 1939–1945: Official History,* Vol. 3, Part 2. London: HMSO, 1961.

Schofield, B. B. *Operation Neptune.* London: Ian Allan, 1974.

Winters, Richard D. (1918–2011)

U.S. Army officer who led several daring missions during World War II, including one during the Normandy (D-Day) invasion on June 6, 1944. Richard "Dick" Winters was born on January 21, 1918, in Ephrata, Pennsylvania. Graduating from Franklin and Marshall College in June 1941, he joined the army in August. In April 1942 he completed Officer Candidate School and was commissioned a second lieutenant that July. Winters was eventually assigned to E Company, 2nd Battalion, 506th Parachute Infantry Regiment, in the 101st Airborne Division and received advanced paratrooper training in England.

Shortly after midnight on June 6, 1944, several hours before the main invasion of Normandy began, E Company embarked on a mission that would drop its men behind enemy lines. En route, one of the aircraft that was carrying the company's headquarters section was shot down, killing all aboard, including the company commander. Winters, jumping from another aircraft, was thus elevated to command of the company.

Winters and a small group of men safely landed outside Sainte-Mère-Église near Utah Beach and moved toward their primary target of a German artillery battery manned by 50 German soldiers. Fire from these guns was cutting down Allied soldiers coming ashore. With just 13 men, Winters's detachment managed to silence the battery and kill or capture the entire German contingent.

Winters saw action throughout much of the Normandy campaign and on July 7, 1944, was awarded the Distinguished Service Cross for his actions. Thereafter, the U.S. Army used Winters's operation against the German batteries to demonstrate how a numerically superior enemy could be vanquished in small actions. In July 1944, Winters was promoted to captain. He remained with the 506th Parachute Infantry Regiment, albeit in a different battalion.

Winters subsequently saw action throughout northern France as well as in Belgium, the Netherlands, and Germany. Promoted to major in March 1945, on May 5, 1945, he participated in the taking of Eagle's Nest, Adolf Hitler's personal retreat in Berchtesgaden, Germany. Winters was demobilized later that year. Although he was recalled to active duty during the 1950–1953 Korean

War, he was never deployed and instead resigned his inactive reserve commission.

Winters ran a small farm in Pennsylvania and then founded a farm-supply company. For many years, he was a frequent guest lecturer at the U.S. Military Academy at West Point. Historian Stephen Ambrose immortalized Winters and his exploits in the 1992 book *Band of Brothers: Easy Company, 506th Regiment, 101st Airborne from Normandy to Hitler's Eagle's Nest*. The popular 2001 television miniseries *Band of Brothers* was based on this book.

Winters died on January 2, 2011, in Campbelltown, Pennsylvania.

Paul G. Pierpaoli Jr.

Further Reading

Ambrose, Stephen E. *Band of Brothers: Easy Company, 506th Regiment, 101st Airborne from Normandy to Hitler's Eagle's Nest*. New York: Simon and Schuster, 2001.

Hevesi, Dennis. "Richard Winters Dies at 92; Led 'Band of Brothers.'" *New York Times*, January 10, 2011, http://www.nytimes.com/2011/01/11/us/11winters.html.

World War II, European Theater: Overview

On September 1, 1939, German forces invaded Poland. Two days later, Britain and France declared war on Germany. World War II had begun.

France and Poland together had the equivalent of 150 divisions. Germany had only 98 divisions, and 36 of these were being organized. Hitler, however, had supported the creation of 14 new type armored, mechanized, and motorized infantry divisions. The armored divisions were to break through weak points followed by motorized infantry and mobile antitank guns, all supported by flying artillery in the Ju-87 Stuka dive-bomber. The Polish campaign was the first example of the blitzkrieg (lightning war).

The Germans were able to invade from three directions simultaneously. The bulk of the Polish forces were dispersed forward along the 800-mile western frontier and could thus be cut off and surrounded. German aircraft prevented concentration and spread panic by attacking cities, including Warsaw. Then on September 17, the Soviets invaded from the east in accordance with secret provisions of the Nazi-Soviet Non-Aggression Pact. The Red Army also proceeded into Estonia, Latvia, and Lithuania. Warsaw surrendered on September 27, and organized Polish resistance ceased on October 5.

In the west the French had an overwhelming strength on the ground and, with the Royal Air Force, in the air. The Allies had promised the Poles immediate air attacks and a French invasion of Germany, but the best the French could do was a slight advance of some 5 miles on a 16-mile front. Despite light casualties, the French halted and, when Warsaw surrendered, withdrew. Had they undertaken a major offensive, it would have reached the Rhine and greatly impacted the war. Britain did even less. The British Expeditionary Force (BEF) had not even completed its assembly by early October, and Polish pleas for the bombing of Germany met no response.

Germany annexed outright about half of the territory taken. The remainder was exploited for cheap labor. Special extermination squads moved in to kill potential leaders and Jews. Poland ultimately became a vast network of work camps and extermination centers, with Jews shipped there from all over Europe. During the war some 6 million Jews were slaughtered in what was called the Final Solution of the Jewish Question but is better known as the

Holocaust. The Russians also imposed a brutal regime in their part of Poland, executing some 15,000 Polish Army officers and Polish intellectuals.

The Poles made an important technological contribution. The Germans had adopted for transmission of classified messages an electromechanical rotor encrypting device christened "Enigma." Japan also used the machine. Enigma enabled encoding in some 150 million combinations, with settings typically changed daily. The Germans believed that such messages were unbreakable. The Poles, however, achieved some success in decoding Enigma and shared this with their allies. The British then assembled a team of experts and developed additional refinements that, with German operator errors, greatly reduced the delay. If it did not enable the Allies to win the war, Enigma intelligence (code-named Top Secret Ultra) undoubtedly shortened it.

Joseph Stalin now demanded territory from Finland to provide security for Leningrad. He offered in return more Russian land but in the north. When the Finns refused to yield land on the Hango Peninsula for a naval base, Stalin ordered an invasion. The ensuing Soviet-Finnish War (November 30, 1939–March 13, 1940), known as the Winter War, was a foregone conclusion but an embarrassment for Stalin. The Red Army sustained enormous casualties and took four months to defeat Finland, which then had to yield far more than the original demand.

In late November 1939 Hitler informed his military chiefs of his determination to secure *Lebensraum* (living space) at the expense of the Soviet Union. That country was then of little military threat, but Germany must first defeat France and Britain. All was then quiet on the Western Front, with the Allies content to wage a war of attrition through economic strangulation by naval blockade, as in World War I. But 1939 was not 1914, for Germany had benevolent neutrals in Italy and the Soviet Union.

Correctly convinced that the British were about to move against neutral Norway, Hitler preempted them, employing virtually the entire German Navy. Beginning on April 9, 1940, the Germans secured Oslo, other cities, and airfields. The British and French landed troops and captured Narvik, but the German invasion of France and the Low Countries on May 10 forced an Allied evacuation on June 7–8. On June 10, Norway surrendered. Denmark had been overrun on April 9.

The Germans had sacrificed half of their cruisers and destroyers but had secured protection for their northern flank as well as Norway's agriculture. Norway also provided bases from which the Germans could strike the Allied North Atlantic convoys and later the Arctic convoys bound for the Soviet Union. But the operation would severely stretch the Reich's manpower resources.

As in World War I, Germany concentrated its naval effort on submarines. In September 1939, Germany had only 55 operational U-boats but gradually built up the numbers. It also had success breaking the British convoy codes and developed new innovative tactics. Certainly the Battle of the Atlantic was one of the most important struggles of the war.

German surface ships carried out commerce raiding. The most spectacular engagement occurred with the sortie of the powerful German battleship *Bismarck*. It sank the British battle cruiser *Hood* and severely damaged the battleship *Prince of Wales* before itself falling prey to pursuing British warships on May 27, 1941.

After Hitler succeeded in his conquest of Norway and Denmark, his next move was against France and the Low Countries of the Netherlands, Belgium, and Luxembourg. Planned for November, the invasion was repeatedly postponed owing to unusually harsh winter conditions and the Allies having secured the German invasion plans.

The original plan had called for a sweeping movement through Belgium and the Netherlands against France, similar to 1914, and would have encountered the best British and French forces. The new plan massed the bulk of the German panzer divisions to southward to push through the hilly and wooded Ardennes region, then drive north to the English Channel, cutting off Allied forces in Belgium. At the point of their planned breakthrough the Germans would have 44 divisions; the French would have 9 divisions and had no reserve to contain a German breakthrough. The Allies had more tanks, but most were scattered in support of infantry. The Luftwaffe had twice the number of Allied combat aircraft and many more antiaircraft guns.

The offensive opened on May 10, 1940, and the best British and French units left their prepared defensive positions and advanced to the relief of Belgium. Although French pilots detected the German Ardennes armor buildup, reports were disbelieved, and no action was taken. On the night of May 12–13 the Germans launched their Ardennes drive. They soon crossed the Meuse, then swung northward to trap the major Allied armies in Belgium.

Hitler now intervened. On May 24 he halted the panzers for three critical days in order to allow the infantry to catch up. General Hermann Göring also assured Hitler that the Luftwaffe could destroy the BEF from the air. On May 28, despite a pledge not to act unilaterally, King Leopold III surrendered Belgian forces.

With the Allies now in great jeopardy, BEF commander Field Marshal John Vereker, Viscount Gort, rejected French appeals to attack southward against the German thrust while the French moved from the south. Believing the battle lost, Gort withdrew the BEF to the coast. During May 28–June 4 the British evacuated their own and some French troops from Dunkirk. The British were forced to abandon virtually all their equipment, but the vast bulk of the BEF escaped to fight another day.

On June 10 Benito Mussolini, believing that Germany had won the war, cast his lot with Hitler and declared war on France and Britain. The Italians made little progress in invading southeastern France before the armistice, however. On June 16 the French cabinet voted to ask for terms. Eighty-four-year-old French marshal Philippe Pétain became premier, and fighting in France ceased on August 25. The Germans occupied two-thirds of the country, including Paris.

On October 28 Mussolini sent Italian forces into Greece from Albania. Italy also attacked the British in Africa. Only Great Britain remained at war. Winston Churchill, who had become prime minister on May 10, appealed to U.S. president Franklin Roosevelt for material assistance.

Roosevelt believed strongly that American security was at stake, but American opinion was still strongly isolationist. American neutrality legislation was, however, amended with repeal of a ban on arms sales, and Roosevelt ordered sharp increases in weapons production, especially aircraft and ships. In 1940 the United States adopted conscription. That September, Roosevelt agreed to provide 50 old destroyers in return for basing rights. Then on March 8, 1941, in an extraordinarily important step, Congress passed Lend-Lease, empowering Roosevelt to provide arms, raw materials, and food to countries fighting the Axis.

Roosevelt also secured bases in Greenland and Iceland and ordered American shipping convoyed as far as Iceland. When in

September 1941 a German submarine fired a torpedo against a U.S. destroyer, Roosevelt issued a "shoot on sight" order. On October 31 German submarines sank the U.S. destroyer *Reuben James,* and 100 men were lost. No doubt war with Germany would have eventually come from the sinking of U.S. ships.

Britain, meanwhile, was in a perilous state. In June 1940 there was only one properly equipped division in all of Britain, and the navy ordered its ships to the far north to escape the Luftwaffe. Hitler, however, had not anticipated the rapid defeat of France and had no plans for the logical next step of an invasion of Britain. Several key advisers urged an immediate airborne effort to secure a British toehold, but Hitler refused. Believing that the British would soon sue for peace, he let a month pass before initiating planning for a sea invasion.

The essential prerequisite was command of the air. The Battle of Britain began on July 10, 1940, and continued until October 31. German mistakes and the shortcomings of the Luftwaffe contributed to the German defeat. On November 1 the Germans shifted to area night bombing. Had Hitler concentrated on air and submarine pressure to starve Britain of resources he could have brought about its defeat, but he pivoted toward the Soviet Union. Hitler claimed that the British continued in the war only because they hoped that Germany and the Soviet Union might come to blows. Defeat the Soviet Union, and Britain would have to give up.

Hitler rejected suggestions for a far better Mediterranean option to secure the Suez Canal and the Persian Gulf oil fields. He ordered an invasion of the Soviet Union not for sound strategic reasons but instead to secure his territorial goals. In taking this decision, he grossly underestimated Soviet resources and ability.

Shocked by the rapid defeat of France, Stalin incorporated Lithuania, Latvia, and Estonia. He also annexed Bessarabia and Northern Bukovina (the latter had not been assigned to the Soviet Union). To counter these moves and secure his southern flank, Hitler pressured Romania, Bulgaria, and Hungary to join the Axis. Yugoslavia, which resisted, was conquered.

The Germans also invaded Greece, rescuing the Italians who had been driven out by the Greeks. Churchill then halted a successful British North African offensive to aid Greece. The BEF was soon defeated and evacuated to Crete, however, which Hitler then took in a successful but costly airborne invasion.

So confident was Hitler of success in the Soviet Union of one campaign of three months' duration that he did not put Germany on full wartime mobilization. Nor did he consider it necessary to coordinate plans with Japan. His Balkans campaign and heavy rains also imposed delay, perhaps the final blow to the chance of German victory. Stalin meanwhile received numerous warnings from Britain and the United States of German intentions but rejected them as an attempt to drive a wedge between the Soviet Union and Germany.

Early on June 22, 1941, the German Army, with Finnish, Romanian, Hungarian, and Italian contingents totaling some 3 million men, moved into the Soviet Union along a 2,000-mile front. The appallingly bad generalship of Stalin had the bulk of Red Army units in forward positions, where they were quickly cut off and surrounded. In the early fighting Stalin repeatedly ignored sound military advice. Ordering his units not to retreat cost the Red Army 665,000 men taken prisoner at Kiev and 457,000 at Smolensk.

Within a week the Germans had advanced 350 miles. By autumn, they had conquered

Belarus (White Russia) and most of Ukraine. In the north the Germans besieged Leningrad, in the center they were driving on Moscow, and in the south they entered the Crimean Peninsula and laid siege to Sebastopol.

The blitzkrieg had worked well in short distances but broke down in the vast expanses of the Soviet Union. An appallingly primitive transportation system and winter temperatures plummeting to 60 degrees below zero greatly hampered German logistics. Hitler also greatly miscalculated Soviet resources. The Germans expected to meet 200 divisions. By mid-August they had defeated these but now had to contend with another 160. The Soviets also greatly outnumbered the Germans in tanks and aircraft. Stalin called on resources from Russian Asia, and in December the Soviets pushed back the Germans from the Moscow suburbs.

Hitler, disgusted by events, assumed personal command, and in the spring of 1942 he shifted the main attack to the south toward the oil fields of the Caucasus. Sebastopol soon fell. But he also sent forces against Stalingrad on the Volga and now experienced the consequences of strategic overstretch.

Major fighting was also occurring in North Africa. It had begun in September 1940 when Mussolini ordered an invasion of Egypt from Libya. Determined to maintain control of the Suez Canal and the vital supply route to India, Churchill diverted vitally needed resources. British forces secured Ethiopia, and a British counteroffensive in Egypt carried well into Libya. It could have cleared Africa of the Axis completely but was halted when Churchill decided to aid Greece.

The Italian breakdown led Hitler to send German reinforcements. Lieutenant General Erwin Rommel's Afrika Korps launched an offensive in Libya in the spring of 1941. But Hitler never did make a major effort in North Africa or the choke points of Gibraltar, Malta, and Suez. Instead, he merely opened a fresh drain on Germany's resources. The fighting in North Africa shifted back and forth, but by mid-1942 Rommel had been halted in the First Battle of El Alamein in Egypt (July 1–27).

In December 1941 the war widened when the Japanese attacked without warning the U.S. Pacific Fleet at Pearl Harbor, Hawaii. This was designed to purchase time for Japan to conquer Southeast Asia and establish a defensive ring. Japan was not to have the time to exploit the resources of the conquered territory.

The United States and Britain formed the Combined Chiefs of Staff and developed a unified strategy. The defeat of Germany was the primary goal, but sufficient resources were available to permit American operations against Japan.

Meanwhile, plans to invade continental Europe had to be delayed, for U.S. forces were unready. This greatly displeased the Soviets, who understandably sought relief from the 300 Axis divisions on their territory. In the meantime, the Western Allies concentrated on the air bombardment of Germany.

British and American air commanders believed strongly that strategic bombing could win the war. Precision daylight bombing proving impossible, the United States in effect accepted the British argument that the way to win was to shatter morale and "unhouse" civilians in the area bombing of cities. Such arguments proved specious, although U.S. strategic bombing was much more effective in the Pacific theater.

At the end of 1942, the tide of European battle began to turn. On November 8, Anglo-American forces landed at Casablanca in

Morocco and at Oran and Algiers in Algeria. Vichy French forces contested the landings, which were, however, successful. The Allies then pushed eastward to meet British general Bernard Montgomery's Eighth Army, which broke out in the Second Battle of El Alamein (October 23–November 4), although Axis forces were able to withdraw in good order into Tunisia.

Too late Hitler reinforced, only to see Axis forces defeated in the Battle of Tunis (May 3–13, 1943). Africa was cleared of Axis forces, and the threat to Egypt and Suez was ended. Meanwhile, by the autumn of 1943 the Allies were winning the Battle of the Atlantic, thanks to convoys, better depth charges, escort carriers, independent hunter-killer groups, new radar sets in long-range aircraft, and Ultra.

The Germans also suffered a major defeat in the Soviet Union in the Battle of Stalingrad (August 24, 1942–January 31, 1943). The Eastern Front might still have been fought to a draw but only with withdrawal and a shortened front. Hitler rejected this, insisting that there be no retreat. This only ensured that inevitable withdrawals were more costly.

By the summer of 1943, the advantage had passed to the Soviets. Increased industrial production and immense quantities of Lend-Lease aid were factors. Still, the Soviet Union bore the brunt of ground combat in the war. It lost more men at Stalingrad alone than the United States did in battle during the entire war in all theaters combined. From June 1941 the Soviets had to contend most of the time with four-fifths and never less than three-fourths of the German Army.

Hitler prepared a major offensive that became the Battle of Kursk (July 5–16, 1943). The Soviets knew the German plans through their spy apparatus in Berlin, and the attackers encountered deep, well-prepared defenses. Kursk was the largest battle of World War II, involving some 4 million Soviet and German troops, some 70,000 artillery pieces, and 12,000 planes. With 13,000 tanks engaged, it was the largest armor battle in history. On July 12 the Soviets launched a counteroffensive, making Kursk the true turning point on the Eastern Front.

U.S., British, and Canadian forces invaded and conquered Sicily during July 9–August 17, 1943. This brought finis to Mussolini's regime (the Germans subsequently rescued him and set him up as head of a rump Italian state in the north), and the new Italian government promptly opened secret talks with the Allies. On September 3 the Allies invaded Italy from the south, but the Germans took over the Italian positions. In October 1943 the Italian government declared war on Germany, but German forces blocked the advance on Rome, and the Italian campaign became a bloody stalemate as Allied resources were drawn off for the invasion of France. Rome was only liberated on June 4, 1944, and the German surrender in Italy occurred on May 2, 1945.

The Allies also continued their strategic bombing of Germany. In the summer of 1943, British and American bombers launched devastating raids against German cities. Heavy bomber losses were reversed in late 1943 with the arrival of new long-range American fighters capable of accompanying the bombers to and from their targets. Strategic bombing was important but not decisive. Germany was actually attaining its highest levels of military production at the end of the war.

General Dwight D. Eisenhower had command of the invasion of France. The Allies invaded from the sea on June 6, 1944, while airborne forces fought to prevent German reinforcements from reaching the beaches.

The Germans had heavily fortified the Atlantic coastline, but the Allies brought their own artificial harbors (Mulberries). Elaborate deceptions convinced Hitler that the Allies would invade Norway and that the Normandy operation was a feint, with the main landing in France to occur in the Pas de Calais.

Some 130,000 men came ashore the first day, and 1 million came ashore within a month. Nonetheless, the going was slower than expected. Not until the end of July were the Allies able to break free. Lieutenant General George Patton's Third Army in a single month liberated most of France north of the Loire. On August 15, meanwhile, the Seventh Army invaded southern France near Cannes, then drove northeast.

The Western Allies wasted several opportunities that would have shortened the war. Failure to close a gap between Argentan and Falaise allowed some 100,000 Germans to escape. Montgomery also halted at Antwerp, and the German Fifteenth Army was able to reach Holland. Most German leaders knew that the war was lost, but it was clear that Hitler was determined to fight to the last, even at the cost of the complete destruction of Germany. Plots to assassinate him failed, however.

Montgomery's effort to cross the Rhine at Arnheim and drive into the Ruhr failed. Meanwhile, the Soviets began a great offensive that destroyed German Army Group Center (June 22–August 19, 1944). The Red Army then halted before Warsaw. After

Bird's-eye view of landing craft, barrage balloons, and Allied troops landing in Normandy, France, on D-Day, June 6, 1944. (Library of Congress)

encouraging the Poles to rise up, the Red Army then sat idly by for two months. Some 300,000 Poles died, making the subsequent Soviet subjugation of Poland far easier. In December, however, the Red Army crossed into Germany as millions of German refugees fled.

Meanwhile, Hitler planned to recapture Antwerp. Substantial German reinforcements were transferred from the Eastern Front for what would be the biggest battle on the Western Front in the war and the largest engagement ever for the U.S. Army. In the Ardennes Offensive, also known as the Battle of the Bulge (December 16, 1944–January 16, 1945), the Germans caught the Americans by surprise. Bad weather grounded Allied aircraft, and the Germans created a bulge in the lines some 50 miles deep and 70 miles wide. Clearing weather and rapid Allied reinforcement turned the tide. Then, before the Germans could shift resources eastward, the Soviets launched their great Vistula–Oder Offensive (January 12–February 2, 1945). In effect, the Ardennes Offensive hastened the end of the war. Hitler meanwhile rejected all appeals to end the slaughter, forbidding retreat.

Soviet forces swept through the Baltic states, White Russia, Ukraine, and Poland and forced the capitulation of Romania, Finland, and Bulgaria. Early in 1945 the Red Army entered East Prussia, Czechoslovakia, and Hungary and began its drive into Germany. On April 16 the Soviets launched an operation to take Berlin. Eisenhower meanwhile sent 18 divisions to clear out the Ruhr. He also sent much of his strength southward to reduce an imagined German alpine redoubt.

Mussolini was captured in northern Italy by the antifascist resistance and shot. Hitler committed suicide in the ruins of Berlin, and the Germans surrendered unconditionally on May 8, 1945. By that time the Western Allies had met the Red Army on the Elbe and in Bohemia and Austria. The war in Europe was over.

Spencer C. Tucker

Further Reading

Beevor, Antony. *The Second World War.* London: Weidenfeld and Nicolson, 2012.

Bellamy, Chris T. *Absolute War: Soviet Russia in the Second World War.* New York: Knopf, 2007.

Black, Jeremy. *World War Two: A Military History.* London: Routledge, 2003.

Davies, Norman. *No Simple Victory: World War II in Europe, 1939–1945.* London: Penguin, 2008.

Evans, Richard J. *The Third Reich at War.* New York: Penguin, 2009.

Glantz, David M. *When Titans Clashed: How the Red Army Stopped Hitler.* Lawrence: University Press of Kansas, 1998.

Hastings, Max. *Inferno: The World at War, 1939–1945.* New York: Knopf, 2011.

Keegan, John. *The Second World War.* New York: Viking, 1989.

Liddell Hart, B. H. *History of the Second World War.* New York: Putnam, 1970.

Morison, Samuel Eliot. *History of United States Naval Operations in World War II.* 15 vols. Boston: Little, Brown, 1947–1962.

Murray, Williamson, and Allan R. Millett. *A War to Be Won: Fighting the Second World War.* Cambridge, MA: Belknap, 2000.

Neillands, Robin. *The Bomber War: The Allied Air Offensive against Nazi Germany.* Woodstock, NY: Overlook, 2001.

Tucker, Spencer C. *The Second World War.* New York: Palgrave Macmillan, 2004.

Weinberg, Gerhard L. *A World at Arms: A Global History of World War II.* New York: Cambridge University Press, 1994.

Willmott, H. P. *The Great Crusade: A New Complete History of the Second World War.* Revised ed. Washington, DC: Potomac Books, 2008.

Primary Documents

Allied Planning for the Normandy Invasion (July 1943)

In 1943, military leaders in Great Britain and the United States began formulating plans to launch a massive invasion of northern France to force the Germans to fight on yet another front and bring World War II to a close. The following is the preliminary planning document for the invasion. It gives the operation the code name OVERLORD, *identifies the Caen area of the Cotentin Peninsula of Normandy as the invasion site, discusses the problems involved and the resources necessary for success, and identifies military objectives following a successful initial landing and a timetable to secure them.*

Object

1. The object of Operation "Overlord" is to mount and carry out an operation, with forces and equipment established in the United Kingdom, and with target date the 1st May, 1944, to secure a lodgment on the Continent from which further offensive operations can be developed. The lodgment area must contain sufficient port facilities to maintain a force of some twenty-six to thirty divisions, and enable that force to be augmented by follow-up shipments from the United States or elsewhere of additional divisions and supporting units at the rate of three to five divisions per month.

Selection of a Lodgment Area

2. In order to provide sufficient port facilities to maintain these large forces, it will be necessary to select a lodgment area which includes a group of major ports. We must plan on the assumption that ports, on capture, will be seriously damaged and probably blocked. It will take some time to restore normal facilities. We shall thus be forced to rely on maintenance over beaches for an extended period.

3. A study of the beaches on the Belgian and Channel coasts shows that the beaches with the highest capacity for passing vehicles and stores inland are those in the Pas de Calais [assumed here to be the area between Gravelines and the River Somme] and the Caen-Cotentin area. ["Caen area" is taken as that between the River Orne and the base of the Cotentin Peninsula. The "Cotentin" area is the peninsula in which Cherbourg is situated.] Of these, the Caen beaches are the most favourable, as they are, unlike the others, sheltered from the prevailing winds. Naval and air considerations point to the area between the Pas de Calais and the Cotentin as the most suitable for the initial landing, air factors of optimum air support and rapid provision of airfields indicating the Pas de Calais as the best choice, with Caen as an acceptable alternative.

4. Thus, taking beach capacity and air and naval considerations together, it appears that either the Pas de Calais area or the Caen-Cotentin area is the most suitable for the initial main landing.

5. As the area for the initial landing the Pas de Calais has many obvious advantages such that good air support and quick turn round for our shipping can be achieved. On the other hand, it is a focal point of the enemy fighters disposed for defense, and maximum enemy air activity can be brought to bear over this area with the minimum movement of his air forces. Moreover, the Pas de Calais is the most strongly defended area on the whole French coast. The defenses would require very heavy and sustained bombardment from sea and air: penetration would be slow, and the result of the bombardment of beach exits would severely limit the rate of build-up. Further, this area does not offer good opportunities for expansion. It would be necessary to develop the bridgehead to include either the Belgian ports as far as Antwerp or the Channel ports Westwards to include Havre and Rouen. But both an advance to Antwerp across the numerous water obstacles, and a long flank march of some 120 miles to the Seine ports must be considered unsound operations of war unless the German forces are in a state not far short of final collapse.

6. In the Caen-Cotentin area it would be possible to make our initial landing either partly on the Cotentin Peninsula and partly on the Caen beaches, wholly in the Cotentin or wholly on the Caen beaches. An attack with part of our forces in the Cotentin and part on the Caen beaches, is, however, considered to be unsound. It would entail dividing our limited forces by the low-lying marshy ground and intricate river system at the neck of the Cotentin Peninsula; thus exposing them to defeat in detail.

7. An attack against the Cotentin Peninsula, on the other hand, has a reasonable chance of success, and would ensure the early capture of the port of Cherbourg. Unfortunately, very few airfields exist in the Cotentin, and that area is not suitable for rapid airfield development. Furthermore, the narrow neck of the Peninsula would give the Germans an easy task in preventing us from breaking out and expanding our initial bridgehead. Moreover, during the period of our consolidation in the Cotentin the Germans would have time to reinforce their coastal troops in the Caen area, rendering a subsequent amphibious assault in that area much more difficult.

8. There remains the attack on the Caen beaches. The Caen sector is weakly held; the defenses are relatively light and the beaches are of high capacity and sheltered from the prevailing winds. Inland the terrain is suitable for airfield development and for the consolidation of the initial bridgehead; and much of it is unfavourable for counter-attacks by panzer divisions. Maximum enemy air opposition can only be brought to bear at the expense of the enemy air defense screen covering the approaches to Germany; and the limited number of enemy airfields within range of the Caen area facilitates local neutralization of the German fighter force. The sector suffers from the disadvantage that considerable effort will be required to provide adequate air support to our assault forces and some time must elapse before the capture of a major port.

After a landing in the Caen sector it would be necessary to seize either the Seine group of ports or the Brittany group of ports. To seize the Seine ports would entail forcing a crossing of the Seine, which is likely to require greater forces than we can build up through the Caen beaches and the port of Cherbourg. It should, however, be possible to seize the Brittany ports between Cherbourg and Nantes and on them build up sufficient forces for our final advance Eastwards.

Provided that the necessary air situation can first be achieved, the chances of a successful attack and of rapid subsequent development are so much greater in this sector than in any other that it is considered that the advantages far outweigh the disadvantages.

The Lodgment Area Selected

9. In the light of these factors, it is considered that our initial landing on the Continent should be effected in the Caen area, with a view to the eventual seizure of a lodgment area comprising the Cherbourg-Brittany group of ports (from Cherbourg to Nantes).

Opening Phase up to the Capture of Cherbourg

10. The opening phase in the seizing of this lodgment area would be the effecting of a landing in the Caen sector with a view to the early capture and development of airfield sites in the Caen area, and of the port of Cherbourg.

11. The main limiting factors affecting such an operation are the possibility of attaining the necessary air situation; the number of offensive divisions which the enemy can make available for counter attack in the Caen area; the availability of landing ships and craft and of transport aircraft; and the capacity of the beaches and ports in the sector.

12. Although the strength of the G.A.F. [German Air Force, or Luftwaffe] available in 1944 on the Western front cannot be forecast at this stage, we can confidently expect that we shall have a vast numerical superiority in bomber forces. The first-line strength of the German fighter force is, however, showing a steady increase and although it is unlikely to equal the size of the force at our disposal, there is no doubt that our fighters will have a very large commitment entailing dispersal and operations at maximum intensity. Our fighters will also be operating under serious tactical disadvantages in the early stages, which will largely offset their numerical superiority. Before the assault takes place, therefore, it will be necessary to reduce the effectiveness of the G.A.F., particularly that part which can be brought to bear against the Caen area.

13. The necessary air situation to ensure a reasonable chance of success will therefore require that the maximum number of German fighter forces are contained in the Low Countries and North-West Germany, that the effectiveness of the fighter defense in the Caen area is reduced and that air reinforcements are prevented from arriving in the early stages from the Mediterranean. Above all, it will be necessary to reduce the overall strength of the German fighter force between now and the date of the operation by destruction of the sources of supply, by the infliction of casualties by bringing on air battles, and, immediately prior to the assault, by the disorganization of G.A.F. installations and control system in the Caen area.

14. As it is impossible to forecast with any accuracy the number and location of German formations in reserve in 1944, while, on the other hand, the forces available to us

have been laid down, an attempt has been made in this paper to determine the wisest employment of our own forces and then to determine the maximum number of German formations which they can reasonably overcome. Apart from the air situation, which is an over-riding factor, the practicability of this plan will depend principally on the number, effectiveness, and availability of German divisions present in France and the Low Countries in relation to our own capabilities. This consideration is discussed below (paragraph 35).

15. A maximum of thirty and a minimum of twenty-six equivalent divisions are likely to be available in the United Kingdom for cross-Channel operations on the 1st May 1944. Further build-up can be at the rate of three to five divisions per month.

16. Landing ships and craft have been provided to lift the equivalent of three assault divisions and two follow-up divisions, without "overheads," and it has been assumed that the equivalent of an additional two divisions can be afloat in ships.

17. Airborne forces amounting to two airborne divisions and some five or six parachute regiments will be available, but, largely owing to shortage of transport aircraft, it is only possible to lift the equivalent of two-thirds of one airborne division simultaneously, on the basis of present forecasts.

18. Even if additional landing ships and craft could be made available, the beaches in the Caen area would preclude the landing of forces greater than the equivalent of the three assault and two follow-up divisions, for which craft have already been provided. Nevertheless, an all-round increase of at least 10 percent in landing ships and craft is highly desirable in order to provide a greater margin for contingencies within the framework of the existing plan. Furthermore, sufficient lift for a further assault division could most usefully be employed in an additional landing on other beaches.

19. There is no port of any capacity within the sector although there are a number of small ports of limited value. Maintenance will, therefore, of necessity be largely over the beaches until it is possible to capture and open up the port of Cherbourg. In view of the possibilities of interruption by bad weather it will be essential to provide early some form of improvised sheltered waters.

20. Assuming optimum weather conditions, it should be possible to build up the force over the beaches to a total by D plus 6 of the equivalent of some eleven divisions and five tank brigades and thereafter to land one division a day until about D plus 24.

Proposed Plan

Preliminary Phase

21. During the preliminary phase, which must start forthwith, all possible means including air and sea action, propaganda, political and economic pressure, and sabotage, must be integrated into a combined offensive aimed at softening the German resistance. In particular, air action should be directed towards the reduction of the German air forces on the Western front, the progressive destruction of the German economic system and the undermining of German morale.

22. In order to contain the maximum German forces away from the Caen area diversionary operations should be staged against

other areas such as the Pas de Calais and the Mediterranean Coast of France.

Preparatory Phase

23. During this phase air action will be intensified against the G.A.F., particularly in North-West France, with a view to reducing the effectiveness of the G.A.F. in that area, and will be extended to include attacks against communications more directly associated with movement of German reserves which might affect the Caen area. Three naval assault forces will be assembled with the naval escorts and loaded at ports along the South Coast of England. Two naval assault forces carrying the follow-up forces will also be assembled and loaded, one in the Thames Estuary and one on the West Coast.

The Assault

24. After a very short air bombardment of the beach defenses three assault divisions will be landed simultaneously on the Caen beaches, followed up on D Day by the equivalent of two tank brigades (United States regiments) and a brigade group (United States regimental combat team). At the same time, airborne forces will be used to seize the town of Caen; and subsidiary operations by commandos and possibly by airborne forces will be undertaken to neutralize certain coast defenses and seize certain important river crossings. The object of the assault forces will be to seize the general line Grandcamp–Bayeux–Caen.

Follow-up and Build-up Phase

25. Subsequent action will take the form of a strong thrust Southwards and South-Westwards with a view to destroying enemy forces, acquiring sites for airfields, and gaining depth for a turning movement into the Cotentin Peninsula directed on Cherbourg. When sufficient depth has been gained a force will advance into the Cotentin and seize Cherbourg. At the same time a thrust will be made to deepen the bridgehead South-Eastwards in order to cover the construction and operation of additional airfields in the area South-East of Caen.

26. It is considered that, within fourteen days of the initial assault, Cherbourg should be captured and the bridgehead extended to include the general line Trouville–Alencon–Mont St. Michel. By this date, moreover, it should have been possible to land some eighteen divisions and to have in operation about fourteen airfields from which twenty-eight to thirty-three fighter-type squadrons should be operating.

Further Developments after Capture of Cherbourg

27. After the capture of Cherbourg the Supreme Allied Commander will have to decide whether to initiate operations to seize the Seine ports or whether he must content himself with first occupying the Brittany ports. In this decision he will have to be guided largely by the situation of the enemy forces. If the German resistance is sufficiently weak, an immediate advance could be made to seize Havre and Rouen. On the other hand, the more probable situation is that the Germans will have retired with the bulk of their forces to hold Paris and the line of the Seine, where they can best be covered by their air forces from North-East France and where they may possibly be reinforced by formations from Russia. Elsewhere they may move a few divisions from Southern France to hold the crossings of the Loire and will leave the existing defensive divisions in Brittany.

It will therefore most probably be necessary for us to seize the Brittany ports first, in order to build up sufficient forces with which we can eventually force the passage of the Seine.

28. Under these circumstances, the most suitable plan would appear to be to secure first the left flank and to gain sufficient airfields for subsequent operations. This would be done by extending the bridgehead to the line of the River Eure from Dreux to Rouen and thence along the line of the Seine to the sea, seizing at the same time Chartres, Orleans and Tours.

29. Under cover of these operations a force would be employed in capturing the Brittany ports; the first step being a thrust Southwards to seize Nantes and St. Nazaire, followed by subsidiary operations to capture Brest and the various small ports of the Brittany Peninsula.

30. This action would complete the occupation of our initial lodgment area and would secure sufficient major ports for the maintenance of at least thirty divisions. As soon as the organization of the L. of C. in this lodgment area allowed, and sufficient air forces had been established, operations would then be begun to force the line of the Seine, and to capture Paris and the Seine ports. As opportunity offered, subsidiary action would also be taken to clear the Germans from the Biscay ports to facilitate the entry of additional American troops and the feeding of the French population.

Command and Control

31. In carrying out Operation "Overlord" administrative control would be greatly simplified if the principle were adopted that the United States forces were normally on the right of the line and the British and Canadian forces on the left.

Major Conditions Affecting Success of the Operation

32. It will be seen that the plan for the initial landing is based on two main principles—concentration of force and tactical surprise. Concentration of the assault forces is considered essential if we are to ensure adequate air support and if our limited assault forces are to avoid defeat in detail. An attempt has been made to obtain tactical surprise by landing in a lightly defended area—presumably lightly defended as, due to its distance from a major port, the Germans consider a landing there unlikely to be successful. This action, of course, presupposes that we can offset the absence of a port in the initial stages by the provision of improvised sheltered waters. It is believed that this can be accomplished.

33. The operation calls for a much higher standard of performance on the part of the naval assault forces than any previous operation. This will depend upon their being formed in sufficient time to permit of adequate training.

34. Above all, it is essential that there should be an over-all reduction in the German fighter force between now and the time of the surface assault. From now onwards every practical method of achieving this end must be employed. This condition, above all others, will dictate the date by which the amphibious assault can be launched.

35. The next condition is that the number of German offensive divisions in reserve must not exceed a certain figure on the

target date if the operation is to have a reasonable chance of success. The German reserves in France and the Low Countries as a whole, excluding divisions holding the coast, G.A.F. divisions and training divisions, should not exceed on the day of the assault twelve full-strength first-quality divisions. In addition, the Germans should not be able to transfer more than fifteen first-quality divisions from Russia during the first two months. Moreover, on the target date the divisions in reserve should be so located that the number of first-quality divisions which the Germans could deploy in the Caen area to support the divisions holding the coast should not exceed three divisions on D Day, five divisions on D plus 2, or nine divisions by D plus 8.

During the preliminary period, therefore, every effort must be made to dissipate and divert German formations, lower their fighting efficiency and disrupt communications.

36. Finally, there is the question of maintenance. Maintenance will have to be carried out over beaches for a period of some three months for a number of formations, varying from a maximum of eighteen divisions in the first month to twelve divisions in the second month, rapidly diminishing to nil in the third month. Unless adequate measures are taken to provide sheltered waters by artificial means, the operation will be at the mercy of the weather. Moreover, special facilities and equipment will be required to prevent undue damage to craft during this extended period. Immediate action for the provision of the necessary requirements is essential.

37. Given these conditions—a reduced G.A.F., a limitation in the number or effectiveness of German offensive formations in France, and adequate arrangements to provide improvised sheltered waters—it is considered that Operation "Overlord" has a reasonable prospect of success. To ensure these conditions being attained by the 1st May, 1944, action must start now and every possible effort made by all means in our power to soften German resistance and to speed up our own preparations.

Source: Offices of the War Cabinet, S.W.1, 30th July, 1943.

Anglo-American Combined Chiefs of Staff, Directive to Supreme Commander Allied Expeditionary Force, February 12, 1944

In early 1944, the Anglo-American Chiefs of Staff issued a directive formally appointing General Dwight D. Eisenhower, who had previously led the North African and Italian campaigns, commander of the Allied forces that would undertake Operation OVERLORD, *the long-awaited Western invasion of Germany. The original invasion date was set for May, though this was later deferred until June 6, 1944.*

1. You are hereby designated as Supreme Allied Commander of the forces placed under your orders for operations for liberation of Europe from Germans. Your title will be Supreme Commander Allied Expeditionary Force.

2. *Task.* You will enter the continent of Europe and, in conjunction with the other United Nations, undertake operations aimed at the heart of Germany and the destruction of her armed forces. The date for entering the Continent is the month of May, 1944. After adequate Channel ports have been secured, exploitation will be directed towards securing

an area that will facilitate both ground and air operations against the enemy.

3. Notwithstanding the target date above you will be prepared at any time to take immediate advantage of favorable circumstances, such as withdrawal by the enemy on your front, to effect a reentry into the Continent with such forces as you have available at the time; a general plan for this operation when approved will be furnished for your assistance.

4. *Command.* You are responsible to the Combined Chiefs of Staff and will exercise command generally in accordance with the diagram at Appendix [not included with this printing]. Direct communication with the United States and British Chiefs of Staff is authorized in the interest of facilitating your operations and for arranging necessary logistic support.

5. *Logistics.* In the United Kingdom the responsibility for logistics organization, concentration, movement, and supply of forces to meet the requirements of your plan will rest with British Service Ministries so far as British Forces are concerned. So far as United States Forces are concerned, this responsibility will rest with the United States War and Navy Departments. You will be responsible for the coordination of logistical arrangements on the continent. You will also be responsible for coordinating the requirements of British and United States forces under your command.

6. *Coordination of operations of other Forces and Agencies.* In preparation for your assault on enemy occupied Europe, Sea and Air Forces, agencies of sabotage, subversion, and propaganda, acting under a variety of authorities, are now in action. You may recommend any variation in these activities which may seem to you desirable.

7. *Relationship to United Nations Forces in other areas.* Responsibility will rest with the Combined Chiefs of Staff for supplying information relating to operations of the Forces of the U. S. S. R. for your guidance in timing your operations. It is understood that the Soviet Forces will launch an offensive at about the same time as OVERLORD with the object of preventing the German forces from transferring from the Eastern to the Western front. The Allied Commander in Chief, Mediterranean Theater, will conduct operations designed to assist your operation, including the launching of an attack against the south of France at about the same time as OVERLORD. The scope and timing of his operations will be decided by the Combined Chiefs of Staff. You will establish contact with him and submit to the Combined Chiefs of Staff your views and recommendations regarding operations from the Mediterranean in support of your attack from the United Kingdom. The Combined Chiefs of Staff will place under your command the forces operating in Southern France as soon as you are in a position to assume such command. You will submit timely recommendations compatible with this regard.

8. *Relationship with Allied Governments—the re-establishment of Civil Governments and Liberated Allied Territories and the administration of enemy territories.* Further instructions will be issued to you on these subjects at a later date.

Source: Gordon A. Harrison, *United States Army in World War II: The European Theater of Operations, Cross Channel Attack* (Washington, DC: Office of the Chief of Military History, Department of the Army, 1951).

Eisenhower's Statement in the Event the D-Day Landings Failed, June 5, 1944

Supreme commander Allied Forces Western Europe U.S. general Dwight D. Eisenhower drafted this note in case the Allied landing in France failed. In it, he takes full responsibility. Hastily written on June 5, 1944, it was accidentally dated July 5, 1944.

Our landings in the Cherbourg-Havre area have failed to gain a satisfactory foothold and I have withdrawn the troops. My decision to attack at this time and place was based upon the best information available. The troops, the air and the Navy did all that Bravery and devotion to duty could do. If any blame or fault attaches to the attempt it is mine alone.

Source: Pre-Presidential Papers, Dwight D. Eisenhower Library, National Archives Identifier 186470.

Order of the Day and Letter to the Troops, Supreme Commander of the Western Allied Expeditionary Force General Dwight D. Eisenhower, June 6, 1944

After long months of planning, on June 6, 1944, the Allies launched their Western offensive against German forces in France and Western Europe. Before the invasion began, General Dwight D. Eisenhower, commander of the Allied Expeditionary Force, issued an order of the day to his troops. Each soldier also received a letter detailing how the Allied troops should conduct themselves in the areas they liberated. In marked contrast to German looting of the conquered areas of Europe, Eisenhower warned soldiers that they must treat the inhabitants generously and respect their rights and property.

To troops of the A.E.F.

Soldiers, Sailors and Airmen of the Allied Expeditionary Force!

You are about to embark upon the Great Crusade, toward which we have striven these many months. The eyes of the world are upon you. The hopes and prayers of liberty-loving people everywhere march with you. In company with our brave Allies and brothers-in-arms on other Fronts, you will bring about the destruction of the German war machine, the elimination of Nazi tyranny over the oppressed peoples of Europe, and security for ourselves in a free world.

Your task will not be an easy one. Your enemy is well trained, well equipped and battle hardened. He will fight savagely.

But this is the year 1944! Much has happened since the Nazi triumphs of 1940–41. The United Nations have inflicted upon the Germans great defeats, in open battle, man-to-man. Our air offensive has seriously reduced their strength in the air and their capacity to wage war on the ground. Our Home Fronts have given us an overwhelming superiority in weapons and munitions of war, and placed at our disposal great reserves of trained fighting men. The tide has turned! The free men of the world are marching together to Victory!

I have full confidence in your courage and devotion to duty and skill in battle. We will accept nothing less than full Victory!

Good luck! And let us beseech the blessing of Almighty God upon this great and noble undertaking.

(Signed) Dwight D. Eisenhower

Source: Papers of Dwight D. Eisenhower, Eisenhower Presidential Library.

U.S. President Franklin D. Roosevelt's Remarks by Radio, June 6, 1944

Only the day before, June 5, President Franklin D. Roosevelt had spoken on the radio on the liberation of Rome. This welcome news was, however, superceded by the Allied invasion of Normandy, when he again addressed the American people via radio. His remarks, originally titled "Let Our Hearts Be Stout," were delivered on the evening of June 6, 1944.

My Fellow Americans:

Last night, when I spoke with you about the fall of Rome, I knew at that moment that troops of the United States and our Allies were crossing the Channel in another and greater operation. It has come to pass with success thus far.

And so, in this poignant hour, I ask you to join with me in prayer:

Almighty God: Our sons, pride of our nation, this day have set upon a mighty endeavor, a struggle to preserve our Republic, our religion, and our civilization, and to set free a suffering humanity.

Lead them straight and true; give strength to their arms, stoutness to their hearts, steadfastness in their faith.

They will need Thy blessings. Their road will be long and hard. For the enemy is strong. He may hurl back our forces. Success may not come with rushing speed, but we shall return again and again; and we know that by Thy grace, and by the righteousness of our cause, our sons will triumph.

They will be sore tried, by night and by day, without rest—until the victory is won. The darkness will be rent by noise and flame. Men's souls will be shaken with the violences of war.

For these men are lately drawn from the ways of peace. They fight not for the lust of conquest. They fight to end conquest. They fight to liberate. They fight to let justice arise, and tolerance and goodwill among all Thy people. They yearn but for the end of battle, for their return to the haven of home.

Some will never return. Embrace these, Father, and receive them, Thy heroic servants, into Thy kingdom.

And for us at home—fathers, mothers, children, wives, sisters, and brothers of brave men overseas, whose thoughts and prayers are ever with them—help us, Almighty God, to rededicate ourselves in renewed faith in Thee in this hour of great sacrifice.

Many people have urged that I call the nation into a single day of special prayer. But because the road is long and the desire is great, I ask that our people devote themselves in a continuance of prayer. As we rise to each new day, and again when each day is spent, let words of prayer be on our lips, invoking Thy help to our efforts.

Give us strength, too—strength in our daily tasks, to redouble the contributions we make in the physical and the material support of our armed forces.

And let our hearts be stout, to wait out the long travail, to bear sorrows that may come, to impart our courage unto our sons wheresoever they may be.

And, O Lord, give us faith. Give us faith in Thee; faith in our sons; faith in each other; faith in our united crusade. Let not the keenness of our spirit ever be dulled. Let not the impacts of temporary events, of temporal matters of but fleeting moment—let not these deter us in our unconquerable purpose.

With Thy blessing, we shall prevail over the unholy forces of our enemy. Help us to conquer the apostles of greed and racial arrogances. Lead us to the saving of our country, and with our sister nations into a world unity that will spell a sure peace—a peace invulnerable to the schemings of unworthy men. And a peace that will let all of men live in freedom, reaping the just rewards of their honest toil.

Thy will be done, Almighty God.

Amen.

Source: "A 'Mighty Endeavor'. D-Day," Franklin D. Roosevelt Library, https://fdrlibrary.org/d-day.

Forrest C. Pogue on D-Day, June 6–7, 1944

Forrest C. Pogue, then a young official army combat historian, was present at the D-Day landings. His group of five combat historians was attached to part of the 175th Infantry, which was supposed to land on the afternoon of June 6, 1944, D-Day itself. Congestion on the invasion beaches meant that the 175th did not land until June 7, while the historical personnel remained aboard ship until the following day. Pogue described what he was able to observe of the day's fighting on June 7.

Naval craft off the beaches fired sporadically. Everyone seemed pleased that the French ships were joining in the attack on shore positions. Destroyers lay near the shore and fired on shore positions several miles in. The Germans replied occasionally to the fire, but without effect, and as for German air, we saw only one enemy plane, a reconnaissance aircraft, during the day. British and American planes were over in force all day. In one fifteen-minute period we counted five flights of eighteen Marauders each.

After three o'clock the skies cleared except for a few clouds over the fighting area and it turned hot, to our great discomfort. We wanted to go ashore, but orders came out that only people with rifles, who were prepared to use them, were to go in. So we parasites, armed for the most part with pistols, stayed aboard as spectators of the second act. Standing on jeeps and trucks, we watched developments off Omaha Beach as if we were at a fair. Actually, we could make out very little on the shore. Signs of movement were obscured by smoke from the firing, fires that had been started by shells, and by the demolition of mines. I did not see how it was possible for troops to have recognized any landmarks, nor have I been able to understand how correspondents, who watched the D-Day attack from ten miles out, ever got such vivid pictures of the shore.

Beginning on 7 June, when various wounded men came aboard his ship, over the next six weeks Pogue conducted numerous interviews with officers and men who had taken part in the D-Day fighting, enabling him to form the following composite picture:

My own picture of D-Day was gleaned from dozens of interviews with officers and men who went in during the morning of 6 June. Some I talked to shortly after they were wounded, others I interviewed as they rested near the front lines, and some gave their stories weeks later. A short outline of that morning is given below.

The ships that took the assault elements to Normandy had been loaded, much like ours, in many coves and inlets in Wales, southern England, and the eastern counties. On the evening of 5 June they had proceeded from the rendezvous area near the Isle of Wight southward toward France. Shortly after midnight, minesweepers of the Allied fleet began to clear channels through the minefields for the ships. British and American airborne units took off from English fields and flew overhead to drop over their objectives—the British east of the Orne and the Americans in the Cotentin Peninsula. The British reached their bridgehead early and secured it, while the American forces, scattered to a considerable degree, had a tough job of assembling for concerted action.

Toward daylight the planes and ships took up their task of softening up the enemy, the chief change in plan being that . . . the air force struck a few miles inland instead of at the beaches. On the western limit of Omaha Beach, the Rangers scrambled ashore to find that the six guns they were to knock out were pulled back out of their way.

By daylight, ship channels had been cleared to the beaches and the small landing craft had been filled with men from the LSTs and larger transports and were on their way in from rendezvous points some ten miles out. The floating tanks were started in, as were guns in small craft. Only five out of thirty-two DDs survived of those that tried to float in under their own power, while most of those in the other tank battalion, sent in at the last minute by boat, got in safely. In one field artillery battalion all but one gun was lost when the craft carrying them capsized.

The accounts of the early landings tend to follow the same pattern. Heavy seas threatened to swamp the smaller craft and made many of the soldiers seasick. Enemy fire struck numerous craft or forced navy crews to unload in deep water. Poor visibility, obstacles, and inexperience led other navy crews to land on the wrong beaches. Many of the soldiers in the first waves had to wade ashore carrying heavy equipment, which they often disposed of in deep water. At the extreme ends of the beaches, the cliffs interfered to some extent with the enemy fire and gave our troops some protection. In front of Vierville, the men hid behind the seawall that ran along the beach, and near Saint-Laurent-sur-Mer they found mounds of shingles to use as cover. Accounts of the first hours on the beaches speak of efforts of officers and non-coms [noncommissioned officers] to organize their units and get them off the beaches, but often those who tried to direct the attack fell as soon as they exposed themselves to the enemy. In some cases, platoons stuck together, but in others sections landed some distance apart—and there were instances where dispersed elements attached themselves to entirely different regiments and divisions and did not return to their parent organization for two or three days.

The first real effort to give direction to the attack came after the regimental commanders landed. The command group of the 116th Regimental Combat Team, which included Brigadier General Norman D. Cota, the assistant division commander, and Colonel C. D. W. Canham, the regimental commander, came in at about 7.30 a.m. The S-4 of the regiment was killed near the water's edge and other members of the command group were hit. Colonel Canham was wounded as he tried to organize the attack, but after receiving first aid he returned to his task. One of the most active commanders was General Cota, who, according to the accounts of the soldiers, was apparently everywhere that morning. Some spoke of his handling the bangalore torpedo that breached the wire at one of the exits, and others had him handling a Browning automatic rifle. His activities in the first weeks ashore made him almost a legendary figure. Noncoms were also called on to give leadership, as heavy casualties were inflicted on the junior officers. In one case, a private who had worked until a short time before in the regimental Post Exchange rallied the men of his unit by calling them by name and persuading them to follow him over the seawall.

On the 16th Infantry's beaches, Colonel George Taylor, the RCT commander, gained lasting fame by saying to his officers and men: "The only people on the beach are the dead and those who are going to die—now let's get the hell out of here." In a short time he had the men in his sector moving. He and Colonel Canham were promoted to the rank of brigadier general for their work on D-Day.

The manner of the advance up the bluffs differed somewhat among the various units. Some stayed behind the seawall until units in the second and third waves came in through them and went up the cliffs. Others, after being reorganized, pressed forward and by noon were on top of the bluffs.

By midnight on 6 June all of the regiments in the 1st Division (the 16th, the 18th, and 26th) and two from the 29th (the 116th and 115th) had been landed on Omaha Beach. The 2d and 5th Ranger Battalions were in position to their right. Heavy seas, landings on the wrong beaches, intense fire from well-entrenched positions, the foundering of DD tanks and artillery pieces, abnormally high casualties among officers, failure to open all the beach exits, beach congestion, the slowness of some of the assault waves to move forward from the seawall, the difficulty of using the full force of naval gunfire because of the fear of inflicting losses on the infantrymen, the lack of sufficient gaps in underwater obstacles and beach obstacles, and the failure, for various reasons, of air bombardment to take out beach fortifications all placed V Corps a considerable distance from its D-Day objectives, and, as a result of the presence of the German 352d Division in the area, in danger of a counterattack before the time estimated. In the face of this situation, the regiments were reorganized, defenses were set up for the night, and preparations made for a vigorous offensive to attain the D-Day objectives as quickly as possible.

Source: Forrest C. Pogue, *Pogue's War: Diaries of a WWII Combat Historian* (Lexington: University of Kentucky Press, 2001), 51–54. Reproduced with permission of University Press of Kentucky via Copyright Clearance Center.

General Dwight D. Eisenhower to General George C. Marshall, July 5, 1944

The supreme commander of the Allied forces in Europe, General Dwight D. Eisenhower, supplemented his official reports with regular personal letters to General George C. Marshall, chief of staff of the U.S. Army. One month after the Normandy landings, American forces faced fierce and difficult fighting in France in conditions that Eisenhower graphically described.

. . . I spent four days in the beachhead. We began attacking southward with the VIII Corps on the 3rd and the VII Corps joined in with one Division on July 4th. I was particularly anxious to visit these Corps and their Divisions during actual operations. The going is extremely tough, with three main causes responsible. The first of these, as always, is the fighting quality of the German soldier. The second is the nature of the country. Our whole attack has to fight its way out of very narrow bottlenecks flanked by marshes and against an enemy who has a double hedgerow and an intervening ditch almost every fifty yards as ready-made strong points. The third cause is the weather. Our air has been unable to operate at maximum efficiency and on top of this the rain and mud were so bad during my visit that I was reminded of Tunisian wintertime. It was almost impossible to locate artillery targets although we have plenty of guns available. Even with clear weather it is extraordinarily difficult to point out a target that is an appropriate one for either air or artillery.

Source: Biennial Reports of the Chief of Staff of the United States Army to the Secretary of War, 1 July 1939–30 June 1945 (Washington, DC: Center of Military History, United States Army, 1996), 137.

General Erwin Rommel, Teletype Message to Hitler, July 15, 1944

Six weeks after the Normandy invasion began, Field Marshal Erwin Rommel, commander of German forces in France, sent Adolf Hitler a teletype message warning that Germany faced defeat by the Allies and should withdraw from France. Ignoring this advice, Hitler ordered what became a disastrous German counterattack against advancing Allied units around Caen. On July 17, Rommel was severely injured when British fighter planes strafed his car. In company with other like-minded German generals, Rommel had intended that if Hitler ignored his advice, he would open negotiations with Allied commanders in France for an armistice and a separate peace in the West, a move that he hoped would spare Germany from invasion by Russian forces from the east. Rommel had also met with a representative of another group of German military officers who intended to assassinate Hitler, though he himself apparently knew nothing of these plans. Rommel had, however, stated his belief that Hitler should be removed from power, albeit without bloodshed. On July 20 the planned coup failed, and the conspirators, who were arrested and tortured, eventually implicated Rommel. In order not to embarrass the German government, he was given the opportunity to commit suicide, which he accepted. After his death Rommel received a hero's funeral with full military honors.

The situation on the Normandy front is growing worse every day and is now approaching a grave crisis.

Due to the severity of the fighting, the enemy's enormous use of material—above all, artillery and tanks—and the effect of his unrestricted command of the air over the battle area, our casualties are so high that the fighting power of our divisions is rapidly diminishing. Replacements from home are few in number and, with the difficult transport situation, take weeks to get to the front. As against 97,000 casualties (including 2,360 officers)—i.e. an average of 2,500 to 3,000 a day—replacements to date number 10,000, of whom about 6,000 have actually arrived at the front.

Material losses are also huge and have so far been replaced on a very small scale; in tanks, for example, only 17 replacements have arrived to date as compared with 225 losses.

The newly arrived infantry divisions are raw and, with their small establishment of artillery, anti-tank guns and close-combat anti-tank weapons, are in no state to make a lengthy stand against major enemy attacks coming after hours of drum-fire and heavy bombing. The fighting has shown that with this use of material by the enemy, even the bravest army will be smashed piece by piece, losing men, arms and territory in the process.

Due to the destruction of the railway system and the threat of the enemy air force to roads and tracks up to 90 miles behind the front, supply conditions are so bad that only the barest essentials can be brought to the front. It is consequently now necessary to exercise the greatest economy in all fields, and especially in artillery and mortar ammunition. These conditions are unlikely to improve, as enemy action is steadily reducing the transport capacity available. Moreover, this activity in the air is likely to become even more effective as the numerous air-strips in the bridgehead are taken into use.

No new forces of any consequence can be brought up to the Normandy front except by weakening Fifteenth Army's front on the Channel, or the Mediterranean front in southern France. Yet Seventh Army's front, taken over all, urgently requires two fresh divisions, as the troops in Normandy are exhausted.

On the enemy's side, fresh forces and great quantities of war material are flowing into his front every day. His supplies are undisturbed by our air force. Enemy pressure is growing steadily stronger.

In these circumstances we must expect that in the foreseeable future the enemy will succeed in breaking through our thin front, above all, Seventh Army's, and thrusting deep into France. Apart from the Panzer Group's sector reserves, which are at present tied down by the fighting on their own front and—due to the enemy's command of the air—can only move by night, we dispose of no mobile reserve for defence against such a break-through. Action by our air force will, as in the past, have little effect.

The troops are everywhere fighting heroically, but the unequal struggle is approaching its end. It is urgently necessary for the proper conclusion to be drawn from this situation. As C.-in-C. of the Army Group I feel myself in duty bound to speak plainly on this point.

Source: Bundesarchiv/Militärarchiv RH 19-IX/8, Bl. 105–108. Translation by Dr. Marcus Jones.

U.S. Army General Dwight D. Eisenhower on Sergeant Curtis G. Culin's Invention of the "Rhino" Tank Modification Preceding Operation COBRA (July 25–31, 1944)

Sgt. Curtis "Bud" Culin's modification to the M4 Sherman tank, which involved welding four, tusklike steel bars to the front of the vehicle, enabled them to smash through the hedgerows in Normandy. Formed over the centuries to separate ancestral fields, these hedgerows were ideal defensive barriers for the Germans. When a tank rode up over the hedgerow, its main gun pointed upward, and the tank exposed its vulnerable unarmored underside and could be more easily destroyed by German antitank devices. It was perhaps the most outstanding example of American ingenuity at work in the war. Allied Expeditionary Force commander General Dwight D. Eisenhower credited the device with saving many lives and contributing greatly to the Allied success.

There was a little sergeant. His name was Culin, and he had an idea. And his idea was that we could fasten knives, great big steel knives in front of these tanks, and as they came along they would cut off these banks right at ground level—they would go through on the level keel—would carry with themselves a little bit of camouflage for a while. And this idea was brought to the captain, to the major, to the colonel, and it got high enough that somebody did something about it—and that was General Bradley—and he did it very quickly.

Because this seemed like a crazy idea, they did not even go to the engineers very fast, because they were afraid of the technical advice, and then someone did have a big question, "Where are you going to find the steel for all this thing?" Well now, happily the Germans tried to keep us from going on the beaches with great steel "chevaux de fries"—big crosses, there were all big bars of steel down on the beach where the Germans left it. And he got it—got these things sharpened up—and it worked fine. The biggest and happiest group I suppose in all the Allied Armies that night were those that knew that this thing worked. And it worked beautifully.

Source: Public Papers of the Presidents of the United States: Dwight D. Eisenhower: 1960–61 (Washington, DC: U.S., Government Printing Office, 1961), 908–909.

Introductions by Priscilla Roberts and Spencer C. Tucker

Appendix A: Ground Forces Order of Battle on D-Day, June 6, 1944

Allied Forces

On June 6, 1944, the Western Allies landed in Normandy more than 156,000 men. These included 75,214 in the British sector of Gold, Juno, and Sword Beaches and 57,500 in the American sector of Omaha and Utah Beaches. In addition, there were some 23,400 airborne forces: 15,500 U.S. and 7,900 British. Thus, total British and Canadian forces (83,114) landed alone outnumbered those of the United States (73,000), consisting of some 53 percent of the total.

The following major units came ashore on June 6:

British and British Commonwealth
6th Airborne Division
I Corps of the 3rd British Infantry Division and the British 27th Armoured Brigade, the 3rd Canadian Infantry Division, and the 2nd Canadian Armoured Brigade
XXX Corps of the British 50th Infantry Division and the 8th Armoured Brigade
British 79th Armoured Division

United States
V Corps of the 1st Infantry Division and the 29th Infantry Division
VII Corps of the 4th Infantry Division, 82nd Airborne Division, and the 101st Airborne Division

German Forces
Units deployed defensively in the actual landing areas:
352nd Infantry Division
709th Infantry Division (Static)
716th Infantry Division (Static)
91st Air Landing Division (a regular infantry division capable of being transported by air)
Units in areas adjacent to the landing beaches:
243rd Infantry Division (Static), along the western coast of the Cotentin Peninsula
711th Infantry Division (Static), in the Pas de Calais area, and the 21st Panzer Division, deployed near Caen

Source: "Invasion of Normandy," Wikipedia, https://en.wikipedia.org/wiki/Invasion_of_Normandy.

Appendix B: Number of Troops Killed on June 6, 1944

British and Canadian	1,914
United States	2,499
German	Estimated at 4,000–9,000

Source: "D-Day: June 6, 1944," The National WWII Museum, http://www.nationalww2museum.org/learn/education/for-students/ww2-history/d-day-june-6–1944.html?referrer=https://www.google.com/.

Appendix C: Army, Corps, and Division Units Involved in the Battle of Normandy (June 6–August 29, 1944)

United States/French Forces

First Army
XII Corps
XV Corps

Third Army
V Corps
VII Corps
VIII Corps
XIX Corps

Armored Divisions
2nd Armored Division (from July 2)
3rd Armored Division (July 9)
4th Armored Division (July 28)
5th Armored Division (August 2)
6th Armored Division (July 28)
7th Armored Division (August 14)
2nd French Armored Division (August 1)

Airborne Divisions
2nd Airborne Division (June 6)
101st Airborne Division (June 6)

Infantry Divisions
1st Infantry Division (June 6)
2nd Infantry Division (June 8)
4th Infantry Division (June 6)
5th Infantry Division (July 16)
8th Infantry Division (July 8)
9th Infantry Division (June 14)
28th Infantry Division (July 27)
29th Infantry Division (June 7)
30th Infantry Division (June 15)
35th Infantry Division (July 11)
79th Infantry Division (June 19)
80th Infantry Division (Aug 8)
83rd Infantry Division (June 27)
90th Infantry Division (June 10)

British/Canadian/Polish Forces
British 21st Army Group
British Second Army

Armored Divisions
Guards Armored Division (June 28)
7th Guards Armored Division (June 8)
11th Armored Division (June 13)
79th Armored Division (Specialized Armor, June 6)

Airborne Division
6th Airborne Division (6 June)

Infantry Divisions
3rd Infantry Division (June 6)
15th Infantry Division (Scottish, June 14)
43rd Infantry Division (Wessex, June 24)
49th Infantry Division (West Riding, June 6)
50th Infantry Division (Northumbrian, June 6)
51st Infantry Division (Highland, June 6)
53rd Infantry Division (Welsh, June 27)

59th Infantry Division (Staffordshire, June 27)

Canadian and Polish Forces Attached to the British Army
4th Canadian Armored Division
1st Polish Armored Division
2nd Canadian Division
3rd Canadian Infantry Division

German Divisions (39)
1st Armored SS Division
2nd Armored Division
2nd Mechanized SS Division
3rd Airborne Division
5th Airborne Division
9th Armored SS Division
9th Infantry SS Division
10th Armored SS Division
12th Armored Division
16th Infantry Division, Luftwaffe
17th Mechanized Division
17th Infantry SS Division
21st Armored Division
71st Infantry Division
77th Infantry Division
84th Infantry Division
85th Infantry Division
89th Infantry Division
91st Infantry Division
116th Armored Division
242nd Infantry Division
243rd Infantry Division
265th Infantry Division
266th Infantry Division
271st Infantry Division
272nd Infantry Division
275th Infantry Division
276th Infantry Division
277th Infantry Division
326th Infantry Division
346th Infantry Division
352nd Infantry Division
353rd Infantry Division
363rd Infantry Division
709th Infantry Division
711th Infantry Division
716th Infantry Division
736th Infantry Division
Panzer Lehr Armored Division

Allied Expeditionary Air Forces

United States Army Air Forces
Ninth Tactical Air Force
Eighth Air Force

Royal Air Force
Second Tactical Force

Source: "Divisions Involved in Normandy," D-Day Overlord, http://www.dday-overlord.com/eng/divisions.htm.

Appendix D: Estimated Casualties in the Battle of Normandy (June 6–August 29, 1944)

	Killed	Wounded	Missing	Total
Allied Ground Forces				
21st Army Group (British, Canadian, Polish)	15,995	57,996	9,054	83,045
United States	20,838	94,881	10,128	125,847
Allied Air Forces				
Royal Air Force	8,178 killed and missing		8,178	
U.S. Army Air Forces	8,536		8,536	
Estimated Allied losses in preinvasion operations, mostly air	12,000		12,000	
Germans		200,000 killed or wounded	200,000 prisoners of war	400,000

Source: Carlo d'Este, *Decision in Normandy* (New York: E. P. Dutton, 1983), 517.

Chronology

1939

Sep 1: German forces invade Poland. Two days later, on expiration of their ultimatum for Germany to withdraw from Poland, Great Britain and France declare war on Germany. World War II has begun.

1941

Dec 7: Japanese forces attack the U.S. Pacific Fleet at Honolulu, Hawaii, and the United States declares war on Japan.

Dec 11: German chancellor Adolf Hitler declares war on the United States.

Dec 22–Jan 14, 1942: In the Arcadia Conference, U.S. president Franklin D. Roosevelt and British prime minister Winston Churchill and their staffs meet in Washington, D.C., to discuss military strategy and cooperative agreements to defeat the Axis powers. The conference leads to the establishment of the Combined Chiefs of Staff, involving the military chiefs from the two states and the Joint Chiefs of Staff, its U.S. component. Establishment of the Combined Chiefs of Staff marks the beginning of perhaps the closest ever collaboration between two sovereign nations at war. The leaders also agree that the war against Germany will have priority over the effort against Japan. Among other items, the conferees discuss the possibility of an Allied invasion of North Africa.

1942

Jun 11: Dwight D. Eisenhower is appointed to command U.S. forces in the European theater.

Jun 25: Eisenhower arrives at U.S. headquarters in London and formally takes command.

Aug 19: British and Canadian forces carry out Operation JUBILEE, a costly, unsuccessful raid on German-occupied Dieppe, France. It convinces even die-hard American advocates that the Western Allies are not ready to assault Festung Europa (Fortress Europe) in 1942. It also demonstrates the need for strong naval and air preliminary bombardment along with thorough training of assault forces, and it proves the difficulty of attacking ports and leads to the decision to develop artificial harbors for the eventual invasion across the English Channel.

Nov 8–10: In Operation TORCH, which had been pushed by Roosevelt, U.S. and British forces invade Casablanca, Oran, and Algiers in French North Africa.

1943

Jul 9–11: In Operation HUSKY, British and U.S. forces invade Sicily.

Aug 14–24: Canadian prime minister William Lyon Mackenzie King, British prime minister Winston Churchill, and U.S. president Roosevelt meet at Quebec, Canada, and endorse the plan to invade France in 1944.

Sep 3: In Operation AVALANCHE, British forces invade Italy.

Sep 9: British forces carry out a secondary landing at Taranto, Italy, while U.S. forces invade Salerno. With the Italian front settling into stalemate, resources are withdrawn from Italy for the cross-channel invasion of France.

Nov 28–Dec 1: Roosevelt, Churchill, and Soviet leader Joseph Stalin confer at Tehran. With British and U.S. troops fighting the Germans on the ground only in Italy and with 14 divisions, while the Soviet Union has 178 divisions locked in combat, Stalin presses the Western leaders on the planned cross-channel invasion of France and insists on learning the name of the commander. Shortly after the conference, Roosevelt names General Dwight D. Eisenhower to that position.

1944

Feb 20–26: Allied forces launch coordinated air strikes, known as "Big Week," against German factories.

Mar 18: The Royal Air Force (RAF) conducts a major raid on Hamburg, Germany.

Apr 1: A visitors' ban is imposed within 10 miles of the southern coast of Britain.

Apr 28: In the Battle of Lyme Bay in England, German E-boats surprise and attack U.S. forces on TIGER, a training exercise for the Normandy invasion, sinking *LST-507* and *LST-531* and heavily damaging *LST-289*, with heavy personnel losses.

May 2–6: Exercise FABIUS, rehearsals for the invasion, are held in Lyme Bay and the Isle of Wight areas.

May 8: General Eisenhower settles on June 5 as the date for the cross-channel Normandy invasion. It is also decided that in the event of bad weather, the invasion could be mounted on June 6 or 7.

May 26: Amid very tight security, Allied forces are concentrated on the southern coast of England, and the camps are sealed, with no one allowed to enter or leave without special authorization.

May 28: All Allied naval personnel are "sealed" within their ships.

Jun 2: Bombardment Force O Eastern Task Force (two battleships, one monitor, five cruisers, and eight Fleet destroyers) sails from Scapa Flow.

Midget submarines *X.20* (assigned to the Juno Beach sector) and *X.23* (Sword Beach sector) depart Portsmouth, England, in tow.

Jun 3: Bombardment Forces E and K (1 battleship, 7 cruisers, 12 fleet destroyers) of the Eastern Task Force depart from the Clyde.

Bombarding Forces A and C (3 battleships, 1 monitor, 9 cruisers, and 17 destroyers) of the Western Task Force sail from Belfast.

Force U of the assault convoys sails from the Start Peninsula.

Jun 4: 5:15 a.m. Operation NEPTUNE is postponed by 24 hours owing to the stormy weather.

Jun 5: 4:00 a.m. General Eisenhower, supreme commander of the Allied Expeditionary Force, takes the "final and irrevocable decision" that the invasion will proceed. The plan drawn up expects 132,715 troops to be landed on five beaches on a spread of some 49 miles, with 23,400 paratroopers to be dropped farther inland and 6,483 ships involved.

9:00 a.m. The first Eastern Task Force assault groups sail from Portsmouth, Shoreham, and other ports.

6:00 p.m. The U.S. minesweeper *Osprey* is mined northwest of Cap d'Antifer.

7:57 p.m. The 14th Minesweeping Flotilla reaches a point within sight of the French coast.

10:00 p.m. Five fleets of assault ships depart their English port bases, overtaking the long columns of troop transports and larger landing craft, all protected by a vast aerial armada.

10:56 p.m. Handley Page heavy bombers towing six Horsa gliders take off from Tarrant Rushton, Dorset. The glidermen aboard are charged with securing two key bridges at the eastern end of the landing beaches.

Jun 6: 0:00 a.m. In Operation TITANIC, part of Operation FORTITUDE, the Allied deception plan to convince the Germans that the Normandy invasion is merely a feint, with the real landings to occur in the Pas de Calais area, RAF aircraft drop hundreds of dummy paratroopers across Seine-Maritime, Calvados, and Manche. A Special Air Service (SAS) team drops into the Cotentin Peninsula five miles west of Saint-Lô, with Lieutenant Norman Poole the first man to land in Normandy. The SAS men install amplifiers to play combat noises, mortar explosions, and the sound of soldiers.

0:10 a.m. The first American pathfinders drop over the Cotentin Peninsula to mark the drop zones for the paratroopers to follow.

0:16 a.m. Three of the British gliders land just 30 yards from the first bridge, over the Caen Canal. Led by Major John Howard, the glidermen capture the bridge, then go on to take the second bridge as well, cutting off German reinforcement to the Normandy beaches from that direction.

0:30 a.m. The Café Gondreé by the Caen Canal Bridge (today known as Pegasus Bridge) is the first building liberated in France. Allied troops there are given champagne by the owner.

0:45 a.m. The German 919th Regiment reports the presence of enemy paratroopers in the Cotentin Peninsula.

0:50 a.m. Paratroopers of the British 6th Airborne Division drop over Ranville, Merville, Trouffeville, and Troarn in Normandy. Their goal is to take out the German artillery battery of Merville, southeast of Cabourg; destroy the bridges; and occupy the crest of Troarn in order to prevent the arrival of German reinforcements during the Allied landings.

1:00 a.m. Paratroopers of the U.S. 82nd and 101st Airborne Divisions jump into the Cherbourg Peninsula at the western end of the beaches. Because of heavy cloud cover, a number miss the drop zone target and drown in flooded swamps, but the wide dispersal has the unintended advantage of confusing the Germans as to the actual Allied objectives.

1:10 a.m. Four teams of Free France paratroopers jump over Brittany in the Duault forest near Plumelec.

1:30 a.m. Colonel General Friedrich Dollmann, commander of the German Seventh Army, orders it on general alert.

2:00 a.m. The first wave of Allied bombers takes off from fields in England for France, targeting German positions in the vicinity of the invasion beaches.

2:45 a.m. Soldiers begin to climb down from the transports into their landing craft, which pitch and roll in every direction in the heavy seas, for the run to the beaches.

3:09 a.m. German radar picks up the Allied invasion fleet, and Admiral Theodor Krancke, commander in chief of German Navy Group Command West, orders shore batteries under his command to prepare to resist the Allied landings and German naval units to engage the Allied ships.

3:48 a.m. German E-boat flotillas and two armed trawlers get under way to engage the Allied invasion fleet.

4:30 a.m. Sainte-Mère-Église is the first town to be liberated in France, taken by the American paratroopers, although many of the paratroopers are killed by the Germans before they can free themselves from their harnesses.

4:40 a.m. German commander in the West Field Marshal Gerd von Rundstedt orders two panzer divisions near Paris to move immediately to Calvados. Colonel General Alfred Jodl, chief of the Operations Staff of the Armed Forces High Command (Oberkommando der Wehrmacht), countermands the order until Hitler is awake.

4:45 a.m. British forces capture the Merville battery, easing the way for the landing on Sword Beach.

5:20 a.m. Sunrise.

5:30 a.m. The Allied naval bombardment of the landing areas begins.

5:35 a.m. German shore batteries commence fire against the Allied invasion ships.

5:37 a.m. A flotilla of three German E-boats operating out of Le Havre launches torpedoes at Allied destroyers screening the invasion fleet, sinking the Norwegian destroyer *Svenner* west of Le Havre and north of Sword Beach. It is the only Allied warship lost to German naval activity on June 6.

6:00 a.m. Aerial bombing of German fortifications at Omaha and Utah Beaches begins. LSTs launch their duplex-drive M4 Sherman tanks.

6:20 a.m. Allied landing craft approach Omaha Beach.

6:30 a.m. American forces land at Omaha Beach. They meet stiff German resistance and sustain heavy casualties. A number of amphibious vehicles sink owing to the unexpected swells and because they entered the water too far from shore.

6:31 a.m. American forces land at Utah Beach. The tide results in the landing craft coming ashore about a mile south, but the landings are a success.

6:41 a.m. The crew of the U.S. Navy destroyer *Cory* is forced to abandon ship owing to a direct hit by a shell from one of the three 210mm (8.5-inch) guns of a German coastal defense battery and probably a German mine.

6:45 a.m. The Royal Navy destroyer escort *Wrestler* is damaged beyond repair by a German mine west of Le Havre off Sword Beach.

7:10 a.m. The U.S. Army 2nd Ranger Battalion commences its assault on Pointe du Hoc.

7:25 a.m. The British 3rd Infantry Division begins coming ashore on Gold Beach. The success of the landing is aided by the "swimming tanks" (duplex-drive M4 Sherman tanks) that are able to reach the shore.

7:35 a.m. Elements of the British 50th Infantry Division begin coming ashore at Sword Beach. Commandos led by the impressive Brigadier Simon Fraser, 15th Lord Lovat, then proceed to reinforce the men at the Caen Canal Bridge.

7:35 a.m. Canadian forces begin landing on Juno Beach, again aided by the Sherman tanks. The German defenders are shocked to see tanks emerge from the sea.

7:45 a.m. U.S. forces at Utah Beach begin moving inland.

8:30 a.m. LCMs, LCTs, and LSTs land tanks at Omaha Beach.

9:00 a.m. The 2nd Ranger Battalion secures Pointe du Hoc and then defends it against German counterattacks.

9:05 a.m. Hitler is finally awakened at the Berghof in Berchtesgaden, Germany, and informed of the news from Normandy. He is in high spirits, believing—thanks to the Allied deception of Operation FORTITUDE—that the Normandy invasion is only a feint, with the main landing to come in the Pas de Calais.

9:15 a.m. With U.S. forces in trouble at Omaha Beach, Lieutenant General Omar N. Bradley, commanding the U.S. landings, considers abandoning the landing there.

9:50 a.m. Disaster is averted at Omaha Beach, thanks largely to destroyers, the commanders of which risk their ships grounding to provide close-in naval gunfire support.

11:10 a.m. Men of the U.S. 101st Airborne Division link up with troops of the 4th Infantry Division at Utah Beach, allowing the infantry to proceed inland.

12:00 noon. American forces are by this time able to advance inland from Omaha Beach.

4:20 p.m. The Liberty ship SS *Sambut* is sunk in the Strait of Dover by German long-range artillery.

6:00 p.m. A prerecorded radio address by Free French leader General Charles de Gaulle is broadcast to the French people.

10:00 p.m. By this time the Allies have established a bridgehead some 60 miles wide and 10 miles deep in Normandy.

Jun 7: The U.S. freighter *Susan B. Anthony* is sunk by a mine off Juno Beach.

The U.S. *LST-715* is sunk by a German E-boat.

The U.S. minesweeper *Tide* is sunk by a mine off Utah Beach.

Fifty-four merchant ships are scuttled to form five protected anchorages, known as Gooseberries.

Jun 7/8: Two Royal Navy LCTs are sunk in the middle of the English Channel by German E-boats.

Jun 8: The U.S. destroyer *Meredith* is mined off Utah Beach. It sinks on June 9 from a bomb in a German air attack.

The Royal Navy frigate *Lawford* is sunk in a German air attack off Juno Beach.

The U.S. destroyer *Glennon* strikes a mine off Utah Beach. It is lost on June 10 after a German shore battery finds the range.

The U.S. destroyer escort *Rich* strikes a mine and is sunk while endeavoring to assist the *Glennon*.

The Royal Navy netlayer *Minster* strikes a mine and is sunk off Utah Beach.

The tanker *Chant 6* is sunk by an air attack. Port-en-Bessin, captured on June 7, is back in operation for coasters and barges.

Jun 8/9: U.S. *LST-314* and *LST-376* are sunk by E-boats in midchannel.

Jun 9: The Royal Navy destroyer *Ashanti* sinks the German destroyer *ZH.1* off Île de Batz, while the Canadian destroyer *Haida* drives the German destroyer *Z.32* ashore on Île de Batz.

Jun 9/10: German E-boats sink the ammunition coasters *Brackenfield* and *Dungrange* in midchannel.

Jun 10: A German air attack sinks the U.S. freighter *Charles Morgan*.

The Gooseberry anchorages are completed.

Jun 11: German E-boats attack and damage beyond repair the British frigate *Halstead*.

The Royal Navy MTB.448 and one German E-boat are sunk in an action in the West Task Force area.

The British coaster *Ashanti* and four tugs are sunk by German E-boats in midchannel.

The U.S. Army V Corps and the British XXX Corps link up.

Jun 13: The British destroyer escort *Boadacia* is sunk by a German aerial torpedo south of Portland, England.

Jun 14: The Canadian destroyer *Ashanti* and the Polish destroyer *Piorun* sink the German minesweepers *M.83* and *M.343* off the Channel Islands.

Jun 15: An Allied air attack on Le Havre sinks the German E-boats *Falke, Jaguar,* and *Möwe* and damages the *Kondor.* Twenty small patrol craft and 19 tugs are also hit and damaged or sunk.

The German submarine *U.767* sinks the British frigate *Mourne* off Uzard.

The German submarine *U.764* sinks the British frigate *Blackwood* off Portland.

Operation PLUTO begins with laying the first cross-channel pipeline to Port-en-Bessin.

The Germans regain control of the east bank of the mouth of the Orne River and intensify their shelling of Sword Beach, damaging two British ships and five LSTs. Unloading troops and supplies is shifted to Juno Beach.

Jun 16: The British Trinity House Vessel *Alert* is mined and sunk in the vicinity of Gold Beach.

Jun 18: The Royal Navy MTYBs *727* and *748* attack and damage beyond repair the German minesweeper *M.133* off Jersey.

The British destroyers *Fame, Inconstant,* and *Havelock* sink the German submarine *U.767.*

A German air attack sinks the coaster *Albert C. Field* south of St. Albans Head.

Jun 19–23: A great category 6–7 storm strikes the Allied assault areas in Normandy. Thirteen merchant and auxiliary vessels and more than 800 smaller vessels are driven aground. The Mulberry Harbor off Omaha Beach at St. Laurent is badly damaged and rendered unusable. All convoy movements are halted on June 19, but they are resumed late on June 21.

Jun 20: The French frigate *La Surprise* is badly damaged by a mine off Omaha Beach.

Jun 21: The British destroyer escort *Fury* is mined off Sword Beach and beached to prevent its sinking.

Jun 22: Soviet forces begin their great Belorussia Offensive.

Jun 23: The coaster *Dunvegan Head* is hit by German shore artillery and destroyed off Sword Beach.

The British antiaircraft cruiser *Scylia* (Rear Admiral Philip Vian's flagship) is damaged beyond repair by a mine off Sword Beach.

The Norwegian destroyer escort *Glaisdale* and the British minesweeper *Persian* are badly damaged by mines off Gold Beach.

Jun 24: The British destroyer *Swift* is mined off Sword Beach.

The freighters *Fort Norfolk* and *Derrycunihy* are mined and sunk in the Eastern Task Force area.

The British cruiser *Arethusa* is severely damaged in a German air attack.

The Canadian destroyer *Haida* and other ships and aircraft sink the German submarine *U.971.*

The German submarine *U.984* damages beyond repair the British frigate *Goodson* in the middle of the English Channel.

The British frigates *Affleck* and *Balfour* sink the German submarine *U.1191,* and the frigate *Bickerton* sinks *U.269.*

Continued German shelling of Sword Beach brings the abandonment of resupply there by all but minor craft.

The first oil pipeline of Operation PLUTO is completed.

Jun 26: The U.S. Army VII Corps liberates Cherbourg.

Jun 27: A German U-boat damages beyond repair the British corvette *Pink* off Barfleur.

Jun 28: The U.S. freighter *Charles W. Elliot* is mined and sunk off Juno Beach.

Jun 29: The German submarine *U.984* attacks Convoy EMC.17 and damages beyond repair the U.S. freighters *James A. Farrell*, *James A. Treutlin*, and *H. G. Blasdel* and also damages the *Edward M. House*.

The German submarine *U.988* attacks Convoy FMT.22 and sinks the freighter *Empire Portia*. Four British warships and British aircraft attack and sink the *U.988*.

Jul 1: German artillery fire forces the closing of Sword Beach for all unloading.

Jul 2: The merchant LSI (large) *Empire Broadsword* is mined and sunk in the Western Task Force area.

Jul 3: Operation NEPTUNE officially ends.

Jul 5: By this date the Allies have landed 1 million men in France.

The British minesweeper *Friendship* is severely damaged by a mine off Gold Beach.

The British destroyer *Wanderer* and frigate *Tavy* sink the German submarine *U.390*.

Jul 6: German midget submarines sink the British minesweepers *Magic* and *Cato* off Sword Beach.

The Canadian destroyer *Ottawa* and destroy escort *Kootenay* sink the German submarine *U.678*.

Jul 7: A German air strike sinks the fighter direction tender (converted LST) *FDT 216* in the Seine Bay.

Jul 8: German midget submarines damage the Polish cruiser *Ort Dragon* and force it to beach to prevent sinking and also sink the British minesweeper *Pylades*, both off Sword Beach.

The battleship *Rodney* and the monitor *Roberts* shell German targets, and the RAF Bomber Command raids Caen.

Some 600 small craft damaged in the great storm of June 19–23 are refloated.

Jul 8–9: British and Canadian forces mount Operation CHARNWOOD in an effort to take the city of Caen.

Jul 18: The British frigate *Balfour* sinks the German submarine *U.672*.

Jul 18–20: Operation GOODWOOD occurs, another British offensive in the ongoing effort to secure Caen.

Jul 20: An assassination attempt on German leader Adolf Hitler fails, as does the associated effort by the German resistance to topple the Nazi regime.

The British destroyer escort *Isis* is lost to an unconfirmed German action off Sword Beach.

The British frigates *St. John* and *Matane* off Ushant are damaged by glide bombs.

Jul 21: The British minesweeper *Chamois* is damaged beyond repair by a mine in the Eastern Task Force area.

The British frigates *Curzon* and *Ekins* sink the German submarine *U.212*.

Jul 24: The British assault HQ ship (escort destroyer) *Goathland* is damaged beyond repair by a mine in the Eastern Task Force area.

Jul 25: The British Admiralty resumes operational control of the English Channel through the normal chain of command.

Jul 25–31: In Operation COBRA, American forces break out from the Normandy perimeter.

Jul 26: The British frigate *Cooke* sinks the German submarine *U.214.*

Jul 30–31: German E-boats attack Convoy FTM.53 off Beachy Head, sinking one freighter, the *Samwake,* and damaging four others.

Jul 30–Aug 7: British forces launch Operation BLUECOAT in support of COBRA, the American breakout.

Jul 31: The British sloop *Starling* and frigate *Loch Killin* sink the German submarine *U.333.*

Aug 2: German chancellor Adolf Hitler orders a concentration of panzer divisions for a counterattack to erase the U.S. 1st Army's gains in Operation COBRA and to cut off the U.S. Third Army, which has advanced into Normandy.

Aug 2–3: German small battle units launch 58 midget submarines and 22 explosive motorboats to attack Allied anchorages in the Eastern Task Force area. Only 17 midget submarines return.

Aug 3: German midget submarines sink the British destroyer escort *Quorn* and trawler *Gairsay,* and an explosive motorboat sinks an LCT.

Aug 4: An RAF air strike on Pauillac in the Gironde sinks the German minesweepers *M.271, M.325,* and *M.422.*

The British destroyer *Wensleydale* and frigate *Stayner* sink the German submarine *U.671.*

Aug 6: The British AA cruiser *Bellona* and destroyers *Ashanti* and *Tartar* and the Canadian destroyers *Haida* and *Iroquois* sink the German minesweepers *M.263* and *M.486,* with four ships in convoy, south of Saint-Nazaire. The German escort *SG.3* (ex-*Sans Pareil*), damaged in this action, is then destroyed by an RAF air attack at Sables d'Olonne.

The British frigate *Loch Killin* sinks the German submarine *U.736.*

An RAF strike on Noirmoutiers sinks the German minesweepers *M.366, M.367, M.428,* and *M.438.*

Caen falls to British and Canadian forces.

Aug 7–13: Commanded by Field Marshal Günther von Kluge, German commander in the West and commander of Army Group B, Operation LÜTTICH, known to the British and Americans as the Mortain Counteroffensive or Battle of Mortain, commences with the goal of reaching the vicinity of Avranches. The Germans achieve surprise but are soon halted in the vicinity of Mortain by a stubborn U.S. ground resistance and Allied tactical airpower, especially British Typhoon aircraft firing rockets. Hitler has merely speeded up the German defeat in France.

Aug 8–13: The First Canadian Army carries out Operation TOTALIZE, an offensive in Normandy.

Aug 10: The British minesweeper *Vestal* is badly damaged by a mine off Gold Beach.

Aug 11: The German minesweeper *M.27* succumbs to a mine off Pauillac.

The British sloop *Starling* and RAF aircraft sink the German submarine *U.385.*

Aug 12: An RAF strike on Royan sinks the German minesweeper *M.370.*

Aug 14: The German minesweeper *M.444* is sunk in Brest Roads, probably by a mine.

The British frigates *Duckworth* and *Essington* and RAF aircraft sink the German submarine *U.618.*

Aug 14–21: In Operation TRACTABLE Canadian and Polish forces, supported by a brigade of British tanks, carry out their last offensive of the Battle of Normandy.

Aug 15: In Operation DRAGOON, Allied forces land in southern France.

Damaged by gunfire from the British cruiser *Mauritius* and destroyer *Ursa* and the Canadian destroyer *Iroquois,* the German minesweeper *M.385* is beached off Sables d'Olonne.

The British corvette *Orchis* sinks the German submarine *U.741*.

Aug 18: The Canadian destroyers *Ottawa, Kootenay,* and *Chaudiere* sink the German submarine *U.621*.

Aug 19: The French Resistance mounts an uprising in Paris.

Aug 20: The British destroyers *Wensleydale, Forester,* and *Vidette* sink the German submarine *U.413*.

Aug 21: Allied forces trap 60,000 Germans in the Argentan–Falaise pocket.

The British corvette *Orchis,* mined off Courseulles, is beached as a total loss.

The Canadian corvette *Alberni* is sunk by a German U-boat in the English Channel.

RAF air strikes sink the German destroyer *Z.23* at La Pallice and the minesweeper *M.292* at Le Verdon in the Gironde.

Aug 22: A German submarine sinks the British minesweeper *Loyalty* in the English Channel.

Aug 24: An RAF air strike sinks the German destroyer *Z.24* and torpedo boat *T.24* off Le Verdon.

The British frigate *Louis* sinks the German submarine *U.445*.

Aug 25: Free French forces liberate Paris.

The British minesweeper *Gleaner* is badly damaged by a mine off Sword Beach.

Aug 27: An RAF air strike in the Seine Bay sinks the British minesweepers *Britomart* and *Hussar* and damages beyond repair the minesweeper *Salamander.*

Aug 28: Allied forces secure Toulon and Marseilles, France.

Aug 31: The Canadian frigates *Swansea* and *St John* sink the German submarine *U.247*.

Sep 12: Le Havre surrenders.

Sep 17–26: Operation MARKET GARDEN, the effort by the Western Allies to secure a crossing over the Rhine River at Arnhem, ends in failure.

Sep 28: Canadian forces liberate Calais, France.

1945

May 7: German forces surrender unconditionally at Rheims, France.

May 8: V-E Day (Victory in Europe).

Bibliography

Ambrose, Stephen E. *D-Day, June 6, 1944: The Climactic Battle of World War II.* New York: Simon and Schuster, 1994.

Ambrose, Stephen E. *Eisenhower: Soldier, General of the Army, President-Elect.* New York: Simon and Schuster, 1983.

Ambrose, Stephen E. *Pegasus Bridge.* New York: Simon and Schuster, 1985.

Baker, A. D., III. *Allied Landing Craft of World War Two.* Annapolis, MD: Naval Institute Press, 1985

Balkoski, Joseph. *Beyond the Beachhead: The 29th Infantry Division in Normandy.* Mechanicsburg, PA: Stackpole Books, 2005.

Barbier, Mary Kathryn. *D-Day Deception: Operation Fortitude and the Normandy Invasion.* Westport, CT: Praeger Security International, 2007.

Baxter, Colin F. *Field Marshal Bernard Law Montgomery, 1887–1976.* Westport, CT: Greenwood, 1999.

Baxter, Colin F. *The Normandy Campaign, 1944: A Selected Bibliography.* New York: Greenwood, 1992.

Bennett, Ralph. *Ultra in the West: The Normandy Campaign of 1944–1945.* New York: Scribner, 1979.

Bercuson, David. *Maple Leaf against the Axis: Canada's Second World War.* Toronto: Stoddart, 1995.

Black, Robert W. *The Battalion: The Dramatic Story of the 2nd Ranger Battalion in World War II.* Mechanicsburg, PA: Stackpole Books, 2006.

Black, Robert W. *Rangers in World War II.* New York: Ivy Books, 1992.

Blair, Clay. *Ridgway's Paratroopers: The American Airborne in World War II.* Garden City, NY: Dial, 1985.

Blumenson, Martin. *Patton: The Man behind the Legend, 1885–1945.* New York: William Morrow, 1985.

Blumenson, Martin. *The U.S. Army in World War II, European Theater of Operations: Breakout and Pursuit.* Washington, DC: U.S. Army, Office of the Chief of Military History, 1961.

Boog, Horst, Gerhard Krebs, and Detlef Vogel. *Germany and the Second World War,* Vol. 7, *The Strategic Air War in Europe and the War in the West and East Asia, 1943–1944/5,* Oxford, UK: Clarendon, 2006.

Bradley, Omar N. *A Soldier's Story.* New York: Holt, 1951.

Bradley, Omar N., and Clay Blair. *A General's Life: An Autobiography.* New York: Simon and Schuster, 1983.

Breuer, William B. *Hitler's Fortress Cherbourg: The Conquest of a Bastion.* New York: Stein and Day, 1984.

Brinkley, Douglas. *The Boys of Pointe du Hoc: Ronald Reagan, D-Day, and the U.S. Army 2nd Ranger Battalion.* New York: W. Morrow, 2006.

Buckley, John. *British Armour in the Normandy Campaign 1944.* Abingdon, UK: Taylor and Francis, 2006.

Bykofsky, J., and H. Larson. *The U.S. Army in World War II: Transportation Corps Operations Overseas.* Washington, DC: Center of Military History, 1957.

Carafano, James J. *After D-Day: Operation Cobra and the Normandy Breakout.* Boulder, CO: Lynne Rienner, 2000.

Carafano, James Jay. *GI Ingenuity: Improvisation, Technology, and Winning World War II.* Westport, CT: Praeger Security International, 2006.

Chalmers, W. S. *Full Cycle: The Biography of Admiral Sir Bertram Ramsay.* London: Hodder and Stoughton, 1959.

Chandler, Alfred D., et al., eds. *The Papers of Dwight David Eisenhower: The War Years,* Vols. 1–4. Baltimore: Johns Hopkins University Press, 1970.

Chesneau, Roger, ed. *Conway's All the World's Fighting Ships, 1922–1946.* London: Conway Maritime, 1980.

Colley, John. *The Day of the Typhoon: Flying with RAF Tankbusters in Normandy.* Wellingborough, UK: Patrick Stephens, 1986.

Collins, J. Lawton. *Lightning Joe: An Autobiography.* Baton Rouge: Louisiana State University Press, 1979.

Coningham, Arthur. "The Development of Tactical Air Forces." *Royal United Services Institution Journal* 91(562) (1946): 211–226.

Craven, Wesley Frank, and James Lea Cate, eds. *The Army Air Forces in World War II,* Vol. 3, *Europe: Argument to V-E Day, January 1944–May 1945.* New Imprint. Washington, DC: Office of Air Force History, 1983.

Crowdy, Terry. *Deceiving Hitler: Double-Cross and Deception in World War II.* Oxford, UK: Osprey, 2008.

Daglish, Ian. *Operation BLUECOAT.* Barnsley, UK: Pen and Sword, 2009.

Daglish, Ian. *Operation Goodwood: Over the Battlefield.* Barnsley, UK: Pen and Sword, 2005.

Daugherty, Leo J. *The Battle of the Hedgerows: Bradley's First Army in Normandy, June–July 1944.* Shepperton, Surrey, UK: Ian Allan, 2001.

Dawes, Kenneth S. *FDR: The War President, 1940–1943; A History.* New York: Random House, 2000.

DeFelice, Jim. *Omar Bradley: General at War.* Washington, DC: Regnery, 2011.

De Gaulle, Charles. *The Complete War Memories of Charles de Gaulle.* Translated by Jonathan Griffin and Richard Howard. New York: Simon and Schuster, 1969.

De Guingand, Francis W. *Generals at War.* London: Hodder and Stoughton, 1964.

Delaney, Douglas E. *Corps Commanders: Five British and Canadian Generals at War, 1939–1945.* Vancouver: University of British Columbia Press, 2011.

Delmer, Sefton. *The Counterfeit Spy.* New York: Harper and Row, 1971.

Demoulin, Charles. *Firebirds! Flying the Typhoon in Action.* Washington, DC: Smithsonian Institution Press, 1988.

D'Este, Carlo. *Decision in Normandy: The Real Story of Montgomery and the Allied Campaign.* London: Penguin, 2004.

D'Este, Carlo. *Eisenhower: A Soldier's Life.* New York: Henry Holt, 2002.

D'Este, Carlo. *Patton: A Genius for War.* New York: HarperCollins, 1995.

Dunn, Walter Scott. *Second Front Now, 1943.* Tuscaloosa: University of Alabama Press, 1980.

Edmonds, Robin. *The Big Three: Churchill, Roosevelt and Stalin in War and Peace.* New York: Norton, 1991.

Eisenhower, David. *Eisenhower at War, 1943–1945.* New York: Random House, 1986.

Eisenhower, Dwight D. *Crusade in Europe.* Garden City, NY: Doubleday, 1948.

Ellis, Lionel F., G. W. G. Allen, A. E. Warhurst, and James Robb. *Victory in the West,* Vol. 1, *The Battle of Normandy.* London: HMSO, 1962.

English, J. A. *Failure in High Command: The Canadian Army and the Normandy Campaign.* Ottawa: Golden Dog, 1995.

Fey, William. *Armor Battles of the Waffen-SS.* Lancaster, PA: Stackpole Books, 2003.

Fischer, Louis. *The Road to Yalta: Soviet Relations, 1941–1945.* New York: Harper and Row, 1972.

Ford, Ken, and Howard Gerrard. *Caen 1944.* Oxford, UK: Osprey, 2004.

Forty, George. *Villers Bocage: Battle Zone Normandy.* Stroud, Gloucestershire, UK: Sutton, 2004.

Fraser, David. *Knight's Cross: A Life of Field Marshal Erwin Rommel.* New York: HarperCollins, 1994.

Futter, Geoffrey W. *The Funnies: The 79th Armored Division and Its Specialized Equipment.* Hemel Hempstead, UK: Model and Allied Publications, 1974.

Gale, Sir Richard Nelson. *Call to Arms: An Autobiography.* London: Hutchinson, 1968.

Gale, Sir Richard Nelson. *With the 6th Airborne Division in Normandy.* London: Smason Law, Marston, 1948.

Gardner, Lloyd C. *Spheres of Influence: The Great Powers Partition Europe, from Munich to Yalta.* Chicago: Ivan R. Dee, 1993.

Gooderson, Ian. *Air Power at the Battlefront: Allied Close Air Support in Europe, 1943–45.* London: Frank Cass, 1997.

Graham, Dominic. *The Price of Command: A Biography of General Guy Simonds.* Toronto: Stoddart, 1993.

Granatstein, J. L. *The Generals: The Canadian Army's Senior Commanders in the Second World War.* Toronto: Stoddart, 1993.

Green, William. *Famous Bombers of the Second World War.* 2nd ed. London: Book Club Associates, 1979.

Green, William. *Famous Fighters of the Second World War.* 2nd ed. London: Book Club Associates, 1979.

Hallion, Richard P. *Strike from the Sky: The History of Battlefield Air Attack, 1911–1945.* Washington, DC: Smithsonian Institution Press, 1989.

Hallion, Richard P. *The U.S. Army Air Forces in World War II: D-Day 1944, Air Power over the Normandy Beaches and Beyond.* Washington, DC: U.S. Air Force History and Museum Program, 1994.

Hamilton, Nigel. *The Mantle of Command: FDR at War, 1941–1943.* Boston: Houghton Mifflin Harcourt, 2014.

Hamilton, Nigel. *Monty.* 3 vols. New York: McGraw-Hill, 1981–1986.

Harrison, Gordon A. *United States Army in World War II: The European Theater of Operations; Cross Channel Attack.* Washington, DC: U.S. Army, Office of the Chief of Military History, 1951.

Hart, Russell A. *Clash of Arms: How the Allies Won in Normandy.* Boulder, CO: Lynne Rienner, 2001.

Hart, S. *Road to Falaise.* Stroud, UK: Sutton, 2004.

Hart, Stephen Ashley. *Montgomery and "Colossal Cracks": The 21st Army Group in Northwest Europe, 1944–1945.* Westport, CT: Praeger, 2000.

Hartcup, Guy. *Code Name Mulberry: The Planning, Building and Operation of the Normandy Harbours.* New York: Hippocrene Books, 1977.

Hastings, Max. *Das Reich: The March of the 2d Panzer Division through France.* New York: Holt, Rinehart and Winston, 1981.

Hastings, Max. *Overlord: D-Day and the Battle for Normandy.* New York: Simon and Schuster, 1984.

Hatfield, Thomas M. *Rudder: From Leader to Legend.* College Station: Texas A&M University Press, 2011.

Hesketh, Roger. *Fortitude: The D-Day Deception Campaign.* New York: Overlook, 2000.

Hirshson, Stanley P. *General Patton: A Soldier's Life.* New York: HarperCollins, 2002.

Hogg, Ian V. *The Biography of General George S. Patton.* London: Hamlyn, 1982.

Howard, John, and Penny Bates. *The Pegasus Diaries: The Private Papers of Major John Howard, DSO.* Barnsley, South Yorkshire, UK: Pen and Sword, 2009.

Hughes, Thomas Alexander. OVERLORD: *General Pete Quesada and the Triumph of Tactical Air Power in World War II.* New York: Free Press, 1995.

Jackson, G. S. *Operations of VIII Corps: Account of Operations from Normandy to the River Rhine.* London: St. Clementa, 1948.

Jarrett, Philip, ed. *Aircraft of the Second World War.* London: Putnam, 1997.

Jeffers, H. Paul. *Theodore Roosevelt, Jr.: The Life of a War Hero*. Novato, CA: Presidio, 2002.

Johns, Glover S., Jr. *The Clay Pigeons of St. Lo*. Harrisburg, PA: Military Service Publishing, 1958.

Kaufmann, J. E., and J. M. Jurga. "Atlantic Wall." In *Fortress Europe: European Fortifications of World War II*, 381–406. Conshohocken, PA: Combined Publishing, 1999.

Keegan, John. *Six Armies in Normandy: From D-Day to the Liberation of Paris, June 6th–August 25th, 1944*. New York: Viking, 1982.

Knight, Bob, Harry Smith, and Barry Barnett. PLUTO*: World War II's Best-Kept Secret*. Bexley, UK: Bexley Council, 1998.

Kohn, Richard H., and Joseph P. Harahan, eds. *Air Superiority in World War II and Korea: An Interview with Gen. James Ferguson, Gen. Robert M. Lee, Gen. William Momyer, and Lt. Gen. Elwood R. Quesada*. Washington, DC: Office of Air Force History, 1983.

Lacouture, Jean. *De Gaulle: The Rebel, 1890–1944*. Translated by Patrick O'Brian. New York: Norton, 1990.

Larrabee, Eric. *Commander in Chief: Franklin Delano Roosevelt; His Lieutenants and Their War*. New York: Simon and Schuster, 1987.

Lewin, Ronald. *Montgomery as a Military Commander*. New York: Stein and Day, 1972.

Lewin, Ronald. *Ultra Goes to War*. New York: McGraw-Hill, 1978.

Lewis, Adrian R. *Omaha Beach: A Flawed Victory*. Chapel Hill: University of North Carolina Press, 2001.

Liddell Hart, Basel H., ed. *The Rommel Papers*. New York: Da Capo, 1953.

Lodieu, Didier. *Dying for Saint-Lô: Hedgerow Hell, July 1944*. Paris: Histoire and Collections, 2007.

Lorelli, John A. *To Foreign Shores: U.S. Amphibious Operations in World War II*. Annapolis, MD: Naval Institute Press, 1995.

Love, Robert W., Jr., and John Major, eds. *The Year of D-Day: The 1944 Diary of Admiral Sir Bertram Ramsay*. Hull, UK: University of Hull Press, 1994.

Ludewig, Joachim. *Rückzug: The German Retreat from France, 1944*. Lexington: University Press of Kentucky, 2012.

Lukacs, John. *Churchill: Visionary, Statesman, Historian*. New Haven, CT: Yale University Press, 2002.

Macksey, Kenneth. *Armored Crusader: A Biography of Major-General Sir Percy Hobart*. London: Hutchinson, 1967.

Marriott, Leo, and Simon Forty. *The Normandy Battlefields and the Bridgehead*. Philadelphia: Casemate, 2014.

Masterman, J. C. *The Double-Cross System in the War of 1939–1945*. New Haven, CT: Yale University Press, 1972.

Masters, Charles J. *Glidermen of Neptune: The American D-Day Glider Attack*. Carbondale: Southern Illinois University Press, 1995.

Mead, Richard. *Churchill's Lions: A Biographical Guide to the Key British Generals of World War II*. Stroud, Gloucestershire, UK: Spellmount, 2007.

Mellenthin, F. W. von. *German Generals of World War II: As I Saw Them*. Norman: University of Oklahoma Press, 1977.

Mellenthin, F. W. von. *Panzer Battles: A Study of the Employment of Armor in the Second World War*. New York: Ballantine Books, 1971.

Messenger, Charles. *The Last Prussian: Biography of Field Marshal Gerd von Rundstedt, 1875–1953*. Washington, DC: Brassey's Defence Publishers, 1991.

Miller, Robert A. *Division Commander: A Biography of Major General Norman D. Cota*. Spartanburg, SC: Reprint Publishers, 1989.

Mitcham, Samuel W., Jr. *Retreat to the Reich: The German Defeat in France, 1944*. Westport, CT: Praeger, 2000.

Mitcham, Samuel W., Jr. *Rommel's Last Battle: The Desert Fox in the Normandy Campaign*. New York: Stein and Day, 1983.

Montgomery, Bernard L. *The Memoirs of Field-Marshal the Viscount Montgomery of Alamein, K.G.* London: Collins, 1958.

Morgan, General Sir Frederick E. *Overture to Overlord.* New York: Doubleday, 1950.

Morison, Samuel Eliot. *History of United States Naval Operations in World War II,* Vol. 11, *The Invasion of France and Germany, 1944–1945.* Boston: Little, Brown, 1957.

Mrazek, James E. *Fighting Gliders of World War II.* New York: St. Martin's, 1977.

Mrazek, James E. *The Glider War.* New York: St. Martin's, 1975.

Munson, Kenneth. *Bombers, Patrol, and Transport Aircraft, 1939–45.* Poole, UK: Blandford, 1975.

Munson, Kenneth. *Fighters, Attack and Training Aircraft, 1939–45.* Poole, UK: Blandford, 1975.

Murray, Williamson. *Luftwaffe.* Baltimore: Nautical and Aviation Publishing, 1985.

Orange, Vincent. *Coningham: A Biography of Air Marshal Sir Arthur Coningham, KCB, KBE, DSO, MC, DFC, AFC.* Washington, DC: Center for Air Force History, 1992.

Orange, Vincent. *A Life of Marshal of the RAF Lord Tedder of Glenguin.* London: Frank Cass, 2002.

Otway, T. B. H. *Official Account of Airborne Forces.* London: War Office, 1951.

Power, Stephen T., and Kevin Dennehy. *The D-Day Assault: A 70th Anniversary Guide to the Normandy Landings.* Denver, CO: GTCI Press, 2014.

Prados, John. *Normandy Crucible: The Decisive Battle That Shaped World War II in Europe.* New York: NAL Caliber, 2011.

Price, Alfred. *World War II Fighter Conflict.* London: Macdonald and Janes, 1975.

Ramsden, John. *Man of the Century: Winston Churchill and His Legend since 1945.* New York: HarperCollins, 2002.

Reynolds, Michael. *Steel Inferno: I SS Panzer Corps in Normandy; The Story of the 1st and 12th SS Panzer Divisions in the 1944 Normandy Campaign.* New York: Sarpedon, 1997.

Richards, Denis, and Hilary St. George Saunders. *Royal Air Force: 1939–1945,* Vol. 2, *The Fight Avails.* London: HMSO, 1954.

Ridgway, Matthew B. *Soldier: The Memoirs of Matthew B. Ridgway, as Told to Harold H. Martin.* New York: Harper, 1996.

Rolf, Rudi. *Atlantic Wall Typology.* Revised ed. Nieuw Weerdinge, Netherlands: Fortress Books, 1998.

Roskill, Stephen W. *The War at Sea, 1939–1945: Official History,* Vol. 3, Part 2. London: HMSO, 1961.

Ross, John. *The Forecast for D-Day and the Weatherman behind Ike's Greatest Gamble.* Guilford, CT: Lyons, 2014.

Rottman, Gordon. *World War II Airborne Forces Tactics.* Oxford, UK: Osprey, 2006.

Roy, Reginald H. *1944: The Canadians in Normandy.* Toronto: Macmillan of Canada in collaboration with the Canadian War Museum, 1984.

Ruge, Friedrich. *Rommel in Normandy: Reminiscences.* San Rafael, CA: Presidio, 1979.

Ruppenthal, Roland G. *The U.S. Army in World War II: The European Theater of Operations; Logistical Support of the Armies.* 2 vols. Washington, DC: Center of Military History, 1953, 1959.

Rutherford, Ward. *The Biography of Field Marshal Erwin Rommel.* London: Hamlyn, 1981.

Ryan, Cornelius. *The Longest Day: June 6, 1944.* New York: Simon and Schuster, 1959.

Sainsbury, Keith. *The Turning Point: Roosevelt, Stalin, Churchill, and Chiang-Kai-shek, 1943; The Moscow, Cairo, and Teheran Conferences.* Oxford: Oxford University Press, 1985.

Saunders, Anthony. *Hitler's Atlantic Wall.* Stroud, UK: Sutton, 2001.

Schmeelke, Karl-Heinz, and Michael Schmeelke. *German Defensive Batteries and Gun Emplacements on the Normandy Beaches.* Atglen, PA: Schiffer, 1995.

Schofield, Brian Betham. *Operation Neptune.* London: Ian Allan, 1974.

Searle, Adrian. *Pipe-Line under the Ocean.* Isle of Wight, UK: Shanklin Chine, n.d.

Seth, Ronald. *Lion with Blue Wings: The Story of the Glider Regiment, 1942–1945.* London: Gollancz, 1955.

Shannon, Kevin, and Stephen Wright. *One Night in June: The Story of Operation Tonga, the Initial Phase of the Invasion of*

Normandy, 1944. Shrewsbury, UK: Airlife, 1994.

Smith, Claude. *The History of the Glider Pilot Regiment.* London: Leo Cooper, 1992.

Smith, Walter Bedell. *Eisenhower's Six Great Decisions: Europe 1944–1945.* London: Longmans, Green, 1956.

Soffer, Jonathan N. *General Matthew B. Ridgway: From Progressivism to Reaganism, 1895–1993.* Westport, CT: Praeger, 1998.

Stafford, David. *Roosevelt and Churchill: Men of Secrets.* London: Little, Brown, 1999.

Stagg, J. M. *Forecast for Overlord.* New York: Norton, 1971.

Stoler, Mark A. *Allies and Adversaries: The Joint Chiefs of Staff, the Grand Alliance, and U.S. Strategy in World War II.* Chapel Hill: University of North Carolina Press, 2000.

Stoler, Mark A. *George C. Marshall: Soldier-Statesman of the American Century.* Boston: Twayne, 1989.

Stoler, Mark A. *The Politics of the Second Front: American Military Planning and Diplomacy in Coalition Warfare, 1941–1943.* Westport, CT: Greenwood, 1977.

Strahan, Jerry E. *Andrew Jackson Higgins and the Boats That Won World War II.* Baton Rouge: Louisiana State University Press, 1994.

Sullivan, John J. "The Botched Air Support of Operation Cobra." *Parameters: The U.S. Army War College Quarterly* 18(1) (March 1988): 97–110.

Taylor, Blaine. *Hitler's Engineers: Fritz Todt and Albert Speer, Master Builders of the Third Reich.* Philadelphia: Casemate Publishers, 2010.

Taylor, John M. *General Maxwell Taylor: The Sword and the Pen.* New York: Doubleday, 1989.

Tedder, Sir Arthur. *With Prejudice: The War Memoirs of Marshal of the Royal Air Force Lord Tedder G.C.B.* Boston: Little, Brown, 1967.

Terraine, John. *A Time for Courage: The Royal Air Force in the European War, 1939–1945.* New York: Macmillan, 1985.

Tout, Ken. *Road to Falaise.* Stroud, UK: Sutton, 2202.

Trew, Simon, and Stephen Badsey. *Battle for Caen.* Stroud, UK: Sutton, 2004.

Unwin, Peter. *The Narrow Sea: Barrier, Bridge, and Gateway to the World; The History of the English Channel.* London: Headline, 2004.

Van Der Vat, Dan. *D-Day: The Greatest Invasion, A People's History.* New York: Bloomsbury, 2003.

Virilio, Paul. *Bunker Archeology.* New York: Princeton Architectural Press, 1994.

Waddell, Steve R. *U.S. Army Logistics: The Normandy Campaign, 1944.* Westport, CT: Greenwood, 1994.

Weigley, Russell F. *Eisenhower's Lieutenants.* Bloomington: Indiana University Press, 1981.

Wilt, Alan F. *The Atlantic Wall: Hitler's Defenses in the West, 1941–1944.* Ames: Iowa State University Press, 1975.

Wood, James A., ed. *Army of the West: The Weekly Reports of German Army Group B from Normandy to the West Wall.* Harrisburg, PA: Stackpole, 2007.

Wright, Robert K., and John T. Greenwood. *Airborne Forces at War.* Annapolis, MD: Naval Institute Press, 2007.

Zaloga, Steven J. *Operation Cobra 1944: Breakout from Normandy.* Oxford, UK: Osprey, 2001.

Spencer C. Tucker

Editor and Contributors

Editor

Dr. Spencer C. Tucker
Retired Professor and Holder of the John Biggs Chair in Military History
Department of History
Virginia Military Institute

Contributors

Lt. Col. William J. Astore, USAF
Defense Language Institute Foreign Language Center
Monterey, California

Lt. Col. Robert L. Bateman
Adjunct Professor
Center for Security Studies
Georgetown University

Dr. Colin F. Baxter
Professor
Department of History
East Tennessee State University

Mr. Andy Blackburn
Independent Scholar
Windsor, United Kingdom

Mr. Brandon S. Boor
Virginia Military Institute

Dr. Patrick H. Brennan
Associate Professor Emeritus of History
University of Calgary

Dr. Robert J. Bunker
National Law Enforcement and Corrections Technology Center, West
Counter-OPFOR Program
El Segundo, California

Mr. Robert W. Duvall
History Department
Hanford West High School/Chapman University
Hanford, California

Brig. Gen. Uzal W. Ent, PNG (Ret.)
Independent Scholar

Dr. Paul E. Fontenoy
Curator of Maritime Research
North Carolina Maritime Museum
Beaufort, North Carolina

Dr. Fred R. van Hartesveldt
Professor of History
Fort Valley State University

Ms. Kathleen G. Hitt
Instructor
Pierce College, L.A. Harbor College, and College of the Canyons

Lt. Col. Edwin L. Kennedy Jr. (Ret.)
Assistant Professor
U.S. Army Command and General Staff College

Col. Cole C. Kingseed, USA (Ret.)
Department of History
U.S. Military Academy
West Point, New York

Dr. Tom Lansford
Professor of Political Science
University of Southern Mississippi

Lt. Col. Guy A. Lofaro
Independent Scholar

Mr. Britton W. MacDonald
History Department
Temple University
Saskatoon, Saskatchewan, Canada

Dr. Wendy A. Maier-Sarti
Professor of History
Oakton Community College

Dr. Martin Moll
Universität Dozent for Modern and Contemporary History
University of Graz
Graz, Austria

Dr. Justin D. Murphy
Department of History
Howard Payne University

Dr. Paul G. Pierpaoli Jr.
Fellow
Military History, ABC-CLIO, Inc.

Mr. Steven J. Rauch
Command Historian
U.S. Army Signal Center
Fort Gordon, Georgia

Dr. Annette Richardson
Educational Policy Studies
University of Alberta

Dr. Priscilla Roberts
Associate Professor of History
University of Hong Kong

Prof. Dr. Jürgen Rohwer
Bibliothek für Zeitgeschichte Stuttgart
International Intelligence History Association (Honorary Chairman)
Weinstadt, Germany

Dr. Elizabeth D. Schafer
Independent Scholar

Mr. R. Kyle Schlafer
Texas Capitol Visitors Center
Austin, Texas

Capt. Carl Otis Schuster, USN (Ret.)
Military Science and Diplomacy, History Department
Hawaii Pacific University

Mr. T. Jason Soderstrum
Independent Scholar

Jason M. Sokiera
Historian/Museum Studies
Allison Park, Pennsylvania

Dr. Christopher H. Sterling
Emeritus Professor of Media and Public Affairs
George Washington University

David M. Toczek
Independent Scholar

Dr. Spencer C. Tucker
Retired Professor and Holder of the John Biggs Chair in Military History
Virginia Military Institute
Department of History
Lexington, Virginia

Dr. Thomas D. Veve
Associate Professor of History
Dalton State College

Dr. John F. Votaw
Executive Director
Cantigny First Division Foundation
Wheaton, Illinois

Dr. Steve R. Waddell
Department of History
U.S. Military Academy
West Point, New York

Dr. David Westwood
Military Library Research Service (MLRS) Ltd.
Buxton, Derbyshire, United Kingdom

Dr. James H. Willbanks, Lt. Col. (Ret.)
General of the Army George C. Marshall Chair of Military History
U.S. Army Command and General Staff College
Ft. Leavenworth, Kansas

Harold Lee Wise
Adjunct Professor
Elizabeth City State University

Dr. David T. Zabecki
Major General
Army of the United States, Retired

About the Editor

Spencer C. Tucker, PhD, has been senior fellow in military history at ABC-CLIO since 2003. He is the author or editor of 62 books and encyclopedias, many of which have won prestigious awards. He taught for 30 years at Texas Christian University and for the last five was chair of its History Department. Tucker's last academic position before his retirement from teaching was the John Biggs Chair in Military History at the Virginia Military Institute in Lexington. He has been a Fulbright scholar, a visiting research associate at the Smithsonian Institution, and, as a U.S. Army captain, an intelligence analyst in the Pentagon. His recently published works include *World War II: The Definitive Encyclopedia and Document Collection, The Roots and Consequences of Civil Wars and Revolution: Conflicts That Changed World History, Modern Conflict in the Greater Middle East: A Country-by-Country Guide,* and *Enduring Controversies in Military History: Critical Analyses and Context,* all published by ABC-CLIO.

Index

A22 Churchill tanks, 188–189
A27 Centaur, 188
A27L (Liberty) tank, 188
ABERLOUR, Operation, 44
Abwehr, Double-Cross System, 77–78
Adder tanks, 190
Administrative amphibious landings, 20
Admiral Scheer, 119
Airborne forces, British and American, **1–4**
   Allied command structure, 61
   Army, Corps, and Division Units in Battle of Normandy (June 6–August 29, 1944), 242
   Casualty Estimates in Battle of Normandy (June 6–August 29, 1944), 243
   Coningham, Sir Arthur "Mary" (1895–1948), 65–66
   European Theater, Overview, 213–219
   Leigh-Mallory, Sir Trafford (1892–1944), 127–128
   Quesada, Elwood Richard "Pete" (1904–1993), 163–164
   Tedder, Sir Arthur William (1st Baron Tedder) (1890–1967), 193
Aircraft, bombers, **4–8**
   close air support, 26–27
Aircraft, fighters and fighter-bombers, **8–11**
   close air support, 26–27
Aircraft, gliders, 1–2, 3, **11–14**
   howitzer transport by, 25
   La Fière Causeway, Battle of (June 6–9, 1944), 122
   Operation NEPTUNE (June 6–Jully 3, 1944), 145–146
   Operation TONGA (June 6), 42, 99
   Pegasus and Horsa Bridges, Battle for (June 6, 1944), 110, 156–157
   transport aircraft, 15
Aircraft, machine guns and, 135
Aircraft, transports, **14–16**
Air support, 26–27
   Coningham, Sir Arthur "Mary" (1895–1948), 65–66
Air warfare, ground-attack aviation, **16–19**
Algeria, 217
Allied command structure, 60–62
Allied Planning for the Normandy Invasion (July 1943), 151–153, 199, 221–227
American Cemetery and Memorial, Colleville-sur-Mer, 47–48
The Americanization of Emily (1964), 88
Americans. *See* United States
Amphibious warfare in the European Theater, **19–22**
   Allied warships, 209–211
   duplex drive (DD) tanks, 190
   Higgins, Andrew Jackson (1886–1952), 105–106
   landing craft, 122–126
   Terrain and Tactical Problems on D-Day, 195–199
Anglo-American Combined Chiefs of Staff, Directive to Supreme Commander Allied Expeditionary Force, February 12, 1944, 227–228
Antitank guns and antitank warfare, **23–24**, 26, 187–188, 190
ANVIL, Operation, 96
Ardennes Offensive, 2, 38
Argentan, 93

Army, Corps, and Division Units in Battle of Normandy (June 6–August 29, 1944), 241–242
Arnold, Henry H. "Hap," 12
Arromanches, Harbor at, 144, 196
Artillery and fire support, **24–28**
Assaults, amphibious landings, 20
Atlantic, Battle of the, **28–31**, 119
ATLANTIC, Operation (July 18–21, 1944), 46, 55
Atlantic Wall, **31–33**, 200
    Festung Europa, 86–87
Australia
    airborne forces, 3
    Coningham, Sir Arthur "Mary" (1895–1948), 65–66
AVALANCHE, Operation (1943), 22
Avranches, 92–93, 200
Avro Lancaster bomber, 5

B-17 Flying Fortress bomber, 6–7
B-24 Liberator bomber, 7
B-25 Mitchell bomber, 7, 17
B-26 Marauder, 7–8, 18
Badger flamethrower tanks, 190
Bambi, 159
Band of Brothers (2001), 89, 211
Barton, Raymond Oscar "Tubby" (1889–1963), **35**
Battle for Pegasus and Horsa Bridges (June 6, 1944), 156–157
Battle of Britain (1940), 16
Battle of Kursk (July 5–6, 1943), 217
Battle of La Fière Causeway (June 6–9, 1944), 121–122, 199
Battle of Le Mesuil-Patry (1944), 43
Battle of Lyme Bay (April 28, 1944), 130–131
Battle of Mortain (August 7–13, 1944), 128–130
Battle of Odon, First (June 26–30, 1944), 44
Battle of Odon, Second (July 18–20, 1944), 45–46
Battle of Saint-Lô (July 11–19, 1944), 179–182
Battle of Slapton Sands (April 28, 1944), 130–131
Battle of the Atlantic, 28–31, 119
Battle of the Bulge (1944–1945), 23, 35, 62, 67, 81–82, 156, 219
Battle of Villers-Bocage (1944), 43
Battleships, 209, 210
    See also Navy

Battle to Secure Caen (June 6–July 18, 1944), 41–47, 92
Bayerlein, Fritz, 43–44
Bayeux War Cemetery, 48
Bazooka, 23, 190
Belarus, 216
Belgium
    airborne forces, 3
    European Theater, Overview, 213–219
Bény-sur-Mer Canadian War Cemetery, 48
Bessarabia, 215
Bf-109 fighter aircraft, 8
Bf-110 fighter aircraft, 8–9
The Big Red One (1980), 88
Black Sea, amphibious landings and, 21
Blaskowitz, Johannes, 63
Bletchley Park, 29–30
BLUECOAT, Operation (July 30–August 7, 1944), **35–36**
Bocage
    Battle to Secure Caen (June 6–July 18, 1944), 42
    Culin, Curtis Grubb, III (1915–1963), 69–70
    Normandy region, overview, 149, 198
    Operation BLUECOAT (July 30–August 7, 1944), 36
    Operation COBRA (July 25–31, 1944), 54, 55
    Saint-Lô, 179–182
    See also Terrain and Tactical Problems on D-Day
Boeing B-17 Flying Fortress, 6–7
Bomber Command, 1
    See also Command structure, Allied
Bombers, 4–8
    Germany, 4–5
    Great Britain, 5–6
    United States, 6–8
Bourguébus Ridge, 45–46
Bradley, Omar Nelson (1893–1981), 2, **37–38**, 152
    Falaise-Argentan Pocket (August 12–24, 1944), 85–86, 129
    France, Campaign (June 6–September 15, 1944), 91–95
    Operation COBRA (July 25–31, 1944), 54–57
    Operation NEPTUNE (June 6–July 3, 1944), 147
Brereton, Lewis H., 61
Brest, 93–94
Bretteville-sur-Laize, 45–46

Bretteville-sur-Laize Canadian War Cemetery, 48
Bristol Blenheim bomber, 17
Britain. *See* Great Britain
Britain, Battle of (1940), 16
Brooke, Sir Alan Francis (First Viscount Alanbrooke), **38–39**, 60, 175
Brotheridge, Herbert "Den," 157
Buckinghamshire Light Infantry, 3
Bucknall, Gerard, 35, 36
Bulgaria, 215
Bulge, Battle of (1944–1945), 23, 35, 62, 67, 81–82, 156, 219

C-47 aircraft, 1, 3, 15
Caen, 149–150
Caen, Battle to Secure (June 6–July 18, 1944), **41–47**, 92
   Operation ATLANTIC (July 18–21, 1944), 46
   Operation CHARNWOOD (July 8–9, 1944), 45
   Operation EPSOM (June 26–30, 1944), 44
   Operation GOODWOOD (July 18–20, 1944), 36, 45–46
   Operation JUPITER (July 10–11, 1944), 45
   Operation MARTLET (June 25–July 1, 1944), 44
   Operation PERCH (June 4–14, 1944), 42–44
   Operation SPRING (July 25–27), 46
   Operation TONGA (June 6, 1944), 42
   Operation WINDSOR (July 4–5, 1944), 44–45
Caen Canal, 3
Calais, Operation FORTITUDE (1944), 90–91
Canada
   airborne forces, 3
   Army, Corps, and Division Units in Battle of Normandy (June 6–August 29, 1944), 241–242
   Bény-sur-Mer Canadian War Cemetery, 48
   Casualty Estimates in Battle of Normandy (June 6–August 29, 1944), 243
   Crerar, Henry Duncan Graham (1888–1965), 68–69
   destroyers and escorts, 210–211
   Doohan, James Montgomery (1920–2005), 76–77
   France, Campaign (June 6–September 15, 1944), 93
   ground forces order of battle on D-Day, 237
   number of troops killed June 6, 1944, 239
   Operation JUBILEE (Dieppe Raid, August 9, 1942), 114–115
   Operation TOTALIZE (August 7–13, 1944), 200–202
   Operation TRACTABLE (August 14–21, 1944), 202–203
   Simonds, Guy Granville (1903–1974), 182
Cap de la Hague, 50
Carpiquet, 45
Casualty Estimates in Battle of Normandy (June 6–August 29, 1944), 243
Cato, 77–78
Cemeteries, Normandy Invasion, **47–48**
Centaur Kangaroos, 188
Centaur (A27L) tank, 188
Challenger tanks, 190
Chamberlain, Leslie, 157
CHARNWOOD, Operation (July 8–9, 1944), 45
Cherbourg, 149–150
Cherbourg, Capture of (June 22–29, 1944), **48–50**
Cherbourg (Cotentin) Peninsula, 67–68
Chief of Staff to the Supreme Allied Commander (COSSAC), 151–153
Choltitz, Dietrich, 55
Chronology of events, 245–253
Churchill, Sir Winston Leonard Spencer (1874–1965), **50–54**, 94
   airborne forces, 1
   on amphibious landings, 21
   Brooke, Sir Alan Francis on, 39
   on Charles de Gaulle, 96
   European Theater, Overview, 214–219
   on Operation JUBILEE (Dieppe Raid, August 9, 1942), 113–115
   Operation OVERLORD, Planning for, 151
   on Operation ROUNDUP (1943), 175
   Roosevelt and, 172–173
   Tehran Conference (November 28–December 1, 1943), 193–195
Churchill tanks, 188–189
Close air support, 26–27
Coastal artillery, 27–28
COBRA, Operation (July 25–31, 1944), 35, 36, 38, **54–57**, 92
Cole, Robert George (1915–1944), **57–59**
Colleville-sur-Mer, American Cemetery and Memorial, 47–48

Collins, Joseph Lawton "Lightning Joe" (1896–1987), 49, 55, **59–60**, 92, 129
Command structure, Allied, **60–62**
Command structure, German, **62–65**, 108–109
Coningham, Sir Arthur "Mary" (1895–1948), 61, **65–66**
Consolidated B-24 Liberator, 7
Conundrums, PLUTO, 158–159
Corncobs, 142
COSSAC (Chief of Staff to the Supreme Allied Commander), 151–153
Cota, Norman Daniel "Dutch" (1893–1971), **66–67**, 181
Cotentin (Cherbourg) Peninsula, 3, 27–28, **67–68**
Countances, 92
Crab flail anitmine tanks, 190
Crerar, Henry Duncan Graham (1888–1965), 61, **68–69**, 92, 200–202
Crimean Peninsula, 216
Crocker, Sir John Treddinick (1896–1963), **69**
Crocodile tanks, 190
Cromwell tanks, 188, 190
Cruisers, Allied warships, 209–210
Cruiser tank, 188
Culin, Curtis Grubb, III (1915–1963), 55, **69–70**, 235–236
Culin's Cutter, 70

DAUNTLESS, Operation (June 25–July 1, 1944), 44
de Gaulle, Charles (1890–1970), **71–74**, 95–97
De Havilland Mosquito, 5–6, 10
Dempsey, Miles Christopher (1896–1969), 61, **74–75**
　Battle to Secure Caen (June 6–July 18, 1944), 43, 54
　France, Campaign (June 6–September 15, 1944), 91–95
　Operation BLUECOAT (July 30–August 7, 1944), 35
　Operation NEPTUNE (June 6–July 3, 1944), 147
Destroyers and escorts, 210–211
　See also Navy
Destroyers for Bases Agreement (1940), 52
Devers, Jacob, 61, 94
Dieppe Raid (August 9, 1942), 21, 113–115
Dietrich, Josef "Sepp" (1892–1966), **75–76**
Dollman, Friedrich (1882–1944), **76**

Dönitz, Karl, 28–31
Doohan, James Montgomery (1920–2005), **76–77**
Doolittle, James H., 61
Double-Cross System, **77–78**
Douglas C-47 Dakota, 1
Douglas C-47 Skytrain, 15
Douhuet, Giulio, 4, 16
Douve River, 198–199
Dragon, 210–211
DRAGOON, Operation (1944), 22, 94
DUKW (landing craft), 125–126
Dumbo, 159
Dunkerque evacuation, 20, 74, 138
Duplex drive (DD) tanks, 190

Eastern Command, 1
　See also Command structure, Allied
Egypt, 216
Ehlers, Walter David (1921–2014), **79–80**
8th Canadian Brigade, 44–45
82nd Airborne Division, 2–4
　Battle of La Fière Causeway (June 6–9, 1944), 121–122
　gliders, use of, 13–14
　Sainte-Mère-Église, 199
　Sainte-Mère-Église museum, 68
Eisenhower, Dwight David (1890–1969), 54, **80–82**
　Allied command structure, 60–62, 61
　Anglo-American Combined Chiefs of Staff, Directive to Supreme Commander Allied Expeditionary Force, February 12, 1944, 227–228
　on Charles de Gaulle, 96
　on Curtis G. Culin's "Rhino" Tank Modification, 235–236
　Falaise-Argentan Pocket (August 12–24, 1944), 85–86
　on fighter aircraft, 9
　France, Campaign (June 6–September 15, 1944), 91–95
　to General George C. Marshall, July 5, 1944, 233–234
　on gliders, 13–14
　on LÜTTICH, Operation (Mortain Counteroffensive, August 7–13, 1944), 129
　Operation OVERLORD, Planning for, 152–153
　Operation ROUNDUP (1943), 175

Order of the Day and Letter to the Troops, June 6, 1944, 229
on PLUTO, 158
on Smith, Walter Bedell (1895–1961), 184–185
Statement in the Event the D-Day Landings Failed, 229
11th Airborne Division, 2, 13
11th Armoured Division, 36, 110
11th Battalion, 3
English Channel, **82–83**
Enigma, 29–30, 213
EPSOM, Operation (June 26–30, 1944), 44
Equipment and resources, planning for, 153, 157–159
Erskine, George, 36
Espionage
 Double-Cross System, 77–78
 Enigma, 213
 French Resistance, 95–96
 Operation FORTITUDE (1944), 90–91
 Operation NEPTUNE (June 6–July 3, 1944), 147
Estonia, 215
Ethiopia, 216
Europe, map under Axis Domination (1941), xiii
European Theater, Overview, 212–219
Evacuations, amphibious landings, 20
Exercise TIGER (April 22–30, 1944), 130–131
Eye of the Needle (1981), 88

Falaise-Argentan Pocket (August 12–24, 1944), **85–86**, 93, 201–203
Festung Europa, **86–87**
Field artillery, 24–26
15th (Scottish) Infantry Division, 44
50th (Northumbrian) Infantry Division, 43
51st (Highland) Division, 43
Films Treating the Normandy Invasion, **87–89**
Firefly tanks, 190
First Battle of the Odon (June 26–30, 1944), 44
I SS Panzer Corps, 46
First U.S. Army Group (FUSAG), 90–91
First Viscount Alanbrooke (Brooke, Sir Alan Francis), 38–39
Flying Fortress, B-17 bomber, 6–7
Focke-Wolf FW-190A, 8, 18
FORTITUDE, Operation (1944), 63–64, 77–78, **89–91**, 147, 152
43rd (Wessex) Infantry Division, 44, 45

4th Armored Division, Canada, 201, 202
4th Armored Division, U.S., 57, 94
4th Armoured Brigade, British, 45
4th Infantry Division, Canada, 46, 201
4th Infantry Division, U.S., 49, 55, 57, 147, 198
France
 airborne forces, 3
 Army, Corps, and Division Units in Battle of Normandy (June 6–August 29, 1944), 241
 de Gaulle, Charles (1890–1970), 71–74
 European Theater, Overview, 212–219
 Free French, destroyers and escorts, 210–211
 map of (1944), xv
 See also Maps
France, Campaign (June 6–September 15, 1944), **91–95**
French Forces of the Interior (FFI), 95
French Resistance, 91–92, **95–97**, 146
 de Gaulle, Charles (1890–1970), 72–74
 Pegasus and Horsa Bridges, Battle for (June 6, 1944), 157
FUSAG (First U.S. Army Group), 90–91
FW-190A fighter aircraft, 8

Gale, Sir Richard Nelson (1896–1982), 2, **99–100**
Gavin, James M., 2, 121–122
General Aircraft Limited GAL 49 Hamilcar, 12
Gerhardt, Charles Hunter (1895–1976), **100–101**, 180
Germany
 airborne forces, 1
 aircraft, bombers, 4–5
 aircraft, fighters and fighter-bombers, 8–9
 aircraft, transports, 15
 Army, Corps, and Division Units in Battle of Normandy (June 6–August 29, 1944), 242
 Casualty Estimates in Battle of Normandy (June 6–August 29, 1944), 243
 command structure, 62–65
 Dietrich, Josef "Sepp" (1892–1966), 75–76
 Dollman, Friedrich (1882–1944), 76
 European Theater, Overview, 212–219
 Festung Europa, 86–87
 Geyr von Schweppenburg, Leo Dietrich Franz Freiherr (1886–1974), 102–103
 gliders, use of, 11–12
 ground-attack aviation, 16
 ground forces order of battle on D-Day, 237
 Jodl, Alfred (1890–1946), 113

Germany (*continued*)
   Kluge, Günther Adolf Ferdinand von (1882–1944), 118–119
   Krancke, Theodor (1893–1973), 119
   La Cambe German War Cemetery, 47
   map, collapse of Germany (1945), xvi
   number of troops killed June 6, 1944, 239
   rifles, 168–169
   Rommel, Erwin Johannes Eugen (1891–1944), 169–171
   Rundstedt, Karl Rudolf Gerd von (1875–1953), 176–178
   tanks, 187–188, 191
   Todt Organization (OT), 199–200
   See also Hitler, Adolf (1889–1945); Maps
Gerow, Leonard Townsend (1888–1972), **101–102**
Geyr von Schweppenburg, Leo Dietrich Franz Freiherr (1886–1974), **102–103**
Gliders, 1–2, 3, 11–14
   howitzer transport by, 25
   La Fière Causeway, Battle of (June 6–9, 1944), 122
   Operation NEPTUNE (June 6–Jully 3, 1944), 145–146
   Operation TONGA (June 6), 42, 99
   Pegasus and Horsa Bridges, Battle for (June 6, 1944), 110, 156–157
   transport aircraft, 15
Gold Beach, 24, 27–28, 150, 196
GOODWOOD, Operation (July 18–20, 1944), 36, 45–46, 55, 74, 92, 139–140
   See also Caen, Battle to Secure (June 6–July 18, 1944)
Great Britain
   airborne forces, 1–4
   aircraft, bombers, 5–6
   aircraft, fighters and fighter-bombers, 9–10
   Allied command structure, 60–62
   Allied warships, 209–211
   Army, Corps, and Division Units in Battle of Normandy (June 6–August 29, 1944), 241–242
   Brooke, Sir Alan Francis (First Viscount Alanbrooke), 38–39
   Casualty Estimates in Battle of Normandy (June 6–August 29, 1944), 243
   Churchill, Sir Winston Leonard Spencer (1874–1965), 50–54
   Coningham, Sir Arthur "Mary" (1895–1948), 65–66
   Crocker, Sir John Treddinick (1896–1963), 69
   Dempsey, Miles Christopher (1896–1969), 74–75
   European Theater, Overview, 212–219
   Gale, Sir Richard Nelson (1896–1982), 99–100
   gliders, use of, 12
   ground forces order of battle on D-Day, 237
   Hobart, Sir Percy Cleghorn Stanley (1885–1957), 109–110
   Howard, John (1912–1999), 110–111
   landing craft, 123–124
   Leigh-Mallory, Sir Trafford (1892–1944), 127–128
   Millin, William "Piper Bill" (1922–2010), 137–138
   Montgomery, Sir Bernard Law (First Viscount Montgomery of Alamein)(1887–1976), 138–140
   Morgan, Frederick Edgeworth (1894–1967), 141–142
   number of troops killed June 6, 1944, 239
   Ramsay, Sir Bertram Home (1883–1945), 165
   rifles, 167
   Stagg, James Martin (1900–1965), 185–186
   tanks, 188–189, 190
   Tedder, Sir Arthur William (1st Baron Tedder) (1890–1967), 193
   Vian, Sir Philip Louis (1894–1968), 207
   See also Maps
Greece, 215, 216
Grenades, 105
Ground-attack aviation, 16–19
Ground forces
   Allied command structure, 61
   Army, Corps, and Division Units in Battle of Normandy (June 6–August 29, 1944), 241–242
   Order of Battle on D-Day, 237
Guderian, Heinz, 64
GYMNAST, Operation, 175

Haislip, Wade, 93
Halifax I bomber, 5
Hamilcar gliders, 12
Hand grenades, **105**
Handly Page Halifax I, 5

Harris, Arthur, 61
Hausser, Paul, 35, 76, 92
Hawker Hurricane, 9
Hawker Tempest, 10
Hawker Typhoon, 9–10, 17, 45, 46, 49, 129
Hedgerows *(bocage)*
  Battle to Secure Caen (June 6–July 18, 1944), 42
  Culin, Curtis Grubb, III (1915–1963), 69–70
  Normandy region, overview, 149, 198
  Operation BLUECOAT (July 30–August 7, 1944), 36
  Operation COBRA (July 25–31, 1944), 54, 55
  Saint-Lô, 179–182
  See also Terrain and Tactical Problems on D-Day
Heinkel HE-177 "Greif" (Griffen), 4–5
Hesse, Kurt, 114
Hexachloroethane smoke, 25
Higgins, Andrew Jackson (1886–1952), **105–106**, 124–126
Higgins Boat, 124
Hitler, Adolf (1889–1945), 61, **106–109**
  bodyguards, 75–76
  command structure, 62, 63
  European Theater, Overview, 213–219
  Festung Europa, 87
  Operation LÜTTICH (Mortain Counteroffensive, August 7–13, 1944), 128, 129
  on Operation NEPTUNE (June 6–July 3, 1944), 146–147
  Rommel's Teletype Message to Hitler, July 15, 1944, 234–235
HMS *Azalea*, 130–131
HMS *Boadicea*, 211
HMS *Erebus*, 209
HMS *Fury*, 211
HMS *Glennon*, 211
HMS *Nelson*, 209
HMS *Ramillies*, 209
HMS *Roberts*, 209
HMS *Rodney*, 27, 45, 209
HMS *Scimitar*, 130–131
HMS *Swift*, 211
HMS *Warspite*, 209
HMS *Wrestler*, 211
Hobart, Sir Percy Cleghorn Stanley (1885–1957), **109–110**

Hobbs, Leland S., 129
Hodges, Courtney, 61
Holland, 2, 3, 146, 177, 218
Holocaust, 212–213
Horrocks, Brian, 36
Horsa Bridge, Battle or (June 6, 1944), 156–157
Howard, John (1912–1999), **110–111**, 156–157, 196
Howie, Thomas D., 181
Huebner, Clarence Ralph (1888–1972), **111**
Hughes-Hallett, J., 114
Hungary, 215
Hurricane fighter aircraft, 9
HUSKY, Operation (1943), 22

ICEBERG, Operation (1945), 22
Ilyushin I1-2 Sturmovik, 17
Infantry mortars, 26
Intelligence
  Double-Cross System, 77–78
  Enigma, 213
  French Resistance, 95–96
  Operation FORTITUDE (1944), 89–91
  Operation NEPTUNE (June 6–July 3, 1944), 147
International Military Tribunal at Nuremberg, 113
Italy, 214, 215, 216

Jagdpanzers, 188
Japan, amphibious warfare, 19–20
Jodl, Alfred (1890–1946), 61, 63, **113**
Joint Chiefs of Staff, 38
JUBILEE, Operation (Dieppe Raid, August 9, 1942), 21, **113–115**
Junkers Ju-52/3m, 15
Juno Beach
  artillery and fire support, 24, 27
  Doohan, James Montgomery (1920–2005), 76
  ground forces, order of battle on D-Day, 237
  landing craft, 123
  Normandy, overview of, 150
  Operation NEPTUNE (June 6–July 3, 1944), 148
  terrain and tactical problems, 196
JUPITER, Operation (July 10–11, 1944), 45

Keitel, Wilhelm, 63
Kesselring, Albert, 63
King, Ernest J., 126

Kirk, Alan Goodrich (1888–1963), 61, **117–118**, 145
Kluge, Günther Adolf Ferdinand von (1882–1944), **118–119**, 128–130
Krancke, Theodor (1893–1973), **119**
Kursk, Battle of (July 5–6, 1943), 217

La Cambe German War Cemetery, 47
La Fière Causeway, Battle of (June 6–9, 1944), **121–122**, 199
Lancaster bomber, 5
Landing craft, 106, **122–126**
    of Great Britain, 123–124
    of United States, 124–126
Lattre de Tassigny, Jean de, 61
Latvia, 215
LCA (landing craft assault), 123
LCI (landing craft infantry), 124
LCM (landing craft mechanized), 124
LCT (landing craft tank Mk4), 123
LCT-R (landing craft tank-rocket), 123–124
LCVP (landing craft vehicle, personnel, aka Higgins Boat), 124
Lee, John Clifford Hodges (1887–1958), **126–127**
Lee, William C., 2
Le Havre, 149–150
Leigh-Mallory, Sir Trafford (1892–1944), 55, 61, **127–128**
Le Mesuil-Patry, Battle of (1944), 43
Liberator bomber, 7
Libya, 216
Lightning fighter aircraft, 10, 17
Lithuania, 215
Lobster antimine tanks, 190
Lockheed P-38 Lightning, 10
The Longest Day (1962), 87–88, 111, 157
Lorient, 94
LST (landing ship tank), 124–125
Lublin government, 53
Luftwaffe
    airborne forces, 1
    aircraft, bombers, 4–5
    aircraft, fighters and fighter-bombers, 8–9
    aircraft, transports, 15
    gliders, use of, 11–12
    ground-attack aviation, 16–19
    operational aircraft on D-Day, 27
LÜTTICH, Operation (Mortain Counteroffensive, August 7–13, 1944), 35, 36, **128–130**
Luxembourg, European Theater, Overview, 213
Lyme Bay, Battle of (April 28, 1944), **130–131**

M4 Sherman tanks, 188, 189–191
Machine guns, **133–135**
MALLARD, Operation, 12
Mallory, Trafford Leigh, 152
Maps
    Collapse of Germany (1945), xvi
    Europe under Axis Domination (1941), xiii
    France (1944), xv
    Normandy Invasion (1944), xiv
MARKET GARDEN, Operation, 2, 3, 14, 74, 140
Marseilles, 94
Marshall, George Catlett (1880–1959), 80, **135–137**
    airborne forces, 2
    Allied command structure, 60
    on landing craft, 126
    Operation OVERLORD, Planning for, 151
    Operation ROUNDUP (1943), 175
Marshall Memorandum, 183
Marshall Plan, 136–137
Martin B-26 Marauder, 7–8, 18
MARTLET, Operation (June 25–July 1, 1944), 44
Masterman, John, 78
McNair, Lesley J., 56
Meindl, Eugen, 180
Merchant ships, 119
    Battle of the Atlantic, 28–31
Merdert River, 198–199
Merville Battery, 3, 27–28
Messerschmitt Bf-109, 8
Messerschmitt Bf-110, 8–9
Meyer, Kurt, 201, 202–203
Middleton, Troy H., 92
Millin, William "Piper Bill" (1922–2010), **137–138**
Mitchell, William, 1
Mitchell bomber, B-25, 7, 17
Mk4 Cromwell tank, 188
Mk VIII tank, 188
Monitors, Allied warships, 209
Montelimar, 94
Montgomery, Sir Bernard Law (First Viscount Montgomery of Alamein)(1887–1976), **138–140**
    Allied command structure, 61

Battle to Secure Caen (June 6–July 18, 1944), 42, 54
Falaise-Argentan Pocket (August 12–24, 1944), 85–86
France, Campaign (June 6–September 15, 1944), 91–95
on Henry Crerar, 68
Operation NEPTUNE (June 6–July 3, 1944), 147
Operation OVERLORD, planning for, 152–153
Operation TRACTABLE (August 14–21, 1944), 202
Moon, Don Pardee (1894–1944), **140–141**
Morgan, Frederick Edgeworth (1894–1967), 60, **141–142**, 151, 199
Morocco, 217
Mortain Counteroffensive, August 7–13, 1944 (LÜTTICH, Operation), 128–130
Mortars, infantry, 26
Mosquito bomber, 5–6
Mosquito fighter aircraft, 10
Moulin, Jean, 72, 95
Mountbatten, Louis, 114, 151
Mount Pinçon, 35–36
Mulberries, 54, **142–144**, 147, 148
Mussolini, Benito, 214, 216
Mustang fighter aircraft, 10–11, 17, 49

National Resistance Council (CNR), 95
Navy
    Allied command structure, 61
    Battle of the Atlantic, 28–31
    European Theater, Overview, 213–219
    Higgins, Andrew Jackson (1886–1952), 105–106
    naval gunfire support, 27
    Ramsay, Sir Bertram Home (1883–1945), 165
    Vian, Sir Philip Louis (1894–1968), 207
    warships, Allied, 209–211
NEPTUNE, Operation (June 6–July 3, 1944), 22, 27, **145–149**
Netherlands
    European Theater, Overview, 94, 213–219
    German air assault, 1, 11
    Operation MARKET GARDEN, 14
9th Air Force, U.S., 49
9th Bomber Command, 49
9th Infantry Division, U.S., 49, 55
9th SS Panzer Division, 45

Normandy, **149–150**
Normandy Invasion (1944), map of, xiv
North Africa, 216–217
Northern Bukovina, 215
Norway
    airborne forces, 3
    destroyers and escorts, 210–211
    Operation FORTITUDE (1944), 89–90
Nuremberg, International Military Tribunal, 113

O'Connor, Richard, 35, 44
Octopus bridging vehicle, 190
Odon, First Battle of (June 26–30, 1944), 44
Odon, Second Battle of (July 18–20, 1944), 45–46
Omaha Beach, 196–198
    coastal artillery, 27–28
    Coningham, Sir Arthur "Mary" (1895–1948), 65–66
    field artillery, 24
    obstacles on, 150
    Operation NEPTUNE (June 6–July 3, 1944), 148
    paratroopers and gliders, 3
    Pointe du Hoc, Seizure of (June 6, 1944), 159–161
Omaha Beach Gooseberry, 143
101st Airborne Division, 2–4
    gliders, use of, 13–14
    Operation NEPTUNE (June 6–July 3, 1944), 145
    order of battle on D-Day, 237
    Sainte-Mère-Église, 179, 198
    Sainte-Mère-Église museum, 68
    Taylor, Maxwell Davenport (1901–1987), 192
    units involved in Battle of Normandy, summary, 241
    Winters, Richard D. (1918–2011), 211–212
Operation ABERLOUR, 44
Operational amphibious landings, 20
Operation ANVIL, 96
Operation ATLANTIC (July 18–21, 1944), 46, 55
Operation AVALANCHE (1943), 22
Operation BLUECOAT (July 30–August 7, 1944), 35–36
Operation CHARNWOOD (July 8–9, 1944), 45
Operation COBRA (July 25–31, 1944), 35, 36, 38, 54–57, 92

Operation DAUNTLESS (June 25–July 1, 1944), 44
Operation DRAGOON (1944), 22, 94
Operation EPSOM (June 26–30, 1944), 44
Operation FORTITUDE (1944), 63–64, 77–78, 89–91, 147, 152
Operation GOODWOOD (July 18–20, 1944), 36, 45–46, 55, 74, 92, 139–140
  See also Caen, Battle to Secure (June 6–July 18, 1944)
Operation GYMNAST, 175
Operation HUSKY (1943), 22
Operation ICEBERG (1945), 22
Operation JUBILEE (1942), 21, 113–115
Operation JUPITER (July 10–11, 1944), 45
Operation LÜTTICH (Mortain Counteroffensive, August 7–13, 1944), 35, 36, 128–130
Operation MALLARD, 12
Operation MARKET GARDEN, 2, 3, 14, 74, 140
Operation MARTLET (June 25–July 1, 1944), 44
Operation NEPTUNE (June 6–July 3, 1944), 22, 27, 145–149
Operation OTTAWA, 44
Operation OVERLORD (D-Day)
  amphibious landings, 22
  paratroopers and gliders, 3
  Planning for, 151–153, 199, 221–227
Operation PERCH (June 4–14, 1944), 42–44
Operation ROUNDUP (1943), 175–176
Operation SLEDGEHAMMER, 175, 183–184
Operation SPRING (July 25–27), 46, 56
Operation TONGA (June 6, 1944), 42, 99
Operation TORCH (1942), 20, 21–22
Operation TOTALIZE (August 7–13, 1944), 200–202
Operation TRACTABLE (August 14–21, 1944), 202–203
Operation VERITABLE, 68
Operation WINDSOR (July 4–5, 1944), 44–45
Order of the Day and Letter to the Troops, Supreme Commander of the Western Allies Expeditionary Forces General Dwight D. Eisenhower, June 6, 1944, 229
Orne bridge landing, 2
Orne River, 3
OTTAWA, Operation, 44
Overlord (1975), 88

OVERLORD, Operation, Planning for, 3, 22, **151–153**, 199
  Allied Planning for the Normandy Invasion (July 1943), 221–227
Oxford Light Infantry, 3

P-38 Lightning, 10, 17
P-47 Thunderbolt, 11, 17
P-51 Mustang, 10–11, 17, 49
Panther tanks, 190
Panzerfaust, 23, 43, 54, 187–188
Panzergrenadier, 56, 63, 65, 75
Panzer Group West, 42, 63, 64, 65
Panzergruppe West
  Geyr von Schweppenburg, Leo Dietrich Franz Freiherr (1886–1974), 102–103
Panzer Lehr Division, 43
Panzerschreck, 43, 190
Parachute force
  Battle for Pegasus and Horsa Bridges (June 6, 1944), 157
  Battle of La Fière Causeway (June 6–9, 1944), 121, 122
  Operation NEPTUNE (June 6–July 3, 1944), 145–146
  Operation OVERLORD (D-Day), 3, 81
  Operation TONGA (June 6), 42
  Sainte-Mère-Église, 179
  Steele, John Marvin (1912–1969), 186
  training for, 3
  transport aircraft, 15
  Winters, Richard D. (1918–2011), 211–212
  See also Airborne forces, British and American
Paris, liberation of, 35
Pas de Calais, Operation FORTITUDE (1944), 90–91
Patch, Alexander M., 61, 94
Patton, George Smith, Jr. (1885–1945), **155–156**
  Allied command structure, 61
  Falaise-Argentan Pocket (August 12–24, 1944), 85–86
  France Campaign (June 6–September 15, 1944), 92, 94
  ground-attack aviation, 19
  Operation COBRA (July 25–31, 1944), 56–57
  Operation OVERLORD, Planning for, 152
Pegasus and Horsa Bridges, Battle for (June 6, 1944), **156–157**

PERCH, operation (June 4–14, 1944), 42–44
Pershing, John J., 136
Phoenixes, 142
PIAT, 23
PLUTO (Pipeline under the Ocean), **157–159**
Plymouth bridging vehicle, 190
Pogue, Forrest C., Primary Document, 231–233
Pointe du Hoc, Seizure of (June 6, 1944), **159–161**, 198
  coastal artillery, 27–28
  Rudder, James Earl (1910–1970), 176
Poland
  1st Parachute Brigade, 3
  Casualty Estimates in Battle of Normandy (June 6–August 29, 1944), 243
  destroyers and escorts, 210–211
  European Theater, Overview, 212–219
  Tehran Conference (November 28–December 1, 1943), 194–195
Polish War Cemetery, 48
Primary Documents
  Allied Planning for the Normandy Invasion (July 1943), 221–227
  Anglo-American Combined Chiefs of Staff, Directive to Supreme Commander Allied Expeditionary Force, February 12, 1944, 227–228
  Eisenhower's Statement in the Event the D-Day Landings Failed, 229
  Forrest C. Pogue on D-Day, June 6–7, 1944, 231–233
  General Dwight D. Eisenhower to General George C. Marshall, July 5, 1944, 233–234
  General Erwin Rommel Teletype Message to Hitler, July 15, 1944, 234–235
  Order of the Day and Letter to the Troops, Supreme Commander of the Western Allies Expeditionary Forces General Dwight D. Eisenhower, June 6, 1944, 229
  U.S. Army General Dwight D. Eisenhower on invention of "Rhino" Tank Modification, 235–236
  U.S. President Franklin D. Roosevelt's Remarks by Radio, June 6, 1944, 230–231
Pujol, Juan, 78
Puntenney, William H., 181
Purple Heart Lane, 58
PzKpfw tanks, 187–188, 190

Queen's Own Regiment of Canada, 43
Quesada, Elwood Richard "Pete" (1904–1993), 18–19, 55, **163–164**

Rae, Robert, 122
Raids, amphibious landings, 20
Ramsay, Sir Bertram Home (1883–1945), 61, 145–149, 148, 152, **165**
Ranville War Cemetery, 48
Rennes, 96
Republic P-47 Thunderbolt, 11
Rhinos, 55, 70, 235–236
Ridgway, Matthew Bunker (1895–1993), 2, 121–122, **166–167**
Rifles, **167–169**
Rodney, Battleship, 45
Romania, 215
Rommel, Erwin Johannes Eugen (1891–1944), 27, **169–171**
  Afrika Korps, 216
  on Atlantic Wall, 33
  command structure, 63–65
  Festung Europa, 87
  on Operation NEPTUNE (June 6–July 3, 1944), 146–147
  Teletype Message to Hitler, July 15, 1944, 234–235
Rommel's asparagus, 87
Ronson, 191
Roosevelt, Franklin D. (1882–1945), **171–173**
  on Charles de Gaulle, 96
  Churchill, Winston and, 52–53
  European Theater, Overview, 214–219
  Operation OVERLORD, Planning for, 151, 152–153
  on Operation ROUNDUP (1943), 175
  Remarks by Radio, June 6, 1944, 230–231
  Tehran Conference (November 28–December 1, 1943), 193–195
Roosevelt, Theodore, Jr. (1887–1944), **173–175**
Rouen, 149–150
ROUNDUP, Operation (1943), **175–176**
Royal Air Force (RAF)
  airborne forces, overview, 1–3
  Coningham, Sir Arthur "Mary" (1895–1948), 65–66
Royal Marines Armoured Support Group, 188
Royal Winnipeg Rifles, 44–45
Rudder, James Earl (1910–1970), 160, **176**, 198

Rundstedt, Karl Rudolf Gerd von (1875–1953), 62–65, 102, 146–147, **176–178**

SACEUR (Supreme Allied Commander, Europe), 60–62
Sainte-Mère-Église, 68, 121–122, **179**, 199, 211
Saint-Lô, Battle of (July 11–19, 1944), 92, **179–182**
Saint-Malo, 93–94
Saint-Nazaire, 93–94
Salamander tanks, 190
Sattler, Robert, 49–50
Saving Private Ryan (1998), 88–89
Schlieben, Karl von, 48–50
Schweppenburg, Leo Geyr von, 64
Scorpion antimine tanks, 190
2nd Army, British
  Allied command structure, 61
  Battle to Secure Caen (June 6–July 18, 1944), 42, 44, 45
  Dempsey, Miles Christopher (1896–1969), 74
  Falaise-Argentan Pocket (August 12–24, 1944), 86
  France, Campaign (June 6–September 15, 1944), 91, 92
  Operation BLUECOAT (July 30–August 7, 1944), 35–36
  Operation COBRA (July 25–31, 1944), 54, 56
  Operation NEPTUNE (June 6–July 3, 1944), 147
  Operation OVERLORD, planning for, 153
2nd Panzer Division, 35–36
Second Battle of Odon (July 18–20, 1944), 45–46
II Canadian Corps, 46, 56
17th Airborne Division, 2
7th Armoured Division, 43, 44–45
79th Infantry Division, U.S., 49
SHAEF (Supreme Headquarters, Allied Expeditionary Force), 60, 153
Sherman tanks, 55, 188, 189–191
Siegfried Line, 35, 200
Simonds, Guy Granville (1903–1974), 46, 56, 68, **182**, 201, 202–203
16th Luftwaffe Field Division, 45
6th Airborne Division, 2, 3
6th Armoured Regiment, Canada, 43
Skytrain, 1
Slapton Sands, Battle of (April 28, 1944), 130–131
SLEDGEHAMMER, Operation, 175, **183–184**

Smith, Walter Bedell (1895–1961), 60, 152, **184–185**
Soviet Union
  airborne forces, 1
  Churchill, Winston and, 52–53
  European Theater, Overview, 212–219
  Soviet Black Sea Fleet, 21
  tanks, 187
  See also Maps; Stalin, Josef
Special Air Service Brigade, 3
Speer, Albert, 86–87, 200
Spitfire fighter aircraft, 9, 135
SPRING, Operation (July 25–27), 46, 56
SS Panzer Corps, 44
Stagg, James Martin (1900–1965), 146, 185–186
Stalin, Josef
  Churchill, Winston and, 52–53
  European Theater, Overview, 213–219
  on Operation JUBILEE (Dieppe Raid, August 9, 1942), 113–115
  Tehran Conference (November 28–December 1, 1943), 193–195
Steele, John Marvin (1912–1969), 179, **186**
Stokes Mortar, 26
Strait of Dover, 82
Strategic amphibious landings, 20
Stuart tanks, 55
Sturmovik fighter aircraft, 17
Submarines
  Battle of the Atlantic, 28–31
  European Theater, Overview, 213–219
Supermarine Spitfire, 9
Supreme Allied Commander, Europe (SACEUR), 60–62
Supreme Headquarters, Allied Expeditionary Force (SHAEF), 60, 153
Svenner, 211
Sword Beach
  Battle for Pegasus and Horsa Bridges (June 6, 1944), 156
  coastal artillery, 27–28
  field artillery, 24
  ground forces, order of battle D-Day, 237
  Millin, William "Piper Bill" (1922–2010), 137
  Operation TONGA (June 6, 1944), 42
  terrain and tactical problems on D-Day, 150, 196

Tactical amphibious landings, 20
Tank landing ships (LSTs), 21

Tanks, **187–191**
    antitank guns and warfare, 23–24, 26, 187–188, 190
    Culin, Curtis Grubb, III (1915–1963), 69–70
    Eisenhower on invention of "Rhino" tank modification, 235–236
    European Theater, Overview, 214–219
    Germany, 187–188, 191
    Great Britain, 188–189
    Hobart, Sir Percy Cleghorn Stanley (1885–1957), 109–110
    machine guns and, 135
    Patton, George Smith Jr. (1885–1945), 155
Tassigny, Jean de Lattre de, 94
Taylor, Maxwell Davenport (1901–1987), 2, **191–193**
Tedder, Sir Arthur William (1st Baron Tedder) (1890–1967), 60, 152, **193**
Tehran Conference (November 28–December 1, 1943), **193–195**
Tempest fighter aircraft, 10
10th Armoured Regiment, 44–45
Terrain and Tactical Problems on D-Day, **195–199**
    Normandy, characteristics of, 150
    Pointe du Hoc, Seizure of (June 6, 1944), 159–161
3rd Canadian Division, 44, 201
3rd Infantry Division, British
    Battle to Secure Caen (June 6–July 18, 1944), 42, 44
    Montgomery, Sir Bernard Law (First Viscount Montgomery of Alamein) (1887–1976), 138
    Operation NEPTUNE (1944), 148
13th Airborne Division, 2, 13
30th Infantry Division, U.S., 55
31st Tank Brigade, 44
Thunderbolt fighter aircraft, 11, 17
TIGER, Exercise (April 22–30, 1944), 130–131
Tiger tanks, 54, 187, 190
Tilly-sur-Seulles, 43–44
Todd, Richard, 157
Todt, Fritz, 86–87, 199–200
Todt Organization (OT), **199–200**
TONGA, Operation (June 6, 1944), 42, 99
TORCH, Operation (1942), 20, 21–22
TOTALIZE, Operation (August 7–13, 1944), **200–202**
Toulon, 94

TRACTABLE, Operation (August 14–21, 1944), **202–203**
Transport aircraft, 14–16
Truscott, Lucian, 94
Twaby Ark bridging vehicle, 190
12th SS Panzer Division, 43, 45
29th Infantry Division
    Battle of Saint-Lô (July 11–19, 1944), 180–181
    Gerhardt, Charles Hunter (1895–1976), 100
27th Armoured Regiment, 46
Typhoon fighter aircraft, 9–10, 17, 45, 46, 49, 129

U-boats
    Battle of the Atlantic, 28–31
    European Theater, Overview, 213–219
Ukraine, 216
Underwater demolition teams (UDTs), 21
United States
    airborne forces, 1–4
    aircraft, bombers, 6–8
    aircraft, fighters and fighter-bombers, 10–11
    aircraft, transports, 15
    Allied command structure, 60–62
    Allied warships, 209–211
    Army, Corps, and Division Units in Battle of Normandy (June 6–August 29, 1944), 241
    Barton, Raymond Oscar "Tubby" (1889–1963), 35
    Bradley, Omar Nelson (1893–1981), 37–38
    Casualty Estimates in Battle of Normandy (June 6–August 29, 1944), 243
    Churchill, Winston and, 52–53
    Cole, Robert George (1915–1944), 57–58
    Collins, Joseph Lawton "Lightning Joe" (1896–1987), 58–59
    Cota, Norman Daniel "Dutch" (1893–1971), 66–67
    Culin, Curtis Grubb, III (1915–1963), 69–70
    Ehlers, Walter David (1921–2014), 79–80
    European Theater, Overview, 212–219
    Gerhardt, Charles Hunter (1895–1976), 100–101
    Gerow, Leonard Townsend (1888–1972), 101–102
    gliders, use of, 12
    ground forces order of battle on D-Day, 237
    Higgins, Andrew Jackson (1886–1952), 105–106
    Huebner, Clarence Ralph (1888–1972), 111

United States (*continued*)
  Kirk, Alan Goodrich (1888–1963), 117–118
  landing craft, 124–126
  Lee, John Clifford Hodges (1887–1958), 126–127
  Marshall, George Catlett (1880–1959), 135–137
  Moon, Don Pardee (1894–1944), 140–141
  number of troops killed June 6, 1944, 239
  Patton, George Smith Jr. (1885–1945), 155–156
  Quesada, Elwood Richard "Pete" (1904–1993), 163–164
  Ridgway, Matthew Bunker (1895–1993), 166–167
  rifles, 167–168
  Roosevelt, Franklin D. (1882–1945), 171–173
  Roosevelt, Theodore, Jr. (1887–1944), 173–175
  Rudder, James Earl (1910–1970), 176
  Smith, Walter Bedell (1895–1961), 184–185
  Steele, John Marvin (1912–1969), 186
  Taylor, Maxwell Davenport (1901–1987), 191–193
  Winters, Richard D. (1918–2011), 211–212
USS *Arkansas*, 209, 210
USS *Cory*, 211
USS *Nevada*, 209
USS *Reuben James*, 215
USS *Rich*, 211
USS *Texas*, 209
U.S. Troop Carrier Command, 3
Utah Beach
  Battle of La Fière Causeway (June 6–9, 1944), 121–122
  Battle of Lyme Bay (April 28, 1944), 130
  coastal artillery, 27–28
  Collins, Joseph Lawton "Lightning Joe" (1896–1987), 59
  Cotentin (Cherbourg) Peninsula, 49, 67–68
  Exercise TIGER (April 22–30, 1944), 130–131
  field artillery, 24
  ground forces order of battle, D-Day, 237
  landing craft, 123
  Moon, Don Pardee (1894–1944), 140–141
  Operation OVERLORD, planning for, 153
  paratroopers and gliders, 3
  Pointe du Hoc, Seizure of (June 6, 1944), 159–161
  Roosevelt, Theodore, Jr. (1887–1944), 174
  Sainte-Mère-Église, 179
  Sainte-Mère-Église museum, 68
  terrain and tactical problems, D-Day, 64, 150, 196, 198–199
  Winters, Richard D. (1918–2011), 211
Utah Beach Gooseberry, 143

Vallentine tanks, 190
VERITABLE, Operation, 68
Vian, Sir Philip Louis (1894–1968), 61, 145, 148, **207**
Villers-Bocage, Battle of (1944), 43
Vimont, 45–46
Vire, 35–36

Waco Aircraft Company, 12
Waco CG-4A glider, 12
Warships, Allied, **209–211**
Weather
  Ardennes Offensive, 219
  Battle of La Fière Causeway (June 6–9, 1944), 121
  Battle to Secure Caen (June 6–July 18, 1944), 44
  Eisenhower's decision to launch D-Day attack, 80–81, 146
  English Channel tides and, 83, 150
  Operation NEPTUNE (June 6–July 3, 1944), 146, 148
  Stagg, James Martin (1900–1965), 185–186
West Wall (Siegfried Line), 200
Weyland, Otto P., 19
Where Eagles Dare (1968), 88
White phosphorus (WP), 25
Whitley bomber, 1
Wiese, Friedrich, 94
WINDSOR, Operation (July 4–5, 1944), 44–45
Winters, Richard D. (1918–2011), **211–212**
Woods, John S., 57
World War II, European Theater: Overview, **212–219**

X Air Corps, 18

Yakovlev Yak-4 fighter, 17
Yalta Conference (1945), 53, 173
Yugoslavia, 215